THE ADVENT OF DEMOCRACY: THE IMPACT OF THE 1918 REFORM ACT ON BRITISH POLITICS

Edited by
Stuart Ball

T0385669

THE ADVENT OF DEMOCRACY: THE IMPACT OF THE 1918 REFORM ACT ON BRITISH POLITICS

Edited by
Stuart Ball

WILEY
for
THE PARLIAMENTARY HISTORY YEARBOOK TRUST

© 2018 The Parliamentary History Yearbook Trust

John Wiley & Sons

Registered Office
John Wiley & Sons Ltd, The Atrium, Southern Gate, Chichester, West Sussex, PO19 8SQ, UK

Editorial Offices
101 Station Landing, Medford, MA 02144, USA
9600 Garsington Road, Oxford, OX4 2DQ, UK
The Atrium, Southern Gate, Chichester, West Sussex, PO19 8SQ, UK

For details of our global editorial offices, for customer services, and for information about how to apply for permission to reuse the copyright material in this book please see our website at www.wiley.com/wiley-blackwell.

The rights of Stuart Ball to be identified as the editor of the editorial material in this work has been asserted in accordance with the Copyright, Designs and Patents Act 1988.

Wiley also publishes its books in a variety of electronic formats. Some content that appears in print may not be available in electronic books.

Library of Congress Cataloging-in-Publication Data
Library of Congress Cataloging-in-Publication data is available for this book

ISBN 9781119511199
A catalogue record for this title is available from the British Library
Set in 10/12pt Bembo
by Aptara Inc., India
Printed and bound in Singapore
by Markono print Media Pte Ltd

1   2018

CONTENTS

Notes on Contributors   vi

STUART BALL, The Reform Act of 1918 – the Advent of Democracy   1

STUART BALL, The Conservative Party and the Impact of the 1918 Reform Act   23

GAVIN FREEMAN, The Liberal Party and the Impact of the 1918 Reform Act   47

CHRIS WRIGLEY, The Labour Party and the Impact of the 1918 Reform Act   64

IAN CAWOOD, The Impact of the 1918 Reform Act on the Politics of the West
Midlands   81

EWEN A. CAMERON, The 1918 Reform Act, Redistribution and Scottish Politics   101

JOHN COAKLEY, The Impact of the 1918 Reform Act in Ireland   116

MARTIN FARR, The Impact of the 1918 Reform Act on the House of Commons   133

ADRIAN BINGHAM, The British Press and the 1918 Reform Act   150

MARI TAKAYANAGI, Women and the Vote: The Parliamentary Path to Equal
Franchise, 1918–28   168

Chronology of the 1918 Reform Act   186

Index   188

NOTES ON CONTRIBUTORS

Stuart Ball is emeritus professor of modern British history at the University of Leicester, where he taught from 1979 to 2016. He has published extensively on the history of the Conservative Party in the 20th century, and his most recent books are *Portrait of a Party: The Conservative Party in Britain 1918–1945* (Oxford, 2013), and *Conservative Politics in National and Imperial Crisis: Letters from Britain to the Viceroy of India 1926–31* (Farnham, 2014). He has also has written a short biography of Churchill, *Winston Churchill* (2003), and edited the political diaries of Sir Cuthbert Headlam (2 vols, 1992 and 1999). He was awarded a CBE (Commander of the Order of the British Empire) in the New Year Honours List 2018.

Adrian Bingham is professor of modern British history at the University of Sheffield. He is author of *Gender, Modernity, and the Popular Press in Inter-War Britain* (Oxford, 2004); *Family Newspapers? Sex, Private Life, and the British Popular Press, 1918–1978* (Oxford, 2009); and, with Martin Conboy, *Tabloid Century: The Popular Press in Britain, 1896 to the Present* (Oxford, 2015).

Ewen A. Cameron is Sir William Fraser professor of Scottish history at the University of Edinburgh. He is the author of *Land for the People? The British Government and the Scottish Highlands, 1880 to 1925* (East Linton, 1996); a biography of the Crofter MP, Charles Fraser Mackintosh; and a general history of modern and contemporary Scotland: *Impaled upon a Thistle: Scotland since 1880* (Edinburgh, 2010).

Ian Cawood is reader in modern history at Newman University, Birmingham. He is the author of *The Liberal Unionist Party: A History* (2012) and co-editor, with Chris Upton, of *Joseph Chamberlain: International Statesman, National Leader and Local Icon* (2016).

John Coakley is professor of politics at Queen's University, Belfast, and a fellow of the Geary Institute for Public Policy at University College, Dublin. He is author of *Nationalism, Ethnicity and the State* (2012) and *Reforming Political Institutions: Ireland in Comparative Perspective* (Dublin, 2013), and co-editor of *Politics in the Republic of Ireland* (6th edn, 2018).

Martin Farr is senior lecturer in contemporary British history at Newcastle University. His publications include books and articles on the politics of the First and Second World Wars, political biography, party politics, and government. He is currently writing a history of the international reception of Thatcherism entitled *Margaret Thatcher's World*. He is also co-editing two books: a Festschrift for John M. MacKenzie, for which he will contribute a chapter on imperial tropes in 1960s British popular culture, and *Presidents and Premiers:*

From McKinley and Salisbury to Obama and Cameron, in which he will be writing about the relationship of Barack Obama and David Cameron.

Gavin Freeman is an associate lecturer at the University of Leicester, where his thesis 'Beyond Westminster: Grass-Roots Liberalism in England, 1910–1929' was awarded a PhD in 2014. His publications include 'The Decline of the Liberal Party in the Heart of England: The Liberals in Leicestershire, 1914–24', which appeared in *Historical Research* in 2016.

Mari Takayanagi is senior archivist at the Parliamentary Archives. Her doctoral thesis was on 'Parliament and Women, c.1900–1945' (King's College London, 2012). She has published articles on the Life Peerages Act 1958, women and parliamentary committees c.1918–1945, and women staff in parliament during the First and Second World Wars. She is joint project manager and co-curator for 'Vote 100', parliament's project to celebrate the Representation of the People Act 1918 in 2018, and is currently working on an essay on suffrage centenaries for the forthcoming *Routledge Companion to British Women's Suffrage*.

Chris Wrigley is emeritus professor of modern British history at the University of Nottingham. His books include *David Lloyd George and the British Labour Movement: Peace and War* (Hassocks, 1976); *Lloyd George and the Challenge of Labour: The Post-War Coalition 1918–1922* (Brighton, 1990); *Arthur Henderson* (Cardiff, 1990); *Lloyd George* (Oxford, 1992); *A.J.P. Taylor: Radical Historian of Europe* (2006); and as editor, *A History of British Industrial Relations* (3 vols, Brighton and Cheltenham, 1982–96). He was president of the Historical Association, 1996–9.

The Reform Act of 1918 – the Advent of Democracy

STUART BALL

1

The Representation of the People Act of 1918 (often referred to as the '1918 Reform Act' or, less frequently, the 'Fourth Reform Act')[1] was a landmark in modern British history and the most substantial and significant change in the composition of the political nation ever to take place.[2] The increase in the electorate was far larger than that of any previous measure, both numerically and proportionately, and the 1918 Reform Act marked a fundamental change in the principles upon which the franchise was based, one element of which was the admission of women to the parliamentary suffrage for the first time.[3] In essence, the vote became a matter of adult citizenship, although at first this was restricted for women by an age limit of 30 years and a basic property qualification, until a further measure in 1928 equalised the terms for both genders as simple residence and legal adulthood (which in this period was 21 years of age). The extent of the change can be measured by the proportion of the adult population registered as electors: this was 29.4% in 1910, 79.5% in 1919, 90.9% in 1929, and 98.6% in 1939 (the latter increase being due to more thorough registration, not to any further change in the electoral system).[4] The greater scale of the 1918 Reform Act than any previous measure is shown in Table 1.

---

[1] This is unlike its predecessors – the First (also known as 'Great') Reform Act of 1832, the Second Reform Act of 1867, and the Third Reform Act of 1884 – which are almost always described in this way.

[2] For the general context of franchise extension from 1832 to 1918, see E.J. Evans, *Parliamentary Reform in Britain c.1770–1918* (Harlow, 1999); Ian Machin, *The Rise of Democracy in Britain, 1830–1918* (Basingstoke, 2000); John Garrard, *Democratisation in Britain: Elites, Civil Society and Reform since 1800* (Basingstoke, 2001).

[3] For the origins, passage and provisions of the Representation of the People Act 1918, see generally, Martin Pugh, *Electoral Reform in War and Peace 1906–18* (1978); D.E. Butler, *The Electoral System in Britain, 1918–1951* (Oxford, 1953); Robert Blackburn, 'Laying the Foundations of the Modern Voting System: The Representation of the People Act 1918', *Parliamentary History*, xxx (2011), 33–52; and for specific aspects, J. Turner, *British Politics and the Great War: Coalition and Conflict 1915–1918* (New Haven, CT, 1992); J.D. Fair, *British Inter-Party Conferences: A Study of the Procedure of Conciliation in British Politics, 1867–1921* (Oxford, 1980); M. Pugh, 'Politicians and the Woman's Vote 1914–1918', *History*, lix (1974), 358–74; J.D. Fair, 'The Political Aspects of Women's Suffrage during the First World War', *Albion*, viii (1976), 274–95; M. Hausmann, 'The Impact of the Great War on the Discussion of Women's Suffrage', in *Change and Inertia: Britain under the Impact of the Great War*, ed. H. Berghoff and R. von Friedeburg (Bodenheim, 1998), 121–40; A. Clark, 'Gender, Class and the Constitution: Franchise Reform in England 1832–1928', in *Re-Reading the Constitution*, ed. J. Vernon (Cambridge, 1996), 230–53; J. Hart, *Proportional Representation: Critics of the British Electoral System 1820–1945* (Oxford, 1992); D. Tanner, 'The Parliamentary Electoral System, the "Fourth" Reform Act, and the Rise of Labour in England', *Bulletin of the Institute of Historical Research*, lvi (1983), 205–19.

[4] Percentages calculated from population and electorate figures in *A History of British Elections since 1689*, ed. C. Cook and J. Stevenson (2014), 253, table 9.39 (the percentages given there are incorrect); the 1910 figure is for the January electorate, not the December electorate. In 1929, half a million men who were entitled to the vote had not bothered to register for it: *Registrar-General's Statistical Review for 1929* (1930–1), ii, 136.

Table 1: *Increases in the United Kingdom Electorate 1831–1929*

Reform Act	Electorate before		Electorate after		Increase	
	year	no.	year	no.	no.	%
1832	1831	515,930	1832	806,050	290,120	56.2
1867	1866	1,366,818	1868	2,462,529	1,095,711	80.2
1884	1883	3,152,912	1885	5,675,461	2,522,549	80.0
1918	1910	7,663,415	1918	21,324,231	13,660,816	178.3
1928	1924	21,648,609	1929	28,735,491	7,086,882	32.7

Notes: The university franchise is not included. The figures up to 1918 include the whole of Ireland, but those for 1924 and 1929 only include Northern Ireland. In December 1910 the electorate in Ireland was 683,767 and in 1918 it was 1,926,274; for comparison, the electorate of Northern Ireland in 1924 was 610,064. The increase in 1885 is affected by the large addition in Ireland, where the number of voters more than trebled from 224,018 in 1883 to 737,965 in 1885, a rise of 329.4%. The 1885 increase in England, Scotland and Wales was 2,008,602 (68.6%).
Sources: Figures for 1831, 1866, and 1884 are calculated from those for Scotland and Ireland by Sir John Lambert, 'Parliamentary Franchises Past and Present', *Nineteenth Century*, xxvi (1889), 958, and those for England and Wales revised by Charles Seymour, *Electoral Reform in England and Wales: The Development and Operation of the Parliamentary Franchise 1832–1885* (1915), 533, in *A History of British Elections since 1689*, ed. C. Cook and J. Stevenson (2014), 252–3. Figures for 1832, 1868, 1886, and 1910–29 are from *British Electoral Facts 1832–1987*, ed. F.W.S. Craig (Aldershot, 1989), 66–9.

The 1918 Reform Act swept away the accumulated variety of property-based qualifications which had previously made electoral registration a complex legal area, and in the process repealed 50 statutes and amended 57 others.[5] The act introduced an almost-universal male franchise from the legal age of adulthood on a simple residential basis.[6] There was no required minimum value of the residence occupied, no necessity to be a ratepayer (the

---

[5] Sir Hugh Fraser, *The Representation of the People Act, 1918, with Explanatory Notes* (1918), xxv. For a summary of the previous franchises, see Blackburn, 'Laying the Foundations of the Modern Voting System', 37.

[6] The act stated that 'A man shall be entitled to be registered as a parliamentary elector for a constituency (other than a university constituency) if he is of full age and not subject to any legal incapacity and (a) has the requisite residential qualification; or (b) has the requisite business premises qualification': Representation of the People Act 1918 (7 & 8 Geo. V, c. 64), section 1, subsection 1; 'the requisite residential qualification' was defined in subsection 2 as simply 'residing in premises in the constituency'. The term 'legal incapacity' was not defined in the 1918 Reform Act itself, although there were separate statements that a person who was not a British subject could not qualify (section 9, subsection 3) and that 'a person who is an inmate or patient in any prison, lunatic asylum, workhouse, poorhouse, or any other similar institution shall not by reason thereof be treated as resident therein for any purpose of this Act'; section 41, subsection 5. However, these clauses were defining an absence of qualification, and as the guide to the act by a legal authority explained: 'a legal incapacity is quite distinct from an absence of the qualifications required by this Act to enable a person to be registered or to vote at an election', but was 'some quality inherent in a person or for the time being irremovable in such person, which, either at Common Law or by Statute, deprives him of the status of a parliamentary elector'. The exclusions of this nature were those which still mainly remain in force: members of the house of lords, holders of a small number of legal and administrative offices related to the conduct of elections, foreign nationals, the insane (defined as 'a lunatic who is not in a lucid interval'), the severely mentally handicapped (two terms were used to define this, the contemporary expression 'an idiot', and 'an imbecile who is not *compos mentis*'), prisoners serving sentences 'with hard labour or exceeding twelve months', and those who within a certain number of previous years had been convicted of corrupt or illegal practices in parliamentary or local government elections: Fraser, *Representation of the People Act*, 4–7.

local government tax), and no longer was there an exclusion of those who had been in receipt of poor relief.[7] The qualifying period was reduced from 12 months to six months, and qualifying was made easier as it was no longer to be affected by changes of residence that were within the same borough or county, or from an adjoining borough or county.

The effect of introducing adult male suffrage was far from uniform across the nation, as the proportion of men enfranchised under the previous system varied greatly between different types of constituency. Although their economic nature was the fundamental factor, the differing degrees of enfranchisement were not a direct extrapolation from their class composition, as it was the type of abode even more than its value that determined the ease or difficulty of obtaining the vote. It did not require much property to qualify under the pre-1918 system, but it did require particular kinds and it also required some permanence of abode. It was comparatively easy for the householder – however humble – to get on the register, and generally difficult for the lodger, about whom there were complicated rules and past judgments in case law concerning exclusive access (the possession of a latchkey, etc.), the relative value of furnished and unfurnished rooms, and so on.[8] A crucial factor was the way in which the registration system operated and the effect of the lengthy qualifying period that was required, as a change in the type of qualification or removal to another constituency (and for certain types of accommodation, such as lodgers, even a change of address within the same constituency) resulted in removal from the register and having to start all over again. The voter had to be in possession of the necessary qualification for 12 months before registering, and then there was a six-month gap between the preparation of the register in July and when it came into effect on the following 1st of January; in consequence, the average period for qualification before 1918 was two years and one month.[9]

This affected the working class in the industrial towns and cities to a greater extent than the less mobile population of the rural areas and small towns. It was estimated that, in the county seats, on average 5% of voters moved constituency each year, whereas in urban industrial areas, it was 20–30%, and in London 30–40%.[10] When combined with other factors, such as the disqualification from having been in receipt of poor relief, this produced large variations in the proportion of adult male enfranchisement between the poorer districts of large cities at one end of the scale and the old-established country towns at the other. The average level of adult male enfranchisement in England and Wales was 59.8% in the boroughs and 69.9% in the counties, but this conceals much wider disparities,

---

[7] Although this was not a radical departure (as removing this bar had been recommended by both the majority and minority reports of the royal commission on the poor laws in 1909), it was not one of the unanimous recommendations of the Speaker's conference on electoral reform and was passed only by an unspecified majority. The recommendation was also not for complete exemption, but 'that no person who has received poor relief other than medical relief for less than thirty days in the aggregate during the qualifying period, shall be disqualified from being registered as a parliamentary elector': *Report of the Speaker's Conference on Electoral Reform*, Cd. 8463, para. 35: the Speaker to the prime minister, 27 Jan. 1917. However, in the eventual act the poor relief disqualification was removed completely: Representation of the People Act 1918, section 9, subsection 1.

[8] Thus Herbert Williams, when living at home with his mother, did not qualify for the parliamentary or local government franchise: Sir H. Williams, *Politics: Grave and Gay* (1949), 44; the pre-1918 system is extensively discussed in D. Tanner, *Political Change and the Labour Party 1900–1918* (Cambridge, 1990), 102–23, and Neal Blewett, 'The Franchise in the United Kingdom, 1885–1918', *Past & Present*, No. 32 (1965), 27–56.

[9] Blewett, 'Franchise in the United Kingdom', 35.

[10] Blewett, 'Franchise in the United Kingdom', 36.

ranging from only 39.3% in Liverpool Everton and 42.6% in Bethnal Green, to 73.1% in Scarborough, 75.0% in Oxford, and 78.6% in the Montgomery Boroughs in Wales.[11] The 1918 Reform Act's simple entitlement and shorter qualifying period resulted in a much more complete and evenly-distributed male enfranchisement, with the consequence that the proportionate increase was much greater in some places than in others. Thus in Scotland, the increase in the male electorate from 1910 to 1921 was 165% in the shipbuilding town of Greenock and 120% in the Dunfermline Boroughs, but in the counties it was only 51% in Argyll, and 35% in Galloway. The contrast can be summed up by the county of Fife, where in the industrial and coal-mining West Fife constituency the male electorate increased by 81%, but in rural and small town East Fife it grew by only 31%.[12]

The act included two special temporary provisions relating to the male franchise: men who had served, or were serving, in the armed forces 'in or in connection with the present war' could vote if aged 19 years or over,[13] while those who had registered as conscientious objectors were disfranchised for the duration of the war and the following five years, unless they had undertaken war service (such as in the army medical corps or on minesweepers) or other 'work of national importance' and had obtained a certificate confirming this from the central tribunal established under the Military Service Act of 1916.[14] The ban on conscientious objectors had not been part of the proposals for reform of the Speaker's conference in January 1917, and resulted from an amendment moved by the Conservative Party chairman, Sir George Younger, in November 1917, but it reflected parliamentary and public attitudes at the time.

The 1918 Reform Act broke new ground in introducing votes for women. This was on a substantial scale, but with limitations: women had to be over the age of 30 years, and – a fact which is often forgotten – there was also a property requirement. As a contemporary guide to the act by a legal expert noted: 'there is a material difference, besides that of age, between the qualifications which confer the parliamentary franchise … on a woman and those which confer it on a man'.[15] A woman had to qualify personally for the local government franchise or be married to a man who did so, either as the occupant of a 'dwelling-house' (for which there was no minimum value or rent), or as the occupier of land or premises with an annual rental value of at least £5.[16] The local government qualification in the 1918 Reform Act remained very similar to the previous parliamentary franchise, and so was

[11] H.C.G. Matthew, R.I. McKibbin and J.A. Kay, 'The Franchise Factor in the Rise of the Labour Party', *English Historical Review*, xci (1976), 727–31.

[12] Michael Dyer, *Capable Citizens and Improvident Democrats: The Scottish Electoral System, 1884–1929* (Aberdeen, 1996), 118.

[13] Representation of the People Act 1918, section 5, subsection 4.

[14] Representation of the People Act 1918, section 9, subsection 2.

[15] Fraser, *Representation of the People Act*, 69.

[16] Representation of the People Act 1918, section 4, subsection 1, provision (c); the exact wording was 'if she … (c) is entitled to be registered as a local government elector in respect of the occupation in that constituency of land or premises (not being a dwelling-house) of a yearly value of not less than five pounds or of a dwelling-house, or is the wife of a husband entitled to be so registered'. Following this, section 4, subsection 3 stated: 'A woman shall be entitled to be registered as a local government elector for any local government electoral area (a) where she would be entitled to be so registered if she were a man; and (b) where she is the wife of a man who is entitled to be so registered in respect of premises in which they both reside'. The term 'dwelling-house' was defined later in section 41, subsection 8: 'The expression "dwelling-house" includes any part of a house where that part is occupied separately as a dwelling-house.'

Table 2: *The Male and Female Electorate 1910–29*

Election	Male electorate		Female electorate		Total
	no.	%	no.	%	
1910 Dec.	7,709,981	100.0	–	–	7,709,981
1918	12,913,166	60.4	8,479,156	39.6	21,392,322
1929	13,657,434	47.3	15,193,925	52.7	28,851,359

Source: *British Electoral Facts 1832–1987*, ed. F.W.S. Craig (Aldershot, 1989), 68, 78.

more restricted than the simple 'residing' which was now all that was necessary for the male parliamentary vote. For both men and women, the local government requirement was to be 'occupying as owner or tenant', and while this covered many forms of accommodation, lodgers in furnished rooms were specifically excluded.[17]

The restrictions to the female parliamentary franchise in the 1918 Reform Act – particularly the age restriction – had been put in place to meet concerns that women, who were slightly more than half of the population, would predominate in the new electorate, which together with adult male suffrage was too much of a leap in the dark. The members of the Speaker's conference had had no precise data upon which to base their eventual compromise proposals, which was partly why their report left it for parliament to decide between the ages of 30 and 35 years.[18] The former was adopted, and it was estimated after the act was passed that it would enfranchise around six million women.[19] This proved to be a significant underestimate (see Table 2), and the new registers for the 1918 general election included nearly 8.5 million women, which was more than the total male electorate of 7.7 million at the previous general election in December 1910. However, the form of the franchise excluded around one-third of adult women, of whom approximately one-third were aged over 30 years but did not meet the property qualification – particularly domestic servants living in their employer's property,[20] lodgers in furnished rooms and hostels, and those living with relatives other than a husband (usually parents or grandparents), where their relative was the owner or tenant and thus the local government elector.

Plural voting was abolished for residential properties – a person owning or renting several abodes might be registered in several constituencies, but could now only cast a residential vote in one of them[21] – but it remained in two other forms. The first of these was the business franchise, under which the owner or occupier of business premises which had an

---

[17] Representation of the People Act 1918, section 3, defined the local government franchise qualification for men as 'occupying as owner or tenant any land or premises', but followed this by stating in section 3, provision (ii): 'for the purposes of this section the word tenant shall include a person who occupies a room or rooms as a lodger only where such room or rooms are let to him in an unfurnished state'; Fraser, *Representation of the People Act*, 40–2, 68–71; Pugh, *Electoral Reform*, 111–12.

[18] *Report of the Speaker's Conference*, para. 33; the recommendation for female suffrage was not unanimous, but by an unspecified majority.

[19] *Daily Telegraph*, 6 June 1917, p. 4; Fraser, *Representation of the People Act*, xxviii.

[20] They did not qualify in the same way as lodgers in furnished rooms, their employer being the householder.

[21] Representation of the People Act 1918, section 8, subsection 1.

annual rental value of at least £10, in another constituency from the one where they were
a residential voter, was entitled to cast a vote in that constituency. Furthermore, each of
the partners in the business qualified for a vote if the value of the premises when divided
gave each of them a share worth £10 or more; however, the business franchise did not
apply to either the directors or the shareholders of limited companies. One significant
change introduced when the bill was passing through parliament was that constituencies
which were divisions of the same city or town would be treated as entirely separate for
the purposes of the business franchise, which had not been the case before. Previously, a
voter who lived in Sheffield Brightside and had business premises in Sheffield Central had
not qualified for a second vote because this was within the same borough, but now they
would do so. The number of plural voters was considerably reduced from the pre-war
level of around 450,000–475,000 in England and Wales,[22] and it was now a much smaller
proportion of the total electorate. However, the business vote remained a significant factor
in a number of urban seats, especially in the central and business districts of the larger cities.
In 1918, the business vote in England and Wales was 159,013 (0.9% of the English and
Welsh electorate), and it grew steadily to reach 211,257 (1.1%) in 1924. The 1918 Reform
Act allowed women who qualified for the business vote in their own right to exercise this
in addition to their residential qualification, but stipulated that women could only vote
once on qualifications derived from their husbands, and naturally almost all women chose
to use the residential vote in the constituency in which they lived. However, the Equal
Franchise Act of 1928 removed this restriction and allowed wives a second vote based on
their husbands' business qualifications. In consequence, in 1929 the number on the business
premises register in England and Wales jumped to 371,594 (1.5% of the enlarged English
and Welsh electorate); it then remained close to this figure in 1931 and 1935.[23]

The second form of plural voting was in the university seats. Cambridge and Oxford
Universities had returned members of parliament since the early 17th century, and in 1800
and 1867 this had been extended to other universities.[24] In the 1918 Reform Act, the further expansion of higher education was recognized by increasing the number of university
seats from nine to 15. The two existing Scottish university seats were merged into a single
constituency, which was given a third MP; single member seats were created for the National University of Ireland, Queen's University, Belfast and the University of Wales, and
a two-member Combined English Universities seat was established for the more recently-
founded English universities of Birmingham, Bristol, Durham, Leeds, Liverpool, Manchester, and Sheffield (to which Reading was added in 1928). However, this number was
reduced to 12 following the Anglo-Irish Treaty of 1921, as the two seats of Trinity College
Dublin and the one of the National University of Ireland were removed from the house

[22]Tanner, *Political Change and the Labour Party*, 100; Blewett, 'Franchise in the United Kingdom', 46, suggests
an overall figure of 500,000–600,000.

[23]Butler, *Electoral System*, 146; the 1928 act also made men eligible for a vote derived from their wives' occupation of business premises, but this was presumably a much smaller number, and also still limited by the rule
that no person could cast more than two votes. Figures from *British Electoral Facts 1832–1987*, ed. F.W.S. Craig
(Aldershot, 1989), 78; the figures for Scotland and Northern Ireland were not published.

[24]Trinity College Dublin was given one seat at Westminster in the Act of Union in 1800 and a second seat in
the 1832 Reform Act, and in the 1867 Reform Act three further university seats were created: one for London,
one jointly for Aberdeen and Glasgow, and one jointly for Edinburgh and St Andrews: J.S. Meisel, *Knowledge and
Power: The Parliamentary Representation of Universities in Britain and the Empire* (Oxford, 2011), 24–32, 36–44.

Table 3: *The Representation of the University Seats 1918–35*

Party	1918	1922	1923	1924	1929	1931	1935
Conservative	9	8	9	8	8	8	7
Liberal	3	4	2	3	2	2	2
Independent	–	–	1	1	2	2	3

Notes: This table analyses the 12 university seats in England, Scotland, Wales, and Northern Ireland; it does not include the three southern Irish university seats, which ceased to exist in 1921.
Source: *British Parliamentary Election Results 1918–1949*, ed. F.W.S. Craig (2nd edn, 1977).

of commons together with the other constituencies in the area that became the Irish Free State. The 1918 Reform Act also expanded the qualification for the university franchise. Before 1918, voting in the Cambridge, Oxford, and Trinity College Dublin constituencies required the possession of a MA degree – which could be obtained simply by paying around £25 to upgrade the bachelor's degree, but many did not choose or could afford to do this.[25] It now became the case in all of the university seats that all graduates were entitled to vote; in addition, in the case of Cambridge and Oxford, which allowed women to attend as students but did not confer degrees upon them, women were qualified to vote if they had fulfilled the university's condition of residence and passed the final examinations.[26] However, the act's age restrictions still applied, and so women had to be over the age of 30 years to exercise the university franchise.

The voters in the university constituencies were scattered throughout the British Isles and Empire.[27] The elections were therefore conducted by postal ballot, and the university seats with more than one MP were the only constituencies in which the 1918 Reform Act introduced proportional representation, using the single transferable vote system.[28] However, the unit size of these three double-member and one triple-member constituencies was too small for the system to be effective, especially as in most cases the Conservative majority among the voters was so large that it swamped any Liberal or Labour minority. What did occur was the election of a few non-party independents, but that was due more to the cultural characteristics of the university electorate than to the voting system (see Table 3). Retaining the university representation had been a recommendation of the Speaker's conference, and both the principle and its logical expansion were uncontroversial during the passage of the bill. However, both university representation and the business franchise were abolished by the post-1945 Labour government in the Representation of the People Act of 1948.

The 1918 Reform Act placed one further limitation on plural voting, that no matter in how many ways or places a person might be qualified to register, in an election they could

[25] Meisel, *Knowledge and Power*, 41; Asquith was one distinguished Oxford graduate who did not do so.

[26] Representation of the People Act 1918, section 4, subsection 2.

[27] The 1918 Reform Act relaxed the witnessing requirements for postal ballots for university electors who were overseas, which previously had required the signature of a JP; it was estimated in 1930 that 8% of university voters lived overseas: Meisel, *Knowledge and Power*, 42.

[28] For details of how this operated, see *British Parliamentary Election Results 1918–1949*, ed. F.W.S. Craig (2nd edn, 1977), appendix i, 676–84.

cast no more than two votes.[29] Thus, a person having a residential vote in one constituency, a business premises vote in another, and – being a graduate – a vote in one of the university seats, could only exercise two of those franchises.

The Speaker's conference unanimously proposed the introduction of proportional representation in the boroughs which were large enough to have three or more MPs; these were to be arranged in constituencies returning between three and five members, in which each elector would have a single transferable vote.[30] More contentiously, the conference passed by a majority the recommendation that, in single-member seats when more than two candidates were nominated, the alternative vote system should be used.[31] However, when the conference report was eventually debated in the house of commons on 28 March 1916, the prime minister, David Lloyd George, undermined these proposals by indicating his lack of enthusiasm for proportional representation; it was not 'in quite the same category' as the other recommendations, and indeed 'not an essential part of the scheme'.[32] This opened the door to the report's recommendations being treated as a list which could be adopted or amended selectively, rather than an indivisible whole, and it overtly encouraged the discarding of proportional representation – about which the views of MPs were certainly divided. The majority of Conservative MPs were opposed to both forms of proportional representation, but there was support among Conservative peers for the single transferable vote as the means of retaining some representation of the middle class in the towns, where they would be a beleaguered minority after the advent of adult male suffrage. On the other hand, many Liberal and Labour MPs favoured the alternative vote; this had been a proposal in the pre-war era of their 'progressive alliance', and they expected to gain from it in Conservative-held areas, especially in the counties. Views on the alternative vote more closely paralleled party lines than did those on the single transferable vote, but there were many unpredictable cross-currents in the house of commons. Some of these were based on past convictions for or against proportional representation, but others were matters of personal expediency in reaction to how their own constituency would be affected. The application of the scheme to London was particularly disliked by most of its MPs, both Conservative and Liberal, and they played an important role in the foundation of the Anti-Proportional Representation Committee in 1917.[33]

The result was a protracted series of motions and amendments, and during the second half of 1917 various proposals were defeated or approved, often by narrow and temporary majorities. Early in the committee stage of the bill, the single transferable vote scheme was defeated on 12 June 1917 by 149 to 141, with 85 Conservative MPs voting against it, and it

---

[29] Representation of the People Act 1918, section 8, subsection 1.

[30] *Report of the Speaker's Conference*, para. 23; P. Catterall, 'The British Electoral System 1885–1970', *Historical Research*, lxxiii, (2000), 156–74. It has been calculated that, after the redistribution proposed by the boundary commissioners, this would have affected 211 of the 569 English, Welsh and Scottish territorial constituencies: Hart, *Proportional Representation*, 181.

[31] *Report of the Speaker's Conference*, para. 36.

[32] Hansard, *Commons Debates*, 5th ser., xcii, col. 492: 28 Mar. 1917; J. Grigg, 'Lloyd George and Electoral Reform', in *The Political Culture of Modern Britain: Studies in Memory of Stephen Koss*, ed. J.M.W. Bean (1987), 165–77. Lloyd George's view was reinforced in briefings to lobby correspondents before the first reading of the bill: *Daily Telegraph*, 12 May 1917, p. 4.

[33] Catterall, 'British Electoral System', 165.

was, again, rejected on 4 July by 201 to 169.[34] On 9 August, when the alternative vote was approved by a single vote, the party division on this issue was clear: the MPs who opposed it consisted of 113 Conservatives and 13 Liberals, while those in favour comprised two Conservatives, 98 Liberals, 17 Labour, and ten Irish Nationalists.[35] At the report stage, the single transferable vote scheme was rejected again by the larger margin of 202 to 126 on 22 November, while later on the same day the alternative vote was reaffirmed by 150 to 121. Finally, on 5 December, two days before the bill passed its third reading in the Commons, the single transferable vote was inserted for application only to Ireland by 181 to 117. The Conservative Party remained strongly opposed to the alternative vote, and when the bill reached the Conservative-dominated house of lords, on 22 January 1918, it was removed and replaced by the single transferable vote. When the bill went back to the Commons, it rejected the Lords' amendments by 223 to 123 on 30 January, and next day, by the much narrower margin of 178 to 170, reinstated the alternative vote. There was then a final flurry, with the house of lords in turn reversing this on 4 February, and on the following day the lower House removing the single transferable vote again by 238 to 141, and restoring the alternative vote by the narrowest of margins (195 to 194), although only for borough constituencies. On 6 February, the Lords then removed the alternative vote for a third time and the Commons again rejected its amendments, after which a compromise was quickly agreed.[36] Liberal and Labour MPs feared losing the bill entirely, and did not wish to risk the attainment of their pre-war objectives of adult male suffrage and the restriction of plural voting by insisting on the alternative vote, while the peers did not wish to press their amendments to the point of provoking a constitutional crisis. The result was that the alternative vote was dropped from the bill entirely, as was the single transferable vote for the territorial constituencies, and the provision was inserted that a royal commission be appointed to draw up a scheme for the application of proportional representation in 100 seats.[37] The Representation of the People Act then completed its passage, and received the royal assent on 6 February 1918.

Chaired by Speaker Lowther, the royal commission worked swiftly, and on 13 April 1918 published its plan, under which the larger towns and cities would be formed into 24 constituencies of between three and seven members each, returning a total of 99 MPs. However, given the extension of the franchise, these multi-member seats would have very large electorates, and few of the MPs sitting for one of the existing smaller divisions liked the prospect of being submerged in the larger unit. The scheme was rejected by the house of commons on 13 May by 166 to 110 votes, and thus apart from its application in the four university constituencies which returned two or three MPs, proportional representation was

[34] Different voting figures for the divisions during the passage of the bill are given in various books and articles (particularly Pugh, *Electoral Reform*, and Hart, *Proportional Representation*); some variations are due to errors, but generally in the case of Commons' divisions the discrepancies are due to whether or not the two tellers on each side are counted as having voted. The division list figures here have been checked with the official record of debates and are the ones given there, which in the case of the house of commons do not include the tellers, as technically they have not voted in the lobby which they are counting.

[35] *The Times*, 11 Aug. 1917, p. 7. These figures included the two tellers on each side, who were two Conservatives for the 'No' vote and two Liberals for the 'Aye' vote; the result recorded for the division was actually 124 against and 125 in favour: Hansard, *Commons Debates*, 5th ser., xcvii, col. 652: 9 Aug. 1917.

[36] *Real Old Tory Politics: The Political Diaries of Sir Robert Sanders, Lord Bayford, 1910–1935*, ed. John Ramsden (1984), 100: Sanders diary, 10 Feb. 1918.

[37] Representation of the People Act 1918, section 20, subsection 2, provision (a).

cast into limbo. By default, the 1918 Reform Act retained the first-past-the-post system for all of the territorial constituencies, which, with the exception of 12 surviving double-member boroughs (see below), were all to be individual single-member seats.

The fewer and more straightforward franchise qualifications in the 1918 Reform Act were paralleled by the introduction of a simpler and less partisan system of registration. Since 1832, the register had been compiled by the Poor Law overseers from the rate-books and any other claims that were lodged, but now the preparation of the registers was made the responsibility of local government officials, who were required to make 'a house to house or other sufficient inquiry'.[38] This did away with the previous system in which party agents could put the cases of some voters to be registered, and make objections to the claims of others, in the annual Revision Court before a barrister appointed to oversee this process; in the smaller electorates before 1914, adding a couple of hundred of your supporters and securing the removal of a similar number of your opponents could be decisive.[39] As part of this change, the costs of the returning officers were to be paid by central government; previously each candidate had paid an equal share of the costs in their constituency (which in December 1910 had averaged £280), in addition to their election expenses, but now they were relieved of this charge. The 1918 Reform Act also introduced two electoral registers in each year, instead of the previous one; the 'spring' register was to come into effect on 15 April for six months, and the 'autumn' register on 15 October for the next six months. However, in 1926, with the government under pressure to economise, this costly and time-consuming procedure was abandoned and a single annual register was reverted to, coming into force on 15 October; at the same time, the residential qualifying period was reduced to three months.[40]

Another new feature in the 1918 Reform Act was a postal ballot for members of the armed forces, who were placed on a list of 'absent voters' in the constituency where they would otherwise have qualified as resident, with their votes to be included in the count there; it was under this provision that servicemen voted in the general election of December 1918, and again in 1945.[41] The act also allowed voting by proxy if they were serving in a location too remote for postal ballots to be returned in time, and gave discretion to registration officers to allow proxies for merchant seamen, harbour pilots, and fishermen if they could show that they were likely to be at sea on polling day.[42] Following the demobilisation of 1919–20, during the interwar period the number of absent voters was relatively small: in 1924, the first election for which there is a national total, it was 184,201, which

[38]Representation of the People Act 1918, 1st schedule, 'Form of Register', rule 6; the act created the position of registration officer, which for a county division was to be the clerk of the county council, and for a borough division the clerk of the borough council: section 12, subsection 2.

[39]G.A. Jones, 'Further Thoughts on the Franchise 1885–1918', *Past & Present*, No. 34 (1966), 134–8; Kathryn Rix, *Parties, Agents and Electoral Culture in England, 1880–1910* (Woodbridge, 2016).

[40]Representation of the People (Economy Provisions) Act 1926 (16 & 17 Geo. V, c. 9); Blackburn, 'Laying the Foundations of the Modern Voting System', 34.

[41]It was only in 1918 and 1945 that the counting of ballots did not take place immediately after the poll and was delayed (by two weeks in 1918 and three weeks in 1945) to allow for the return of the servicemen's postal votes from overseas. After causing frustrating delays in the counting at by-elections since 1918, an amending act in 1920 limited postal voting to within the United Kingdom and instead servicemen overseas could appoint proxies; by this time the armed services had been much reduced in number: Butler, *Electoral System*, 49.

[42]Representation of the People Act 1918, section 23, subsections 1, 2, 4, and 1st schedule, rules 16, 17.

was 0.84% of the whole electorate.[43] However, this was an innovation from which much wider civilian postal balloting was to develop after 1948.

The legislation setting limits on election expenses, which was enacted in 1883, had proved effective in tackling corrupt practices, and there was no need to do anything substantial in that area.[44] However, the average election expenses of candidates had risen since 1885, reaching a peak of £861 in January 1910, and the Speaker's conference was 'strongly and unanimously of opinion that the expenditure at present entailed in fighting a contested election is unjustifiable, and should be materially reduced'.[45] A new formula was needed in relation to the much larger electorate, and so the 1918 Reform Act stipulated that the maximum expenditure was 7*d*. per voter in a county constituency and 5*d*. per voter in the more compact borough seats.[46] This had the desired effect and the average of candidates' expenses in the general elections of 1922–9 was £683; following the reduction of the permitted amount in county seats to 6*d*. per voter in 1929, the average fell further to £506 in 1931 and £536 in 1935.[47] The one innovation in 1918 was the requirement that a candidate, upon nomination, had to lodge a deposit of £150 with the returning officer, which was returned to them only if they received at least one-eighth of the votes cast; otherwise, it was forfeited to the crown.[48] This was a substantial sum in these times: in 1925, the average annual income of an agricultural labourer was £73–109, and of a building labourer £143; among skilled workers, a railway engine driver earned £187–234 per annum, and a printing compositor £192.[49] However, this was less of a problem for Labour Party candidates than it might appear, as many of them were sponsored by a trade union for their election expenses. In the 1918 general election, only six Labour and three Conservative candidates lost their deposits, although 44 Liberals did so; however, that was the Liberal Party's highest number until 1945. Both Labour (35) and the Conservatives (18) had their highest total in the 1929 general election, but this was a consequence of both parties nominating their largest number of candidates in the interwar period and contesting many hopeless prospects.[50]

Three other provisions in the 1918 Reform Act related to election campaigns. The first of these entitled candidates to make use of rooms in public elementary schools in the constituency to hold election meetings. This was not free, as is sometimes stated, as the local education authority or school managers were permitted to make a charge for preparing the room beforehand and returning it to its normal state afterwards, and for heating, lighting and cleaning (and for any damage incurred).[51] However, these costs were very small and, as they did not include any element for the use of the room as such, they were considerably less than

[43] *British Electoral Facts*, ed. Craig, 97.

[44] C. O'Leary, *The Elimination of Corrupt Practices in British Elections, 1868 to 1911* (Oxford, 1962); W.B. Gwyn, *Democracy and the Cost of Politics in Britain* (1962); K. Rix, 'The Elimination of Corrupt Practices in British Elections? Reassessing the Impact of the 1883 Corrupt Practices Act', *English Historical Review*, cxxiii (2008), 65–97.

[45] *Report of the Speaker's Conference*, preamble to para. 28.

[46] Representation of the People Act 1918, 4th schedule.

[47] *British Electoral Facts*, ed. Craig, 61–2.

[48] Representation of the People Act 1918, section 26.

[49] Calculated from ministry of labour statistics provided in reply to a question: Hansard, Commons Debates, 5th ser., clxxxvii, cols 671–3: 30 July 1925.

[50] *British Electoral Facts*, ed. Craig, 82.

[51] Representation of the People Act 1918, section 25.

hiring a meeting place commercially. Of equal significance, in the rural constituencies they provided reasonably accessible venues among the scattered villages. This provision of the act was helpful to all candidates in keeping their expenses down, especially in the county divisions; it may have marginally been most helpful to Labour candidates in these seats, because their party was weakest in the agricultural areas and there was less trade union sponsorship.

The second provision was that each duly nominated candidate was entitled to one free postal delivery to every registered elector in the constituency, 'containing matter relating to the election only, and not exceeding two ounces in weight'.[52] This was almost always used by candidates for their election address, which was a printed leaflet containing their personal message and policy statement. However, while the Royal Mail delivered this without charge, it had to be prepared by the candidates and their supporters, at their own expense. This was not just a matter of printing sufficient thousands of copies of the election address, but also of putting these into envelopes addressed to each voter – the latter was not part of the postal service's responsibility. One consequence of this was that local constituency associations would often keep in stock a sufficient supply of envelopes, ready to be addressed by the voluntary members when a general election was announced, with the aim of being the first to get their candidate's address into the hands of the voters.

Finally, a significant change in the conduct of elections was the provision that polling should take place everywhere on the same day.[53] This was quite different from the practice which had been followed from the earliest times, in which different districts selected their own day. In the general elections from 1885 to 1910, the polling in different constituencies had been spread over a period of between 15 and 17 days, which had the effect that the results in the early seats could affect opinion in those who voted later, such as when the Conservative Party leader, Arthur Balfour, lost his seat in 1906.[54] The previous system had also made it easier to use plural votes, but as these were now being limited to just one additional vote, the change to a uniform polling day made little extra difference in this respect. The 1918 Reform Act's new provision standardised the length of campaigns, as all seats now had the same interval between the announcement of the election and the polling day. This marked a final stage in the evolution of elections from being a collection of local contests, with local issues and the standing of local candidates playing an important, and even determining, role, into a more uniform national experience in which the programmes, propaganda, and leaders of the parties at the national level were the crucial factors, and candidates were mostly voted for according to their party label.

As had been the case with the previous Reform Acts, the 1918 act included a redistribution of constituencies and redrawing of their boundaries. The same procedure was adopted, of appointing three Boundary Commissions (one for England and Wales, one for Scotland, and one for Ireland) to draw up detailed proposals in accordance with the instructions passed by parliament; the innovation in 1918 was that all three commissions were chaired by the Speaker. In 1885, the Third Reform Act had made the most radical and extensive changes

---

[52]Representation of the People Act 1918, section 33, subsection 2.

[53]Representation of the People Act 1918, section 21, subsection 1; the deadline for the nomination of candidates would also be on the same day everywhere.

[54]The period of 15–17 days does not include the Orkney and Shetland constituency and the university seats, which usually held their poll about a week after the other constituencies had completed: *British Electoral Facts*, ed. Craig, 151.

in the political map, by introducing large numbers of single-member constituencies, particularly through partitioning the cities into many smaller seats. The Speaker's conference recommended 'the principle that each vote recorded shall, as far as possible, command an equal share of representation in the House of Commons',[55] and the Reform Bill based upon its proposals sought to achieve this by having constituencies based upon a standard population size. The initial instructions to the commissioners in May 1917 specified that the number of MPs for each county or parliamentary borough would be one for every 70,000 population, plus an additional member if the remaining population was above 50,000; a county or borough with a population of between 50,000 and 70,000 would retain one MP, while those with less than 50,000 'shall cease to have separate representation'. However, the strict application of these mathematical criteria was made more difficult by two of the other instructions; first, that the total number of MPs 'shall remain substantially as at present', and second, that the boundaries of constituencies should, 'as far as practicable', coincide with the local government boundaries.[56]

There were concerns that the geographical size of constituencies in thinly-populated rural regions would become unmanageable, and together with the desire of the Conservative Party to defend the agricultural interest, this led to a resolution being passed by the house of commons on 18 June 1917 which amended the instructions. The commissioners were now given more freedom of action, and could 'depart from the strict application of these Instructions in any case where it would result in the formation of constituencies inconvenient in size or character'. The resolution also abandoned proportional representation: the original instructions had been that boroughs whose population entitled them to between three and five MPs should be a single constituency, and those entitled to six or more MPs should be divided into constituencies each returning between three and five MPs, but, following the rejection of the single transferable vote six days earlier, the resolution of 18 June laid down that 'the Commissioners shall act on the assumption that proportional representation is not adopted'.[57]

The Boundary Commissions worked quickly, with that for England and Wales reporting its proposals on 27 September 1917, and that for Scotland on the next day. There then followed a stage of representations from the public, which came mostly from local authorities and the constituency associations of the political parties, after which Local Inquiries were held – there were 120 of these in England and Wales, affecting a total of 465 constituencies.[58] These resulted in some minor revisions of boundaries, which in some cases worked to the advantage of the political party that had been most active and effective in presenting its case (generally the Conservatives), but no substantial changes. However, even with the greater flexibility that the amended instructions had allowed, the eventual proposals found

---

[55] *Report of the Speaker's Conference*, para. 13.

[56] Instructions to the Boundary Commission for England and Wales, May 1917, reproduced in D.J. Rossiter, R.J. Johnston and C.J. Pattie, *The Boundary Commissions: Redrawing the United Kingdom's Map of Parliamentary Constituencies* (Manchester, 1999), 52–3.

[57] Amended instructions, 22 June 1917, reproduced in Rossiter *et al.*, *Boundary Commissions*, 54.

[58] These were conducted by the assistant commissioners, of whom 11 had been appointed for England and Wales, 11 for Scotland and seven for Ireland: Rossiter *et al.*, *Boundary Commissions*, 51–2.

it necessary to add 31 more territorial MPs; together with the six additional university seats, this increased the house of commons from 670 to 707 members.[59]

The revision of boundaries and reallocation of seats which took place in 1918 was primarily caused by the changes in population patterns since 1885. There had been a continued growth in the urban population, particularly in the cities, and a consequent decline in the rural areas, especially the more remote. Thus while Wales, Scotland, and Ireland each received just one more territorial seat, London gained three seats and the number of English borough constituencies rose from 166 to 193, even though a number of ancient boroughs (including five county towns)[60] lost their status and were merged into their counties. The largest additions were in the biggest cities: Glasgow expanded from seven to 15 seats, Birmingham from seven to 12, and Manchester from six to 10. As Table 4 shows, while the Conservative Party was able to maintain its share of wins in the large cities after 1918, the Liberals' share slumped to one-third of the pre-war level; the beneficiary of this was the Labour Party, whose overall proportion of wins rose to match the previous Liberal share.

The region with the most marked increase was south-east England, and especially in the two northern 'home counties' of Middlesex and Essex, where the number of constituencies more than doubled, from 18 to 37. At the other end of the scale – and country – the 'District of Burghs' constituencies in Scotland, each of which grouped together a number of small towns, were reduced from 13 to six; even so, the remainder still had electorates under 32,000.[61] The 1918 Reform Act also marked a further stage in the extinction of the medieval form of the two-member borough seat, in which each elector had two votes. This now survived in only ten English, one Scottish and one Irish towns of compact size where the population merited two MPs,[62] and in the special case of the City of London;[63] elsewhere, the single-member division had become the universal pattern in the territorial constituencies.

The amended instructions to the commissioners to take the character of the area into account had the effect of creating more economically-homogenous constituencies than previously, especially in industrial areas. After 1918, there was a larger number of seats which had a high proportion of working-class voters, and particularly more dominated by coal mining; the number of constituencies with more than 30% of occupied men working in the coal industry increased from around 35 before 1914 to 66, of which 30 had over 50% engaged in coal mining.[64] This pattern benefited the trade union-based Labour Party,

---

[59] *Representation of the People Bill, 1917: Redistribution of Seats, Report of the Boundary Commission (England & Wales)*, Cmd. 8756–8 (3 vols, 1917).

[60] Canterbury, Colchester, Peterborough, Shrewsbury, and Warwick.

[61] M. Dyer, 'Burgh Districts and the Representation of Scotland, 1707–1983', *Parliamentary History*, xv (1996), 302–4.

[62] These were Blackburn, Bolton, Brighton, Derby, Norwich, Oldham, Preston, Southampton, Stockport, and Sunderland in England, which had an average electorate of 69,405 in 1922 (two constituencies were not contested in 1918); Dundee in Scotland, which had 83,676 electors in 1918, and Cork City in Ireland (until the Anglo-Irish Treaty of 1921). Other towns which merited two MPs were divided into separate seats, such as Birkenhead, Croydon, East Ham, Middlesbrough, and Rochester.

[63] Instruction no. 8 in the original instructions of May 1917 was that 'The City of London shall continue to return two Members': Rossiter *et al.*, *Boundary Commissions*, 52. The City was a special case partly due to its historic prestige and economic importance, and because it had few residents but a large business vote; in the 1931 census, only 7,085 of the electorate of 43,902 had qualified on the basis of residence.

[64] M. Kinnear, *The British Voter: An Atlas and Survey since 1885* (2nd edn, 1981), 116.

Table 4: *The Effects of Constituency Redistribution in the Cities 1895–1929*

		1895–1910							1918–29						
		Cons. wins		Liberal wins		Labour wins			Cons. wins		Liberal wins		Labour wins	
City	No. seats	no.	%	no.	%	no.	%	No. seats	no.	%	no.	%	no.	%
Glasgow	7	18	51	13	37	3	9	15	31	41	4	5	38	51
Birmingham	7	35	100	0	0	0	0	12	52	87	0	0	7	12
Liverpool	9	37	82	3	7	0	0	11	41	75	2	4	7	13
Manchester	6	11	37	13	43	6	20	10	25	50	7	14	18	36
Sheffield	5	16	64	7	28	2	8	7	16	46	5	14	14	40
Leeds	5	5	20	17	68	3	12	6	12	40	5	17	13	43
Bristol	4	7	35	13	65	0	0	5	9	36	9	36	7	28
Edinburgh	4	7	35	13	65	0	0	5	11	44	6	24	8	32
Total	47	136	58	79	34	14	6	71	197	55	38	11	112	32

Notes: This table analyses the cities of mainland Britain which after 1918 returned five or more MPs, and compares party performances in the five general elections before and after the 1918 Reform Act. In 1895–1910, Liberal Unionists are counted as Conservatives, and in 1918 coalition Liberals are counted as Liberals. Independents and minor parties are not included; generally these were only elected occasionally, but it should be noted that throughout the period 1895–1929 one of the seats in Liverpool returned an Irish Nationalist MP.
Sources: *British Parliamentary Election Results 1885–1918*, ed. F.W.S. Craig (1974); *British Parliamentary Election Results 1918–1949*, ed. F.W.S. Craig (2nd edn, 1977).

and it has also been argued that the number of safe Conservative seats was increased, with more constituencies having a significant middle-class element together with the retention of a substantial number of agricultural seats – 86 constituencies had more than 30% of their occupied male population engaged in agriculture.[65] Some of the highly-agricultural areas had been Liberal strongholds and continued to return Liberal MPs in the 1920s, but in general that party benefited least from the redistribution, which added to the problems that it faced after 1918.

The 1918 Reform Act established our contemporary electoral system in almost every recognizable way, and it can be argued that the changes since then have been little more than tinkering – none have been a departure in principle, and none have added more than a relatively limited proportion of new voters. The most significant subsequent measure, the Equal Franchise Act of 1928,[66] is often regarded as simply a delayed instalment of the 1918 Act, completing its work by removing its largest anomaly. It led to the second-largest admission of new voters, and there were 7.1 million more electors on the registers for the May 1929 general election than there had been four-and-a-half years previously in the election of October 1924. However, not all of this increase was previously disqualified female voters, as during these several years the general growth of population had added more men aged over 21 years and women over 30 years who met the existing criteria. David Butler has calculated that the increase in the number of women registered from 1928 to 1929 was 5,299,301, which was 18.4% of the electorate at the general election in May 1929 (for which a special register came into force on 1 May).[67] Of those who were newly qualified by the 1928 act, about one-third were aged over 30 years but had been excluded by the property restrictions, while those aged between 21 and 30 years were certainly not mostly the frivolous and hedonistic 'flappers' characterised by the opponents of the measure.[68] Many of them were working women, in factories, shops and offices (the 1921 census found that 62.2% of women aged 20–24 years were working outside the home), while a high proportion of those aged over 25 years were married.[69]

The only change in the franchise that has occurred since 1928 was not primarily an electoral reform, but rather the necessary consequence of the change in the legal definition of adulthood when this was reduced from 21 to 18 years in 1969. The consequent increase in the electorate from 1969 to 1970 was 2,630,134; at 7.1%, this was proportionately by far the smallest of any franchise extension.[70] The next substantial redistribution of constituencies

---

[65] J. Ramsden, *The Age of Balfour and Baldwin 1902–40* (1978), 123; Kinnear, *British Voter*, 119–24.

[66] Representation of the People (Equal Franchise) Act 1928 (18 & 19 Geo. V, c. 12).

[67] Butler, *Electoral System*, 145.

[68] *Daily Mail*, 30, 31 Mar. 1927; Adrian Bingham, ' "Stop the Flapper Vote Folly": Lord Rothermere, the *Daily Mail*, and the Equalization of the Franchise 1927–28', *Twentieth Century British History*, xiii (2002), 17–37. For the effects of extending the franchise, see J. Rasmussen, 'Women in Labour: The Flapper Vote and Party System Transformation in Britain', *Electoral Studies*, iii (1984), 47–63; J. Rasmussen, 'The Political Integration of British Women: The Response of a Traditional System to a Newly Emergent Group', *Social Science History*, vii (1983), 61–95; P. Lynn, 'The Impact of Women: The Shaping of Political Allegiance in County Durham 1918–1945', *The Local Historian*, xxviii (1998), 159–75.

[69] *Census of England and Wales, 1921: Occupation Tables* (1924), 54, shows that 62.2% of women aged 20–24 years were working outside the home, and that 66.3% of women aged 25–34 years were married or widowed.

[70] *British Electoral Facts*, ed. Craig, 76.

after 1918 took place in 1948,[71] and in 1949 a consolidating act established a procedure of recurring periodic reviews. The first of these resulted in only minor changes in 1958 and the second, which reported in 1969 but was delayed by the Labour government and not implemented until 1970, was more extensive;[72] in more recent decades, the boundary commissioners have engaged upon a more frequent cycle of revision to match the shifting pattern of population. Other than this, there have been only minor changes in the electoral machinery established in 1918, of which the most important has been the expansion of postal voting in recent decades, including allowing British citizens living overseas to cast a vote. When more radical change was proposed in the referendum of 2011 on the introduction of proportional representation, it was rejected by the electorate, just as the house of commons had done during the passage of the 1918 Reform Act.

2

Despite its scale and lasting legacy, the 1918 Reform Act has attracted remarkably little attention from historians. Its main provisions were described (with some simplifications) in David Butler's account of the contemporary electoral system, first published in 1953;[73] apart from this, specific analysis of the act as a whole is limited to a single monograph published in 1978 and one more recent article.[74] There is a vast literature on women's suffrage up to 1914 and a growing body of work on women and politics in the interwar period, but comparatively little – and still less recently – that directly focuses upon even this most famous aspect of the 1918 enfranchisement.[75]

The 1918 Reform Act was followed by a period of unparalleled turbulence in the party system, this being the only occasion when a long-standing party of government declined to minor party status and was replaced by an alternative governing party. However, at first the impact of the changes introduced by the act was almost invisible in the historiography, which focused upon political issues and conflicts during the First World War and their consequences for the Liberal and Labour Parties. The early and influential analysis of the decline of the Liberal Party by Trevor Wilson published in 1966 had no listing in its index for the 1918 Representation of the People Act (or even for broader terms such as 'electoral reform' or 'franchise'), and, curiously, neither did Ross McKibbin's pioneering examination of the development of the Labour Party between 1910 and 1924, although his introduction declared that it was founded 'upon a proposition argued implicitly in the book: that the 1918 Representation of the People Act ... transformed the conditions under which Labour

---

[71] The national government considered a redistribution measure after 20 years, in 1937–8, but did not proceed with it: TNA, PREM 1/255. If they had done so, it would have made a Labour victory at the next election (expected in summer or autumn 1940) even more unlikely, because the population increase in London and the Home Counties had continued since 1918, and, as on the latter occasion, a redistribution would have divided existing Conservative seats into a larger number of new ones.

[72] Rossiter *et al.*, *Boundary Commissions*, 83–104.

[73] Butler, *Electoral System*.

[74] Pugh, *Electoral Reform*; Blackburn, 'Laying the Foundations of the Modern Voting System'.

[75] Pugh, 'Politicians and the Woman's Vote'; Fair, 'Political Aspects of Women's Suffrage'; Hausmann, 'Impact of the Great War on the Discussion of Women's Suffrage'.

grew'.[76] Later on the same page, he made two linked assertions: 'Much of this new electorate voted Labour in 1918, but had it been enfranchised it would probably have done so in 1914 as well.' From this a considerable controversy developed over the following two decades, in particular following the fuller argument for the significance of the 'franchise factor' in the rise of the Labour Party, written jointly by McKibbin with H.C.G. Matthew and J.A. Kay, which appeared in the *English Historical Review* in 1976.[77] They argued that the 1918 Reform Act was 'of first importance in Labour's replacing the Liberal Party', in which 'the introduction of universal franchise … was a critical element', and that there was 'a latent Labour vote in the pre-war electorate, which would have been mobilised with more candidates'.[78] The contention of the 'franchise factor' thesis was that the change in the electoral system was more significant for the rise of Labour (and, therefore, the decline of the Liberals) than the events of the First World War (especially the Liberal split of 1916), which historians examining the Liberal Party – particularly Wilson and Peter Clarke – had put centre stage.[79]

During the following decade, the case for the 'franchise factor' was questioned first by Peter Clarke, then Michael Hart, and finally, and most extensively, by Duncan Tanner. Clarke's response mainly focused on the appendix to the 'franchise factor' article which had contested his previous argument that there was a correlation between high levels of enfranchisement and Liberal support before 1914, as evidence of a continuing Liberal appeal to working-class voters.[80] Hart further developed the argument that the war was the crucial factor in the Liberal decline, as it left the party divided, lacking in new policies and effective leadership, and in an apparently right-of-centre orientation, and that it was these problems rather than the expansion of the franchise which gave Labour the opportunity to displace it in the industrial constituencies after 1918.[81] He also pointed to the remaining size of the Liberal vote under the new franchise in the 1922 and 1923 general elections, and to Liberal electoral successes in the interwar period in constituencies where there had been low levels of enfranchisement before 1914 and thus the largest increases after the 1918 Reform Act.

Tanner's seminal article scrutinised the nature of the pre-war electorate and questioned the extent to which the unenfranchised male population was composed of the working class.[82] He showed that 'the system discriminated against lodgers more than anyone else', who were mostly 'younger and single people', both working class and middle class, while the large number who qualified under the household franchise were older men, generally married or widowed, but from all social strata including some of the poorest. Tanner's

---

[76] T. Wilson, *The Downfall of the Liberal Party, 1914–1935* (1966); Ross McKibbin, *The Evolution of the Labour Party 1910–1924* (Oxford, 1974), xv.

[77] Matthew, McKibbin and Kay 'Franchise Factor', 723–52, reprinted in R. McKibbin, *The Ideologies of Class: Social Relations in Britain 1880–1950* (Oxford, 1990), 66–100.

[78] Matthew, McKibbin and Kay, 'Franchise Factor, 736, 740.

[79] P. Clarke, *Lancashire and the New Liberalism* (Cambridge, 1971).

[80] P.F. Clarke, 'Liberals, Labour and the Franchise', *English Historical Review*, xcii (1977), 582–9, with a response by Kay, McKibbin and Matthew, 589–90; see also P. Clarke's review of McKibbin, *Evolution of the Labour Party*, in *English Historical Review*, xci, 157–63.

[81] M. Hart, 'The Liberals, the War, and the Franchise', *English Historical Review*, xcvii (1982), 820–32.

[82] Tanner, 'Parliamentary Electoral System'; these arguments were further set out in Tanner, *Political Change and the Labour Party*, 102–23; D. Tanner, 'Elections, Statistics and the Rise of the Labour Party 1906–1931', *Historical Journal*, xxxiv (1991), 893–908.

calculation of the increase in the working-class proportion of the electorate from 67% before 1914 to 78% after the 1918 Reform Act was significantly below that of previous studies, which had suggested a rise from 60–62% to 80%.[83] For these reasons, he argued that the new male voters under the 1918 Reform Act were not mainly drawn from a social 'sub-class' who might have significantly different views from existing working-class voters, but were younger men who were of the same class as their older householder fathers and more likely to share their outlook than greatly diverge from it. This has seemed to conclude the 'franchise factor' debate, although another aspect of the effect of the First World War and the changes in the electoral system was examined in the article by Michael Childs on the effects of changing generations.[84]

The only other work to focus specifically on the impact of the 1918 Reform Act has been Michael Dawson's article of 1992, which highlighted the significance of the changes to the limits on election expenses.[85] He argued that these particularly benefited the Labour Party and enabled it to become a truly national party by contesting a large number of seats, and, further, that Labour's ability to run candidates in rural and suburban seats where they had little hope of winning had the effect of preventing Liberal victories and thereby undermining their main rival. In the same year there appeared John Turner's major study of politics during the First World War, which concluded with a detailed statistical analysis of the 1918 general election.[86] In the mid 1990s, Michael Dyer examined the nature and operation of the electoral system in Scotland from the Third Reform Act to 1929, and in an article traced the fortunes of the Scottish 'District of Burghs' type of constituency over a longer period.[87]

During the last two decades, the focus has moved to the impact of democracy on political culture, both generally and within particular parties. Kevin Jefferys has written a history of democracy in Britain since 1918, while Clare Griffiths has discussed mid-20th-century attitudes to mass democracy.[88] The changes in the public culture of politics during election campaigns in the interwar period, particularly relating to violence and concepts of masculinity, which were due mainly to the legacy of the war but also to the inclusion of women, have been discussed by Jon Lawrence and Kit Good.[89] The political culture of the interwar period has been discussed by Pat Thane, particularly in relation to the role

---

[83] Tanner, 'Parliamentary Electoral System', 216; Matthew, McKibbin and Kay 'Franchise Factor', 733; Neal Blewett, *The Peers, the Parties and the People: The General Elections of 1910* (1972), 363–4.

[84] M. Childs, 'Labour Grows Up: The Electoral System, Political Generations, and British Politics 1890–1929', *Twentieth Century British History*, vi (1995), 123–44.

[85] Michael Dawson, 'Money and the Real Impact of the Fourth Reform Act', *Historical Journal*, xxxv (1992), 369–81.

[86] Turner, *British Politics and the Great War*; see also the preliminary findings in J. Turner, 'The Labour Vote and the Franchise after 1918: An Investigation of the English Evidence', in *History and Computing*, ed. P. Denley and D. Hopkins (Manchester, 1987), 136–43; J. Turner, 'Sex, Age and the Labour Vote in the 1920s', in *History and Computing II*, ed. P. Denley, S. Fogelvik and C. Harvey (Manchester, 1989), 243–54.

[87] Dyer, *Capable Citizens*; Dyer, 'Burgh Districts'.

[88] K. Jefferys, *Politics and the People: A History of British Democracy since 1918* (2007); C. Griffiths, 'Dubious Democrats: Party Politics and the Mass Electorate in Twentieth-Century Britain', in *Twentieth-Century Mass Society in Britain and the Netherlands*, ed. B. Moore and H. von Nierop (Oxford, 2006), 30–46.

[89] Jon Lawrence, 'The Transformation of British Public Politics after the First World War', *Past & Present*, No. 190 (2006), 185–216; Jon Lawrence, *Electing Our Masters: The Hustings in British Politics from Hogarth to Blair* (Oxford, 2009); K. Good, ' "Quit Ye Like Men": Platform Manliness and Electioneering 1895–1939', in *Public Men: Masculinity and Politics in Modern Britain*, ed. M. McCormack (Basingstoke, 2007), 143–64.

of women after gaining the suffrage,[90] by Helen McCarthy in relation to new non-party voluntary movements,[91] and by David Thackeray on women's roles within Conservative politics in the period spanning before, during, and after, the achievement of suffrage.[92] As far as the political parties are concerned, most attention has been given to the Conservatives' adaptation to the developments of the First World War and their successful navigation of the new democratic environment between the wars.[93] There has been no comparable national analysis of the fortunes during the war and the immediate post-war period of the Labour Party since Duncan Tanner's major study published in 1990,[94] or of the Liberals for much longer, although there have been valuable regional and local case studies.[95]

The consequence is that the 1918 Reform Act is almost always in the background, and the spotlight of historical enquiry rarely shines directly upon it. Even more than in its origins and passage, this is the case with its provisions and impact, and for that reason this centennial collection has concentrated upon the latter. The first three essays examine the main political parties, assessing their response to the act and its consequences for their fortunes in the interwar era. Stuart Ball discusses the Conservative Party, which before 1914 opposed adult male suffrage and was divided over the question of female suffrage; as the party of property and privilege, it might have been expected to struggle in the environment of a mass electorate overwhelmingly dominated by the working class. Instead, it became the dominant party of the interwar period and it has been the most electorally successful party

---

[90]P. Thane, 'The Impact of Mass Democracy on British Political Culture, 1918–1939', in *The Aftermath of Suffrage: Women, Gender and Politics in Britain, 1918–1945*, ed. J.V. Gottlieb and R. Toye (Basingstoke, 2013), 54–69; P. Thane, 'What Difference did the Vote Make? Women in Public and Private Life in Britain since 1918', *Historical Research*, lxxvi (2003), 268–85; see also M. Hilson, 'Women Voters and the Rhetoric of Patriotism in the British General Election of 1918', *Women's History Review*, x (2001), 325–47; Cheryl Law, *Suffrage and Power: The Women's Movement, 1918–1928* (1997); J. Alberti, *Beyond Suffrage: Feminists in War and Peace 1914–1928* (Basingstoke, 1989); H. Jones, *Women in British Public Life 1914–1950: Gender, Power and Social Policy* (Harlow, 2000).

[91]Helen McCarthy, 'Parties, Voluntary Associations, and Democratic Politics in Interwar Britain', *Historical Journal*, l (2007), 891–912.

[92]D. Thackeray, 'Home and Politics: Women and Conservative Activism in Early Twentieth-Century Britain', *Journal of British Studies*, xlix (2010), 826–48.

[93]J. Stubbs, 'The Impact of the Great War on the Conservative Party', in *The Politics of Reappraisal 1918–1939*, ed. G. Peele and C. Cook (1975), 14–38; Ramsden, *Age of Balfour and Baldwin*, 114–27; R. McKibbin, 'Class and Conventional Wisdom: The Conservative Party and the "Public" in Inter-War Britain', in McKibbin, *Ideologies of Class*, 259–93; D. Jarvis, 'British Conservatism and Class Politics in the 1920s', *English Historical Review*, cxi (1996), 59–84; A. Taylor, 'Speaking to Democracy: The Conservative Party and Mass Opinion from the 1920s to the 1950s', in *Mass Conservatism: The Conservatives and the Public since the 1880s*, ed. S. Ball and I. Holliday (2002), 78–99; M. Hendley, 'Constructing the Citizen: The Primrose League and the Definition of Citizenship in the Age of Mass Democracy in Britain 1918–1928', *Journal of the Canadian Historical Association*, vii (1996), 125–51; N. Keohane, *The Party of Patriotism: The Conservative Party and the First World War* (Farnham, 2010); D. Thackeray, 'Building a Peaceable Party: Masculine Identities in British Conservative Politics c.1903–1924', *Historical Research*, lxxxv (2012), 651–73; David Thackeray, *Conservatism for the Democratic Age: Conservative Cultures and the Challenge of Mass Politics in Early Twentieth Century England* (Manchester, 2013); S. Ball, *Portrait of a Party: The Conservative Party in Britain 1918–1945* (Oxford, 2013), 35–93, 168–71, 331–7, 512–22; N. Fleming, 'Women and Lancashire Conservatism between the Wars', *Women's History Review*, xxvi (2017), 329–49.

[94]Tanner, *Political Change and the Labour Party*; there is also a useful summary essay by C. Wrigley, 'The Impact of the First World War on the Labour Movement', in *Strategy and Intelligence: British Policy during the First World War*, ed. M. Dockrill and D. French (1996), 139–59.

[95]G.L. Bernstein, 'Yorkshire Liberalism during the First World War', *Historical Journal*, xxxii (1989), 102–29; M. Dawson, 'Liberalism in Devon and Cornwall 1910–1931: The Old-Time Religion', *Historical Journal*, xxxviii (1995), 425–37; G. Freeman, 'The Decline of the Liberal Party in the Heart of England: The Liberals in Leicestershire, 1914–24', *Historical Research*, lxxxix (2016), 531–49.

during the century since 1918. There were several reasons for this, but one of them was the way in which the Conservatives took the maximum possible benefit from the changes brought about by the 1918 Reform Act, while also managing to avoid the most dangerous potential threats. Gavin Freeman analyses the role of the electoral changes in the decline of the Liberal Party, and argues that its problems were exacerbated not by any inevitable effects of the 1918 Reform Act itself, but by the failure of the leadership, organisation and constituencies to make any rapid and effective response to the changes that it brought. This was due to the divided state of the Liberal Party, together with a lack of drive and vision from Asquith, who remained party leader even when out of the house of commons in the crucial period of 1918–20; in that sense, it was the contingent event of the First World War that was the prime factor in the Liberal decline. Chris Wrigley analyses the role of the act in the dramatic advance of the Labour Party from its limited Edwardian base to becoming a governing party and the accepted alternative to the Conservatives, and argues that its passage compelled Labour to overhaul its organisation and expand its appeal beyond its pre-war core base of male working-class trade unionists, to appeal to working-class women and white-collar workers. In a parallel with Freeman's analysis, Wrigley concludes that the expansion of the trade union movement during the war provided the Labour Party with greatly-enhanced financial resources and an organisational base at a crucial moment when the Liberals were in disarray.

The middle three essays take a regional perspective, and analyse the impact of the 1918 Reform Act in three parts of the United Kingdom which had very different socio-economic environments, political cultures and previous electoral histories. Ian Cawood examines the ways in which the act affected politics in the wider west midlands area. He finds significant elements of continuity with pre-war politics, although the change in the scale and nature of the electorate led the parties to seek new methods of mass communication. The Conservative and Unionist Party was the most successful in doing this, and this was a factor in enabling it to continue to dominate politics in the region – especially in Birmingham until 1929 – despite the advance of Labour. Ewen Cameron assesses the impact of the 1918 Reform Act in Scotland, focusing particularly on the effects of the redistribution proposals. Although the overall number of Scottish constituencies remained almost unchanged, within this there was a substantial reallocation of seats from the rural regions of the north and south to industrial west Scotland, and especially to Glasgow which was awarded an additional eight seats. In this process, more than half of the 'districts of burghs' type of constituency were eliminated and many of the remainder were recast. These developments aroused much controversy and opposition, and the arguments deployed in defence of the seats proposed for abolition are analysed. The essay concludes that the changes in Scotland created conditions that were favourable to the rise of the Labour Party in the 1920s. John Coakley looks at the 1918 Reform Act in Ireland – a topic largely neglected by historians – and considers it in the context of Ireland's different previous franchise history, which led to a near-tripling of its electorate in 1918, and the recent political events which enabled Sinn Fein to exploit the opportunity provided by the enlarged electorate. He assesses the nature of the act's provisions as they applied to Ireland, the outcome in Ireland of the first general election under its terms, the extent to which this was conditioned by the terms of the act, and the longer-term consequences of the measure. He concludes that the 1918 Reform Act has had a powerful and lasting impact upon Irish Republicans, as for the first time it enabled the whole Irish nation (or rather its adult male component, which for many contemporaries was all that mattered) to voice its demands, and that this mandated the establishment of an independent republic in a united Ireland, which in their eyes no subsequent election has had the authority to annul.

The final three essays examine other significant impacts and legacies of the 1918 Reform Act. Martin Farr considers its consequences for the place that gave it birth, the house of commons, and he examines the expectations and realities of parliament in the democratic age. There was some disillusion, with criticism from both within the chamber and outside that the outcome had been an unrepresentative, and therefore undemocratic, house of commons, and that the legislature had become merely an appendage of the executive. He analyses how the implications of the act were envisaged and how they were experienced, and discusses the legislature that resulted, its members, and how they changed its procedures and conventions, and adapted to the new political environment. Adrian Bingham looks at the view of the 1918 Reform Act and its effects from outside, through the reactions of the press during its passage and afterwards. In this darkest period of the First World War, newspapers across the political spectrum revealed a deep disillusionment with the divisiveness of partisan politics and the party machines. Much of the national press hoped for a revitalised democracy that could face the challenges of post-war reconstruction, and, in their hope of breaking away from the party machines, he finds widespread support for the introduction of proportional representation. Finally, Mari Takayanagi examines how the Speaker's conference of 1916–17 affected the position of women, and looks forward from the 1918 Reform Act to the attainment of equal suffrage in 1928. She considers the hurriedly-passed measure of October 1918 which allowed women to become MPs and the related legislation which removed other sex disqualifications, and traces progress in parliament towards the Equal Franchise Bill of 1928, which followed from pledges given by the Conservative leader, Stanley Baldwin, in the 1924 general election campaign and, controversially, by the home secretary in the following Conservative government, Sir William Joynson-Hicks, in February 1925.

The Conservative Party and the Impact of the 1918 Reform Act

STUART BALL

Before the First World War, the Conservative Party feared the extension of the suffrage to all adult males, and was divided over even a limited granting of votes to women. However, the patriotic public response to the war moderated these attitudes, and by 1916 the Conservatives were in favour of giving the vote to all servicemen. Although the Conservatives were represented in the Speaker's conference which drew up proposals for electoral reform, when its report was published in January 1917, these were almost entirely opposed by the party organisation. However, the Conservatives came to accept adult male suffrage as the only practicable way of recognizing the servicemen's contribution. During the passage of the electoral reform bill, they successfully amended it in several respects and secured gains from the redistribution of constituencies. This essay assesses the Conservative response to the reform proposals and the impact of the Representation of the People Act 1918 upon the party's fortunes, organisation, and culture. During the following decade, the Conservative Party made substantial efforts to reach the female, younger, and working-class voters. While it was reassured by electoral success, and especially support from women, there remained concerns about the nature of democracy and demands from the grass roots for a defensive restoration of powers to the house of lords. However, by 1928, giving the vote to women on equal terms of adult citizenship was seen as the inevitable completion of the new electoral system – in which the Conservatives became the most successful party.

Keywords: Andrew Bonar Law; Conservative Party; electoral reform; Equal Franchise Act 1928; female suffrage; franchise; house of lords; proportional representation; redistribution; Representation of the People Act 1918

1

The Reform Act passed in 1918 (formally titled the Representation of the People Act) was by far the most extensive expansion in the political nation of any franchise measure, and the dozen years after it took effect saw the only substantial and long-term change that has taken place in the British party system. The collapse of the Liberals as a governing party, their replacement on the left by the rise of Labour, and the re-establishment of the Conservative Party[1] as the most successful securer of power, was (like the Reform Act itself) mainly caused by the First World War, but the transformation of the electoral system also made a significant contribution. Even if the 1918 Reform Act was more the

---

[1] The term 'Conservative' is used in this essay for clarity, although the customary name used by the party from the early 1890s to the early 1920s was 'Unionist'. The latter derived from the centrality of defending the union with Ireland as a political issue after 1886 and the alliance with the Liberal Unionists; the latter was formalised by merger in 1912, after which the official name became 'Conservative and Unionist'.

conduit of change than its cause, post-war developments would have had different contours if the act had taken a different form. This essay examines its impact on the Conservative Party – the party of established authority, social hierarchy, privilege and property, which might be thought the most vulnerable and unappealing to mass citizenship-based democracy. Instead, it was to prosper the most in the new environment, and generally has continued to do so throughout the century since 1918 – winning the most seats in 17 of the 27 general elections that have taken place between 1918 and 2017, and being the sole government or the largest party in a coalition for just over two-thirds of the last 100 years.

During the decade before the outbreak of the First World War, the most contentious issues between the Conservative and Liberal Parties were the protectionist programme of 'tariff reform', the powers of the house of lords, and the prospect of the passage of home rule for Ireland. However, alongside these were differences on other matters, including electoral reform – particularly the Liberals' wish to curtail plural voting, the Conservatives' objections to the over-representation of Ireland, and the complexities for both parties in responding to the increasingly prominent but problematic question of votes for women. Conservative attitudes towards the latter were far from monolithic, and while the majority of those who vehemently opposed any measure of female enfranchisement were Conservatives, complete negation was not the position of the majority of the party.[2] There was a spectrum of opinion ranging from the inflexible 'antis' to active suffrage campaigners, such as Lady Knightley and Lady Selborne, who were organised in the Conservative and Unionist Women's Franchise Association.[3] Although there was a reaction against the violence of the militant suffragettes, support for giving votes for women on the same property basis as men was growing among both the leadership and MPs, though less so among peers.[4] Many Conservative MPs took a pragmatic attitude to the question of votes for women, and viewed it mainly in the context of the possible introduction of full adult male suffrage, which they generally assumed would be detrimental to their interests.

Conservative responses were more uniform, negative, and defensive, on other aspects of electoral reform. This was simple enough in the case of plural voting, where an elector might qualify for additional votes due to the ownership of property in another constituency from the one in which they resided, or if a graduate might have a vote in one of the university seats. By their nature, the plural franchises were the preserve of the wealthier strata of society, and all observers were agreed that a large majority of these votes were given to the Conservatives. Although the 'out-voters' were generally a small proportion of the electoral roll, in a number of urban and marginal constituencies they were enough to swing the result in Conservative favour – and hence the wish of the Liberal and Labour parties to abolish them, and the Conservative determination to keep them. In 1912 and

---

[2] G.E. Maguire, *Conservative Women: A History of Women and the Conservative Party 1874–1997* (1998); L. Maguire, 'The Conservative Party and Women's Suffrage', and P. Vervaecke, 'The Primrose League and Women's Suffrage 1883–1918', in *Suffrage Outside Suffragism: Women's Vote in Britain 1880–1914*, ed. M. Boussahba-Bravard (2007), 52–76, 180–201.

[3] For the opponents, see B. Harrison, *Separate Spheres: The Opposition to Women's Suffrage in Britain* (1978), and J. Bush, *Women Against The Vote: Female Anti-Suffragism in Britain* (Oxford, 2007); for Conservative suffragism, see M. Auchterlonie, *Conservative Suffragists: The Women's Vote and the Tory Party* (2007).

[4] Martin Pugh, *The March of the Women: A Revisionist Analysis of the Campaign for Women's Suffrage, 1866–1914* (Oxford, 2000), 102–19.

1913, bills to abolish plural voting were passed in the house of commons, but rejected by the Conservative majority in the house of lords.

2

As in so many other aspects of British politics, the First World War produced transformative changes – not at first, but as a consequence of the conflict's continuation and the increasing demands that it placed upon the nation. The mass enthusiasm for enlistment in the army in 1914–15 and the public acceptance of the introduction of conscription in 1916 changed attitudes towards the expansion of the franchise to full manhood suffrage. Lord Selborne, one of the party leaders, wrote in August 1916 that 'the way that the men of our race have behaved in this war has made adult manhood suffrage inevitable; we shall have to do in one stage what I should have preferred to do in several'.[5] The evident sense of duty and the sacrifice of the young men serving in the armed forces created a consequent entitlement, but under the existing system many of those who enlisted did not qualify for the vote, as the franchise was conferred upon householders and ratepayers, who tended to be older; there was also no mechanism by which those who were serving overseas – or at sea – could cast their vote even if they had one. It had been decided in 1915 to postpone the preparation of the electoral register, and by the time that the issue was returned to in 1916 there was widespread acceptance by politicians in all parties that the contribution of the servicemen must be recognized by extending the male franchise. While many Conservatives would have preferred to limit this to those serving in the armed forces, in practice there was no means of doing so that did not raise more issues than it resolved. As the party leader, Andrew Bonar Law, explained at a special party conference in November 1917 (the only one held during the war):[6]

> Once we had the whole nation practically fighting for us, it was obvious that these men must have votes. (Hear, hear and applause) If you start with that hypothesis it is very difficult to see – I never could see – how you could stop much short of the Bill which is now before the House of Commons.

In consequence, with some reluctance, manhood suffrage became accepted as the price of obtaining the vote for servicemen, which by late 1916 Conservatives at all levels considered necessary and desirable.[7] Additionally, once extending the male franchise became accepted, for most Conservatives this removed the barrier to granting votes for women in at least some form.

It was in this context that Walter Long, one of the Conservative Party's leading figures and, as president of the Local Government Board, the minister overseeing electoral registration, believed that there was a unique opportunity for consensus, and in August 1916 he

---

[5] *The Crisis of British Unionism: The Domestic Political Papers of the 2nd Earl of Selborne 1885–1922*, ed. D.G. Boyce (1987), 194–5: earl of Selborne to marquis of Salisbury, 25 Aug. 1916.

[6] Bodl., Conservative Party Archive [hereafter cited as CPA], NUA/2/1/35: National Unionist Association [hereafter cited as NUA] special conference, 30 Nov. 1917.

[7] N. Keohane, *The Party of Patriotism: The Conservative Party and the First World War* (Farnham, 2010), 131–9.

proposed an inter-party conference.[8] This was established in the following month when the Speaker of the house of commons, James Lowther, agreed to become its chairman and selected as its members 27 back-bench MPs and five peers who reflected a balanced range of opinion. The conference met 26 times between 12 October 1916 and 26 January 1917; Lowther's approach was designed to find the common ground as quickly as possible, and only after that, tackle the more contentious points; the result was that all the participants felt that they were gaining some part of their objectives, and so confrontation was minimised and a breakdown prevented. The proceedings took place in secret and there is no record of them, but it seems clear that there was a compromise between the Conservatives and Liberals, in which the former accepted adult male suffrage and the latter accepted the retention of some plural voting and a redistribution of constituencies. A majority of the conference recommended the inclusion of female suffrage in a more limited form (their report suggested an age limit of 30 or 35 years, leaving it to parliament to decide) and, more surprisingly, there was a unanimous proposal for the introduction of proportional representation.

The eventual outcome of the conference's recommendations would turn out to be more beneficial for the Conservatives than for their opponents, but initially many MPs, the party organisers, and the grass roots, did not see it in that light at all. The secretary of the constituency association in Bath gave his executive committee a bleak summary: 'the recommendations ... will be fatal to the Conservative Party, and that any hope that might have been entertained of their coming into office soon would be swept away into the dim and distant future'.[9] Ominously, the influential Sir Edward Carson, recently appointed a cabinet minister in Lloyd George's new coalition, circulated a petition against the report which was signed by over 100 Conservative MPs.[10] The outgoing chairman of the party organisation, Sir Arthur Steel-Maitland, wrote to Long on 3 February that the proposals were 'absolutely disastrous',[11] and the view of the party's professional local agents was that the Conservative members of the conference had been outmanoeuvred by their Liberal counterparts, partly through failing to seek expert advice.[12] The executive committee of the National Unionist Association, the body of the voluntary membership, appointed a subcommittee to go through the proposals, and its report was strongly critical.[13] Not unnaturally, it focused more on what was being definitely conceded than on what might be hypothetically gained. There were concerns about so sweeping an extension of the male franchise in the middle of a major war, while the redistribution of seats which Conservatives had pressed for before the conflict might now produce very different – or at least, unpredictable – results with such a

[8] Hansard, *Commons Debates*, 5th ser., lxxxv, col. 1949: 15 Aug. 1916; J.D. Fair, *British Inter-Party Conferences: A Study of the Procedure of Conciliation in British Politics, 1867–1921* (Oxford, 1980), 170–2.

[9] Bath and North-East Somerset RO, Acc. 12: Bath Conservative Association [hereafter cited as CA], special executive committee, 22 Feb. 1917.

[10] Parliamentary Archives [hereafter cited as PA], Lloyd George MSS, LG/F/6/2/19: Sir E. Carson to D. Lloyd George, 8 Mar. 1917; Fair, *British Inter-Party Conferences*, 177.

[11] Wiltshire and Swindon Archives, Long MSS, 947/675: Sir A. Steel-Maitland to W. Long, 3 Feb. 1917; National Records of Scotland [hereafter cited as NRS], Steel-Maitland MSS, GD193/202: memorandum by Steel-Maitland, 'Notes on the Report of the Speaker's Conference', 3 Feb. 1917.

[12] *Conservative Agents' Journal*, Apr. 1917, pp. 54, 59–61.

[13] Bodl., CPA, NUA/4/1/2-3: NUA executive committee, 8 Feb., 13 Mar. 1917; NUA/6/1/1: NUA executive subcommittee to consider electoral reform, 20 Feb. 1917.

broadened, and possibly radicalised, electorate.[14] By early May, the Central Office reported that 81 constituencies had sent resolutions or letters against the bill and only four in favour; although in 56 cases the reason given for opposition was that such a measure should not be dealt with in wartime, rather than its provisions, that may also have been the easiest way of saying that it should not be tackled at all, or not in this way.[15] Of those expressing a more specific opinion, 15 constituencies had opposed proportional representation (none being recorded in favour),[16] while of the 15 that had given a verdict on female suffrage, nine had approved of it and six were against.[17]

Reflecting these rising concerns, in mid-April the executive committee urged the party leaders to take a completely different course. Their plan was 'to re-establish registration on a normal basis' by means of 'a new Register to be prepared in the normal way under the existing Law', but with the inclusion of servicemen based on whatever qualification they had before enlisting, and that 'munitions workers should be provided for in the same way or by shortening the qualifying period' (the latter point was because many of these workers had moved to where the new factories had been established).[18] However, the leadership was aware that this was no longer a tenable position in the wake of the Speaker's conference report and in the context of both parliamentary and public opinion. On 28 March, the house of commons had approved Asquith's motion accepting the report and calling for legislation based upon it to be promptly introduced, by 341 to 62, with all of the latter being Conservatives.[19] Bonar Law later explained at the special party conference of November 1917, in reply to a question as to why the simpler procedure of a registration bill amended to include servicemen had not been followed, that 'you have to look at things as they were in the House of Commons'; such a measure would have been open to amendments from all sides, and 'it would have been impossible to get through the trouble that would have been raised'. A limited male enfranchisement was not practicable, and he called upon his audience not just 'to make the best of the situation which has arisen', but to seize the opportunity 'to make our party what Disraeli called it – and what, if it is to have any existence, it must be – a really national party'.[20]

---

[14]Bradford RO, 36D78/14: Bradford CA, finance and general purposes committee, 19 June 1917: J. Fawcett to Sir J. Boraston (principal agent).

[15]Sheffield Central Library, LD2103: Sheffield Central CA, special meeting, 20 Feb. 1917. Lord Derby told the party leader that the Lancashire Provincial Division was 'very much opposed to the Speaker's proposals': PA, Bonar Law MSS, BL/81/6/13: earl of Derby to A. Bonar Law, 15 May 1917.

[16]This balance of opinion is reflected in the surviving city and constituency association minute books, with several hostile resolutions and only one favourable view, but even here opinion was divided and only narrowly came down in favour: Sheffield Central Library, LD2107: City of Sheffield CA, annual general meeting, 27 Mar. 1918. This is a notably different pattern from the Conservative-supporting national press, which were strongly in favour of proportional representation throughout the passage of the bill: see the editorial columns of the *Daily Telegraph*, *Observer* and *The Times*.

[17]Bodl., CPA, NUA/4/1/3: NUA executive, 8 May 1917.

[18]Bodl., CPA, NUA/3/1/1: NUA report of executive to central council, 17 Apr. 1917.

[19]Different voting figures for the divisions during the passage of the bill are given in various books and articles; some variations are due to errors, but generally in the case of Commons' divisions the discrepancies are due to whether or not the two tellers on each side are counted as having voted. The division list figures here have been checked with the official record of debates and are the ones given there, which in the case of the house of commons do not include the tellers, as technically they have not voted in the lobby which they are counting.

[20]Bodl., CPA: NUA special conference, 30 Nov. 1917.

This was more than a pious hope; the war had demonstrated the loyalty of the working class and had strengthened patriotic and national feeling, with the latter shifting the political centre of gravity in a rightwards direction. This, in turn, fostered the Conservative Party's sense that it was in tune with public opinion; as the chairman of the party conference of November 1917 declared in his opening remarks: 'the note of patriotism has always resounded through the length and breadth of our ranks'.[21] On the only national issue that mattered in 1917 and 1918 – the vigorous and unconstrained prosecution of the war to achieve decisive victory – this was the case to an extent that could not be matched by either the fractured Liberals or the Labour Party, with its highly-publicised wing of doubters and critics who were pilloried as supposed 'pacifists'. While there were certainly Conservative fears about the growing strength and militancy of the labour movement, and its evolution in a socialist, syndicalist, and perhaps even revolutionary, direction, these were outweighed (although not removed) by the conviction that the large majority of the working class were dependably patriotic. By mid 1917, there was acceptance that the war had made political change inevitable, and that following the February revolution in Russia and the entry of the United States in April, 'the very war itself is now a war of democracy against autocracy', which 'must have a direct bearing on the policy of the [Conservative] party'.[22] Trust in the people became not just a viable strategy, but the best means of assuring social stability and national cohesion. As Bonar Law told the special conference: 'our Party if it is properly conducted has no reason to fear that the mass of the people in this country will not support it'.[23]

The formal first reading of the Representation of the People Bill in the house of commons took place on 15 May 1917 without a division, and on 23 May the second reading was passed by 329 to 40. While all of those voting against were Conservatives, it was more significant that 110 Conservative MPs supported the bill; this also showed the evolving balance of opinion since Asquith's motion of 28 March, which had been opposed (including the tellers) by 64 Conservatives and supported by 79. By early June, as the bill entered the committee stage of detailed debate, the Conservative Party had generally come to accept the inevitability of substantial reform, especially if the key element of votes for servicemen was to be achieved.[24] This position had not been attained without management and effort; the Conservative Party chairman informed Lloyd George regarding 'the Franchise Bill' that 'Bonar Law will be able to tell you by what a narrow squeak I managed to secure acceptance of the general principles of that measure.'[25] Thus the central council, the largest body representative of the constituencies, in 'not too easy a meeting to guide',[26] on 8 June unanimously approved the report of the executive's subcommittee, which with some simplification of past history declared that the Conservative Party 'has always been

[21] Bodl., CPA: NUA special conference, 30 Nov. 1917.

[22] *Daily Telegraph*, 29 May 1917, p. 4.

[23] Bodl., CPA: NUA special conference, 30 Nov. 1917; National Library of Scotland, 10424/28: Scottish Unionist Association, western divisional council, 28 Feb. 1917.

[24] However, in some areas, expressions of opposition continued for some time; in late June, the Yorkshire Area unanimously passed a resolution that 'The Franchise Bill at present before Parliament is in most of its essential features in direct conflict with the views of the [Conservative] Party in Yorkshire': Leeds Central Library: Yorkshire Area, council, 29 June 1917.

[25] PA, Bonar Law MSS, BL/82/1/10: Sir G. Younger to Lloyd George, 8 June 1917.

[26] PA, Bonar Law MSS, BL/82/1/11: Younger to Lloyd George, 9 June 1917.

in favour of … an extension of the franchise', although this was conditional upon it being accompanied by a redistribution of constituencies and a restoration of powers to the house of lords.[27] However, while the main provisions of the bill were now accepted, Conservative Party managers certainly did not embrace the measure in all its aspects.[28] There was much that could be adjusted in defence of the party's interests, and in preparation for this a new subcommittee of the National Unionist Association executive was established on 22 May.[29] Led by the chairman of the party organisation, Sir George Younger, it included the joint principal agents and several prominent members of the executive, and was advised by a group of experienced constituency agents; its role was to consider 'in what direction amendments should be made' and give advice to the MPs moving them.[30] Over 150 amendments were tabled, and in several cases the minister in charge of the bill, the home secretary, Sir George Cave, was forced to concede a free vote and the amendment was carried.

One of the latter was important for its symbolism rather than the relatively small number of voters who were affected. The disenfranchisement of conscientious objectors was a topic about which Conservatives felt strongly; it was not among the proposals of the Speaker's conference, but was inserted after an amendment moved by Younger was passed in a free vote by 209 to 171 on 21 November 1917.[31] This was not a matter of the number of conscientious objectors, which was insignificant even on the pre-war franchise, but because of what they represented – to Conservatives, and it must be said to many others as well, the pacifists had failed the test not just of patriotism but more basically of citizenship, having placed their personal moral purity above the safety of the community. They were, therefore, not entitled to exercise the privileges of that citizenship, and to allow them to do so would be an insult to the fallen and an affront to the living servicemen who had fulfilled their duty. Although the numbers were vastly different, there was a direct relationship of principle between giving the vote to servicemen and taking it away from pacifists.

The most important changes for the Conservatives were in two areas. The first of these was the defence of the agricultural interest, with which the party was traditionally linked and which generally supported it. As well as a likely reduction in the number of agricultural seats due to their lower population, there was concern that their rural nature would be diluted as a consequence of the smaller boroughs losing their separate representation and being absorbed into the neighbouring county divisions. On 18 June 1917, Conservative support secured an amendment of the instructions to the boundary commissioners, so

[27] Bodl., CPA, NUA/3/1/1: NUA central council, 8 June 1917, 'Electoral Reform "Representation of the People Bill", Report of the Sub-committee to the Executive Committee'.

[28] Keohane, *Party of Patriotism*, 137–42.

[29] Bodl., CPA: NUA executive, 22 May 1917.

[30] Bodl., CPA, NUA/6/1/1: NUA executive subcommittee to consider the Representation of the People Bill, 24, 25 May, 1 June 1917; NUA executive, 7 June 1917; NUA report of executive to central council, 10 July 1917; *Conservative Agents' Journal*, July 1917, report of special registration committee, 147–9; Martin Pugh, *Electoral Reform in War and Peace 1906–18* (1978), 105–6.

[31] This was first proposed in an amendment moved by the Conservative MP, Ronald McNeill, during the committee stage on 26 June 1917, which was defeated in a whipped vote; it probably originated from the NUA executive subcommittee to consider the Representation of the People Bill, which on 24 May 1917 considered 'that Conscientious Objectors ought to be disfranchised'; see also Pugh, *Electoral Reform*, 113–14, 125–6.

that the scale and economic composition of a constituency would be taken into account as well as its population.[32] This was intended to avoid the rural constituencies from becoming unmanageable in physical size, and thereby retain a larger number of them. The second area was the business premises franchise, which the original proposals for proportional representation would have rendered useless in the cities – the very places where it was most numerous and effective. The abandonment of the scheme for large multi-member borough constituencies using the single transferable vote did much to restore the efficacy of the business franchise. In addition, an amendment was carried in November 1917 under which a voter resident in one constituency of a town or city which was divided into separate single-member seats could qualify for the business vote in another constituency within the same town or city; thus, a factory owner or shopkeeper who lived in Newcastle North and occupied business premises in Newcastle Central could now cast a vote in both, which had not been the case previously. The 1918 Reform Act limited the ways in which people could qualify for an additional vote, and this considerably reduced the number of plural votes from the pre-war level in England and Wales of 450,000–475,000 to 159,013 in 1918 and 211,257 in 1924;[33] the act also introduced a new restriction that no one could cast more than two votes in total, even if they might qualify for more.[34] However, enabling the use of the business vote within the same divided town or city made it more useful and more likely that it would be cast, and this was certainly advantageous to the Conservative Party.[35]

The main controversy as the bill proceeded through its stages was the proposed introduction of proportional representation, by means of creating constituencies in the cities and largest towns which would return between three and five MPs using the single transferable vote system. While it might be thought that this would benefit the Conservatives where their support was a minority, in practice the partitioning of the cities into individual divisions by the Third Reform Act in 1885 had often worked well for them.[36] In several cities, the party had been able to win a high proportion of the seats through effective organisation and the assistance of the business vote. In this context, proportional representation could only undermine the party's position; hence the vehemently-hostile response from Liverpool, where the Conservatives had won eight of the nine seats in December 1910, whose leaders painted an apocalyptic scenario and threatened to resign if proportional representation was applied to it.[37] However, the prime minister, Lloyd George, had indicated his lack of support for proportional representation in the original debate on the Speaker's

[32]Sanders diary, 10, 15 June, 20 July 1917, in *Real Old Tory Politics: The Political Diaries of Sir Robert Sanders, Lord Bayford, 1910–1935*, ed. John Ramsden (1984).

[33]D. Tanner, *Political Change and the Labour Party 1900–1918* (Cambridge, 1990), 100; *British Electoral Facts 1832–1987*, ed. F.W.S. Craig (Aldershot, 1989), 78.

[34]In fact, very few did so; Central Office estimated that only around 2,000 men had four or more votes: NRS, Steel-Maitland MSS, GD193/202: memorandum by W. Gales, Oct. 1916.

[35]Sanders diary, 22 Nov. 1917; J. Ramsden, *The Age of Balfour and Baldwin 1902–1940* (1978), 121.

[36]See Table 4 in the introduction to this volume (p. 15). The NUA executive subcommittee 'were strongly of opinion that single member constituencies were to be preferred': NUA executive subcommittee to consider electoral reform, 24 Feb. 1917.

[37]PA, Bonar Law MSS, BL/83/3/2, BL/83/3/12: C. Petrie and A. Salvidge to Bonar Law, 1, 3 May 1918; this was in response to the scheme proposed by the royal commission set up by the act, which reported in Apr. 1918.

conference report on 28 March 1917,[38] and this made it easier for Conservatives to oppose it without seeming to be partisan or disloyal to the government.

Some Conservatives favoured the single transferable vote as the means by which a moderate majority of opinion could block socialist, or even revolutionary, extremism, or more pessimistically as the way of retaining some representation in the cities from being swept away by a working-class Labour tide under adult suffrage; these views were held more widely in the house of lords than in the Commons, and led to disagreement between the two Houses during the final stages of the bill.[39] However, many Conservative MPs were opposed to the single transferable vote, and even more strongly to the alternative vote, because they expected – probably correctly, given the pre-war Liberal-Labour pact – that in both systems the second preferences of Liberal and Labour voters would be given to each other, with the result that the Conservatives would be defeated in seats which in a three-way contest under the first-past-the-post system they would win. Other objections to proportional representation included the unworkable size of the multi-member constituencies that were required for it to work effectively, and the view that it would increase, rather than diminish, the dependency of candidates on the party machine for selection and election. One critical constituency resolution observed that 'Members of Parliament should be in close relation with their constituents; they are responsible not to their political partisans only but to the whole of the electors. Under PR this will be lost.'[40]

While there was also a considerable number of Liberal MPs who were dubious about, or felt threatened by, the single transferable vote scheme, the pattern of party attitudes was apparent in the votes at various stages during the passage of the bill. Proportional representation was first defeated during the committee stage of the bill on 12 June 1917, when a resolution amending the instructions to the boundary commissioners to proceed on the basis that it would not be implemented was passed by 149 to 141, with 85 Conservatives among the majority and only 38 in the minority. Subsequently, the alternative vote was approved twice during the bill's passage, although on 9 August this was by the margin of just a single vote: 125 MPs (including only two Conservatives) voted in favour, while 124 (of whom 111 were Conservatives) voted against.[41] It was approved by the much larger margin of 150 to 121 during the report stage on 22 November (when the single transferable vote was again defeated), but when the bill was considered in the house of lords in January 1918, the Conservative-dominated upper chamber three times removed the alternative vote and replaced it with the single transferable vote. The Lords' amendments were rejected on each occasion by the house of commons, leading to a brief confrontation between the two chambers. In the end, a compromise was agreed under which both the alternative vote and the single transferable vote were dropped from the bill, and so the final form of the

---

[38] Hansard, *Commons Debates*, 5th ser., xcii, col. 492: 28 Mar. 1917. A similar view, that 'its disappearance would in no way disturb the other parts of the structure', had been expressed in the long letter supporting the conference proposals from 'Unionist MP', in the *Daily Telegraph*, 8 Mar. 1917.

[39] Sanders diary, 10 Feb. 1918; for a discussion of varying Conservative responses, within and between both Houses, see Pugh, *Electoral Reform*, 158–67; J. Hart, *Proportional Representation: Critics of the British Electoral System 1820–1945* (Oxford, 1992), 182, 186–7, 190–1; Keohane, *Party of Patriotism*, 142–3.

[40] Surrey History Centre, 353/3/2/1: Reigate CA, executive committee, 3 Apr. 1918.

[41] Hansard, *Commons Debates*, 5th ser., xcvii, col. 652: 9 Aug. 1917; the figures published in *The Times*, 11 Aug. 1917, p. 7, included the two tellers on each side, who were two Conservatives for the 'No' vote and two Liberals for the 'Aye' vote.

Representation of the People Act which received the royal assent on 6 February 1918 retained the existing first-past-the-post system everywhere, except for the four university constituencies that returned two or more MPs.[42] The Conservative peers certainly assisted their party's prospects by securing the elimination of the alternative vote; while David Butler's estimates of the outcomes of the general elections from 1923 to 1945 if it had been operating give results almost as large for the three big Conservative victories of 1924, 1931, and 1935, the projection for the three defeats is much poorer. In 1923, the Conservatives with 195 MPs would have been one behind Labour and the Liberals would have been the largest party with 217 MPs, with the incalculable consequences of a Liberal government and the potential stemming of that party's decline; in 1929, Labour would have been very close to an overall majority, with 301 MPs to 167 Conservatives (nearly 100 fewer seats than they won under first-past-the-post) and 137 Liberals, and in 1945 Labour would have had 32 more MPs than their actual landslide, and the Conservatives at 171, over 40 fewer, which would have given them a harder task in recovery.[43]

3

The 1918 Reform Act contained more provisions that were advantageous to the Conservative Party than those that were detrimental, although there were initial fears about several aspects and the benefits only became apparent over time. The area of greatest concern and potential danger was the extension of the male franchise to include almost all adults, and the fear that the wartime expansion of trade unionism, the other economic and social effects of the war, and the ending of the disqualification from voting of those who had been in receipt of poor law relief would mainly benefit the Labour Party, which 'will have a majority of voters throughout the whole of the country'.[44] This was a particular concern of Conservatives in industrial areas, and the chairman of the party in Liverpool – a key location in a key region for the Conservatives – sent a pessimistic assessment of the future consequences to the party leader in the autumn of 1917.[45] More generally, the expert advice given to the National Unionist Association executive's subcommittee in February 1917 was that the new male voters resulting from the change to a simple residence qualification would probably be against the party in the proportion of six to four.[46] Concern about the loyalty and stability of the industrial working class was fanned by the increase in strikes in 1917–18, but was also partly offset by confidence in the patriotic attitudes of the servicemen.[47]

When the war came to an end, rather unexpectedly quickly, with the Armistice of 11 November 1918, this removed the justification for further extensions of the parliament that had been elected in December 1910. This was also Lloyd George's opportunity to consolidate his position and secure a personal mandate before the peace negotiations. The

[42]As part of the compromise, the act contained the provision that a royal commission would be appointed to draw up a proposal for the application of the single transferable vote in seats that would in total return around 100 MPs; this was published on 13 Apr. 1918 but rejected by the house of commons on 13 May.

[43]D.E. Butler, *The Electoral System in Britain, 1918–1951* (Oxford, 1953), 191.

[44]Bodl., CPA: NUA special conference, speech by Lord Chaplin, 30 Nov. 1917.

[45]PA, Bonar Law MSS, BL/82/5/7: Petrie to Bonar Law, 13 Oct. 1917.

[46]NUA executive subcommittee to consider electoral reform, 20 Feb. 1917.

[47]Ramsden, *Age of Balfour and Baldwin*, 115–17.

popularity of the 'man who won the war' was certainly a factor in the decision of the Conservative leaders, which was endorsed by a meeting of the parliamentary party, to continue the coalition into peacetime and contest the imminent general election in alliance with Lloyd George and his wing of the Liberal Party. However, the other key element in this decision was concern about the potential volatility of the new electorate and uncertainty about how it would behave, especially in the context of industrial militancy at home and spreading Bolshevik revolution in central and eastern Europe. In fact, the transformation of the electorate, in which many men as well as women would be casting a ballot for the first time, was not as great a danger for the Conservatives as the overall numbers suggested. Before 1914, the rural areas and country towns with their more settled populations had higher proportions of male enfranchisement than was the case in the industrial towns and the cities, with some agricultural counties reaching an average of 81%.[48] With male enfranchisement in 1918 of around 95% in these areas, the increment was relatively modest in that gender and most of the new voters were women, to whom the Conservative Party was able to project an inclusive appeal. Many of these areas already returned Conservative MPs and continued to do so in the new democracy, and other similar constituencies followed this pattern as the Liberal Party declined.

The restrictions on female suffrage tilted that electorate in directions likely to be more favourable to the Conservatives, particularly by excluding younger women. This was partly due to the proportion of Conservative support increasing in older age groups, a pattern which has been observed over a long period and still applies, and partly to the economic and social structure of the interwar period. Many working women – the group most likely to come into close contact with trade unionism and the Labour Party – were too young to vote under the 1918 Reform Act; of the 3,671,596 women aged over 20 years which the 1921 census recorded in occupations, 1,060,058 (28.9%) were aged 20–24 years, and 1,051,191 (28.6%) were in the next age band of 25–34 years; if it is assumed that half of the latter were aged 25–29 years, then 43.2% of working women were under the qualifying age of 30 years. Most women left work on marriage, which was usually by their mid-20s and was soon followed by motherhood. According to the 1921 census, 72.6% of women aged 20–24 years were single, while 78.5% of women aged over 25 years were either married or widowed; the latter groups also comprised 90.2% of the women aged over 25 years who were not in occupations outside the home.[49] In the interwar period, the Conservative Party pitched its appeal to female voters primarily to the married woman, based upon the cross-class values of home and family, and in contrast to the masculine (often misogynistic) and confrontational environment of the workplace. Women were expected to take a common-sense approach and be less attracted to socialist theories, and married women were assumed to put their family interests first. This was thought to be particularly the case in the working class, where they would exert a moderating influence upon their trade unionist and Labour-supporting husbands. Conservative propaganda in the 1920s often portrayed the working-class wife and mother (or an older experienced working woman) as seeing through the false rhetoric of the socialist agitator and preventing destructive industrial conflict.[50] The

---

[48] W.L. Miller, *Electoral Dynamics in Britain since 1918* (1977), 3.

[49] *Census of England and Wales, 1921: Occupation Tables* (1924), 54.

[50] David Jarvis, 'Mrs Maggs and Betty: The Conservative Appeal to Women Voters in the 1920s', *Twentieth Century British History*, v (1994), 129–52.

property restriction on female suffrage was of less assistance than the age limit, and may even have been disadvantageous to the Conservative Party. The largest single category of women aged over 30 years who did not qualify for the vote after 1918 was the group of domestic servants, of whom there were nearly half a million in the early 1920s.[51] These women may have been most likely to identify with the opinions or economic interests of their employers, and certainly were least likely to be members of trade unions or be living in the poorest districts of towns and cities (although they may well have had relatives who were).

The retention of plural voting was certainly of most help to the Conservative Party (and the least help to Labour); the new limitation to using only two votes was not a very significant handicap, as in most cases practicality made casting any more difficult to manage. Contemporary observers had no doubt that the business vote was overwhelmingly Conservative. At the time of the 1931 census, there were 21 constituencies where the non-resident voters comprised more than 5% of the electorate,[52] and a further 37 where they were more than 2%; sometimes, this was more than the winning candidate's majority. In the first category, which comprised 22 parliamentary seats as it included the double-member City of London, out of the 154 possible wins in the seven interwar general elections of 1918–35, the Conservative candidate was elected on 104 occasions, a success rate of 67.5%.[53] The other form of plural voting, the university seats, continued to be of much more benefit to the Conservatives than any other party. Of the 12 university seats in England, Wales, Scotland, and Northern Ireland, in the general elections from 1918 to 1935, the Conservative Party normally won eight or nine of these, with Liberals and Independents accounting for the rest, and no success for the Labour Party (see Table 3 in the introduction to this volume, p. 7).[54] In view of these advantages, it is not surprising that the first Labour government to enjoy a parliamentary majority abolished both the business vote and the university seats in the 1948 Representation of the People Act.

Several of the other provisions in the 1918 Reform Act were either marginally helpful or mainly neutral in their impact upon Conservative MPs and the party organisation. While its candidates were recruited from the small minority of the wealthier strata of society, the

[51] In census category 900, 'Domestic Servants – Indoor', there were 357,707 women aged over 35 years and 234,567 aged 25–34 years; if it is assumed that half of the latter were aged 30–34 years, this gives a total of 474,990: *Census of England and Wales, 1921*, 104.

[52] These were the business and central districts of the larger cities, and in descending order: City of London (83.9%), Manchester Exchange (31.6%), Holborn (30.5%), Westminster Abbey (27.7%), Liverpool Exchange (27.8%), Leeds Central (12.0%), Finsbury (11.8%), Sheffield Central (11.3%), Bradford Central (9.9%), St Marylebone (9.6%), Birmingham Edgbaston (9.3%), Newcastle Central (9.2%), Birmingham West (8.3%), Bristol Central (8.3%), Westminster St George's (7.8%), Hull Central (7.2%), Shoreditch (7.2%), Southwark North (6.6%), Nottingham Central (6.4%), Whitechapel and St George's (6.3%), and St Pancras South-West (5.8%); figures from the election and census database constructed for S. Ball, *Portrait of a Party: The Conservative Party in Britain 1918–1945* (Oxford, 2013), see appendix ii.

[53] Only official Conservative candidates have been counted. This figure probably underestimates Conservative strength, as in four of the constituencies no Conservative candidate was nominated in 1931 and 1935 against sitting National Labour or Liberal National MPs; if these eight contests are removed from the possible wins, the Conservative success rate becomes 71.2%. David Butler estimated the number of seats won due to the business vote in the general elections of 1922–35 as between the lowest probability of 43 and the highest probability of 75, an average of 7–12: Butler, *Electoral System*, 148.

[54] There was a dip to seven Conservatives in 1935 because three Independents were elected under the 'National' label; J.S. Meisel, *Knowledge and Power: The Parliamentary Representation of Universities in Britain and the Empire* (Oxford, 2011), 73–8.

expectation that they would personally not only pay their election expenses but also give a substantial annual subscription to their constituency association (often as much as the MPs' salary of £400 per annum) placed strains on the pockets of many in the upper-middle and even upper class, especially in the post-war era of greatly-increased taxation and economic difficulty. This led to the safest seats being effectively auctioned to the highest bidder by choosing their candidates on their wealth rather than their ability, a problem that was often denounced in the interwar era but only finally tackled in the Maxwell-Fyfe Report of 1949. Thus, the lower limit on election expenses in the 1918 Reform Act was generally welcome to Conservatives, as there was an inevitable tendency (and even an expectation from their associations) of spending up to whatever the limit was. On the other hand, finding the money for the new requirement of the candidate's deposit of £150 was not a problem – it was not only much less than the election expenses, which could be around £800–900, but not getting it back was a rare event for a Conservative – of the party's 3,753 candidates in the general elections from 1918 to 1935, only 29 (0.8%) forfeited their deposit. The free postal delivery helped to keep down expenses and was useful, as it was 'frequently the only way in which a communication from the candidate can reach isolated voters'.[55] However, this and the free use of school rooms for meetings were of most assistance to the candidates with the least financial resources, and generally they were not the Conservatives. The provision that all constituencies polled on the same day placed a practical restriction on the use of the business premises vote, but this had much less impact as plural voting was now limited to casting only one extra vote, and it was more than outweighed by the new ability to use the second vote in a constituency that was part of the same borough or county.

The one reform for which Conservatives had unitedly and wholeheartedly pressed before 1914 was the redistribution of constituencies. There were two aspects to this, of which the first was that since the boundaries had been drawn in 1885, migratory trends in mainland Britain had swollen the population not only within, but also around, the major cities, and nowhere more so than in the capital and its suburban sprawl – between the 1901 and 1911 censuses, the population of Middlesex increased by 42%. The largest electorates were to be found in the 'home counties'; in 1910, Romford had 53,002 voters, Walthamstow had 39,117, Harrow had 35,379 and Wimbledon had 34,719, when most constituencies were in the 8,000–15,000 range and few exceeded 20,000. There was a strong case that these areas were under-represented and should be divided into a larger number of constituencies; as they were predominantly represented by Conservatives, this would almost certainly increase the party's number of MPs (as it did after 1918, see Table 1). The same demographic causes had diminished the population of rural areas, especially the more remote and less prosperous. This particularly affected the border and highland regions of Scotland; they were mainly represented by Liberal MPs, and so the Liberal Party had resisted a mainland redistribution from which it was likely to be doubly disadvantaged.

The second aspect of redistribution was also inimical to the continuation of Liberal government, although in this case indirectly. This was the change in the balance of population between Ireland and mainland Britain since the Act of Union of 1800, which meant

---

[55] *Conservative Agents' Journal*, Oct. 1920, p. 10.

Table 1: *The Effects of Constituency Redistribution in the Home Counties*

County	December 1910		1922	
	no. seats	no. Cons. wins	no. seats	no. Cons. wins
Essex	11	6	20	13
Kent	15	12	15	14
Middlesex	7	6	17	14
Surrey	7	7	12	11
Total	40	31	64	52

Notes: This table compares the number of seats and the number won by the Conservative Party in the general elections of December 1910 and 1922 in the four counties bordering London. The 1918 general election has not been used because the Conservative Party was then part of a coalition and did not contest a significant number of seats. Only official Conservative candidates have been counted (for 1910 this includes official Liberal Unionist candidates).
Sources: *British Parliamentary Election Results 1885–1918*, ed. F.W.S Craig (1974); *British Parliamentary Election Results 1918–1949*, ed. F.W.S Craig (2nd edn, 1977).

that the 100 Irish seats in the house of commons created by that measure was now a considerable over-representation.[56] Whereas in 1821 the population of Ireland had been 32.5% of the United Kingdom total, by the census of 1911 it had greatly diminished, through the combined effects of the Great Famine of 1845–51, continued emigration, and changes in family structure, and Ireland now accounted for only 9.7%.[57] In the elections from 1885 to 1910, Irish Nationalist MPs were returned for between 80 and 85 of the seats, and this over-representation of Ireland had benefited the Liberal Party ever since Gladstone's adoption of home rule as Liberal policy in 1886. After the 1910 elections, in which the Conservatives and Liberals won almost the same number of seats, to Conservative fury it was Irish Nationalist support – even more than the much smaller Labour Party – which had maintained the Liberal government in office and enabled it to crush the power of the house of lords in the 1911 Parliament Act and embark on the disestablishment of the anglican church in Wales and, worst of all, a Home Rule Bill that would now reach the statute book.

In this context, Conservatives considered that, if electoral reform was to be 'dealt with on a sound basis', 'an Equitable scheme of Redistribution ... to be applicable to the *whole* of the U[nited] K[ingdom]' was an essential element.[58] This objective was only partially achieved, as although there were some changes within Ireland, the total number of Irish seats was not reduced. However, the wholesale revision of constituency boundaries in mainland Britain did substantially benefit the Conservatives, as can be seen in Table 1.

[56]This became 101 seats after the creation of a second seat for Trinity College Dublin in the 1832 Reform Act, and remained at that number in the 1867 and 1884 Reform Acts.
[57] *Census of England and Wales, 1911: General Report, with Appendices* (1917), 263, appendix C, 'Tables Relating to the United Kingdom'.
[58]Bodl., CPA: NUA central council, 8 June 1917, 'Electoral Reform "Representation of the People Bill", Report of the Sub-committee to the Executive Committee'.

In Scotland, the disappearance of the smaller 'District of Burghs' type of constituency through merger into their surrounding county divisions was more often than not to Conservative advantage.[59] In one notable example, it contributed to the defeat of Asquith in the enlarged East Fife constituency in 1918.[60] Overall, it has been suggested that the Conservative Party made a net gain of around 30 seats from the redistribution.[61]

It has also been argued that the number of safe Conservative seats increased, as more constituencies had a substantial element of their population that was either middle class or engaged in agriculture. Two hundred constituencies had 20% or more of their occupied male population in the census categories used by Michael Kinnear to identify the middle class, although the accuracy of the calculation is affected by the insoluble problem that census data exist only for each borough as a whole, and not for the individual constituencies within a divided borough.[62] Thus the city of Manchester, which comprised ten single-member constituencies, had 23.3% middle-class population as a whole, and so all ten seats are included in Kinnear's total – of course, the middle-class voters were not evenly distributed across the city, with some divisions having more and others less. As that cannot be identified statistically there is no alternative to this rather crude methodology, but it is more likely that the actual number of seats with a middle-class population of more than 20% was around 150 to 160. There were also 86 county constituencies with more than 30% of their occupied male population engaged in agriculture. The Conservative Party won most of these seats in every general election apart from 1923, when the Liberals won 43 and the Conservatives 38; however, with the Liberal decline after this, the Conservatives won 74 in 1924, and even in defeat in 1929 they won 55.[63] While being very highly agricultural did not always correlate with Conservative success, as several of the most agricultural seats had a strong nonconformist and Liberal tradition, nevertheless the Conservative Party could count most of rural England and much of rural Scotland among its bedrock, and increasingly so after 1929.

Taking together the seats with significant middle-class and agricultural sectors, John Ramsden concluded that, in the interwar period, 'well over 200 seats [were] unshakably safe', and as many as 300 were 'reliable enough to be won except in a very bad year'.[64] With the house of commons reduced to 615 seats after the Anglo-Irish Treaty of 1921, the advantage of such a solid base was clear – not only in winning general elections but also in defeats, when the Conservatives were able to prevent the Labour Party from gaining an overall majority. However, although the redistribution is often discussed in terms of conferring an advantage on the Conservatives, it would be more accurate to say that it removed a disadvantage which they had suffered in the pre-war years and broadly restored a level

[59] M. Dyer, 'Burgh Districts and the Representation of Scotland, 1707–1983', *Parliamentary History*, xv (1996), 302–4; Michael Dyer, *Capable Citizens and Improvident Democrats: The Scottish Electoral System, 1884–1929* (Aberdeen, 1996), 107–12.

[60] Bodl., Asquith MSS, 33/25: A. Birrell to H. Asquith, 28 Dec. 1918; 33/60: J. Hogge to Asquith, 30 Dec. 1918; S.R. Ball, 'Asquith's Decline and the General Election of 1918', *Scottish Historical Review*, lxi (1982), 44–61.

[61] Ramsden, *Age of Balfour and Baldwin*, 123; Keohane, *Party of Patriotism*, 146–53.

[62] M. Kinnear, *The British Voter: An Atlas and Survey since 1885* (2nd edn, 1981), 122–4.

[63] Kinnear, *British Voter*, 119–21. For evidence of the role of agriculture in Conservative support between the wars, see Ball, *Portrait of a Party*, 112, Table 2.7.

[64] Ramsden, *Age of Balfour and Baldwin*, 123. For a statistical analysis of the middle-class correlation with Conservative support in the interwar period, see Ball, *Portrait of a Party*, 109–11.

playing field. Of course, the same demographic trends continued, and 20 years further on it was again the home counties which had constituencies with excessively large electorates and their Conservative MPs who were pressing the national government in 1937–8 to take steps to remedy the situation before the next election, as once again 'we as a Party are placed under a considerable disadvantage'.[65]

A more immediate impact of the boundary changes was to stimulate, in 1917–18, a revival of the local constituency associations, many of which had lapsed into inactivity since the early part of the war, with their leading figures and professional agents away on military service or absorbed into the expanded wartime bureaucracy.[66] This occurred in two stages, the first of which was in response to the proposals of the boundary commissioners, in attempts to avoid changes that would be detrimental to Conservative prospects. The party headquarters in London often advised and supported these efforts, but they were primarily local in origin, and a logical case based upon local topography and traditions could influence the boundary commissioners when they visited the localities. The second stage followed from the enactment of the new arrangements, for as legal entities, the associations for the former constituencies had to be dissolved, which entailed winding up their financial affairs, and new associations established.[67] In some places, where the extent of the constituency remained broadly similar, this was a fairly nominal and straightforward evolution from the old association, with the new inheriting its funds, premises and staff, and continuing under the same leadership.[68] In others, where the core of a former constituency – often a moderate-sized borough – gained an accretion of outlying districts, it was a case of transferring the branches for these areas from their previous parent body and giving them a share of representation on the central committees of the new association.[69] The most difficult category was where constituencies disappeared and radically new ones replaced them, and it was here most of all that the frictions of personal ambition and status and of local particularism or resentments could cause problems. An example of all these elements occurred in the new Shrewsbury constituency, which was a merger of the former Shrewsbury borough seat and parts of three neighbouring county divisions. At the first meeting to organise the new association, two candidates were proposed as chairman, one from a county district and the other the former chairman of the borough seat; rather than having a vote, the latter suggested settling the question with the toss of a coin, which

---

[65]TNA, PREM 1/255: Sir A. Pownall to the prime minister, 13 Feb., 16 June 1937, 13 May 1938. In the 1935 general election, supporters of the national government (mostly Conservatives) represented 44 of the 48 seats with the largest electorates.

[66]Ramsden, *Age of Balfour and Baldwin*, 124–5; Yorkshire Area, council: 'Report for the six months ending the 30th of June 1917', 'Redistribution Meetings'.

[67]Lancaster CA: central committee, 27 Oct. 1917.

[68]These constituencies also generally continued using the same minute book, while in other cases these were passed on to the successor constituency, such as Strand CA, 1886–1918, in St George's CA deposit (Westminster City Library, 487/5); Mid-Kent CA, 1885–1918, in Maidstone CA deposit (Kent History and Library Centre, U1634); Suffolk North-West CA, 1893–1917, in Bury St Edmunds CA deposit (Suffolk RO, GK501); Truro and Helston CA, 1908–16, in Penryn and Falmouth CA deposit (Cornwall RO, X.551/10), North West Norfolk CA, 1897–1918, continues after merger as King's Lynn CA (North West Norfolk CA); see S. Ball, 'National Politics and Local History: The Regional and Local Archives of the Conservative Party 1867–1945', *Archives*, xxii (1996), 48–9, and for specific details, see S. Ball, 'A Summary List of the Regional and Local Records of the Conservative Party 1867–1945', unpublished list deposited at the Conservative Party Archive.

[69]Canterbury CA: first meeting, 15 May 1918; Knutsford CA: executive committee, 7 Mar. 1918.

he lost. However, at the next meeting a letter was received from him declaring that the borough association had decided to withdraw from the merger and proposing two separate associations in the constituency, one for the town and the other for the rest. This was obviously impracticable, but unity was achieved only by revisions of the proposed new rules and by the chairman from the county stepping down in favour of the former borough chairman.[70]

4

The effects of the 1918 Reform Act on the Conservative Party were felt not only in the immediate wake of its passage, but also in the decade (and decades) that followed. The victorious outcome of the December 1918 general election gave some reassurance, although the increase in the Labour vote and the low turnout of 57.2% were matters of concern. One aspect which stood out was that women had voted in substantial numbers, and mainly for the coalition candidates; in the industrial town of Rotherham, as in many other places, the 'womens franchise had helped to secure success'.[71] This pattern was to continue, and by the time of the next general election the view of party headquarters was 'that the larger the poll of women voters the better it would be for the Conservatives'.[72] After 1918, the party made sustained efforts to adapt its structures and methods, and to reach not only the women but also the other main categories of new voters. However, these were developments of existing institutions and were changes of scale rather than of function. This was particularly the case with the expansion of the representative bodies of the party membership; after an overhaul of the rules in 1924, the average attendance at the central council rose from the pre-war figure of 102 to 681 in the period 1925–39, while by 1929 the attendance at the annual conference had reached almost 4,000.[73] The party's other response to the enlarged electorate was the development of new methods of communication and campaigning to reach a mass audience. More emphasis was placed on propaganda, mainly through leaflets, and the party made its own propaganda films which were shown around the country by a fleet of cinema vans, which were especially effective in rural areas.[74]

The party chairman moved rapidly, after the passage of the Representation of the People Act, to encourage women's participation and integrate them into the organisation. In April 1918, the rules of the National Unionist Association were adapted to admit women to membership of the executive committee and central council, and Younger negotiated the transformation of the Women's Amalgamated Unionist and Tariff Reform

[70]Shrewsbury CA: first meeting, 23 Feb., provisional committee, 4 May, meeting of deputations, 1 June, provisional committee, 8 June 1918.

[71]Rotherham CA: annual general meeting, 12 May 1919; Hampshire RO, 114M84/1: Aldershot CA, executive committee, 6 Feb. 1919; Liverpool, RO, Derby MSS, 920/DER(17)/20/1: P. Woodhouse to earl of Derby, 1 Jan. 1919.

[72]*Daily Telegraph*, 2 Nov. 1922, p. 11.

[73]Ball, *Portrait of a Party*, 248–9, 254.

[74]A. Taylor, 'Speaking to Democracy: The Conservative Party and Mass Opinion from the 1920s to the 1950s', in *Mass Conservatism: The Conservatives and the Public since the 1880s*, ed. S. Ball and I. Holliday (2002), 78–85; T.J. Hollins, 'The Conservative Party and Film Propaganda between the Wars', *English Historical Review*, xcvi (1981), 359–69.

Association, which before the war had been a large and active campaigning body outside the formal party structure, into a vital constituent element within it, under the new name of the Women's Unionist Organisation.[75] This now had a supporting staff housed within the party headquarters, which grew in number during the following decade. The effectiveness of these national developments mutually reinforced the rapid expansion of women's membership in the constituencies, especially in the suburbs, small towns and countryside.[76] By the summer of 1920, the agent at Weymouth was reporting that more women than men had attended his association's annual general meeting; in a typical example, one Somerset county division had grown to 50 local women's branches with a claimed membership of over 4,000 by the end of 1924.[77] A preponderance of female membership became the common pattern at local level in the interwar period, and in the safer seats particularly this could be as large a ratio as four times the number of men. The claims in the later 1920s that the party had a million women members may have been inflated, but not greatly, and the true figure was probably between 750,000 and one million.[78] This large female membership, which included many middle-class women with time and energy available for voluntary activities, was very useful, given the need for more party workers, due to the combination of the larger electorate and the reduced limit on election expenses.[79]

Younger also devoted much effort, but with less reward, to create a new wing of the party organisation aimed at male working-class trade unionists.[80] The Unionist Labour Movement developed from some active pre-war 'labour' organisations in Lancashire, and for that reason held its inaugural conference at Southport on 6 March 1920.[81] It was never able to recruit on a large scale, and remained more of a sounding board than a campaigning asset. Younger and his successors as party chairman also encouraged constituencies to establish their own Labour Advisory Committees, but this tended to happen only in areas where Labour and trade unionism was strong, and consequently to have little effect.[82] The third organisational initiative in response to the extension of the franchise bore more fruit. This was the creation of a youth movement, which, similarly to the women's organisation, was established by integrating an existing separate body into the structure of the party at every level from local branches in constituencies to its own regional committees, national

[75]Bodl., CPA: NUA executive, 21 Jan., 9 July 1918; NUA central council, 11 Mar. 1919; N.R. McCrillis, *The British Conservative Party in the Age of Universal Suffrage: Popular Conservatism 1918–1929* (Columbus, OH, 1998), 20–2; Keohane, *Party of Patriotism*, 157–60.

[76]For the development of the women's organisation after 1918, see Ball, *Portrait of a Party*, 153–4, 167–8, 245, 268–9; Maguire, *Conservative Women*, 73–93; McCrillis, *Conservative Party in the Age of Universal Suffrage*, 22–4, 46–82; D. Thackeray, 'Home and Politics: Women and Conservative Activism in Early Twentieth-Century Britain', *Journal of British Studies*, xlix (2010), 836–8, 845; N. Fleming, 'Women and Lancashire Conservatism between the Wars', *Women's History Review*, xxvi (2017), 329–49.

[77]*Conservative Agents' Journal*, July 1920, p. 17; Wells CA: finance committee, agent's report, 9 Dec. 1924.

[78]Ball, *Portrait of a Party*, 167–8.

[79]Edinburgh City Archives, Acc. 198/11: Edinburgh North CA, agent's report to executive committee, 30 Oct. 1918.

[80]For the development of the trade unionist organisation after 1918, see Ball, *Portrait of a Party*, 157–60, 245, 269–70, 289; J. Greenwood, *The Conservative Party and the Working Classes: The Organisational Response* (Warwick, 1974); McCrillis, *Conservative Party in the Age of Universal Suffrage*, 110–44.

[81]*Conservative Agents' Journal*, Apr. 1920, p. 15, May 1920, pp. 5–9.

[82]*Conservative Agents' Journal*, Mar. 1920, pp. 1–5.

executive, and annual conference.[83] The Junior Imperial League had been founded by Henry Imbert-Terry in 1906 for men aged 18–30 years, most of whom would not have been voters under the pre-war franchise. Having lapsed during the war, as its members were engaged in war work, it was revived in 1920 and now admitted female members. Its expansion was further encouraged by the party chairman from 1926 to 1930, J.C.C. Davidson, partly in response to the equalisation of the franchise in 1928. It proved popular as a respectable way for young men and women to meet, and like the women's movement much of its activity was in social events; by 1930 its national membership was between 150,000 and 200,000.

The nature of local political activity changed after 1918 due to the huge increase in the electorate and the simplification of the registration system. This particularly affected the work of the professional party agents; in the complicated previous system, they had principally focused upon canvassing to identify the party allegiance of voters, the compilation of the register and the annual battle of the revision courts. In the smaller pre-1918 electorates, getting 200 or 300 of your own marginally-qualified voters onto the register and successfully objecting to a similar number of your opponent's could swing the balance in many constituencies, and 'elections were won in the Revision Courts'.[84] After 1918, the straightforward nature of the residential qualification meant that there was little need to substantiate claims to the franchise and fewer opportunities for objections, while the neutral efficiency of the local government officials who now oversaw the register meant that few voters were omitted (apart from some problems with the first registers in 1918). The consequence was that making a regular thorough canvass of the voters was impracticable due to their number and no longer the most productive use of the time and resources available, and as early as 1921, one agent noted the 'growing tendency to ignore registration'.[85] Instead, during the 1920s, the activities of local agents and their constituency associations moved towards campaigning, propaganda, recruitment and fund-raising.[86] This process was further encouraged by the 1918 Reform Act's limits on election expenditure, which allowed much less per voter than before, at the same time as costs had risen due to the wartime inflation. In combination with the massive expansion of the electorate, as an experienced local Conservative agent observed in 1920, 'all this entails a complete re-casting of the electoral machinery'.[87] It also accelerated the changes that were developing in the Conservative agents' profession, as their work ceased to be mainly legal, and thus often carried out on a part-time basis by a local solicitor, and became, instead, organisational and managerial, and increasingly a full-time occupation with its own career structure and recognized qualification.

The expansion of the franchise in 1918 had an impact on the role and responsibilities of being a member of parliament. While this affected all parties, it had particular consequences for the Conservatives; first, because they had – or felt – a more evident need than

---

[83] *Conservative Agents' Journal*, Dec. 1920, pp. 17–20, Mar. 1921, pp. 11–15. For the development of the youth organisation after 1918, see Ball, *Portrait of a Party*, 154–7, 288–9; McCrillis, *Conservative Party in the Age of Universal Suffrage*, 83–109.

[84] *Conservative Agents' Journal*, Aug. 1919, p. 2.

[85] *Conservative Agents' Journal*, Sept. 1921, pp. 1–3. An article contributed by a local agent in 1923 shows that considerable work had resulted in a net gain on the register of 152 voters, which in most constituencies was less than 0.3% of the electorate: *Conservative Agents' Journal*, Nov. 1923, p. 253.

[86] Ball, *Portrait of a Party*, 174, 191–3.

[87] *Conservative Agents' Journal*, Sept. 1920, p. 15.

Labour MPs to demonstrate their concern for, and practical engagement with, the needs of the ordinary citizen, and second, because the party's success in most elections resulted in a considerable number of Conservative MPs defending vulnerable majorities in urban and industrial constituencies. The period after 1918 saw a substantial increase in the demands of constituency casework due to the confluence of franchise extension with three other factors: the legacy of the war in claims for disability and widows' pensions, the expanded responsibilities of local and national government, and the growth in legislation and regulation; whereas in 1906–13 the sessional volume of statutes averaged 355 pages, by 1929–38 it had reached 995 pages.[88] Constituents thus placed greater demands on, and had greater expectations of, their member of parliament.[89] These were partly conflicting: the MP should be an assiduous attender of the House, asking questions and taking part in divisions; an effective and persistent communicator of constituents' cases and claims to Whitehall ministries and local town halls, and also increasingly an active local presence – regular visits and speech-making became the norm, and there were fewer places where a brief annual speaking tour was still sufficient.[90] Concern about the expectations of the democratic electorate and the need to find their feet quickly and demonstrate effectiveness was the principal motivation for a number of the Conservative MPs who were first elected in the 1922 general election, to form a self-help group, 'the Conservative Private Members' (1922) Committee'.[91] Such was the utility of this forum that by 1926 it had expanded to include all Conservative back benchers irrespective of when they had entered the House, an evolution which led to the 1922 Committee becoming a permanent institution which has long outlived its founders.

The 1918 Reform Act gave further stimulus to the vexed question of the reform of the house of lords, as was underlined when the central council resolution of April 1917 which declared 'strongly in favour of an extension of the franchise' explicitly linked this with 'the absolute necessity of concurrently establishing a reformed Second Chamber possessed of adequate powers'.[92] The Conservatives sought to hold the pre-war Liberal government and its coalition successors to the promise made in the preamble to the 1911 Parliament Act of further reform, which they took to mean a reappraisal of the upper House that would strengthen its powers, not diminish them further.[93] This was no theoretical aspiration, for with the advance of the Labour Party and the alarming signs of industrial militancy between 1917 and 1922, the need for a second chamber that could act as an effective barrier to the depredations of a possible socialist majority in the house of commons seemed ever more necessary to the Conservative grass roots and many back-bench MPs – the upper chamber's present capacity for resistance being limited to delaying a bill for up to two years, and

[88] S. Ball, 'Parliament and Politics in Britain 1900–51', *Parliamentary History*, x (1991), 250, 265–6.

[89] Harry Brittain, *Happy Pilgrimage* (1949), 48; Brittain became MP for Acton in 1918.

[90] National Library of Wales, Brogyntyn MSS, PEC/10/1/11/15: W. Ormsby-Gore to his mother, 15 Nov. 1919.

[91] S. Ball, 'The 1922 Committee: The Formative Years 1922–45', *Parliamentary History*, ix (1990), 130–3.

[92] Bodl., CPA: NUA central council, 17 Apr. 1917.

[93] For discussion of this issue, see Ball, *Portrait of a Party*, 388–90; David H. Close, 'The Collapse of Resistance to Democracy: Conservatives, Adult Suffrage, and Second Chamber Reform, 1911–1928', *Historical Journal*, xx (1977), 893–918; N.R. McCrillis, 'Taming Democracy? The Conservative Party and House of Lords' Reform 1916–1929', *Parliamentary History*, xii (1993), 259–80; G. Thomas, 'Conservatives, the Constitution, and the Quest for a "Representative" House of Lords 1911–1935', *Parliamentary History*, xxxi (2012), 419–43.

financial bills not at all. Conservatives envisaged conceding changes in the composition of the house of lords that would make it a broader and more representative institution, so that it would not seem provocatively anti-democratic to restore some of its powers. The Conservatives made several attempts during the interwar period to find an acceptable formula for second chamber reform, but all of these foundered between the twin rocks of the fear of appearing reactionary and encouraging class hostility on the one hand, and on the other the reluctance of MPs to cede power to the upper chamber, especially if it should acquire rivalling legitimacy through being transformed into an elected senate, or even having a significant elected component.[94] However, this left the vulnerable breach in the constitution unfilled, and in the early 1920s the dangers seemed so great that the demand for second chamber reform became one of the most extensive, persistent and urgent concerns of the Conservative constituencies, and this was repeatedly expressed through the executive committee, central council and annual conference of the National Union.[95]

The disappointment of Conservative right-wing MPs and the party's grass roots more generally at the failure of their leaders to grasp the nettle of second chamber reform was augmented by the Representation of the People (Equal Franchise) Act of 1928, which substantially expanded the female electorate by putting the qualification on the same basis as that for men. Although it was widely accepted that the age compromise in the 1918 Reform Act could only be temporary and that eventually equalisation was inevitable,[96] many Conservatives were reluctant to take this final step towards full adult suffrage. This was due not to any remaining hostility to the principle of women's inclusion but to the age range of the new female voters, who were often assumed to be inexperienced, impulsive, and easily influenced by emotional appeals. In general, by the mid 1920s, women voters were welcomed by Conservatives for their contribution to political stability, and this, together with the desire to avoid appearing reactionary, contributed to Bonar Law's personal endorsement of franchise equalisation in the 1922 general election and Baldwin's more definite statement during the 1924 election campaign that the party was 'in favour of equal political rights for men and women'.[97] He proposed that the question be examined by an inter-party conference on the model of 1916, but when the Conservatives were returned to office this was not an immediate priority, partly because of the convention that any franchise extension should come near the end of a parliament's life so that it might soon be followed by an election on the new basis. However, a crucial exchange occurred in the house of commons on 20 February 1925, when the home secretary, Sir William Joynson-Hicks, moved the rejection of a Labour MP's private members' bill to give women the vote on the same basis as men. Joynson-Hicks promised legislation 'within the lifetime of the present Parliament' on the basis of Baldwin's pledge, when he was interrupted by a question from the Conservative

[94] Warwick University Library, Leslie Scott MSS, 119/3/5/CO/3-4: secretary's notes of a meeting between the cabinet house of lords reform committee and a deputation from the executive committee of the second chamber committee of Conservative MPs, 7 Dec. 1925; Headlam diary, 12, 20 May, 10 June, 16 Dec. 1925, 27 June, 6 July 1927, 28 Mar. 1932, in *Parliament and Politics in the Age of Baldwin and MacDonald: The Headlam Diaries 1923–1935*, ed. Stuart Ball (1992), 62–5, 75, 125–6, 234; A.D. Cooper and C.M. Headlam, *House of Lords or Senate?* (1932).

[95] Bodl., CPA: NUA executive, 13 Apr., 12 Oct. 1920, 8 Mar. 1921, 11 May 1922; NUA central council, 11 Mar., 20 May 1919, 23 Feb., 21 June 1921, 27 June 1922; PA, Bonar Law MSS, BL/96/2: Younger to Bonar Law, 3 Jan. 1920; BL/100/2/30: Younger to Bonar Law, 23 Feb. 1921.

[96] *Daily Telegraph*, 13 Mar. 1928, p. 10; 30 Mar. 1928, p. 10.

[97] *The Times*, 11 Nov. 1922, p. 12; 18 Oct. 1924, p. 12.

MP, Lady Astor, asking if he meant equal votes at the age of 21 years. The home secretary's response was:[98]

> It means exactly what it says. ... The Prime Minister's pledge is for equal rights and at the next election. I will say quite definitely that means no difference will take place in the ages at which men and women go to the polls at the next election.

Joynson-Hicks was known for his impulsiveness, and because of this and the fact that Baldwin had been sitting beside him on the front bench and had not demurred, it was taken by everyone that he had committed the government to equalisation at 21 years; in fact, he had left the question of the age open and had only – and uncontroversially – reaffirmed the principle of equality.

However, his cabinet colleagues, somewhat aggrieved at the perceived lack of consultation, considered that he had sold the pass and put them in a position from which they could not honourably retreat. The leader of the party in the house of lords, Lord Salisbury, echoed the general acceptance that a change from 30 years was inevitable, but pessimistically concluded that equalisation at 21 years 'is going to do us a lot of harm now – though hereafter it may possibly pay'.[99] The reason for his concern was the very vocal pressure from the party grass roots, shared by many MPs and strongly supported by the *Daily Mail*, for a voting age of 25 years for both men and women.[100] This was based partly on a crude stereotyping of the younger women as foolish and irresponsible 'flappers', and partly on the more realistic perception that most working-class women aged under 25 years were in employment and more susceptible to the appeal of the Labour Party – this was the basis of the advice from the party chairman and Central Office 'that equal franchise at 21 would prejudice the Party in industrial areas'.[101] However, despite the chorus of support for equalisation at 25 years, its consequence of denying the vote to the estimated two and a half million men aged 21–24 years was too damaging.[102] Taking away a franchise once given was seen as too reactionary and anti-democratic, and the gain would be too small to be worth the penalty of alienating those who, within a short period, would gain the vote at the higher age anyway. After three meetings of a subcommittee which considered various forms of equalisation, the full cabinet decided in April 1927 to proceed with legislation to equalise the franchise at 21 years, and this was passed in July 1928.[103]

[98] Hansard, *Commons Debates*, 5th ser., clxxx, cols 1479, 1503–4: 20 Feb. 1925.

[99] *Conservative Politics in National and Imperial Crisis: Letters from Britain to the Viceroy of India 1926–31*, ed. S. Ball (Farnham, 2014), 135: marquis of Salisbury to Lord Irwin, 24 Apr. 1927.

[100] *Conservative Politics in National and Imperial Crisis*, ed. Ball, 137: G. Lane-Fox to Lord Irwin, 28 Apr. 1927; Ball, *Portrait of a Party*, 229–30; Adrian Bingham, '"Stop the Flapper Vote Folly": Lord Rothermere, the *Daily Mail*, and the Equalization of the Franchise 1927–28', *Twentieth Century British History*, xiii (2002), 17–37; Close, 'Collapse of Resistance to Democracy', 915–17.

[101] TNA, CAB 27/336: equal franchise committee, 21 Feb. 1927, 2 and appendix i. Not all Conservatives were opposed: the delegate who moved a resolution in support of equalisation at age 21 years at the 1927 annual conference objected to the 'plethora of abuse ... such as "Votes for flappers" and they ought to protest against such an offensive term being applied to women of twenty-one, tens of thousands of whom were married and blessed with families', and in the same debate Ian Fraser MP pointed out that one-third of those who would be enfranchised were aged over 30 years and one-third aged 25–30 years; the resolution was carried 'with loud acclamation': Bodl., CPA, NUA/2/1/43: NUA conference, 6–7 Oct. 1927.

[102] *Daily Telegraph*, 19 Apr. 1928, p. 10; Butler, *Electoral System*, 33.

[103] TNA, CAB 27/336: equal franchise committee, 15 Dec. 1926, 14, 21 Feb. 1927; *Conservative Politics in National and Imperial Crisis*, ed. Ball, 132: earl of Birkenhead to Lord Irwin, 13 Apr. 1927.

The increase in the number of women on the register between 1928 and 1929 has been calculated as 5,299,301, which was 18.4% of the electorate at the general election in May 1929.[104] By this time, the tide of public opinion was flowing away from the Conservative government. Its final 18 months had contained little to arouse enthusiasm: middle-class hopes for substantial reductions in spending and taxation had been impossible to fulfil; unemployment had remained stubbornly high; agriculture was in severe depression; the Labour Party had strengthened its position since 1924 and had an attractive programme, and the Liberal Party had been revived by Lloyd George with money (if of dubious origin) and economic plans (if of dubious practicality), while from the Conservative local associations came reports of widespread apathy. All of this would have led to defeat even if there had been no equalisation of the female franchise, but many Conservatives chose to give it the lion's share of the blame, together with the Liberal revival.[105] Its actual effect is harder to determine, especially as the predisposition of many Conservatives may have led them to see what they had expected. The majority of views were negative, such as in the industrial city of Dundee where it was thought that 80% of the new votes had gone to Labour,[106] but on the other hand, the experienced former party chairman and only cabinet minister to lose his seat, Sir Arthur Steel-Maitland, considered 'particularly that the "flapper vote" did not influence matters in the least'.[107] What can be said is that, when the other contingent circumstances changed, full adult suffrage for both genders did not prevent Conservative electoral victories in 1931, 1935, and after 1945.

5

In the form that finally reached the statute book, the Representation of the People Act of 1918 was, as Ross McKibbin has argued, 'the most conservative piece of legislation that could have been devised in the circumstances'.[108] The war had made adult male suffrage both unavoidable and less alarming, the almost-equally unavoidable accompaniment of female suffrage had been limited by age and, to a lesser extent, property, in ways beneficial to the Conservatives, plural voting had been retained although reduced, the threat posed by proportional representation had been avoided, and the under-representation of the areas of Conservative support around London had been corrected. While the advent of full male suffrage and the inclusion of another large new element in the female voters required the reappraisal of existing methods and structures, the Conservative Party proved more able to adapt to the challenges and take advantage of the opportunities than its hitherto main rival, the Liberals. In response to the expansion of the electorate and the rise of the Labour Party, after 1918 the Conservative Party made effective efforts to adapt its organisation, expand its membership, and broaden its appeal.

[104] Butler, *Electoral System*, 145.

[105] See the analysis of constituency responses on the causes of defeat in S. Ball, *Baldwin and the Conservative Party: The Crisis of 1929–1931* (1988), appendix i, 220–1.

[106] Cambridge University, Baldwin MSS, 37/204: E. Wallace to Baldwin, 12 June 1929. The local chairman in another Labour area 'considered the flapper vote went against us', and perhaps it was more likely to do so in such environments: Gloucestershire Archives, D7411: Forest of Dean CA, executive committee, 29 July 1929.

[107] NRS, Steel-Maitland MSS, GD193/120/3/212: Steel-Maitland to Swaby, 10 July 1929.

[108] Ross McKibbin, *Parties and People: England 1914–1951* (Oxford, 2010), 27.

Despite continuing concerns over the ignorance of the mass electorate and its potential receptiveness to demagogic and despoilatory appeals,[109] in the two decades after the 1918 Reform Act, the Conservative Party was able to attract substantial support from both new voters and old. The Conservatives won more seats than any other party in every general election from 1918 to 1935, with the single exception of 1929, when they still polled 285,000 votes more than Labour. There was a 'franchise factor' in this record of success, in which the inclusion of women voters certainly played an important part – although it should not be accorded too prominent a role. From the early 1920s, the Conservative Party projected an effective appeal to 'the man in the street' (a category which encompassed both working men and the white-collar lower middle class), based upon national solidarity over class conflict, patriotism and pride in the Empire, the defence of property (which need not be large), anti-socialism and moderate social reform.[110] Under generally moderate and cautious leadership, the Conservative Party prospered in the new environment, grew in confidence, and eventually came to embrace it. The response of the electorate in giving the national government an overwhelming mandate after the economic crisis of 1931 settled most remaining fears,[111] so that by the late 1930s 'democracy' had become something of which to be proud and to defend.[112] After 1918, the internal culture of Conservatism absorbed the self-image later expressed by one young army officer during the Second World War, that 'the tradition of the Conservative Party is to win the people's trust by putting its trust in the people',[113] and this had become so entrenched that the landslide defeat of 1945 could not shake it.

[109] This was a particular concern of Baldwin and a frequent theme in his speeches; see P. Williamson, *Stanley Baldwin: Conservative Leadership and National Values* (Cambridge, 1999), 203–12.

[110] Ball, *Portrait of a Party*, 82–93, 106–21, 507–12. In 1937, the party's central council passed a resolution defining its 'fundamental and inseparable principles' as 'empire unity, social progress and constitutional democracy': NUA central council, 23 Mar. 1937.

[111] The Conservative Party alone received 55% of the votes cast in the October 1931 general election, and returned 470 MPs; the national government as a whole received 67.7% of the poll and won 558 seats.

[112] E.g., see the final two collected volumes of Baldwin's speeches: S. Baldwin, *This Torch of Freedom* (1935), 39, 51; S. Baldwin, *An Interpreter of England* (1939), 45.

[113] D. Stelling, *Why I Am A Conservative* (1943), 12.

The Liberal Party and the Impact of the 1918 Reform Act[*]

GAVIN FREEMAN ⓘD

This essay challenges the conventional wisdom concerning the impact of the 1918 Reform Act on the Liberal Party. It was not the extension of the franchise or any other feature of the act that led to the downfall of the Liberal Party. Instead, it was the division between Asquith and Lloyd George and the resulting 'Coupon election' of 1918 which severely harmed the Liberals, and the provisions of the act only caused difficulties for the Liberal Party in the context of the split. This essay explores the four facets of the 1918 Reform Act (the enlarged franchise, the redistribution of constituencies, the new registration system, and the method of election), and examines how these affected the Liberal Party. The response of the Liberal elite to these changes is found to be wanting, with the leadership of Asquith particularly criticized. It was the failure of the party leaders to engage with the changed circumstances, and particularly the ways in which they viewed the new electorate, that disadvantaged the Liberals. The coincidental timing of the act, when the Liberals were at their most divided for a generation, provides the most persuasive explanation of why they struggled while the Labour and Conservative Parties prospered under the new system.

Keywords: Coupon election; electoral reform; franchise; Herbert Gladstone; Herbert Henry Asquith; Liberal Party; proportional representation; redistribution; registration; Representation of the People Act 1918

1

The reasons for the decline of the Liberal Party and the rise of the Labour Party have generated much debate over the years. In their seminal article, Matthew, McKibbin and Kay argued that the Representation of the People Act of 1918 'was of first importance in Labour's replacing the Liberal Party as the principal party of progress'.[1] The authors also argued that the Liberal Party faced difficulties in the post-1918 period because of their 'reluctance' to 'take electoral organisation seriously' and their 'incapacity to make the necessary "demagogic" appeals to the mass electorate created by the 1918 act'.[2] However, Tanner has attacked their assumption that all of the four million men who were excluded from the franchise before 1914 were working class. Tanner argues that, due to the nature of the pre-war franchise and registration laws, a number of men from the upper and middle classes were excluded as

[*]I wish to thank Professor Stuart Ball (University of Leicester) and Professor John Martin (De Montfort University) for their helpful comments on earlier drafts of this essay.

[1]H.C.G. Matthew, R.I. McKibbin and J.A. Kay, 'The Franchise Factor in the Rise of the Labour Party', *English Historical Review*, xci (1976), 736.

[2]Matthew, McKibbin and Kay, 'Franchise Factor', 742.

well.[3] Clarke has argued that, before 1914, there was a high correlation between Liberal success and high levels of enfranchisement.[4] This undermined much of Matthew, McKibbin and Kay's central argument. Consequently, Hart has argued that it was the First World War that was 'a vital factor in the decline of the Liberals' because of its 'deliquescent' effect on the party.[5] Therefore, he argues that the 'franchise factor' had 'little or nothing to do' with the Liberals rapid decline.[6] However, what has hitherto been little explored is how the other provisions of the Representation of the People Act 1918 affected the party. This essay will assess the importance of the 1918 Reform Act for the Liberal Party, while also taking into account the comparative importance of Liberal disunity and the 'Coupon election' of December 1918. Its conclusions will reassess the ways in which the 1918 Reform Act contributed to the downfall of the Liberal Party.

2

To what extent was the Representation of the People Act of 1918 responsible for the decline of the Liberal Party? The available evidence suggests that the increased franchise contributed to Liberal difficulties, but not necessarily for the reasons commonly assumed. Matthew, McKibbin and Kay admitted that they could not 'say how many votes the introduction of universal franchise was worth to Labour', but added that they thought it was a 'critical element in the emergence of the party as a major political force'.[7] At first glance, their evidence appears convincing, but certainly not irrefutable. In December 1910, Labour secured 371,772 votes and 7.1% of the total vote. In December 1918, they secured 2,385,472 votes and 22.2% of the poll – a clear progression since 1910.[8] So there appears to be a correlation between the changes to the franchise and an improvement in Labour's fortunes. However, in the 1924 general election, Labour secured 5,489,077 votes and 33% of the total vote, yet there had been no further change in the franchise since 1918.[9] So, if the change in Labour's vote between 1918 and 1924 was not related to the franchise, then the same logic could be extended to the changes between December 1910 and 1918. Hence, there is a need to focus on the general election of 1918. It is the timing of the increase in the electorate that was the primary issue for the Liberals, not who was enfranchised. The work by Childs on political generations contains much merit, but the change

---

[3] D. Tanner, 'The Parliamentary Electoral System, the "Fourth" Reform Act and the Rise of Labour in England and Wales', *Bulletin of the Institute of Historical Research*, lvi (1983), 205–19.

[4] P.F. Clarke, 'Liberals, Labour and the Franchise', *English Historical Review*, xcii (1977), 582–9.

[5] M. Hart, 'The Liberals, the War, and the Franchise', *English Historical Review*, xcvii (1982), 820.

[6] Hart, 'Liberals, the War, and the Franchise', 822.

[7] Matthew, McKibbin and Kay, 'Franchise Factor', 740.

[8] However, much of this is due to the fact that Labour ran more candidates in 1918 compared with December 1910. In fact, Labour's average poll per candidate was lower in 1918 than in December 1910, although the significance of this is reduced, as in 1910 Labour were contesting their very best prospects, and had the advantage of the Lib-Lab Pact which resulted in mainly two-way contests.

[9] The comparable figures for the Liberal Party are: in December 1910, it obtained 2,295,888 votes, which was 43.9% of the total vote. In 1918, the Independent Liberals had 1,298,808 votes cast in their favour, which was 12.1% of the total vote share. In 1924, the reunited Liberal Party secured 2,928,747 votes, which was 17.6% of the votes cast. The only change was that conscientious objectors were disfranchised for five years after the war, and by 1924 this bar would have been removed.

between December 1910 and 1918 cannot solely be explained by this or by an enlarged franchise.[10] Furthermore, Turner's statistical analysis suggests that 'the more new voters, the less the constituency tended towards the Labour Party'.[11] In a similar way, Hart dismissed the franchise factor, as he noted that the areas of lowest enfranchisement in London in 1911 were those where the Liberals retained their only foothold after 1918. The link between low enfranchisement before 1914 and the election results after 1918 are, Hart argues, tenuous.[12] This is especially the case given that Labour made greater advances at the municipal level after 1918, even though the local government franchise was more restricted than the parliamentary one.[13] These arguments reinforce the need to examine factors other than the franchise to explain the prospects of both progressive parties, and hence the primacy of the 1918 election, as an explanatory framework.

The general election that was called after the Armistice for December 1918 has generated much debate in the political historiography of this period.[14] Lloyd George's decision to seek the continuation of the coalition into peacetime by an alliance with the Conservative Party, while excluding half of the Liberal Party, affected both the course of the 1918 general election and the unity of the Liberal Party for the next decade. Those candidates formally endorsed by Lloyd George and Andrew Bonar Law, the leader of the Conservative Party, were distinguished by means of a letter signed by them both which affirmed that the recipient was the official coalition nominee in that constituency. As this device implicitly condemned all non-recipients as opponents of the coalition, Asquith famously dubbed the letter as a 'Coupon' and gave the election the name by which it is known.[15] The outcome was that the coalition had 523 MPs returned, against 184 MPs for all of the other parties combined.[16] It was clearly a landslide victory for the coalition and a crippling result for the Independent Liberals (also known as the Free Liberals, or 'Wee Frees'), who were able to obtain only 36 MPs. This put them behind Sinn Fein, which had 73 MPs, and the Labour Party, which had 57. As Sinn Fein never took up its seats in parliament, this allowed Labour, as the largest remaining party, to obtain the status of His Majesty's Official Opposition. This led to the prime importance of the 1918 general election in the historiography of the fortunes of the Liberal Party, as it has been argued that this election 'was the crucial event in destroying the political viability of the Liberal Party'.[17]

Liberal division was manifest to the electorate in the 1918 general election. In one response, the Liberal candidate for Coventry appealed for the voters to preserve the unity of the Liberal Party: 'The Tories have sacrificed their principles to gain Liberal seats and to break up as far as they can the Liberal Party. It is for you, ladies and gentlemen, it is for you

[10] M. Childs, 'Labour Grows Up: The Electoral System, Political Generations, and British Politics, 1890–1929', *Twentieth Century British History*, vi (1995), 123–44.

[11] J. Turner, 'The Labour Vote and the Franchise after 1918: An Investigation of the English Evidence', in *History and Computing*, ed. P. Denley and D. Hopkins (Manchester, 1987), 139–40.

[12] Hart, 'Liberals, the War, and the Franchise', 823–4.

[13] Hart, 'Liberals, the War, and the Franchise', 824.

[14] B. McGill, 'Lloyd George's Timing of the 1918 Election', *Journal of British Studies*, xiv (1974), 109–24.

[15] R. Douglas, 'The Background to the "Coupon" Election Arrangements', *English Historical Review*, lxxxvi (1971), 318–36.

[16] The coalition figure includes the 50 non-Coupon Conservative candidates who were returned.

[17] G.L. Bernstein, 'Yorkshire Liberalism during the First World War', *Historical Journal*, xxxii (1989) 129.

to preserve the unity of the Liberal Party and to prevent their scheme from succeeding.'[18] A few days later, the same candidate said: 'For Liberals to recommend a Conservative candidate when there is a Liberal candidate standing is stabbing the Liberal Party and Liberal Principles in the back', an indirect reference to Lloyd George.[19] This Liberal disunity deflated Liberal activists in the election. The secretary of the Midland Liberal Federation said that he had never known any election in which 'there was such general apathy amongst Liberal workers', and he attributed this 'to the general bewilderment arising between the national and the party position'.[20] Such confusion and apathy was noted all around the country. One coalition Liberal who was successfully returned for Luton, noted that 'this Coalition business puzzles and disconcerts' Liberals.[21] An election being held at all caught the Liberals off guard, with Asquith commenting a few days before the Armistice was signed that 'it will be difficult to make any plans' for an election campaign.[22] It is evident that the first election under the 1918 Reform Act was unfortunately timed from the Liberal perspective. Their party was divided and demoralised, and this accidently gives the franchise changes greater prominence than they merit in the decline of the Liberal Party.

Away from the immediate Liberal divisions of the 1918 election, there was another reason why the expanded franchise raised difficulties for the Liberals. They were no longer able to feel the pulse of the majority of the electorate. In 1924, Herbert Gladstone, a former chief whip, outlined the position: 'Up to the war, it was possible, given some shrewdness, to estimate the move of opinion in the electorate. Now it is guess work.' Although this would affect all of the political parties, Gladstone also inadvertently revealed some particular Liberal difficulties in this period:

> In the days when canvassing was thorough, expert officials knew with approximate accuracy the texture and strength of the Parties in the constituencies.... Everyone knew that the Conservatives last month [October 1924] would gain seats. As regards the actual result, not one single Liberal Official ever hinted at some such possibility. In 1922–23 there was no accurate forecasting.[23]

Clearly, the Liberals no longer canvassed as thoroughly as they had done before 1914, the explanation being that the post-1918 electorate was too large for such a task. It seems that the increased franchise harmed the Liberals simply because they were intimidated by its size, and this took them out of their Edwardian comfort zone where they had seemed to be the natural governing party. Immediately after the 1918 election, Liberal local constituency agents commented on how difficult it was to communicate with the new electorate and

[18] *Midland Daily Telegraph*, 2 Dec. 1918.

[19] *Coventry Herald*, 6, 7 Dec. 1918.

[20] Birmingham University, Cadbury Research Library [hereafter cited as CRL], WMLF/3, Midland Liberal Federation, executive committee, 31 Jan. 1919.

[21] *Parliament and Politics in the Age of Asquith and Lloyd George: The Diaries of Cecil Harmsworth, MP, 1909–1922*, ed. A. Thorpe and R. Toye (Cambridge, 2016) [hereafter cited as Harmsworth diary], 285, 14 Dec. 1918.

[22] *H.H.A.: Letters of the Earl of Oxford and Asquith to a Friend, First Series 1915–22*, ed. D. MacCarthy (1933) [hereafter cited as *H.H.A.*], 81–2, 6 Nov. 1918.

[23] BL, Herbert Gladstone MSS, Add. MS 46480, ff. 129–37: memorandum by Gladstone, 'Confidential reflections and suggestions on the general organisation of the Liberal Party', 18 Nov. 1924.

that even among Liberals there was a lack of engagement, reinforcing Gladstone's perspective.[24] Furthermore, there are other tangible weaknesses from which Gladstone felt that the Liberals suffered in 1918–24. He felt that the Liberals lacked an adequate grasp of political movements in the country: 'is not an effective Intelligence Department among the first if not the first of our requirements?'. He was also critical of the National Liberal Federation. Similarly, Asquith had a low opinion of Liberal headquarters, describing them 'with one or two exceptions, a simple-minded and dunder-headed lot, with no experience of politics, and a plentiful supply of ingenuous vanity'.[25] It was due to the Liberals' own organisational weaknesses that the increased electorate proved to be an obstacle rather than an opportunity for them. Quite clearly, the Liberals did not adapt themselves to the changed political situation of an enlarged electorate.

Matthew, McKibbin and Kay also argued that the 1918 Reform Act not only enlarged the electorate, but also 'transformed its character by significantly lowering its political awareness'.[26] Such a statement is hard to prove or disprove empirically. However, the authors may have been focusing their attention in the wrong direction. What if the intelligence of the electorate had always been 'low', or if the level of political discourse of the elite became reduced after 1918? Gladstone's analysis would suggest the latter possibility:

> In past days, one of the highest aptitudes of great leaders lay in starting and advancing great public questions in true relation to the probabilities or actualities of public opinion. Now, big propositions are pitchforked to the public quite speculatively in the hope that they will catch on. This is all wrong.[27]

Matthew, McKibbin and Kay's assumption that the political intelligence of the voters was reduced, and that this therefore harmed the Liberals, is therefore far from conclusive. The Liberals had populist slogans in 1906, such as accusing the Conservatives of wanting to introduce 'Stomach Taxes'. If the Liberals did not have a popular message after 1918, this does not mean that the electorate had become less sophisticated, but rather it highlights how the Liberals had lost their populist edge and that the Labour and Conservative Parties found their respective narratives more suited to a mass franchise, whether this be based on the rhetoric of class or of patriotism.[28]

One possible explanation for the Liberals losing their populist edge was of how dismissive some of them were towards the new electorate, as Liberal constituency agents commented on their 'neurotic and butterfly minds'.[29] After quoting a Liberal agent who mourned the passing of the 'virile' pre-war elector, Lawrence has suggested that 'many of the attacks on the supposedly "neurotic" and "irrational" post-war electorate represented nostalgia

[24] *Liberal Agent*, Jan. 1919.

[25] *H.H.A.*, 189, 28 June 1921.

[26] Matthew, McKibbin and Kay, 'Franchise Factor', 749. This is particularly interesting, as an editorial in the *Daily Chronicle* on 21 June 1917 felt that it would lead to 'a gradual general quickening of the people's political intelligence' because it was now the duty of both sexes to be interested in politics, and therefore that interest would be 'deepened and widened'.

[27] BL, Herbert Gladstone MSS, Add. MS 46480, ff. 129–37: 'Confidential reflections and suggestions'.

[28] For the Conservatives, see S. Ball, *Portrait of a Party: The Conservative Party in Britain 1918–1945* (Oxford, 2013); for Labour, see David Howell, *MacDonald's Party: Labour Identities and Crisis 1922–1931* (Oxford, 2002).

[29] *Liberal Agent*, July 1924.

for the exclusively male pre-war polity'.[30] The evidence suggests that it might be less the franchise that was important, and more the ways in which the Liberals perceived the new electorate and democracy. Naturally enough, the Liberal intelligentsia saw it through a prism of principle rather than hard-headed political calculation. A *Manchester Guardian* leader at the time of the passage of the 1918 Reform Act observed:

> It will now rest more largely with women themselves to develop and perfect all that is best in themselves and most helpful to the community. The vote is from one point of view a vulgar instrument, and the spiritual weapon must ever be vastly higher and more potent than the political. Yet the one may be the key to the other, and it is in that hope and belief that we welcome the new electors.[31]

How the Liberal elite viewed the coming of democracy and the reasons why the Liberal Party polled poorly among women voters merits further detailed study. For our purposes, it is sufficient to state that the 1918 Reform Act was not responsible for causing these problems. The responsibility falls on the party for failing to appeal successfully to sufficient numbers of female voters.

In the 1918 general election, the coverage of the Liberal press was initially distracted by the fact of an election taking place so immediately after the war, and then it was dominated by how soldiers were voting 'blindfold' in the general election because it was being rushed and they were abroad.[32] Roughly halfway through the election campaign, more articles aimed at women began to appear, such as 'How women should vote' and 'To the women voter'.[33] Significantly, these started to appear regularly after the *Daily News* claimed that there was 'a Coalition Scheme to capture the women's vote' by using the Political Information Offices for women to campaign for the coalition on 'non-party grounds'.[34] Besides the difficulties over the existence of the coalition, a further reason that the Liberals were slow in appealing to women was because, after the Representation of the People Act was passed, they presumed that men and women would vote the same way, 'as a class'.[35] The Liberals were late in appealing to women, and never really recovered from this. The way in which Asquith blamed 'these damned women voters' for the party's defeat in the Spen Valley by-election of December 1919 helps to explain why he was not able to provide more effective leadership to help the Liberals reach these newly-enfranchised voters.[36] Similarly, during his own by-election campaign for Paisley in 1920, he described the approximately 15,000 women on the electoral register as 'a dim, impenetrable, for the most part ungettable, element – of whom all that one knows is that they are for the most part hopelessly ignorant of politics, credulous to the last degree, and flickering with gusts of sentiment like a candle in the wind'.[37] With

[30] *Liberal Agent*, Apr. 1924, p. 26, in Jon Lawrence, 'The Transformation of British Public Politics after the First World War', *Past & Present*, No. 190 (2006), 207.

[31] *Manchester Guardian*, 7 Feb. 1918.

[32] *Daily News*, 16 Nov. 1918, see also 23 Nov. 1918 for an article showing the form that discharged soldiers and sailors should use to register to vote.

[33] *Daily News*, 29 Nov., 10 Dec. 1918.

[34] *Daily News*, 26 Nov. 1918.

[35] *Daily Chronicle*, 21 June 1917.

[36] *H.H.A.*, 120, 4 Jan. 1920.

[37] *H.H.A.*, 124–5, 30 Jan. 1920.

such attitudes at the head of the party, it is little wonder that the Liberals failed to attract the support of the female half of the electorate. After 1918, the Liberals also suffered from a lack of press support; Asquith believed that the only newspaper of use to the Liberals during the coalition government was the *Manchester Guardian*. Combined with the lack of appeal to women voters, this weakness of communication spelt trouble for the Liberal Party.[38]

The 1918 Reform Act retained two forms of plural voting which continued to aid the Conservative Party. University graduates had another vote in one of the university constituencies, which after the Anglo-Irish Treaty of 1921 cumulatively elected 12 MPs. As a historian of the tory party has noted, 'although the university seats had a certain tradition of independence, they were in practice dominated by the Conservative Party'.[39] However, the Liberals were able to secure some representation in this way; after the disastrous result of 1924, when the party was reduced to 40 MPs, the three members sitting for university seats accounted for 7.5% of the parliamentary party, and it was the Labour Party which suffered disproportionately the most from the university seats. The other form of plural voting that was retained was the business vote, for which those in occupation of a business premises in another constituency from their residence with an annual rental value of at least £10 qualified. Even though the 1918 Reform Act placed a limit on plural voting, that no one could cast more than two votes, it certainly provided much of the upper and upper-middle classes' additional electoral strength which mostly benefited the Conservatives.[40] On the other hand, there is no evidence that the disenfranchisement of conscientious objectors for the five years following the war had any discernible effect on the political fortunes of the Liberal Party.

The enlarged electorate is important as it contributed, both in reality and perception, to a more industrial and working-class electorate, which, in turn, led to class-based issues becoming more important after 1918 than before. Although evidence of class-based appeals can be seen in Edwardian England, this process was accelerated by the 1918 Reform Act and the changed political landscape after the Bolshevik revolution in Russia. Therefore, it is more accurate to say that the expanded franchise underwrote the basis for class appeals after 1918, but only in the context of the increased relevance of socialism and long-term social and economic trends. As many traditional Liberal shibboleths, such as home rule for Ireland, were not based on class lines, this would necessitate some evolution of the party programme. After the Anglo-Irish Treaty in December 1921, the executive of the Midland Liberal Federation recognized that their 'great struggle' of over 35 years since Gladstone's first Home Rule Bill was introduced in 1886 was at an end.[41] It was the end of an era as far as Ireland being a decisive party political issue was concerned. Freddie Guest, admittedly a partisan observer in his role as coalition Liberal chief whip, summed up the difficulty of the independent Liberals: the old Liberal war cries of free trade, temperance and home rule 'limits the possible audiences to whom they appeal to people over 50 years of age'.[42] The

[38] For more on the press, see Adrian Bingham's essay in this volume.
[39] Ball, *Portrait of a Party*, 105.
[40] Ball, *Portrait of a Party*, 106.
[41] CRL, WMLF/4: Midland Liberal Federation, executive committee, 9 Dec. 1921.
[42] Parliamentary Archives, Lloyd George MSS, LG/F/35/1/1: 'The Political Situation', not dated but most likely not long after 5 Jan. 1922.

Liberals now needed to formulate new policies from which to try to gain the support of the newly-enfranchised under the 1918 Reform Act.

The Conservative Party responded to the 1918 franchise by relaunching their junior movement and founding organisations for women and trade unionists to try and attract some of the new voters.[43] At the same time, Liberal constituency agents were wondering whether canvassing was outdated, given the increased franchise.[44] Crucially, there was no equivalent attempt at reorganisation from the Liberal Party. This was because of the division between Asquith and Lloyd George, which was essentially formalised in the general election of 1918 after simmering for two years following the ousting of Asquith in December 1916. At the parliamentary level, there is evidence that the treatment of Asquith by Lloyd George left Liberals 'burning with indignation' and a 'deadly loathing'.[45] The split carried on long after the 1918 general election, and its effects were evident when Sir Robert Hudson, the party's chief organiser, as secretary of the Liberal Central Association, suggested to Sir Donald Maclean, the chairman of the parliamentary party, that a course of inaction be adopted because the party was divided. Hudson felt that 'to call the LCA together at this juncture might invite a split. It had better be kept in cold storage until present differences between "co[alition] Libs" and "Libs" are at an end.'[46] Consequently, while the Conservatives were adapting their party structure to the changes brought by the 1918 Reform Act, the Liberals were paralysed due to division and the fear of widening that division further.

The Liberal paralysis meant that they never focused on trying to win over the most famous aspect of the 1918 act, the enfranchisement of most women. The secretary of the Home Counties Liberal Federation contacted the former MP and minister, Walter Runciman, in 1920 with a suggestion from one of the associations in the group: what was asked for was not speeches on general Liberal principles, but, instead, 'a course of lectures similar to those held on the Insurance Act, with special reference to woman electors'.[47] The demand for this shows how negligent the Liberals had been in the first year after the First World War. If the Labour and Conservative parties benefited more from the enfranchisement women, this was not because they were automatically the partisans of either party. It is because Labour and the tories made more of an effort to cultivate their support after the Representation of the People Act was passed. The Liberals were not only out of touch with the wider electorate, but also with their own activist base who wanted pragmatic, and not vague theoretical, responses to the post-war challenges.

3

The effect of the redistribution of seats is well established in the historiography. The demographic changes, particularly the increased population in the home counties, meant that many new constituencies were created. Many of these were in traditionally Conservative

---

[43] Stuart Ball, 'Local Conservatism and the Evolution of the Party Organisation', in *Conservative Century: The Conservative Party since 1900*, ed. Anthony Seldon and Stuart Ball (Oxford, 1994), 297–8.

[44] *Liberal Agent*, Jan. 1920.

[45] Harmsworth diary, 237, 270, 9 May, 7 Dec. 1916.

[46] Bodl., Maclean MSS, Dep. c.465, f. 124: Sir R. Hudson to Sir D. Maclean, 12 Jan. 1919.

[47] Newcastle University Library, Special Collections, Runciman MSS, WR 185/24: W.M. Crook to W. Runciman, 19 Jan. 1920.

areas and continued to vote tory after 1918. This meant that the Conservatives benefited the most from redistribution, and Kinnear calculated their net benefit was 34 seats.[48] Many of the smaller seats, particularly in northern England, Wales, and Scotland, the areas where Liberal support had traditionally flourished, were either abolished or merged with neighbouring constituencies. This is directly relevant as many of these seats were Liberal and the redistribution, while fair on the basis of demographic changes, was disadvantageous to the Liberals. An example of this was Asquith's constituency: the elimination of many of the grouped 'district of burghs' seats in Scotland resulted in the former St Andrews Burghs constituency, which had been represented by a Liberal MP for only just over three years during the period 1885–1918, being merged with his East Fife seat.[49] Historians of the Labour Party have tended to stress the demographic changes that created a high number of working-class constituencies, particularly the mining seats.[50] While the redistributive element of the 1918 Reform Act cannot be blamed entirely for the troubles of the Liberal Party, it did add emphasis to the results. This would especially be the case in close general elections, such as 1923, when there were returned 258 Conservative MPs, 191 Labour MPs, and 158 Liberal MPs.

However, an even more significant change that needs to be registered was the removal of the MPs from what became the Irish Free State after the Anglo-Irish Treaty of 1921. Although not directly connected with the 1918 Reform Act, this development was important because it removed constituencies which, while they never voted Liberal, returned Irish Nationalist MPs who normally supported the Liberals in the house of commons between 1886 and 1918. This was made worse for the Liberals as the remaining MPs in Northern Ireland were mostly Unionists, and therefore added to the Conservative benches. A leading historian of the Conservative Party has recognized the relevance of this, and pointed out that Ireland had been transformed from being a 'major hindrance' to their prospects of securing a majority to becoming 'a minor help'.[51] The Liberals lost an ally – admittedly one that was sometimes a liability (the cause of home rule for Ireland was not always popular in much of England), but an ally, none the less. What they were left with were more Conservatives to add to the others that had emerged from the 1918 redistribution on the mainland.

There were individuals at the grass roots of the Liberal Party who used the redistribution of parliamentary seats brought about by the 1918 Reform Act to provide some explanations for the reluctant and patchy start to reorganisation after 1918. In the autumn of 1919, the secretary of the Midland Liberal Federation stated that Liberals were still 'adjusting' to the new constituency boundaries created by the Reform Act. Yet, it must also be noted that he recognized that other factors were responsible for Liberal problems as well, including 'the difficulty arising from Labour'. Crucially, the secretary also explained that problems were 'arising from Liberal hesitation in view of the present political situation'.[52] Therefore, the Liberal paralysis prevented adaption both at the grass roots and at the elite level. Meanwhile,

[48] M. Kinnear, *The British Voter: An Atlas and Survey since 1885* (2nd edn, 1981), 72.

[49] S.R. Ball, 'Asquith's Decline and the General Election of 1918', *Scottish Historical Review*, lxi (1982), 48–9.

[50] D. Tanner, *Political Change and the Labour Party 1900–1918* (Cambridge, 1990), 384; Tanner rightly recognizes that, while redistribution did benefit Labour, 'structural changes alone cannot explain Labour's development'.

[51] Ball, *Portrait of a Party*, 509.

[52] CRL, WMLF/3: Midland Liberal Federation, executive committee, 14 Oct. 1919.

the Conservatives appointed their first deputy chairman in order 'to deal with the major redistribution of constituencies' following the 1918 Act.[53] In stark contrast to the other political parties, the Liberals failed to adapt to the new political landscape.

It was perhaps the radical changes to the system of registration that had the most impact on the organisation of the Liberal Party. The partisan battles in the registration courts, so common in the Edwardian era, ceased as 'the cumbrous machinery of registration courts and revising barristers was abolished'.[54] This meant that local associations and their agents were freed from the registration work which had occupied so much of their time before the Great War. However, this would benefit all parties, and not just the Liberals. Butler claims that the administrative costs of the election were 'transferred from the shoulders of the candidate to those of the tax payer'.[55] While this is true, it did not mean that the financial contribution expected from Liberal candidates diminished, and they were often still expected to pay a significant sum to their local association. Furthermore, the introduction of the candidate's deposit of £150 ended up disproportionally affecting the Liberal Party, as when they became the third party of British politics and so most likely to fail to secure the necessary one-eighth of the poll, they had to bear the loss of many more forfeited deposits. In the general elections from 1918 to 1951, the Liberals forfeited 635 deposits, in stark comparison to 140 for Labour and only 37 for the Conservatives.[56] The 1918 Reform Act cannot be blamed for the frequency of elections in the 1920s, and the occurrence of three general elections in the two years from November 1922 to November 1924 stretched the finances of the Liberals, although that would also have been the case before 1914. However, the introduction of the deposit did mean that, because of their poor showing in elections, the new system was more demanding for the Liberals than for their rivals.

Yet the question still remains, how did the revised electoral system affect the finances of the Liberal Party? Pinto-Duschinsky has argued that the Liberal finances after 1918 were 'extremely strong'.[57] While this is an exaggeration, the underlying point is valid. Certainly, between 1919 and 1923 (and arguably from 1918 to 1929), lack of financial resources was not the party's major problem.[58] Pinto-Duschinsky points out that, in the years after the First World War, the Liberal Party was living off capital accumulated in the Edwardian era. This is useful as it highlights, once again, how well run the party had been in that period, and it demonstrates that the Liberals could financially survive one bad election in 1918. This underlines that the downfall of the Liberal Party in the early interwar years was not due to finance. Instead, Liberal paralysis due to the split between Asquith and Lloyd George was responsible. Hudson wrote to Maclean that 'under present conditions' it was 'difficult to say who is with us and who is against us', which meant that 'begging for funds on any considerable scale may consequently be undesirable'.[59] This inaction in 1919

[53]S. Ball, 'The National and Regional Party Structure', in *Conservative Century*, ed. Seldon and Ball, 182.

[54]D.E. Butler, *The Electoral System in Britain, 1918–1951* (Oxford, 1953), 8–9.

[55]Butler, *Electoral System*, 9.

[56]Butler, *Electoral System*, 168.

[57]Michael Pinto-Duschinsky, *British Political Finance, 1830–1980* (Washington, DC, 1981), 83.

[58]Pinto-Duschinsky argues that the Liberals' financial situation was a weakness – but only because they had too much funds; he argues that this cushioned the Liberals 'against reality', 84. For the purposes of this essay, it can be agreed that the new electoral laws did not by themselves hinder the Liberal Party.

[59]Bodl., Maclean MSS, Dep. c.465, f. 129: Sir R. Hudson to Sir D Maclean, 12 Jan. 1919.

Table 1: *General Election Results 1918–35*

Year	Conservative	Liberal	Labour	Others
1922	346	115	142	12
1923	258	159	191	7
1924	419	40	151	5
1929	260	59	288	8
1931	521	37	52	5
1935	431	21	154	9

Source: D.E. Butler, *The Electoral System in Britain, 1918–1951* (Oxford, 1953), 188.

prevented the Liberals from even attempting to recover from the difficult results of the 1918 general election. The psychological impact of the new rules also needs to be considered. The initial reaction of Liberal constituency agents at the time that the electorate was nearly trebled by the 1918 Reform Act was to avoid expensive pictorial posters, drop photographs and expensive lithographic work, and hold fewer meetings, because it would no longer be possible to 'spend money in the old-time way'.[60] This response was incredibly ineffective and, when combined with the difficult context of the 1918 general election, helps explain the disastrous Liberal result.

4

The 1918 Reform Act had almost included an element of proportional representation.[61] The Speaker's conference from which the act evolved had recommended this be introduced on a substantial scale, but after much debate it was eventually applied only in the handful of university seats that returned two or more MPs.[62] Therefore, it is relevant to consider whether or not the method of election after 1918 had any effect on the fortunes of the Liberal Party. As can be seen in Tables 1 and 2, under a proportional electoral system the Liberals would have secured substantially more seats. This is especially the case in the two years where the electoral system hindered them the most, in 1924 and 1929.

It would be fair to suggest that the retention of the first-past-the-post electoral system was the most important aspect of the 1918 Reform Act in relation to the subsequent fortunes of the Liberal Party. However, while this shows how they were disadvantaged once they were in the third party trap, it does not explain why they came into that position.

---

[60] *Liberal Agent*, July 1918.

[61] The *Liberal Magazine* reported in Apr. 1917 that the National Liberal Federation welcomed the Speaker's Report even though they felt it did not go as far as the reforms which had been advocated by the Liberal Party, but the Liberal agents' journal offered only its 'qualified support': *Liberal Agent*, Apr. 1917.

[62] Asquith appealed for a trial of proportional representation, but this was eventually rejected by the house of commons. The editorial of the *Daily Chronicle* was not concerned that the proposed proportional representation experiment was rejected, but was concerned that the alternative vote had not been passed: *Daily Chronicle*, 14 May 1918. As the general election was in full swing, the *Daily News* lamented the loss of both the alternative vote and proportional representation: *Daily News*, 30 Nov. 1918.

Table 2: *General Election Results 1918–35 if under Proportional Representation*

Year	Conservative	Liberal	Labour	Others	Difference to the Liberals
1922	235	179	181	20	+64
1923	234	182	188	11	+23
1924	298	108	202	7	+68
1929	235	143	228	9	+84
1931	413		189	13	n/a
1935	330	41	232	12	+20

Note: Butler, *Electoral System*, 191, provides tables for the election results 1923–51 under the alternative vote.

Source: D.E. Butler, *The Electoral System in Britain, 1918–1951* (Oxford, 1953), 188.

Many Liberals at the grass roots grasped early on the position that they were in and realized that there should be further electoral reform. To take just two examples, the Blackpool Liberal Association approved the 'principle of proportional representation' in early 1922, and the Walthamstow Liberals wanted a resolution in favour of the alternative vote passed as early as the National Liberal Federation conference in 1919.[63] The executive committee of the Midland Liberal Federation comprehended 'the difficulty and danger to which Liberals are exposed where they find it necessary to take part in three-cornered fights', and concluded 'that the only way out lies in a re-arrangement of the method of voting'.[64] The grass roots across the country seem to have recognized this as well, but there was no agreement on whether to seek the alternative vote or some other system of proportional representation.[65] As the Liberals understood that the change would greatly benefit them, they were more wholeheartedly converted to electoral reform. However, for Labour and the Conservatives, who were the beneficiaries of the first-past-the-post system, there was no incentive for change.

The outcome of the 1922 general election showed precisely why the Liberal Party needed electoral reform: the secretary of the Midland Liberal Federation's election report highlighted that, in the 33 seats the Liberals had contested in the region, the party had polled 309,148 votes and had eight MPs elected, which was a ration of over 38,000 votes per MP, while in those same contests the Conservative poll of 316,620 had gained them 19 seats, which was an average of around 16,500 votes for every MP. Unsurprisingly, he concluded that this proved the need for electoral reform. Demoralised, he added that there was a 'disparity of reward occurring to effort put forth'.[66]

[63]Lancashire RO, DDX 1404/1/1/2: Blackpool Liberal Association [hereafter cited as LA], executive committee, 20 Mar. 1922; Vestry House Museum, W32.6 BA/1: Walthamstow LA, executive committee, 26 Sept. 1919.

[64]CRL, WMLF/4: Midland Liberal Federation, executive committee, 4 Feb. 1921. The *Daily News* discussed the 'Split vote peril' during the election on 27 Nov. 1918.

[65]Lancashire RO, Blackpool LA, executive committee, 20 Mar. 1922; Derbyshire RO, D4612/6/1, Chesterfield Women's LA, committee meeting, 30 Mar. 1920; Vestry House Museum, Walthamstow LA, executive committee, 26 Sept. 1919.

[66]CRL, WMLF/4: Midland Liberal Federation, executive committee, 8 Dec. 1922.

Yet, it must be highlighted that, of the 76 contestable seats in the region, Liberal candidates had stood in only 34 (one candidate being returned unopposed at Chesterfield), which was not enough to take even half of the seats even if they had won all that they contested. The advantage the Liberal Party had lost at the general election of 1918 of being either the governing party or the main opposition was reinforced in this election, as it never contested enough seats to become the government in its own right. The Liberal Party contributed to its own downfall by not giving the appearance of being a government in waiting. Potential Liberal MPs were disillusioned and believed that they would not get elected; hence they did not stand, and so it became a self-fulfilling prophecy.

One major change as a result of the 1918 Reform Act was that all polls across the country took place on the same day, instead of being spread across two to three weeks. Although this was a non-partisan change, some of the Liberal elite felt that it had adversely affected them in the 1918 general election. The Liberal *Westminster Gazette* argued that the results had been 'intensified on this occasion by the multiplicity of three-cornered contests, the absence of any provision for minority representation, and the holding of all elections on one day, which deprived the electors of the opportunity they had in 1900 of correcting the excesses of the early returns'.[67] However, holding elections on the same day should have been considered the least important factor of those identified. A more logical conclusion that the Liberals came to was that a consequence of the new arrangement was that heavyweight speakers would not be as available in the same way as before to undertake speaking tours during the last stages of the campaign.[68]

As previously discussed, the lack of proportionality adversely affected the Liberals, and the continued growth of the Labour Party since 1900 was also vitally significant. During the war, the Labour Party clearly developed its ambitions to become a national party, and to that effect undertook reorganisation and drafted a new constitution which was formally adopted in February 1918.[69] The Liberal elite recognized this a couple of months later. The *Westminster Gazette* realized the potential of the Labour Party, and warned that it aimed 'at getting adherents from all classes, and is preparing to contest a very large number of seats at the next election, whenever that may come. This Labour Party is a fact which has to be reckoned with by all politicians, and it may easily upset many plans based on the old politics.'[70] The reason that the Liberals did not combat this cannot be blamed on the 1918 Reform Act, and they have to take much of the responsibility on their own shoulders. The *Westminster Gazette* blamed the inactivity of all the parties, apart from the coalition, as the reason for the latter's dominant victory: 'the elector, being put to the choice of supporting the only organised party which appeared capable of governing the country or of voting for disarmed and disorganised groups which could not even bid for power, inevitably chose the former alternative'.[71] Consequently, the responsibility should rest with the Liberal leadership. Even the loyal *Westminster Gazette* noted that some of Asquith's

---

[67] *Westminster Gazette*, 30 Dec. 1918.

[68] *Liberal Agent*, Jan. 1920.

[69] Matthew Worley, *Labour Inside the Gate: A History of the British Labour Party between the Wars* (2005), 11.

[70] *Westminster Gazette*, 11 May 1918.

[71] *Westminster Gazette*, 30 Dec. 1918.

supporters felt that 'in recent months he seems to some of his followers to have carried modesty and self-effacement to excess'.[72]

There are other relevant weaknesses of the Liberal position after the First World War which make it appear that the 1918 Reform Act was an important factor only because they are apparent in the period after the legislation was passed. The Liberals' lack of a distinctive agenda with which to attract the electorate after the Great War is vitally important. However, this is not as simple as suggesting that, because most women aged over 30 years and all working-class men aged over 21 years now had the franchise, political concerns had changed.[73] Although to some extent this was the case, they had clearly been becoming more class-based in the late Edwardian period as well. The core of the Liberals' problem in appealing to the new electorate was not only that their policies had not moved forward, but they had arguably reverted back to 19th-century shibboleths. When the Liberal candidate for Blackpool was adopted, he was praised as 'a man with the spirit of Gladstonian Liberalism'.[74] The political philosophy of the Grand Old Man still held deep importance for Liberals in 1922; the candidate for Harborough was proud to stick to 'the old watchwords of the party, "peace, retrenchment, and reform" ', as he felt that they were just as applicable in 1922 'as they were to Gladstonian times'.[75] Gladstone had been dead for 24 years, and in the early 1920s most Liberals seemed to have forgotten the success of the new liberalism in between.[76] In many ways, the Liberals had relinquished the progressive flag which they had flown before 1914. It was a rather worrying situation when the prime minister who had imposed the Parliament Act of 1911 should feel that 'the best safeguard for true Liberalism would be found in an unreformed House of Lords and the Cecil Family'.[77] This sums up the plight of the interwar Liberal Party succinctly.

While methods of election are important, the political context of elections are more vitally so. The 'Coupon' election was not fertile ground for the half of the Liberal Party who were outside the coalition that had just successfully concluded what contemporaries called the Great War. This was compounded as the coalition government was putting forward a domestically-progressive manifesto and was headed by a Liberal known for radical reforms. The predicament for Liberals is aptly summarized in a letter to the *Westminster Gazette* on 27 November 1918, in which the Liberal writer said that he would vote for a coalition candidate, as the coalition's programme 'is without flaw or blemish'. However, he took issue with the 'vow of servility' that was 'being extracted from all Coalition candidates'.[78]

---

[72] *Westminster Gazette*, 27 Nov. 1918.

[73] Not all women over the age of 30 years had the vote; either she or her husband had to qualify as a local government elector, by being either a householder or the occupier of land or premises with an annual rental value of at least £5. Lodgers in furnished rooms were not local government electors, and so a domestic servant living at her employer's home did not qualify: Representation of the People Act 1918 (7 & 8 Geo. V, c. 64), section 4, clause 1.

[74] Lancashire RO, Blackpool LA: special meeting of the Liberal Council, 28 Oct. 1922.

[75] *Market Harborough Advertiser*, 14 Nov. 1922.

[76] The main difference between post-1918 Liberalism and Gladstonian Liberalism was the former's support of the League of Nations; however, the League's aims of international arbitration would fit perfectly under the Gladstonian banner of peace.

[77] *H.H.A.*, 118, 22 Dec. 1919.

[78] *Westminster Gazette*, 27 Nov. 1918.

Contemporaries recognized the political shift that had occurred once the results of the election were known. The *Westminster Gazette* described the 1918 general election as 'the spectacle of the old British political system in ruins', with 'one historic party [the Liberals] reduced to a contemptible minority'.[79] However, the evidence suggests that in 1918 the Liberal elite did not think that their party was down and out: 'Past experience has proved to us that Liberalism and Radicalism have never been so strong in the country as within a few months of their greatest reverses at the polls, and we have no doubt that it will prove so on this occasion.'[80] The *Westminster Gazette* continued: 'If Liberals and their leaders are temporarily excluded from Parliament, they must turn with the greater zeal to the work which is imperatively needed from them in the country. They must devise new machinery and new forms of propaganda to meet the circumstances.'[81] The fact that this did not occur was due to internal division leading to paralysis.

Consequently, in 1919 the Liberal drift led some to doubt as to whether the Liberal Party even had a future. Murray Elibank, Liberal MP for Midlothian from January 1910 to 1912, when he became Baron Murray of Elibank, felt 'that a powerful Free Trade Party should be formed immediately'.[82] He had no faith in the current party label, as 'Liberalism for the moment is thoroughly unpopular. The present generation has most obstinately got into its head that Liberals, particularly the chiefs of the Party, did not pull their full strength in the bout [the war], a ridiculous misconception, but the English character is such that it is perfectly mulish over a "fancy", and the only way to eradicate it is to start another one.'[83] Elibank added to Maclean: 'you should be the leader of this new Free Trade Party, because all of the old Liberal leaders are, for the moment, passing through the valley of suspicion'.[84] As Elibank clearly points out, the events of the First World War had the most significant impact on the political fortunes of the Liberal Party. Asquith's leadership of the Liberal Party since the start of the war became a weakness for the Liberals, and was a more significant factor in Liberal decline than the 1918 Reform Act.

5

As has been seen, while the 1918 Representation of the People Act is relevant to the Liberal Party's fortunes, it is not the primary factor when considering the party's difficulties. Instead, the focus should be on the Liberal divisions between Asquith and Lloyd George, which were essentially formalised and deepened in the general election of 1918. The provisions of the 1918 Reform Act are not responsible for this key cause of Liberal decline. Hart has argued that the war and its consequences made the Liberals inadequate and lacking in direction.[85] Similarly, he focused on Liberal division as a reason why the party was unable to recruit the support of 15 million new electors, and how the war had caused the party to break up

---

[79] *Westminster Gazette*, 30 Dec. 1918.

[80] *Westminster Gazette*, 30 Dec. 1918.

[81] *Westminster Gazette*, 30 Dec. 1918.

[82] Bodl., Maclean MSS, Dep. c.465, f. 184: Murray Elibank to Maclean, 10 June 1919.

[83] Bodl., Maclean MSS, Dep. c.465, f. 184: Murray Elibank to Maclean, 10 June 1919.

[84] Bodl., Maclean MSS, Dep. c.465, f. 184: Murray Elibank to Maclean, 10 June 1919.

[85] Hart, 'The Liberals, the War, and the Franchise', 829.

'intellectually'.[86] The 1918 Reform Act is relevant to the Liberals because it took effect at the point when the Liberals were divided and at their lowest ebb. Why should any of the new – or existing – electors vote for the dispirited Liberal Party, when they had the choice of the coalition that successfully prosecuted the war, or a reorganised Labour Party that had also contributed to victory and had a radical agenda?

Several elements of the 1918 Reform Act were secondary factors in the difficulties of the Liberal Party in the interwar years, such as the increased franchise, the redistribution of seats, the retention of plural voting, the retention of the first-past-the-post electoral system, and the introduction of deposits for candidates. With the benefit of hindsight, it is clear that the electoral system negatively affected the Liberals more than the other parties. However, that was only significant after the Liberals became the third party in an essentially two-party system, as its vote was squeezed. The redistribution of seats and plural voting were negative factors for the Liberals, but were only critical in tight elections. The real causes of the Liberal difficulties were self-inflicted.

Asquith was arguably the most significant weakness for the Liberal Party after 1916. While it is admirable that 'no clear-cut' separation of Liberal MPs occurred, due to Asquith's support for the government until the Maurice Debate of May 1918, in other respects his leadership was uninspired.[87] His decision to decline the post of lord chancellor when it was offered by Lloyd George in May 1917 seems catastrophic, as this could have kept the Liberal Party together and moderated the political direction of the coalition in 1918–22. Bentley highlights that there was no concerted Liberal response to socialism before 1918, and this had a knock-on effect in the early 1920s.[88] Clearly, having half the party under Lloyd George in coalition with the Conservatives and half in opposition under first Maclean and later Asquith did not help. Furthermore, Asquith was no longer an electoral asset or force in the post-war world. He described having to 'go on the stump to a variety of places' in the 1918 election as an 'accursed business'.[89] While it is possible to feel that way and still perform effectively, that was not the case for him in this election.

While the responsibility for the Liberal split cannot solely be laid at Asquith's door, he deserves much of the blame. Asquith was dismissive of reconciliation with the coalition Liberals in 1919.[90] If he had an alternative plan to reunion this would not matter as much but Asquith was not particularly interested in politics that year.[91] Thus, crucial time was wasted while politics was in flux. Consequently, the Liberals had few new policies or ideas with which to shape the post-war world. Even when he returned to parliament, he was more of a hindrance than a help to the party; for example, he doubted whether he could 'say anything useful' on the Coal Bill, and so, instead, 'thought it better to be silent'.[92] It would have been best for his historical reputation and the fortunes of the Liberal Party had he retired from public life in 1918. In many ways, Asquith was right when he said

[86] Hart, 'The Liberals, the War, and the Franchise', 831.

[87] T. Wilson, *The Downfall of the Liberal Party, 1914–1935* (1966), 114.

[88] M. Bentley, 'The Liberal Response to Socialism, 1918–29', in *Essays in Anti-Labour History: Responses to the Rise of Labour in Britain*, ed. K.D. Brown (1974), 42–73.

[89] *H.H.A.*, 85, 19 Nov. 1918.

[90] *H.H.A.*, 92, 3 Apr. 1919; see also 114, 13 Nov. 1919.

[91] *H.H.A.*, 106, 23 Oct. 1919, and *passim* 1919 entries.

[92] *H.H.A.*, 158–9, 19 Oct. 1920.

that 'the disintegration of the Liberal party began with the Coupon election'.[93] This has been explored in recent scholarship, and this essay shows not only how the Liberals were unable to take advantage of the 1918 Reform Act, but how its timing severely hindered the Liberals as they were at their weakest moment.[94]

[93] Earl of Oxford and Asquith, *Memories and Reflections, 1852–1927* (1928), 205.

[94] G.J. Freeman, 'The Decline of the Liberal Party in the Heart of England: The Liberals in Leicestershire, 1914–24', *Historical Research*, lxxxix (2016), 531–49.

The Labour Party and the Impact of the 1918 Reform Act

The Representation of the People Act 1918 compelled the Labour Party to respond by changing its organisation. Labour was already in the process of changing its organisation, policies and constitution because of the transformed economic, social, and political circumstances of the Great War. Labour took particular care to adjust its organisation to appeal to women voters, especially working-class ones. It also aimed its electoral appeal to white-collar workers, male and female. Labour benefited in 1919–20 from the wider local government franchise in London and some other urban areas, but such advances were thereafter countered by the Conservatives and Liberals avoiding dividing the anti-Labour vote. It is possible that Labour benefited to a small extent in a few inner-city constituencies by the ending of electoral disqualification for receiving out relief under the poor law. By the 1922 general election, Labour was establishing electoral strongholds in many mining, industrial and inner-city parliamentary seats. Labour welcomed the changes proposed by the Speaker's conference but, to the dismay of some of its supporters, it accepted the loss of the proportional representation proposals in the compromises made as the Representation of the People Bill went through parliament. In the longer term, the lack of proportional representation enabled Labour to form majority governments in 1945 and later.

Keywords: co-operative movement; electoral reform; food; Labour Party; miners; profiteering; proportional representation; Representation of the People Act 1918; white-collar workers; women's suffrage

At the end of 1918, a Newcastle newspaper reflected on what it deemed to be 'the greatest and most revolutionary Reform Bill ever brought before a British Parliament'. It pointed to the great increase in the number of electors and especially to the 8,479,156 women electors. A Rochdale newspaper, making a similar point, referred both to women voters and to the expectation that the Labour Party would run 300 candidates in a 1918 election.[1] How did the Labour Party respond to the reform proposals and how significant was the act in the rise of the Labour Party?

By 1915 it was clear to all interested in politics that the pre-war register of electors was badly outdated and that the war made a revision of the franchise inescapable. Widespread support for giving the vote to soldiers and sailors raised the issue of which other adults would be enfranchised. The Labour Party's subcommittee on electoral reform resolved in March 1916:

[As] the electoral machinery throughout the country has broken down and the electors scattered, and that insuperable obstacles lie in the way of bringing them back to their

---

[1] *Newcastle Journal*, 31 Dec. 1918; *Rochdale Observer*, 29 Oct. 1917.

constituencies, no election should take place until a scheme of franchise reform (including Women's Enfranchisement, Registration and Redistribution) has been effected.

Arthur Henderson followed this resolution with a cabinet paper, 'Necessary Electoral Reform', which made, as Martin Pugh has summarized, 'a proposal for male suffrage based on a simple residential qualification, and votes for women over 25'.[2]

In mid 1916, Labour's War Emergency Workers' National Committee backed Arthur Balfour's suggestion of 2 June 1916 for a select committee to be formed from all the parties to consider franchise and electoral reform. When this proposal ran into difficulties, Asquith took up another suggestion. This was a conference to be chaired by the Speaker of the house of commons to seek a compromise agreement on Reform. The Labour Party nominated three of its MPs, all trade unionists, George Wardle (Railwaymen and chair of the executive committee in 1916); Frank Goldstone (National Union of Teachers) and Stephen Walsh (Lancashire and Cheshire Miners' Federation). The Speaker's conference met 26 times between 12 October 1916 and 26 January 1917. It reached compromise agreements on the major issues and, apart from proportional representation, these became the basis of the 1918 act.[3]

The reorganisation of the Labour Party started after the Representation of the People Bill began to be discussed in the house of commons in June 1917. Arthur Henderson, who was constructively dismissed from Lloyd George's war cabinet on 12 August 1917, raised the issue of reorganisation of the Labour Party with the joint committee of its executive and the parliamentary committee of the Trades Union Congress (TUC) on 6 September. The trade union leaders were suspicious of changes which might affect their dominance in the party.[4] Henderson presented a memorandum on reorganisation to Labour's executive committee on 26 September 1917, in which he outlined the need for 'a wider extension of membership, the strengthening and development of local bodies in the constituencies, together with the promotion of a larger number of candidatures, and the suggestion that a party programme should be adopted'. The executive committee gave Henderson plenary powers to visit affiliated trade unions' executive and district committees in order to strengthen Labour organisation at constituency level.[5] In his report to the January 1918 Labour Party conference, Henderson commented: 'The prospective enactment of the Representation of the People Bill ... has rendered it necessary for the Executive Committee seriously to consider whether the present Party structure and machinery are adequate to cope with the new circumstances.'[6]

The Labour Party welcomed the compromises agreed by the political parties at the Speaker's conference, deeming the agreed proposals to be 'long-delayed and much

[2] Martin Pugh, *Electoral Reform in War and Peace 1906–18* (1978), 62–3.

[3] People's History Museum, Manchester [hereafter cited as PHM], War Emergency Workers' National Committee Papers [hereafter cited as WEWNC], Box 29; Isobel White and Andrew Parker, 'Speakers' Conferences', House of Commons Library, 1 Dec. 2009, 3–4; *Report of Speaker's Conference*, reprinted as appendix 5, in Sir Hugh Fraser, *The Representation of the People Acts, 1918 to 1921* (2nd edn, 1922), 594–602: James Lowther to David Lloyd George, 27 Jan. 1917; Pugh, *Electoral Reform*, 68–86.

[4] Ross McKibbin, *The Evolution of the Labour Party 1910–1924* (Oxford, 1974), 93.

[5] PHM, Labour Party Archive: executive committee minutes, morning meeting, 26 Sept. 1917.

[6] PHM, Labour Party Archive: report of the executive committee, in *Report of the Annual Conference of the Labour Party Held at the Albert Hall, Nottingham on Wednesday, January 23 1918 and Two Following Days, and the Adjourned Conference Held in the Central Hall, Westminster, London SW., on Tuesday February 26th 1918* (1918), 15.

overdue democratic reform'. The Joint Labour Party and TUC committee was outraged in September 1917 at suggestions that, despite its advanced stage in the house of commons, the Representation of the People Bill should be suspended until the reform of the house of lords reached the statute book. The meeting stated that 'any attempt to hold a general election upon the present obsolete register would amount to a national scandal'. The joint committee sent a delegation to see Lloyd George to protest at any such delay.[7] For Labour, the Speaker's conference proposals were a considerable advance, but did not go far enough. J.R. Clynes welcomed the proposals as moving towards recognition that 'the right that a man has for a vote is that he is a man'.[8] The adoption of such a principle would cut through the Gordian knot of franchise and registration restrictions which hitherto had kept so many adult males from the vote.

The Speaker's conference proposals also opened the franchise to some women, but without recognition that the right of a woman to vote was because she was a woman. Jim Middleton, who was Labour's assistant secretary and also the secretary of the War Emergency Workers' National Committee, was active in ensuring that at least one trade union pressed the TUC in 1916 to discuss women's enfranchisement.[9] At the Women's Labour League conference in early 1917, Mary Macarthur had predicted: 'Votes were denied to the mothers of men; she thought they would be given to the makers of infernal machine-guns.'[10] In fact, the powerful argument of war service which was used to enfranchise many men was not applied to women, of whom many of those working in munitions and other war work were aged under 30 years and excluded.

At the June 1918 Labour Party conference there was no opposition to a motion moved by John Bromley of the Associated Society of Locomotive Engineers and Firemen (ASLEF), part of which stated that the defects of the Representation of the People Act included that it:

> failed to give votes to women under 30 years of age, denied them the right to sit in Parliament, maintained for both sexes an unnecessarily long period of residence as a qualification for the register, ignored the rights of the civilian electors who may be compulsorily away from home on polling day and omitted any provision which would have prevented the scandal of large sections of the voters remaining unrepresented whilst Members are returned to Parliament by a minority of their voting constituency.

In moving the motion, Bromley echoed Clynes:

> Although the Government had thrown a sop to women, the great Labour Movement must never be content until they had the fullest freedom of exercising the franchise which was due to them as human beings. They must see to it that ... the right of becoming electors in this kingdom was based on a basis of humanity and not property.

[7] PHM, Labour Party Archive: joint committee of the parliamentary committee of the TUC and the executive committee of the Labour Party minutes, 26 Sept. 1917. Earlier, *The Times* had stated that use of the old register would be 'a mockery of representative government': *The Times*, 31 May 1916.

[8] In a house of commons debate on 28 Mar. 1917, quoted in H.C.G. Matthew, R.I. McKibbin and J.A. Kay, 'The Franchise Factor in the Rise of the Labour Party', *English Historical Review*, xci (1976), 726.

[9] He wrote on 7 June 1916 to J.R. Clynes, Margaret Bondfield and Ben Turner in their capacities as leading trade unionists, to seek their help in ensuring that a motion on women's suffrage went to the TUC in Sept. 1916; in the event, the parliamentary committee put women's suffrage before Congress: PHM, WEWNC, Box 29.

[10] Eleventh conference of the Women's Labour League, Salford, 22 Jan. 1917: *The Times*, 23 Jan. 1917.

Labour was also opposed to the disfranchisement of conscientious objectors and in favour of the abolition of the house of lords.[11]

There was also substantial but minority support within the Labour Party and the trade unions for an alternative to the first-past-the-post system in elections. At the Labour Party conference in January 1914, there was a thoughtful debate on alternative voting systems, with Ramsay MacDonald making a strong case against immediate change. The conference voted against supporting proportional representation or the alternative vote by nearly two to one majorities. However, there remained much enthusiasm for proportional representation among activists. During the First World War, there was also growing support for the alternative vote, much favoured by the party's election specialists such as Arthur Henderson and Egerton Wake and by part of the Parliamentary Labour Party, as a means of protecting Labour candidates in three-way contests. Henderson had been encouraged to press for far more Labour candidates than in 1910 because he believed that the next election would be fought under the alternative vote and this system would make it safer for Labour to break from any electoral reliance on the Liberals.[12] Proportional representation for boroughs had been in the Speaker's conference proposals but alternatives to the first-past-the-post system had divided the parties and the two houses of parliament, the Commons favouring the alternative vote and the Lords favouring a form of proportional representation. Due to the differences between the two houses of parliament, no change was made to the voting system.[13]

Some Labour Party members were angered when some Labour MPs voted in the house of commons against proportional representation after the Labour Party at a Special Conference had agreed to accept the Speaker's conference programme. In June 1917, the National Union of Clerks protested to the Labour Party executive committee. At the Labour Party annual conference held in January 1918, Herbert Elvin, secretary of the National Union of Clerks, moved a motion which stated that no reform settlement was satisfactory which did not include the 'proportional representation of all opinions and interests by means of the single transferable vote, with constituencies returning at least five members'. It was passed without dissent. When both proportional representation and the alternative vote failed to pass in parliament, the Labour parliamentary report included the observation: 'It is the one serious blot on what is otherwise a most comprehensive Franchise Reform.'[14] Proportional representation, in the form of the single transferable vote, was only enacted for the multi-member university seats.

Martin Pugh has argued convincingly that proportional representation would have made 'Labour a substantial minority party but never more than that'.[15] Enthusiasm for alternative systems diminished within Labour as the party succeeded in gaining many seats under the existing system. In 1929, when the Labour Party secured the largest number of MPs,

---

[11] *Report of the Annual Conference, 1918*, 28 June 1918, p. 68.

[12] Ross McKibbin, *Parties and People: England 1914–1951* (Oxford, 2010), 29–30; Pugh, *Electoral Reform*, 8–11, 162–4; Vernon Bogdanor, *The People and the Party System: The Referendum and Electoral Reform in British Politics* (Cambridge, 1981), 130–1; *Report of the Special and Annual Conference of the Labour Party, 1914*, 104–13: debate on proportional representation, 29 Jan. 1914.

[13] G.R. Searle, *A New England? Peace and War 1886–1918* (Oxford, 2004), 831–2.

[14] PHM, Labour Party Archive: executive committee minutes, 27 June 1917; *Report of the Annual Conference, 1918*, 21.

[15] Pugh, *Electoral Reform*, 11.

Labour observed that the other parties had not prioritised proportional representation or the alternative vote in the 1918 or 1928 Reform Acts, but with Labour in office there was a clamour for change. In response, the Labour Party's executive printed figures for single member constituencies where more than two candidates stood which showed that Labour had a majority of votes in 98 seats (45.5% of its total) and a minority in 118 seats, in contrast to the Conservatives with a majority in 60 seats (28.6%) and a minority in 150 seats and the Liberals four (9.1%) and 40. Labour also noted that, in 1924, Labour had four seats with majorities over 10,000 and 25 with majorities between 5,000 and 10,000, while in 1929 the figures were 67 and 91.[16]

When Ramsay MacDonald argued against changing from the first-past-the-post system in 1914, he made much of the cost of fighting the big three- or four-member constituencies required for proportional representation. He observed that it would involve 'a large number of meetings, considerable printing, agents, committee rooms and so on' and he was 'not going to consider Proportional Representation ... until the cost of elections had been materially reduced'.[17] *The Times* editorial on the Speaker's conference commented that the 'central pivot' of the scheme would 'replace the present haphazard methods of registration (under which a qualified voter may even be disfranchised for a couple of years) by a simple six months' qualification, registered automatically, at the public expense, and by the local authorities'. The editorial added: 'It sweeps away at one stroke the whole system of owner, occupier, householder and lodger votes, does away with the main work of registration agents and local party organization, greatly reduces the burden of unnecessary expenditure, and places what remains on the proper shoulders.'[18] Labour welcomed these changes, not least for reducing costs. Although Henderson had been able to leave foundry work for registration and other electoral work, he did not wish to prolong the old ways. The Conservatives and Liberals had greater funds to pay for registration work, and some of it was more to do with limiting democracy (by getting hostile voters excluded from the register) than enlarging it. In contrast to Henderson, Joseph Gould, chairman of the National Society of Conservative Agents, complained that the Representation of the People Bill:

> sweeps away all the old registration machinery without putting anything better in its place, and very largely curtails the power of the political organisation to do the work they have been accustomed to do at election times. The setting up of a registration officer to take the place of the Returning Barrister is an extremely doubtful experiment.

As for the proposed reduction of the time required to be in residence to qualify for the register from 12 to six months, Labour called for a reduction to three months.[19]

The Speaker's conference provisions for proportional representation in local elections fell when the Representation of the People Bill was going through parliament. The local

---

[16] PHM, Labour Party Archive: report of the executive committee 1928–9, in *Report of the 29th Annual Conference, 1929*, 6–7.

[17] PHM, Labour Party Archive: *Report of the Special and Annual Conference, 1914*, 110.

[18] *The Times*, 1 Feb. 1917.

[19] Interview with Joseph Gould in *Western Morning News*, 29 May 1917; PHM, Labour Party Archive: electoral reform motion at the conference, 25 Jan. 1918, in *Report of the Annual Conference, 1918*, 135.

government franchise was wider than the parliamentary one, as it was given to women on the same terms as men, including from the age of 21 years. The bill was estimated to add seven million women to those eligible to vote in local elections. During the bill's passage, Labour extended the vote in local elections to wives of electors and to men who inhabited houses because of their office, service or employment, such as caretakers.[20] It is probable that part of the reason that Labour did especially well in London was due to the franchise changes, though much was due to wartime economic and social pressures as well as to the divided anti-Labour vote in 1919–20.

The removal of the electoral disqualification for 'receipt of poor relief or other alms, either by the elector or some other person for whose maintenance he is responsible' would have benefited many poor people, but poor people were not necessarily Labour supporters. However, the legislation still disfranchised workhouse inmates along with those in prisons or asylums. In England and Wales, usually just over a third of those receiving relief were workhouse inmates. In 1921, the year of the revolt of a majority of the Poplar councillors and poor law guardians, the total of those receiving relief in or out of workhouses amounted to 14.3 per thousand of the population. Hence the likely electoral impact of enfranchised receivers of out relief was unlikely to be great outside of very poor urban areas or during long-running big industrial disputes. However, in such poor areas as Poplar, there were many people receiving out relief who could vote for George Lansbury and the others who struggled to pay out relief sufficient for families' needs.[21]

As with the Reform Acts of 1832, 1867, and 1884, redistribution of seats was a major feature of reform in the 1918 act. The intention was to make populations of 70,000 the standard size for one MP, although boroughs of 50,000 and higher kept their representation.[22] While the Conservatives prioritised safeguarding county agricultural seats and secured some 15–17 more seats than the standardised size of electorates would have given, Labour benefited from the greater number of borough seats, including in London, and often from the removal of nearby rural areas from industrial boroughs.[23]

Labour gained from the new franchise, but not by as much as was suggested in 1976 by Colin Matthew, Ross McKibbin and John Kay. In their article 'The Franchise Factor in the Rise of the Labour Party', they argued that franchise change was 'of first importance' in explaining Labour's replacement of the Liberal Party as 'the principal party of progress'. In so doing, much of their emphasis was on the shortcomings of the Liberal Party, allegedly relying on a small, but sophisticated, electorate. They also largely discounted the importance of the war in bringing about such political change. Their work set off a fruitful debate as to the importance of the Representation of the People Act in the rise of the Labour Party. Computer analysis of election results indicated that the Labour Party did not gain markedly from the franchise changes but the Conservatives did, and that the Liberals were damaged

---

[20] Fraser, *Representation of the People Acts*, xxv; 'Parliamentary Report' published in the annual report section; *Report of the Annual Conference, 1918*, 52.

[21] Fraser, *Representation of the People Acts*, xxvi, 96. Sidney Webb and Beatrice Webb, *English Poor Law History. Part II: The Last Hundred Years, Volume 2* (1929), 814–15, 1044–5; Karel Williams, *From Pauperism to Poverty* (1981), 181–2; John Shepherd, *George Lansbury* (Oxford, 2002), 190–4.

[22] Fraser, *Representation of the People Acts*, xxv.

[23] Pugh, *Electoral Reform*, 109; D. Tanner, *Political Change and the Labour Party 1900–1918* (Cambridge, 1990), 391, 403.

by the declining significance of religion in politics.[24] Some other studies pointed to continuities, such as regional patterns and the longer-term trajectory of Labour's parliamentary growth to 1929.[25] Duncan Tanner argued that the new male electors were not as different in social composition in comparison with the pre-war electorate as was usually assumed, and so adding them to the franchise did not transform Labour's electoral strength.[26] Understandably, part of the debate on the franchise issue has focused on the decline of the Liberals. In contrast, the emphasis here is on the impact of the war in greatly strengthening the Labour Party, with the electoral reform stimulating Labour to revamp its structure and image.

The First World War had changed the political landscape in ways mostly favourable to the Labour Party. The scale of Britain's war effort changed attitudes towards the organisation of society and the economy. The needs of war production soon moved Britain away from 'Business as usual' to ever-widening controls of industry, mining and agriculture under the Defence of the Realm Acts of August and November 1914, the Munitions of War Acts of 1915, 1916, and 1917, and the Corn Production Act of 1917. While state control was not nationalisation, it did move collectivisation from limited practice and socialist aspirations to reality. Alongside this were increased expectations of fairness in social matters, from the freezing of rents under the Increase of Rent and Mortgage Interest (War Restrictions) Act of 1915, to limited food rationing, beginning with sugar, in big urban areas in 1917–18. There was also considerable hardship stemming from wartime inflation, especially for those on fixed incomes. The board of trade's monitoring of the price of food for a family of five found that its cost rose by 93% from July 1914 to February 1917.[27] There was widespread popular support for better provision for soldiers' and sailors' dependants, a cause which the Labour Party took up.

Of special importance for the Labour Party was the enhanced position of labour in the wartime economy. During the war, some 5,670,000 men joined the armed forces, representing roughly 38% of the pre-war male labour force. Despite this, British male trade unionism grew from 3,681,000 in 1914 to 5,280,000 in 1918, a rise in trade union density from 31.8% to 44.8% (union density being the proportion of trade union members out of those legally eligible to join a union). Women workers were prominent among replacement labour, and their numbers rose from 3,277,000 in 1914 to 4,940,000 in 1918. Many women moved from working in sectors unorganised, or poorly organised, by trade unions, to better-paid war work. British trade union membership among female workers rose from 436,000 in 1914 to 1,182,000 in 1918, a rise in density from 8.6% to

[24]J. Turner, 'The Labour Vote and the Franchise after 1918: An Investigation of the English Evidence', in *History and Computing*, ed. P. Denley and D. Hopkins (Manchester, 1987); K.D. Wald, *Crosses on the Ballot: Patterns of British Voter Alignment since 1885* (Princeton, NJ, 1983).

[25]J.P.B. Dunbabin, 'British Elections in the Nineteenth and Twentieth Centuries: A Regional Approach', *English Historical Review*, xcv (1980), 241–67; J. Turner, *British Politics and the Great War: Coalition and Conflict 1915–1918* (New Haven, CT, 1992), 401.

[26]D. Tanner, 'The Parliamentary Electoral System, the "Fourth" Reform Act and the Rise of Labour in England and Wales', *Bulletin of the Institute of Historical Research*, lvi (1983), 205–19; Tanner, *Political Change and the Labour Party*, 386–412.

[27]The Board of Trade's standard working-class budget was based on 1,944 family budgets collected in 1904. The wartime figures are reprinted in PHM, Labour Party Archive: *Report of the Annual Conference of the Labour Party, 1917*, 159–60.

22.8%.[28] This was despite much male hostility towards women entering hitherto male work preserves.

Government intervention in industry, and consequently in industrial relations, led to wider trade union recognition and national wage agreements. Such enhanced status brought more trade union members in hitherto weakly-organised industries, such as hosiery, jute, and pottery, and among white-collar workers. Trade union membership among British white-collar occupations, male and female, jumped by 58% from 3,582,100 in 1914 to 5,645,800 in 1918. There were notable increases of trade union membership in sectors boosted by the war, such as chemicals and allied industries, where membership rose by 156.7% between 1914 and 1918, and in electricity, with an increase of 93.2% in those years.[29] While income from trade union membership rose, the unions paid out less, for there was very low unemployment and under the Munitions Acts there were supposedly no official strikes. Part of the trade union movement's enhanced financial reserves was spent in backing union members as parliamentary candidates. The unions' political funds rose from £37,999 in 1913 to £133,000 in 1918, and then to £185,000 in 1920. The Miners' Federation of Great Britain funded 51 candidates in the 1918 general election, and many other unions sponsored a few candidates, including the Amalgamated Society of Engineers, the National Union of Railwaymen, the National Union of General Workers, the Steel Smelters' Association, the Textile Factory Workers' Association and the Postmen's Federation.[30]

In reorganising in response to an electorate which had risen from the pre-war 7.7 million electors to 21.4 million, the Labour Party needed to move away from relying mostly on trade unionists. Henderson stated in January 1918 that in the executive committee:

> it was felt very strongly that our machinery should be adapted so as to bring into the ranks of the Party those large sections of the public, who for various reasons, have neither the necessity or opportunity of joining trade unions on the one hand, or, on the other, who are not prepared to associate with the Socialist organisations already affiliated with the Party.[31]

After the passage of the Representation of the People Bill, Labour's rhetoric needed to be directed towards the new, wider electorate. In January 1920, in a speech at Widnes, Henderson said: 'Do not believe those who say the Labour Party is merely the party of the trade unions. It is the party of all who work and whose labour enriches the common life in contradiction to those who do not work but live parasitically on the labour of others.'[32] However, proclaiming that the Labour Party was for all of labouring people was one thing, and securing the votes of poor people, agricultural workers and women, most of whom were not trade unionists, was another matter.

---

[28] George Sayers Bain and Robert Price, *Profiles of Union Growth: A Comparative Statistical Portrait of Eight Countries* (Oxford, 1980), 39.

[29] Bain and Price, *Profiles of Union Growth*, 41, 49, 65.

[30] PHM, Labour Party Archive: report of the executive committee, June 1918–June 1919, Labour Party, *Report of the Nineteenth Annual Conference, 1919*, 28. On the huge role of the Durham miners in County Durham, see Tanner, *Political Change and the Labour Party*, 465.

[31] *Report of the Annual Conference, 1918*, 15.

[32] *The Times*, 9 Jan. 1920.

The December 1918 general election was the first held under the 1918 Representation of the People Act. The result was poor for Labour, but this was not surprising given that it was called soon after the Armistice and the campaign took place while the euphoria of victory was strong. Unlike 1945, when service people's votes were gathered in, in 1918 there was a failure to ensure that their votes were received, and this may well have adversely affected pro-war Labour candidates.

Yet, despite the timing of the election, there were good reasons for optimism for the future. Henderson's Widnes speech of January 1920 expressed the realistic view that, in the 1918 general election, the Labour Party had 'polled its minimum vote'.[33] The 1918 general election showed the initial continuities and changes of the Labour Party under the new electoral law. The most marked continuity was the dominance of the trade unions in the party. While Henderson was right in January 1920 to say that the Labour Party was 'not merely the party of the trade unions', nevertheless the trade unions were central to the party. In 1918–19 trade unions accounted for 98.25% of affiliations, in contrast to the socialist societies' 1.75% of affiliations.

In 1918, there was great enthusiasm for running candidates. In some constituencies, such as Lowestoft and Wimbledon, the enthusiasm was there but, in the time available, funding and organisation were not.[34] In many cases, local parties did raise sufficient money. The Representation of the People Act 1918, through cutting the amount that candidates could spend in elections, helped Labour field more candidates in less-promising areas. In mid 1918, Arthur Henderson wrote that 'the question of finance will have to be met. There is no other limit to the number of candidates or the enthusiasm in the ranks of the Movement.'[35] Michael Dawson has argued that this financial change played a vital part in the Labour Party becoming a nationwide challenger for power in the 1920s.[36] Whether or not it was as significant as Dawson claimed, the 1918 electoral law changes certainly made funding of rural candidatures easier for the Labour Party.

At the 1923 Labour Party conference there was a debate on party finance during which members pressed for immediate action on raising money for contesting by-elections and general elections in less-promising seats. The Labour candidate in Dorset East urged: 'They were never going to be a government until the rural districts were effectually organised.' His views were endorsed by Ramsay MacDonald. The conference immediately gave or pledged money for a Special Election Fund, and this was followed by a scheme in which constituency parties pooled a sum of money annually.[37]

Yet the greatest number of candidates came from trade union sponsorships. In the 1918 general election, there were 57 successful candidates who had been endorsed by the Labour Party, 49 of whom were sponsored by trade unions, five by local Labour Parties and three by the Independent Labour Party. In addition, there were four successful candidates not

[33] *The Times*, 9 Jan. 1920.

[34] Don Matthew, *From Two Boys and a Dog to Political Power: The Labour Party in Lowestoft, 1918–1945* (Lowestoft, 1979), 9–12; Gillian Hawtin, *Early Radical Wimbledon, c. 1880–c. 1931* (Wimbledon, 1993), 61, 133–5.

[35] PHM, Labour Party Archive: report of the executive committee, Jan.–June 1918, in *Report of the Annual Conference, 1918*, 3.

[36] Michael Dawson, 'Money and the Real Impact of the Fourth Reform Act', *Historical Journal*, xxxv (1992), 369–81, esp. 379–80.

[37] PHM, Labour Party Archive: *Report of the 23rd Annual Conference, 1923*, 203–5, 216.

endorsed (three Independent Labour and one Co-operative), all of whom promptly joined the Parliamentary Labour Party.

The number of parliamentary seats rose from 670 in 1910 to 707 in 1918. Labour responded to the end of its pre-war electoral understandings with the Liberals, the far bigger electorate and the additional number of seats by putting forward a national body of candidates. This greater electoral ambition began with Labour running 361 candidates in the 1918 general election, a big increase on the 78 endorsed candidates in January 1910 and the 56 who ran in the December 1910 general election.

Of the unsuccessful candidates in 1918, 184 were sponsored by either local Labour Parties (133), the Independent Labour Party (47) or the British Socialist Party (four), whereas the trade unions sponsored the other 120 unsuccessful candidates, while there were six unsuccessful candidates for the university seats. The university seats had been increased from nine to 15, with women entitled to vote. Where a university did not admit women to a degree, women could vote if they had fulfilled the conditions for a man to be admitted to a degree (as well as meeting the age and other requirements). Sidney Webb argued that Labour must contest the university seats if it were to be considered a national party.[38]

The unsuccessful local party-sponsored candidates in 1918 reflected local enthusiasm, sometimes in unlikely seats. For instance, the Labour candidate in Chertsey polled only 3,232 votes and was the last Labour parliamentary candidate there until 1945. In contrast, some local candidates put down a marker for future success. For instance, at Llanelli the Labour candidate polled 14,409 votes but still lost to a coalition Liberal, although the seat was held by Labour thereafter.

The trade unions had a higher success rate with their candidates than did the local Labour Parties, the socialist societies and the Co-operative Party (which ran ten candidates). The Miners' Federation of Great Britain saw 25 of its 51 sponsored candidates elected. Nineteen of their unsuccessful candidates did well in seats that would become either Labour bastions or be won by Labour in good years. The textile unions also did relatively well from their 1918 sponsorships. Like the miners, they had the benefit of many textile working people living in some constituencies. In 1918 they sponsored 12 candidates, five of whom won. The Amalgamated Society of Engineers rarely had the advantage of its members living in concentrated groups and being the dominant employed group, as was the case with many mining communities. Although sponsoring 17 candidates, the Engineers secured the election of only one, Robert Young at Newton. The growing vigour of constituency Labour Parties was indicated by the declining proportion of trade union sponsored MPs by 1929, as it fell from 53% to 40%.[39]

Henderson, in reporting on the 1918 general election, wrote that 'the position secured promises well for future success'. His optimism was due in part to there being many seats where Labour candidates beat Liberal candidates. Labour won seven of the four-cornered contests and beat the Liberal in 11 of the 12 others (the third place being Oldham, where the Labour candidate secured 15,178 votes). In 68 of the three-cornered contests, Labour beat the Liberal candidate.[40]

[38] Beatrice Webb's diary, 16 June 1918, in *Beatrice Webb's Diaries 1912–1924*, ed. Margaret Cole (1952), 122.

[39] PHM, Labour Party Archive: *Report of the 24th Annual Conference, 1924*, 12, and *Report of the 30th Annual Conference, 1930*, 8.

[40] PHM, Labour Party Archive: report of the executive committee, June 1918–June 1919, 29, 194–5.

Labour's performance in 1918 showed very distinct regional strengths. The bulk of its seats were in northern England, in Lancashire, Yorkshire, and the north-east. There were nine seats won in Wales and six in Scotland. In London, West Ham Plaistow, Woolwich East, and Deptford, were held by well-established Labour MPs, while the new seat of Silvertown was won by the unendorsed Jack Jones. The only other seat won in southern England was the Forest of Dean, which was held in every other election apart from 1931.[41]

Labour, like the Liberals, believed rightly that its performance had been harmed by the speed with which the election was called after the Armistice of 11 November 1918. Labour's reorganisation had only been approved in February 1918 and so, as Henderson reported after the general election, 'only about eight months were available' before the election 'for organising the constituencies of the country'. Labour needed to appeal to the new voters, who were in a majority in the 1918 electorate. Moreover, local Labour agents experienced 'the greatest difficulty' in obtaining from registration officers the addresses of the four million military and naval voters, and so often could not use the free postal delivery.[42]

Time was even tighter for women as candidates. It was only on 23 October 1918 that the house of commons approved by 374 to 25 votes that there should be a bill brought forward to ensure women could be parliamentary candidates, thereby not leaving their candidatures liable to rejection by returning officers. Women made up 39.6% of the 1918 electorate, but only 17 women contested seats in the 1918 general election. Four of these were Labour candidates. These women were all distinguished for their trade union, socialist, or suffrage activities. Mary Macarthur was sponsored for Stourbridge by the National Federation of Women Workers, a TUC-affiliated body which she had set up. Her candidature was adversely affected by the returning officer insisting that she be put on the ballot paper under her less-well-known married surname of Anderson. Even so, she was the most successful female Labour candidate, coming in second place; she polled 7,587 votes (32.7%) and lost by only 1,333 votes.[43] The other women candidates were Charlotte Despard, who had been twice jailed for her suffragist activities, in Battersea North; Millicent Hughes Mackenzie, the first female professor in Wales and an active suffragist, for the Welsh university seat, and Emmeline Pethick-Lawrence, a major figure in the suffragette movement, for the Manchester Rusholme Division.[44]

Women formed one of the biggest groups of new electors whose support Labour needed to attract following the 1918 Reform Act. Labour's publicity department, which had been set up in late 1917 as part of the party's reorganisation, arranged the publication of two books in the period before the 1918 general election. One was a set of essays edited by Dr Marion Phillips, *Women and the Labour Party* (1918). Henderson, in his foreword, emphasized Labour's long support of 'the claims of women on the ground of sex equality', stated that in 'the coming era of social reconstruction' Labour's policies aimed to promote 'the common interests of both sexes', and expressed the hope that these policies should be appreciated

---

[41] Matthew Worley, *Labour Inside the Gate: A History of the British Labour Party between the Wars* (2005), 21.

[42] *The Times*, 24 Oct. 1918.

[43] Angela John, 'Macarthur, Mary Reid, 1880–1921', *ODNB*; Cathy Hunt, *The National Federation of Women Workers, 1906–1921* (2014).

[44] Ando Linklater, *An Unhusbandable Life: Charlotte Despard, Suffragette, Socialist and Sinn Feiner* (1980), 200–2; Margaret Mulvihull, 'Despard, Charlotte, 1844–1931', *ODNB*; Brian Harrison, 'Pethick-Lawrence, Emmeline, 1867–1954', *ODNB*; Elizabeth Crawford, *The Women's Suffrage Movement: A Reference Guide, 1866–1928* (1999), 97, 165–9, 534–40.

by women, who 'will recognise separate sex organisations are fundamentally undemocratic and reactionary'.[45] The party also issued a series of new leaflets and pamphlets, the third of which was *Why Women Should Join the Labour Party* (1918). For at least four years after the end of the war, the *Daily Herald* and the Labour Party generally paid special attention to the concerns of women.[46]

Since 1908, Labour had had an affiliated organisation for women in the Women's Labour League. It was subsumed in the Labour Party, along with its journal *Labour Woman*, with the adoption of the new party constitution in February 1918. Many of the women who were paid organisers or parliamentary candidates had learned much about organising in the Women's Labour League and in women's suffrage bodies.[47] Most of the Labour Party's full-time women's organisers were working class. A major exception was Marion Phillips, the chief women's officer from 1918 to 1932, who was able, indefatigable, and an accumulator of positions of influence in the Labour Party and public service. In this she was much like Arthur Henderson, with whom she worked well. She was well established in the socialist and women's movements before the war, but further made her mark on the War Emergency Workers' National Committee as a strong advocate of women's rights.[48]

Two national women organisers for England were appointed in early 1918, and a third in September 1918. A fourth national organiser was appointed in October 1918 for Scotland, but a fifth for Wales was only appointed in March 1919. Agnes Hardie, the Scottish organiser, 1918–23, had been an organiser for the National Union of Shop Assistants, was the first woman on Glasgow Trades Council, and had been elected to the school board in Glasgow. She was a very effective speaker for the Independent Liberal Party and a pacifist. Elizabeth Andrews, Welsh organiser from 1919 to 1948, was a miner's daughter from Hirwaun. Other organisers also had lengthy tenures: Lillian Fenn for 35 years, Gertrude Francis for 33 years, and Annie Townley for 23 years.[49]

Before the 1918 general election, efforts were made to maximise the votes of women in all constituencies. After the election, these efforts were focused on the West Riding of Yorkshire, Lancashire and Cheshire, and the Black Country, as the areas which had proved to be the most promising. By mid 1919, one organiser was focused on Lancashire and Cheshire, the second in Nottinghamshire and Derbyshire, and the third in the Home Counties. The setting up of Labour women's sections was rapid. In 1923 there were over 1,000, with a total membership of over 120,000. Then the biggest women's sections were in Woolwich,

[45] *Women and the Labour Party*, ed. Marion Phillips (1918); David Howell, *MacDonald's Party: Labour Identities and Crisis 1922–1931* (Oxford, 2002), 334.

[46] Pamela Graves, *Labour Women: Women in British Working-Class Politics 1918–1939* (Cambridge, 1994), 18–21. For instance, in denouncing war office proposals to place wives of soldiers under police surveillance, see PHM, WEWNC, Box 32: Phillips to Middleton, 8 Nov. 1914.

[47] Christine Collette, *For Labour and Women: The Women's Labour League, 1906–18* (Manchester, 1989); Krista Cowman, *Women of the Right Spirit: Paid Organizers of the Women's Social and Political Union, 1906–18* (Manchester, 2007).

[48] Beverley Kingston, 'Phillips, Marion (1881–1932)', *Dictionary of Labour Biography*, v (1979), 171–9; Brian Harrison, 'Phillips, Marion (1881–1932)', *ODNB*; Marian Goronwy-Roberts, *A Woman of Vision: A Life of Marion Phillips MP* (Wrexham, 2000); Howell, *MacDonald's Party*, 333–5.

[49] June Hannam, 'The Victory of Ideals must be Organised: Labour Party Women's Organizers in the Interwar years', *Management and Organizational History*, v (2013), 331–48; W.W.J. Knox, 'Hardie (nee Pettigrew), Agnes Agnew (1874–1951)', *ODNB*; Elizabeth Andrews, *A Woman's Work is Never Done* (1952).

which had 1,000 members, Barrow with 900, followed by Blackburn, Watford, and York, each with 400. By 1929, the National Agent, G.R. Shepherd, believed that there would be little further expansion beyond the 1,196 women's sections of local parties, 450 of wards, and 221 of two or more wards. The membership then was about a quarter of a million.[50]

During the war years, Labour had ensured that it became identified with efforts to protect people's quality of life, and not just with male trade union issues. As June Hannam has commented, there was a 'war generation' of women who attributed their decision to join the Labour Party to their experiences then.[51] Labour was adroit at being associated with social issues during the war, not least through its War Emergency Workers' National Committee, which sought to improve working-class conditions, including food supplies, housing, fuel, and allowances for service personnel's dependants. Clynes, chair of the Parliamentary Labour Party in 1921–2, was food controller from July 1918 to January 1919. Wartime scarcities and wartime profiteering fostered, as in the era of the Napoleonic wars, a belief in a moral economy rather than an unfettered economic free-for-all. There was outrage in the Labour movement at profiteering, especially by wholesalers, which was reminiscent of Tudor complaints against 'middlemen'.[52]

The government's wartime discrimination against co-operative trading radicalised part of the co-operative movement, encouraging it to break its old links with the Liberal Party and set up the Co-operative Party in 1917.[53] The Labour Party had been keen to work with co-operators from its beginning. However, while the Labour Party was eager to set up a 'United Co-operative and Labour Board', the co-operators at their annual conference in Aberdeen in May 1913, while approving concerted action with the trade unions, resolved that 'the Central Board be instructed strictly to maintain the neutrality of the movement in respect of party politics, so that political dissension may be avoided'.[54] The war reinforced Henderson's already strong resolve to secure agreement with the co-operative movement. The Co-operative Party ran ten candidates in the 1918 general election, of whom Alf Waterson, an active railway trade unionist and councillor in Derby, was the only successful candidate. Although he lost in 1922, four other Co-operative candidates won in that election, as did six in 1923, five in 1924, and nine in 1929.

With the greater-sized electorate from 1918, Labour also needed more than ever to attract the support of non-union working people. Henderson's book, *The Aims of Labour* (1918), was a major success, both in terms of sales and the attention it received. It expressed sentiments for a better post-war Britain which included some not dissimilar, albeit on a much lesser scale, from those put forward in William Beveridge's report, *Social Insurance and Allied Services*, in 1942. Henderson drew on the arguments of Beatrice and Sidney Webb when he wrote of:

[50]PHM, Labour Party Archive: *Report of the 23rd Annual Conference, 1923*, 60–1; *Report of the 29th Annual Conference, 1929*, 21.

[51]June Hannam, 'Women and Labour Politics', in *The Foundations of the British Labour Party: Identities, Cultures and Perspectives, 1900–1939*, ed. Matthew Worley (Farnham, 2009), 184–5.

[52]London Trades Council, *Sixtieth Annual Report, 1919* (1920), 7.

[53]Nicole Robertson, *The Co-operative Movement and Communities in Britain, 1914–1960* (Farnham, 2010), 155–79.

[54]PHM, Labour Party Archive: report of the executive, 1913; *Report of the Special and Annual Conferences of the Labour Party, Glasgow, 27–30 January 1914*, 21–3.

the reconstruction of society, which will guarantee freedom, security and equality. We propose, as a first step, a series of national minima to protect the people's standard of life. For the worker of all grades and both sexes we demand and mean to secure proper legislative provision against unemployment, accident, and industrial disease, a reasonable amount of leisure, a minimum rate of wages. We shall insist upon a large and practicable scheme to protect the whole wage-earning class against the danger of unemployment and reduction of wages, with a consequent degradation of the standard of life when the war ends and the forces are demobilised and the munitions factories cease work.

Henderson further stated that Labour's taxation policy would be 'regulated by the claims of the professional and housekeeping classes, whose interests are identical with those of the manual workers'.[55]

Many white-collar workers were coming to the Labour movement through unionisation. The wartime inflation and wartime labour restrictions had brought together in trade unionism different groups of workers, skilled, unskilled, and white-collared. Trade unionism among white-collar workers (which included many women) grew substantially during the war and the post-war boom. For instance, trade union density in insurance, banking, and finance has been estimated to have risen from 6.7% to 22.4% between 1911 and 1921.[56] The second leaflet in the Labour Party's 1918 series was *Why Brainworkers Should Join the Labour Party*. This was part of the publicity department's policy of 'stratification'. Sidney Webb outlined this policy in 1922:

We should, as far as possible, 'stratify' our electioneering; appealing to each section of the electorate in the language which that section understands; emphasising just the points in which that section is interested; subordinating the question that each section finds dull or unpleasant; addressing to each section the literature most appropriate to it.[57]

In the 1918 general election campaign, Labour was helped in its efforts to appeal to various groups of electors by Lord Northcliffe, who allowed the party to put its case in the *Daily Mail* in eight columns from 2 December until polling day on 14 December. Labour's *Daily Mail* articles were directed at different groups of electors. The writers included pro-Labour senior clerics, military men, the novelist, J.D. Beresford, and the Oxford political scientist, Ernest Barker.

In the circumstances of an election called amidst the euphoria of the Armistice, Labour did reasonably well. Indeed, the much greater electorate under the 1918 Reform Act and the turmoil in eastern and central Europe added to wartime expectations and fears among many well-to-do people of the Labour Party taking office before long. Nevertheless, turnout was low at 57%, perhaps because there was limited choice of candidates due to the coalition government.

Labour's often remarkable success in local elections in 1919 and 1920 further boosted expectations of a Labour government within a few years. The most notable feature of the

[55] Arthur Henderson, *The Aims of Labour* (1918), 23–5.

[56] Bain and Price, *Profiles of Union Growth*, 41.

[57] Sidney Webb, *London Labour Chronicle*, Dec. 1922, quoted in Laura Beers, *Your Britain: Media and the Making of the Labour Party* (Cambridge, MA, 2010), 37.

London County Council elections in March 1919 was the increase in Labour's proportion of the vote, from 4.4% in 1913 to 34.1%, albeit on a low turnout.[58] One of the cabinet reports on revolutionary organisations noted in April 1919:

> There is a great rejoicing in Socialist and Labour circles at the results of the elections for [Poor Law] Guardians. Forgetting that only about 30 percent of the electorate voted and that opposition to Labour candidates was very half hearted, they think it is certain that a Labour Government will be returned at the next general election.[59]

As threats of revolution diminished in western Europe and fears of industrial militancy became less pressing, the possibility of a Labour government became less worrying for most of the political elite. For instance, in December 1919, Sir Maurice Hankey, the secretary to the cabinet, reassured Jan Smuts, who had been a member of the Imperial War Cabinet:

> although our economic conditions create a good deal of distress and terrible difficulties for the Government, the people as a whole seem extraordinarily sound. I am not afraid of Labour at all. I believe that their leaders are thoroughly patriotic and even the extremists are more patriotic than they make themselves out to be.[60]

Earlier in the year, Lord Esher, perhaps the establishment's greatest eminence grise, wrote to Hankey:

> If, as it may happen, a Labour Government is within the orbit of practical politics, some preparations should be made for its advent, by educating as far as possible Clynes and Thomas and even Smillie. This can be done quietly and judiciously by personal contact with your Secretariat, just as you have always kept in touch with the leaders of the Opposition in times past.[61]

With the severe economic recession of 1921–2, trade unions' actions were defensive and trade union membership fell by 35% from 1920 to 1923. In Europe, the spread of Bolshevism halted, and then receded. Far fewer people feared Labour in 1922 than in 1919–20, although its parliamentary challenge grew, as demonstrated by a series of by-election wins from July 1920 to March 1922.[62]

Labour's early post-war local government successes were eventually curtailed by the Conservatives and Liberals often fielding a single anti-Labour candidate. The policy of avoiding splitting the opposition to Labour was also used in the 1922 general election and after. Michael Kinnear has listed over 200 seats in 1922 where there was Liberal-Conservative co-operation.[63] In the 1923 general election, Labour's substantial gains were offset by only 16 losses, and 13 of these were due to local agreements between the Conservatives and

[58] *Morning Post*, 6 Mar. 1919.

[59] TNA, CAB 24/78/385, f. 388: cabinet paper GT7196, circulated by the home secretary, 30 Apr. 1919.

[60] Churchill Archives Centre, Churchill College, Cambridge [hereafter cited as CAC], Hankey MSS 4/11: Hankey to Smuts, 18 Dec. 1919.

[61] CAC, Hankey MSS 4/11: Esher to Hankey, 15 Feb. 1919.

[62] *By-Elections in British Politics*, ed. Chris Cook and John Ramsden (1973), 361–3.

[63] Michael Kinnear, *The Fall of Lloyd George: The Political Crisis of 1922* (1973), 243–55.

Liberals not to split the anti-Labour vote.[64] Such co-operation in 1922 delayed Labour winning several Liberal coalition seats until the 1923 general election. Nevertheless, in the 1922 general election, with 414 endorsed candidates, Labour increased its number of seats to 142 and polled 4,237,769 votes (29.4%) to the Conservatives' 327 seats and 5,281,555 votes (38.5%). Labour became the second largest party in the house of commons, as the combined Asquith and Lloyd George Liberals secured 116 seats and 4,182,982 votes (29.1%). Nearly half of Labour's gains were in mining seats, and nearly half were in Glasgow, Newcastle, Gateshead, Sheffield, and Greater London.[65]

The general elections of 1918 and 1922 underlined the importance of the affiliation of the Miners' Federation of Great Britain to the Labour Party in 1909. The miners dominated the party in 1918–22, to the irritation of Independent Labour Party and former Liberal figures. The dominance of miners in the parliamentary party was reflected by the election to its chair (and so, in effect, to the party leadership) in 1917 of William Adamson, who held the post for over four years. In the most recent reappraisal of Adamson, William Knox has given the assessment that 'his leadership was competent if rather uninspiring and undynamic. He was a safe pair of hands.'[66] Adamson was succeeded in 1921–2 by Clynes. In 1918 under Adamson, and in 1922 under the more effective but still modest leadership of Clynes, the Labour Party made substantial advances. However, these advances can hardly be ascribed to an outstanding party leadership.

The 1918 and 1922 general elections were important stages under the 1918 Reform Act for Labour becoming the largest party in the house of commons. Between December 1918 and the general election of May 1929, the number of Labour candidates increased by 58%, the number of MPs by 405% and its vote by 273%. After 1922, the Labour Party's organisation continued to spread, so that by mid 1923 it was organised in 597 of the 603 English, Welsh, and Scottish constituencies. In the 1923 general election, Labour ran 427 candidates and 191 were elected, but its vote rose only to 4,348,379 (an increase of just 2.7%). In 1924, the number of candidates was 514 and the number of MPs dropped to 151, yet the Labour vote rose in defeat to 5,487,620 (a 26.2% rise) as Liberal support crumbled. In 1929, Labour fielded 569 candidates and secured the largest number of MPs (287), with a further MP joining the Parliamentary Labour Party after the election.

During the First World War, the Labour Party steadily moved away from being an auxiliary party to the Liberals to becoming a credible contender for forming governments. The party's overhaul, supervised by Arthur Henderson, positioned it to take advantage of the new electoral and social conditions at the end of the First World War. Labour's enlarged trade union base gave the party much organisational and financial power at a time when the Liberal Party's organisation had not recovered from the war. The 1918 Reform Act came at a propitious time for the Labour Party, but a bad one for the still-divided Liberals.

What difference did the 1918 Reform Act make to the Labour Party? It ensured that the Labour Party had greatly to improve its organisation for an enlarged electorate. Combined

---

[64] Searle, *A New England?*, 831–2.

[65] Michael Kinnear, *The British Voter: An Atlas and Survey since 1885* (1968), 40–4; his figure for Labour's total vote in 1922 is a little higher than in the Labour Party's reports. J.J. Smyth, *Labour in Glasgow, 1896–1936: Socialism, Suffrage, Sectarianism* (East Linton, 2000), 94; Sidney Pollard, *A History of Labour in Sheffield* (Liverpool, 1959), 266.

[66] W.W.J. Knox, 'George Nicol Barnes and William Adamson', in *British Labour Leaders*, ed. Charles Clarke and Toby S. James (2015), 85; see also Beatrice Webb's diary, 14 Jan. 1919, in *Beatrice Webb's Diaries 1912–1924*, ed. Cole, 142.

with the economic, social and political impact of the war, it provided a changed context for the party's growth and one in which it secured many rock–solid Labour heartlands for decades, except for 1931. Had the 1918 Reform Act been passed with either the initial proposal for proportional representation or the alternative vote, then the Parliamentary Labour Party might have been larger in 1922–5 and later, but it would have found it harder to secure majority governments after the Second World War.

The Impact of the 1918 Reform Act on the Politics of the West Midlands

IAN CAWOOD

Despite the impact of the Representation of the People Act of 1918 on the political culture of the west midland region in the interwar years, the elements of continuity in the politics of the region are striking. The Labour Party failed to dislodge the Unionists' political control in the region (with the exception of the Black Country) for most of the 1920s and 1930s, notwithstanding the presence of a significant industrial working-class population in the bulk of the region's constituencies. The essay argues that the lack of a significant redistribution of seats in the region, in spite of wartime growth in all urban areas, enabled the well-organised and well-funded Unionist organisations controlled by Stanley Baldwin and Neville Chamberlain to adapt their cross-class, non-denominational message to appeal to the newly-enlarged electorate. Although the Labour Party appeared on the brink of a breakthrough in the west midlands, owing to this 'franchise factor', the Unionists adapted better to the new age of mass communications and political sloganeering which replaced the Edwardian politics of confrontation and public meetings. The Representation of the People Act of 1918 may have changed the political culture of elections in Britain, but, in the west midlands at least, it did not alter the Unionists' ability to manage the outcomes of the elections.

Keywords: British political history; impact of the First World War; Representation of the People Act 1918; 20th-century party politics; 20th-century political culture; west midlands politics

The Representation of the People Act of 1918 (also known as the 1918 Reform Act) had a greater impact on British politics than any other single piece of legislation since the Great Reform Act of 1832. The introduction of universal male suffrage and the extension of the franchise to most women aged 30 years and over significantly increased the parliamentary electorate, while a redistribution of constituencies increased the importance of large cities and industrial counties. Only one in four of the electorate in 1918 would have been on the electoral roll in 1910. In Birmingham, for example, the act increased the electorate from 95,000 to 427,084 voters (165,000 of whom were women aged over 30 years). Across the whole of the west midland region, the number of registered voters increased between 1910 and 1918 from 573,231 to 1,581,439. Despite this transformation, Pat Thane has noted that the political system created by the 1918 Reform Act was remarkably stable, when compared with the rest of Europe.[1] The best symptom of that stability in the west midlands was the preservation of largely pre-war voting patterns across the region, despite the mass enfranchisement and the effects of the First World War. William Miller asserted

---

[1] Pat Thane, 'The Impact of Mass Democracy on British Political Culture, 1918–1939', in *The Aftermath of Suffrage: Women, Gender and Politics in Britain, 1918–1945*, ed. J.V. Gottlieb and R. Toye (2013), 54.

in 1977 that 'the West Midlands were always pro-Conservative and anti-Labour'.[2] While this judgment is rather crude, as it fails to understand the uniquely 'Unionist' nature of politics in the region and takes no account of the breakthrough of Labour in the Black Country and the Staffordshire Potteries after 1918, it is true that the region was at the heart of the Unionists' national dominance between 1918 and 1939. This was achieved despite an apparent transformation in the political culture of Britain after the First World War, which demonstrates the continued resilience, adaptability and successful leadership of the Unionist Party in the region.

Before 1918, west midland politics had been dominated by Joseph Chamberlain's radical Liberal Unionists, although the party's control had retreated towards the city of Birmingham as his older son, Austen, failed to prevent Conservatives from being allocated the outlying constituencies on the retirement of Liberal Unionist MPs and the Liberal Party was resurgent in the region after 1900 (although this was not as extensive as elsewhere).[3] While the trades councils had proved less antagonistic during the First World War than in most areas, there was clear evidence of growing militancy in towns such as Wolverhampton and Wednesbury.[4] Any potential growth of the Labour Party to challenge the middle-class political hegemony in the region had largely been stifled by the limited franchise in the Edwardian period. However, after 1918, Labour was increasingly able to offer itself as an alternative to the traditional message of cross-class Unionism and the carefully-presented rural appeal of Baldwin.[5] Labour made a sufficiently large breakthrough in the region in December 1918, winning six seats in the Black Country and the Potteries, that they were able to persuade one of the few National Democratic and Labour MPs, Eldred Hallas, who had won Birmingham Duddeston, to cross the floor of the Commons and join them in 1919. Although Hallas retired at the 1922 election, Birmingham had seen its first Labour MP, albeit one who the Unionist newspaper, *Straight Forward*, derided as having 'deserted those who had made easy his pathway into Parliamentary life'.[6] Labour also made some significant progress in local politics, with the Birmingham Labour Party stealing a march on the complacent local Unionist Associations and launching an effective municipal campaign nearly six months before the local elections were held, focusing on 'housing, our Municipal Services … Gas and Tram charges and the elimination of a narrow, selfish policy'.[7] They consequently experienced a significant increase in their vote in the ward elections and, in November 1919, won 12 of the 20 municipal seats contested in Birmingham and a third of the seats in Coventry.[8]

---

[2] W.L. Miller, *Electoral Dynamics in Britain since 1918* (1977), 203.

[3] Ian Cawood, *The Liberal Unionist Party: A History* (2012), 211–41.

[4] Paul Fantom, 'Community, Patriotism and the Working Class in the First World War: The Home Front in Wednesbury, 1914–1918', University of Birmingham PhD, 2015, pp. 51–69, 135–60.

[5] Ian Cawood, 'Life after Joe: Politics and War in the West Midlands, 1914–1918', *Midland History*, xlii (2017), 92–117.

[6] Library of Birmingham, Archives and Heritage Service: *Straight Forward: A Journal of Constitutional Progress*, no. 4 (Dec. 1920).

[7] Library of Birmingham, Archives and Heritage Service, 329.94249LAB: Birmingham Central Labour Party minutes, 27 June 1919.

[8] Library of Birmingham, Archives and Heritage Service, LB 76.22: *Town Crier*, new ser., no. 6, 7 Nov. 1919; 329.94249Con: Birmingham Conservative and Unionist Association executive committee minutes, 21 Nov. 1921; Peter Walters, *Great War Britain: Coventry, Remembering 1914–1918* (Stroud, 2016), 136.

In the historiography of post-1918 British politics, the Labour Party has been traditionally seen as the chief beneficiary of the expansion of the electorate, and the sudden decline of the Liberal Party in the west midlands seems to confirm the arguments of those who believe in the 'franchise factor'.[9] Those who supported 'progressive' policies in the region now tended to vote for the Labour candidate who offered the stronger challenge to the Unionist candidate. As Michael Dawson has explained, the restriction of electoral expenses meant that 'Labour could now afford to fight more seats than before the war, which created an insurmountable challenge for a divided and demoralised Liberal party.'[10] By contrast, Duncan Tanner has pointed out that 'there were no inherent sociological reasons why the newly enfranchised men should have voted solidly for Labour'.[11] It should be noted that, after their initial breakthrough, Labour failed to make much more significant progress in the region until the later 1920s, which suggests that the effects of the 1918 Reform Act were more complex than have hitherto been recognized.

The implications of the act for party organisation were swiftly realized, with the Unionist *Gleanings and Memoranda* reporting on the likely outcomes of the Speaker's conference as early as February 1917.[12] This presented a serious challenge for all of the parties which had been largely dormant in the latter years of the conflict. The Conservative Party Archive at the Bodleian Library notes that 'no pamphlets were issued by the Conservative [*sic*] Party during the war years 1915, 1916 and 1917' (although *Gleanings and Memoranda* continued to be printed monthly until February 1917).[13]

In the same way that party organisation had had to respond to the advent of a mass electorate in 1884, with the increased professionalisation of Liberal, Conservative and, subsequently, Liberal Unionist Associations, so there was a need for greater efforts in management of both party and electoral issues once the age of near-full democracy arrived in 1918. Neville Chamberlain took the opportunity to press the much-overdue fusion of Liberal Unionist and Conservative organisations in Birmingham in early 1918 and, similarly, he ensured that the regional body, the Midland Union, was also revitalised.[14] The central National Unionist Association attempted to challenge the new Birmingham Unionist Association when it involved the patriotic National Democratic and Labour Party in the 1918 electoral campaign.[15] When its leading figures, such as Eldred Hallas and Victor Fisher, were forced upon west midland constituencies, Chamberlain 'objected to this procedure on the part of the Central Office', as his father had done before him in the 1890s, and Fisher's

[9]H.C.G. Matthew, R.I. McKibbin and J.A. Kay, 'The Franchise Factor in the Rise of the Labour Party', *English Historical Review*, xci (1976), 732–52.

[10]Michael Dawson, 'Money and the Real Impact of the Fourth Reform Act', *Historical Journal*, xxxv (1992), 369–81.

[11]D. Tanner, 'The Parliamentary Electoral System, the "Fourth" Reform Act and the Rise of Labour in England and Wales', *Bulletin of the Institute of Historical Research*, lvi (1983), 219.

[12]Bodl., Conservative Party Archive [hereafter cited as CPA], X Films 64/20: 'Electoral Reform', *Gleanings and Memoranda*, Feb. 1917, pp. 6–7.

[13]Bodl., CPA, X Films 63/3: pamphlets and leaflets part 3, 1915–25.

[14]Bodl., CPA, ARE/MU/1/5: minutes of the annual meeting of the Midland Union Council, 15 July 1918; Roger Ward, *The Chamberlains: Joseph, Austen and Neville, 1836–1940* (Stroud, 2015), 123.

[15]Library of Birmingham, Archives and Heritage Service, 329.94249Con: Birmingham Conservative and Unionist Association executive committee minutes, 14 July 1918.

disastrous campaign in Stourbridge allowed Chamberlain to demonstrate his superior local political knowledge.[16] In April 1919, the Unionist central office handed effective control of the choice of west midland candidates to Chamberlain. He now held the wires of party patronage firmly in his hands and he insisted upon local constituencies accepting his chosen candidates.[17] When 'dissentient Unionists' in King's Norton objected to his choice of Sir Herbert Austin as their candidate on unspecified 'questions of policy' in October 1918, they were swiftly slapped down.[18] The revitalised Midland Union also spread its influence in the immediate post-war years, resisting an attempt by Derbyshire to break away, and taking Gloucestershire under its control.[19]

If the years before the First World War had required an increasingly professionalised party organisation,[20] the effects of the 1918 Reform Act tested the resources of all the parties. The Unionist Party's apparatus may have rested during the war, manned by a skeleton staff, but it emerged far more united and capable of fighting the series of four general elections that ensued between 1918 and 1924, appointing W.A.J. Gibbs as the organising agent for the midlands in August 1920, putting up candidates in all of the seats that were uncontested by 'Couponed' non-Unionists in 1918 and then contesting every seat with a Unionist candidate in 1922, 1923, and 1924.[21] The style of organisation had to evolve, however, as the scale of campaigning was now the crucial work of the local association, rather than making challenges to the electoral register.[22] The Birmingham Unionist Association quickly identified the need for:

> polling-district committees and their officers, the arranging of frequent meetings of such committees, the splitting up of the polling districts into streets or parts of streets so that each particular member of a polling-district committee should be responsible for the electors in a particular street or part of such a street.[23]

The Association consequently established a Propaganda Society and organised a well-attended free 'Demonstration and Garden Fete' at the Birmingham Botanical Gardens on 18 September 1920, where the political speeches were interspersed with an 'amusement side' which featured performances by 'the Birmingham Small Arms band, concert parties,

---

[16]University of Birmingham, Cadbury Research Library, Neville Chamberlain MSS, NC18/1/190: Neville Chamberlain to Ida and Hilda Chamberlain, 9 Nov. 1918; Bodl., CPA, ARE/MU/2/5: Midland Union executive committee minutes, 19 June 1918; N. Keohane, *The Party of Patriotism: The Conservative Party and the First World War* (Farnham, 2010), 127.

[17]Bodl., CPA, ARE/MU/2/5: Midland Union executive committee minutes, 28 Apr. 1919; Robert Self, *Neville Chamberlain: A Biography* (Aldershot, 2006), 69–70.

[18]Library of Birmingham, Archives and Heritage Service, 329.94249Con: Birmingham Conservative and Unionist Association executive committee minutes, 17 Oct. 1918.

[19]Bodl., CPA, ARE/MU/2/5: Midland Union general purposes and finance subcommittee minutes, 3 Dec. 1920.

[20]See Kathryn Rix, *Parties, Agents and Electoral Culture in England, 1880–1910* (Woodbridge, 2016).

[21]The minutes of the Midland Union Council reveal the strong financial position of the party by 1920: Bodl., CPA, ARE/MU/1/5: Midland Union Council annual meeting minutes, 3 Dec. 1920.

[22]Stuart Ball, 'Local Conservatism and the Evolution of the Party Organisation', in *Conservative Century: The Conservative Party since 1900*, ed. Anthony Seldon and Stuart Ball (Oxford, 1994), 261–311.

[23]Library of Birmingham, Archives and Heritage Service, 329.94249Con: Birmingham Conservative and Unionist Association minutes, 'Memorandum by Ald. Davis and Mr Walthall', 29 Jan. 1919.

conjuror, ventriloquist, concertina performers and other artistes'.[24] As well as the Women's organisations, a Junior Unionist Association was launched in Ladywood in July 1921.[25] The result of all this activity was that, in the municipal elections of November 1920, the feared socialist advance failed to materialise, with the Unionists winning 22 out of 23 contested wards.[26] The divided Liberal Party, starved of funds, was swiftly pushed to the margins in the region in the 1918 general election, with only two Asquithian Liberals returned,[27] together with one Independent Liberal[28] and just one 'Couponed' Liberal.[29] Any coalition Liberals standing in municipal elections were entirely dependent on Unionist organisational support. The Labour Party swiftly overtook the Liberals as the chief opposition to the Unionists, standing in 27 west midland constituencies in 1918, and it was the sole opposition to the Unionists in ten of these seats. Labour organisation, largely funded by the growth of trade union membership during the war, took time to develop, with eight Unionists and one coalition Liberal candidate in the region who faced no contest in the general election of 1918. This allowed the Unionists to build a strong parliamentary tradition in the county seats and larger boroughs which Labour was unable to overturn fully, even in 1929.[30]

The War Emergency Workers' National Committees, which David Powell identifies as providing vital support for Labour in the post-war years elsewhere, were noticeably absent in the west midlands.[31] The Birmingham branch of the Independent Labour Party (ILP) was, unlike elsewhere, also distinctly ineffective at first, spending most of autumn 1918 focusing on attending national conferences, passing resolutions protesting against issues such as the imprisonment of John Maclean, and discussing the release of Karl Liebknecht by the new Socialist government in Germany, rather than preparing for the imminent general election. Councillor Mundy warned the branch in February 1919 'that elections couldn't be won from platforms'.[32] The Birmingham Central Labour Party and Trades Council had largely been captured by pacifists and anti-conscription campaigners in 1915 and their 1918 election campaign was as hapless as that of the local ILP. This was in marked contrast to the effective organisation of the local party in the Black Country, and even in such unpromising rural constituencies as Oswestry and Shrewsbury.[33] However, after its electoral rout in 1918, the Birmingham Labour Party quickly learned its lesson and swiftly reorganised, appointing a new executive committee and divisional organisers, a professional clerk

[24]Library of Birmingham, Archives and Heritage Service, 329.94249Con: Birmingham Conservative and Unionist Association management committee report, 15 Oct. 1920.

[25] *Straight Forward*, no. 12, Aug. 1921.

[26]Library of Birmingham, Archives and Heritage Service, 329.94249Con: Birmingham Conservative and Unionist Association management committee minutes, 12 Nov. 1920.

[27]George Thorne in Wolverhampton East, and J.W. Wilson in Stourbridge.

[28]Josiah Wedgwood in Newcastle-under-Lyme, who faced no contest.

[29]Sir Courtenay Warner in Lichfield.

[30]Labour finally won in Birmingham in the 1929 general election, capturing half of the city's seats and coming within 43 votes of defeating Austen Chamberlain, but all of these were regained by the Unionists in 1931.

[31]David Powell, *British Politics, 1910–1935: The Crisis of the Party System* (Abingdon, 2004), 88.

[32]Library of Birmingham, Archives and Heritage Service, A329.94249IND: ILP, Birmingham city branch minutes, 1915–21. The decision of the secretary of the Birmingham ILP, R. Warden Briggs, to refer to all those present at meetings as 'comrade' between Nov. and Dec. 1918, is, perhaps, a small indication of just how out of touch the Birmingham branch was with its electorate; this practice ceased in January 1919.

[33]Brock Millman, *Managing Domestic Dissent in First World War Britain 1914–1918* (2000), 106–7.

and offices equipped with a telephone.[34] Funds were raised for elections, well in advance, with George Cadbury annually contributing £50.[35] They also adopted a new slogan to distance themselves from their previous mistakes: 'Not Pious Resolutions, but WORK & VOTE FOR LABOUR CANDIDATES.'[36]

It was the development of the *constituency* Labour Parties which harnessed the enthusiasm of individual party members and which gradually enabled the Labour Party to organise sufficiently so that it was able to contest 11 seats successfully in the 1923 election (including the capture of Coventry, the Wrekin, and Lichfield) and even to gain 46% of the vote in Neville Chamberlain's own seat at Ladywood.[37] The Labour Party also began organising a plethora of affiliated social organisations such as choirs, cycling clubs and drama groups. The Birmingham Labour *Town Crier* was also a far less overtly party political publication than the Birmingham Unionist *Straight Forward*, continuing the vibrant print culture of pre-war Birmingham by including book and theatre reviews, 'our children's corner', a gardening column, a serial story and items on socialist history. By contrast, *Straight Forward* failed to print anything more than encomiums of party leaders, details of Unionist events and endless exhortations for 'armchair Unionists' to rouse themselves. Even with the backing of local Unionist businesses such as Mitchells and Butlers, Bird's of Wolverhampton, and Birmingham Small Arms, *Straight Forward* was only ever a monthly publication, with often more illustrations than editorial material, while *Town Crier* survived as a weekly until after the Second World War, despite only carrying adverts from Westwood's (kitchenware) and the S.M. Company ('shirts and overalls … made by trade union labour') in its early editions and only achieving an estimated circulation of 1,500 copies.[38] This was probably due to the response to regular appeals for financial support such as that issued to local trade unionists in November 1920.[39]

The Labour Party did attempt to appeal beyond its traditional support base among unionised industrial workers, as soon as the war was over. In the west midlands, Labour contested county seats such as Oswestry and Evesham for the first time in December 1918 even though, as Clare Griffiths notes, 'most rural areas had no Labour organisation before 1918'.[40] Yet in 1918, Labour won 40% of the votes in Oswestry, where Tom Morris was the sole opponent to the coalition MP, William Bridgeman. This was partly due to what Nicholas Mansfield has described as 'the ambivalence to the war on the part of many of

[34]Library of Birmingham, Archives and Heritage Service, 329.94249LAB: Birmingham Central Labour Party minutes, 16 Jan. 1919.

[35]Library of Birmingham, Archives and Heritage Service, 329.94249LAB: Birmingham Borough Labour Party minutes, i, 1919–21, Labour Party municipal election fund, [1919?].

[36]Library of Birmingham, Archives and Heritage Service, 329.94249LAB: Birmingham Central Labour Party minutes, agenda for meeting, 13 Nov. 1919.

[37]David Howell, *MacDonald's Party: Labour Identities and Crisis 1922–1931* (Oxford, 2002), 18.

[38]*Town Crier*, new ser., no. 2, 10 Oct. 1919; Peter Drake 'The *Town Crier*: Birmingham's Labour Weekly, 1919–1951', in *Worlds of Labour: Essays in Birmingham Labour History*, ed. Anthony Wright and Richard Shackleton (Birmingham, 1983), 103–26. The editor of the *Town Crier*, W.J. Chamberlain, sought 'immediate financial assistance' for his paper from the Birmingham Borough Labour Party within six months of its launch: Library of Birmingham, Archives and Heritage Service, 329.94249LAB: Birmingham Borough Labour Party minute book, i, 1919–21, 12 Feb. 1920.

[39]Library of Birmingham, Archives and Heritage Service, 329.94249LAB: Birmingham Borough Labour Party minute book, i, 1919–21.

[40]C.V.J. Griffiths, *Labour and the Countryside: The Politics of Rural Britain 1918–1939* (Oxford, 2007), 45.

the rural poor'.[41] Although the local party in Oswestry admitted after the election that it had been poorly organised and it was hampered by a lack of support in the Shropshire press, Labour central office provided effective focused propaganda such as the leaflet, 'Why the men and women who work on the land should join a union and vote for the Labour candidate', which asserted that 'the Labour representatives on the District Wages Commission have wrung A HIGHER MINIMUM WAGE from the farmers' and promised 'a still higher minimum wage … if the Labour party is sufficiently strengthened in Parliament'.[42]

Likewise, the Unionists 'gradually develop[ed] a variety of popular appeals after 1900, rooted in class, gender and regional identities', as David Thackeray has noted.[43] One of the most successful Unionist leaflets in 1918 was 'Cards and Coupons' which made effective political capital out of the popular antipathy towards rationing and regulations that was marked in a region such as the west midlands where the working class still prized what John Tosh has termed 'manly independence'.[44] The leaflet promised that, under a coalition government, Britons would not be 'regulated more than is indispensable for a day longer than is necessary', and contrasted their position with that of 'the theoretical socialists of the ILP and the Labour Party' who wanted 'tickets for everything and officials to look after everybody'.[45] Although the Unionists did manage to appeal to working-class men in this way, the most important achievement of the party after 1918 was in its appeal to the newly-enfranchised female voter.

Nicoletta Gullace has convincingly argued that the female voters who were enfranchised in 1918 were those 'who had proved their aversion to pacifism and their support for the war', and that limiting the franchise to those aged over 30 years was designed to reward those mothers who had sacrificed 'the blood of their sons'.[46] Not surprisingly, an electoral discourse of sacrifice which focused on the 'glorious dead' of the previous four years emerged across the west midlands among Unionists and those who wished to benefit from association with the coalition's victory.[47] The Unionists worked hard to tailor their message to this new group, with the Birmingham Unionist Association appointing 'a woman under-secretary to organise the woman vote'.[48] The Association also produced a series of

---

[41] Nicholas Mansfield, 'Farmworkers and Local Conservatism in South-West Shropshire, 1916–1923', in *Mass Conservatism: The Conservative and the Public since the 1880s*, ed. Stuart Ball and Iain Holliday (2002), 38.

[42] *Llangollen Advertiser*, 28 Feb. 1919; Nicholas Mansfield, 'Farmworkers, Local Identity and Conservatism, 1914–1930', in *The English Countryside between the Wars: Regeneration or Decline?*, ed. Paul Brassley, Jeremy Burckhardt and Lynne Thompson (Woodbridge, 2006), 84–5; Bodl., Archives of the British Labour Party, X Films, 81 81/18/59, ser. II: pamphlets and leaflets.

[43] David Thackeray, *Conservatism for the Democratic Age: Conservative Cultures and the Challenge of Mass Politics in Early Twentieth Century England* (Manchester, 2013), 5.

[44] John Tosh, *Manliness and Masculinities in Nineteenth-Century Britain* (Harlow, 2005), 93.

[45] Bodl., CPA, X Films 63/3: 'Cards and Coupons', pamphlet 1918/15.

[46] Nicoletta F. Gullace, *'The Blood of our Sons': Men, Women and the Renegotiation of British Citizenship during the Great War* (New York, 2002), 193. Martin Pugh described female support for the coalition as a 'vicarious blow' against Germany: Martin Pugh, *The Making of Modern British Politics* (3rd edn, Oxford, 2002), 163.

[47] A female speaker in Leamington Spa commented that women had 'a debt of honour to pay' following the war: *Leamington Spa Courier*, 22 Nov. 1918.

[48] Library of Birmingham, Archives and Heritage Service, 329.94249Con: Birmingham Conservative and Unionist Association executive committee minutes, 'Memorandum by Ald. Davis and Mr Walthall', 29 Jan. 1919; David Jarvis, 'Mrs Maggs and Betty: The Conservative Appeal to Women Voters in the 1920s', *Twentieth Century British History*, v (1994), 129–52.

effective campaign leaflets in 1918 (including one entitled *A Word to the Ladies!* which focused on the need for adequate children services).[49] Candidates such as Edward Manville, who successfully stood in Coventry, included pledges of 'equal pay for equal work done by women' in their campaign literature.[50] The Liberals, still wedded to the electoral value of the public meeting, organised women-only meetings in Wednesbury and Stourbridge and relied on electoral material from the Liberal Publications Department which stressed pre-war issues such as temperance and free trade, even in leaflets ostensibly aimed at women.[51] Labour also struggled to focus its appeal to women at first. Even the 1918 election leaflet, *Why women should join the Labour Party*, tellingly described the targets of its appeal as 'every worker, man and woman'. Labour also failed at first to develop its women's organisation in the west midlands, beyond trade unions such as the National Federation of Women Workers.[52]

On the other hand, there is much evidence that, in the west midlands, women were not immediately accepted as fit to exercise the franchise, which tallies with Laura Beers's conclusion that 'the media represented and appealed to [women] as unequal citizens'.[53] In 1918 the *Rugby Advertiser* mocked the female voters' electoral choices, commenting that 'women's logic is perplexing' and citing a female canvasser who, when challenged, said 'don't ask me anything about politics!' even though there was an active branch of the Unionist Women's Citizen Association in the town.[54] The *Birmingham Post* adopted a patronising tone in the final days before voting:

> In these notes nothing has been said on any 'woman's question'. Why? Because the reasons for supporting the Coalition are precisely the same for you as for your brothers and husbands and sons. You now possess full citizenship and the first duty of the citizen is patriotism.[55]

Similarly, the Birmingham Unionist organ, *Straight Forward*, commented that women needed 'training ... by reason of their inexperience in politics' and cited a recruiter for a 'newly formed Women's Unionist Association' who was unable to explain the nature of the Association to those she sought to enlist.[56] The dismissive attitude towards female vot-

[49]University of Birmingham, Cadbury Research Library, Neville Chamberlain MSS, NC18/1/38: *A Word to the Ladies!*, [Nov. 1918].

[50]Herbert Local History Centre, Coventry, PA1177/41/2: Edward Manville's election leaflet, 1918.

[51]*Birmingham Daily Gazette*, 6 Dec. 1918; *Dudley Chronicle*, 30 Nov. 1918; Bodl., Archives of the British Liberal Party, X Films 90/18/27&29: *To Every Woman Voter: The Message of Liberalism*, and *A Word to the Women*, ser. 1: pamphlets and leaflets.

[52]The limited appeal of these bodies was demonstrated when Mary MacArthur, the organiser of the Cradley Heath women chainmakers' successful strike of 1910, was defeated in Stourbridge in the 1918 general election, despite only facing an Asquithian Liberal and Victor Fisher, honorary secretary of the National Democratic and Labour Party, who had been forced on the Unionist local association against their wishes: *The Times*, 29 Nov. 1918; *Birmingham Daily Gazette*, 6 Dec. 1918; *Daily Mail*, 14 Dec. 1918.

[53]Laura Beers, ' "A Timid Disbelief in the Equality to which Lip-Service is Constantly Paid": Gender, Politics and the Press between the Wars', in *Brave New World: Imperial and Democratic Nation-Building in Britain between the Wars*, ed. Laura Beers and Geraint Thomas (2012), 130.

[54]*Rugby Advertiser*, 14 Dec. 1918.

[55]*Birmingham Post*, 13 Dec. 1918; the newspaper changed its name from *Birmingham Daily Post* on 21 May 1918.

[56]*Straight Forward*, no. 16, Jan. 1922.

ers in the local press is in contrast to the largely inclusive and egalitarian attitude towards women voters in the national press, identified by Adrian Bingham.[57] In the west midlands, women appear not to have been immediately welcomed into the public sphere.

The political parties soon realized that supposed female ignorance of politics was, in fact, a symptom of women's antipathy towards party politics, as demonstrated by the rise of non-political groups such as the Townswomen's Guild and the Women's Institute in the interwar years.[58] Although Beatrice Chamberlain expressed concern during the war that women were leaving Unionist Associations in favour of organisations such as the National Union of Women Workers which were 'ostensibly outside politics', in fact the Conservatives were well placed to exploit this trend, having organised the Primrose League as a largely social group in the pre-war years with a message of national unity and domestic renewal specifically aimed at female voters.[59] The Midland Union Council swiftly added an amendment to its rules, decreeing that the executive committee of the council should include at least three women.[60] It must be noted, however, that a distaste for party politics following the collective war effort was not merely restricted to women, as the Birmingham Unionist Association noted the popular anger against party in their review of the 'khaki' election.[61] To counter female voters' avowed dislike of organisations that were too overtly political, Anne Chamberlain, wife of Neville, founded Unionist Women's Institutes (UWI) in Ladywood and Rotton Park and used the resources of the West Midlands Women's Unionist Organisation to promote this clear attempt to hijack the growth of non-partisan women's social gatherings by giving talks on issues relevant to women aged over 30 years and holding children's tea parties, limelight lectures, and sewing parties.[62] Neville Chamberlain was astonished when he spoke at the UWI meeting in his own constituency to find that the meeting 'seemed more like an infant welfare centre than a political gathering'.[63] The organisation soon spread across Birmingham and into the wider west midlands, and Anne Chamberlain found herself running the West Midland Women's Unionist Organisation.[64] The Unionist women's organisation also benefited from the decision of the Women's Unionist and Tariff Reform Association and branches of the Primrose League formally to amalgamate with the party and to rebrand themselves as the Women's Unionist Association.[65] Although some within the party criticized the 'segregation' of the party into

---

[57] Adrian Bingham, 'Enfranchisement, Feminism and the Modern Woman: Debates in the British Popular Press, 1918–1939', in *Aftermath of Suffrage*, ed. Gottlieb and Toye, 87–104; Adrian Bingham, *Gender, Modernity, and the Popular Press in Inter-War Britain* (Oxford, 2004), 120–7.

[58] Thane, 'The Impact of Mass Democracy', 61–2.

[59] University of Birmingham, Cadbury Research Library, Neville Chamberlain MSS, NC1/13/2/156: Beatrice to Neville Chamberlain, 10 Feb. 1917.

[60] Bodl., CPA, ARE/MU/1/5: minutes of the annual meeting of the Midland Union Council, 15 July 1918.

[61] Library of Birmingham, Archives and Heritage Service, 329.94249Con: Birmingham Conservative and Unionist Association executive committee minutes, 29 Jan. 1919.

[62] *Straight Forward*, no. 5, Jan. 1921; no. 8, Apr. 1921. The National Unionist Association conference, held in Birmingham in June 1920, had also included a 'mass meeting of women' at the Midland Institute with over 700 present: Library of Birmingham, Archives and Heritage Service, 329.94249Con: Birmingham Conservative and Unionist Association management committee minutes, 9 July 1920.

[63] *The Neville Chamberlain Diary Letters, i: The Making of a Politician, 1915–1920*, ed. Robert Self (Aldershot, 2000), 388: Neville Chamberlain to Hilda Chamberlain, 26 Sept. 1920.

[64] *Straight Forward*, no. 9, May 1921; no. 10, June 1921; no. 5, Dec. 1921.

[65] Thackeray, *Conservatism for the Democratic Age*, 125.

gender-based organisations, others welcomed the contribution that these bodies could offer. As one writer to the *Conservative Agents' Journal* put it, success in an age of mass democracy 'stands or falls on … whether or not there is a good women's organisation in the constituency'.[66] This judgment appeared to be proved correct when 115 women canvassed Ladywood on behalf of Neville Chamberlain during the 1923 electoral campaign and enabled him to retain his seat, despite a sustained Labour challenge.[67] The Unionist Party's ascendancy was, in David Thackeray's opinion, 'built, in part, on its ability to develop a substantial women's movement, dwarfing its rivals', which, in turn, was due to the creation of separate men's and women's branches of the Midland Unionist Association.[68] By contrast, the Labour organisations were much slower to organise, with the Birmingham branch of the ILP only organising a conference on women's organisations in February 1922 and then failing to discuss the issue again for at least a year.[69]

The Women's Party, founded in autumn 1917, was savagely anti-Bolshevik and anti-pacifist, but simultaneously progressively feminist, supporting equal pay for equal work, equal marriage and reform of the divorce laws, equal opportunities in employment, state provision of maternity and infant care, and co-operative housing schemes with the provision of hot water, crèches, nurseries and laundries, medical services, and even gymnasiums.[70] Although the policies were popular, the failure to identify their audience clearly had serious consequences. Following the hasty decision by parliament in November 1918 to allow women stand for election, an unprepared Christabel Pankhurst was parachuted into the newly-created seat of Smethwick in the Black Country. Lloyd George fulfilled his sense of obligation to the Pankhursts by granting Christabel the Coupon, but she was no match for a Labour candidate who had been nursing the seat for years. Pankhurst was accurately seen as a candidate who had been, in the words of the ousted Unionist candidate, 'sent down for the good of the country and possibly for the good of the women's cause'. In a ludicrous attack, in a seat where the Labour candidate had led wartime recruitment drives and the National Union of Women Workers had a strong membership, Pankhurst claimed that 'the Labour Party … was, in fact, a Bolshevist party because it was led by Bolshevists'.[71] Pankhurst clearly lacked electoral literature, as the *Daily Mail*, one of the most enthusiastic backers of the Women's Party, claimed that her campaign was hindered by rain which washed her supporters' chalked slogans away.[72] She lost by 755 votes and, with this setback, as June Purvis puts it, the Women's Party swiftly 'faded away'.[73] The local Unionist

[66]Bodl., CPA, Pub/3/3: *Conservative Agents' Journal*, Apr. 1923, p. 68.

[67]Thackeray, *Conservatism for the Democratic Age*, 144.

[68]Thackeray, *Conservatism for the Democratic Age*, 147; University of Birmingham, Cadbury Research Library, Neville Chamberlain MSS, NC5/10/11: Neville Chamberlain to Anne Chamberlain, 1 Feb. 1918; Bodl., CPA, ARE/MU/1/5: minutes of the annual meeting of the Midland Union Council, 3 Dec. 1920.

[69]Library of Birmingham, Archives and Heritage Service, A329.94249IND: ILP, Birmingham city branch minutes, 2 Feb. 1922.

[70]*Britannia*, 2 Nov. 1917.

[71]*Birmingham Post*, 11 Dec. 1918; George J. Barnsby, *Socialism in Birmingham and the Black Country, 1850–1939* (Wolverhampton, 1998), 229.

[72]*Daily Mail*, 12 Dec. 1918.

[73]June Purvis, 'Emmeline Pankhurst in the Aftermath of Suffrage, 1918–1928', in *Aftermath of Suffrage*, ed. Gottlieb and Toye, 21; see also Nicoletta F. Gullace, 'Christabel Pankhurst and the Smethwick Election: Right-Wing Feminism, the Great War and the Ideology of Consumption', *Women's History Review*, xxiii (2014), 330–46;

Association determined to develop female politicians more locally, with two female councillors elected in 1918. Although both, together with a third female candidate, stood for the 1921 Birmingham municipal elections, only one was successful and the Birmingham Unionist Association's enthusiasm for female candidates swiftly waned.[74] There were no female Unionist candidates in the 1923 Birmingham municipal elections. Anne Chamberlain, Neville's tireless wife, continued to demonstrate that the chief political contribution that women could make in such a highly-patriarchal society was that of the organiser and canvasser, playing a vital role in the 1924 Ladywood contest between Neville and Oswald Mosley, which the former won by only 77 votes, thus guaranteeing that Neville's swift political rise would not be halted.[75] Labour seemed equally reluctant to put women forward, with only Mrs C.M. Mitchell standing (successfully) in the Birmingham municipal election in November 1919, and Mrs M.E. Cottrell standing unsuccessfully in November 1920.[76]

A crucial factor in the outcome of all elections is the social composition of the constituencies. The contrast between rural and urban seats was clearly evident between 1886 and 1910, with the Liberals, both Unionist and Gladstonian, dominating the more heavily-industrial urban areas and the Conservatives operating an effective control of the rural and suburban seats. Pelling draws a clear, if somewhat questionable, distinction between 'working-class' constituencies such as Coventry and 'middle-class' seats such as Shrewsbury, before 1914.[77] The effect of the redistribution of constituencies which accompanied the 1918 Reform Act was to heighten the distinction between constituencies where the numbers of manual workers dominated and those more suburban and light industrial areas where there was a more professional and business profile to the electorate.

While there were certainly fewer problems in reorganising the constituencies of the west midlands than there were in Ireland,[78] as the *Birmingham Daily Post* reported in January 1918, there was 'considerable interest' in the redistribution of seats in the city, largely owing to the dramatic change in Birmingham's constituency boundaries. It noted that appealing to old loyalties (which had saved Birmingham for Unionism in 1906) would no longer suffice, as 'each of the present members who seeks re-election will have to ask for the suffrage of voters in new districts as well as those of old supporters'.[79] In the whole of Great Britain, the number of constituencies increased from 670 to 707 in 1918. Across England, the number of borough and county seats increased by 29, so it is striking how little the west midlands benefited from the redistribution. In 1910, the region returned 47 MPs and this did not change in 1918, in contrast to the increase in representation that was afforded to Wales and Scotland. What did occur in the west midlands was a redressing of

June Purvis, 'The Women's Party of Great Britain (1917–1919): A Forgotten Episode in British Women's Political History', *Women's History Review*, xxv (2016), 638–51.

[74]The re-elected councillor, Henrietta Bartleet, was returned with a majority of only 89 in her Soho ward: *Straight Forward*, no. 14, Oct. 1921.

[75]Peter Marsh, *The Chamberlain Litany: Letters within a Governing Family from Empire to Appeasement* (2010), 193.

[76]*Town Crier*, new ser., no. 6, 7 Nov. 1919; no. 58, 5 Nov. 1920.

[77]Henry Pelling, *Social Geography of British Elections, 1885–1910* (1967), 173–203.

[78]J.D. Fair, *British Inter-Party Conferences: A Study of the Procedure of Conciliation in British Politics, 1867–1921* (Oxford, 1980), 179–80.

[79]*Birmingham Daily Post*, 26 Jan. 1918.

the balance between borough and county seats, with *The Times* suggesting, in November 1917, that the redistribution amounted to 'an increase in the political power of the great towns'.[80]

In 1910, Birmingham itself had eight MPs, Joseph Chamberlain's famous 'seven'[81] and Aston Manor, which was effectively part of Birmingham and had been recognized as such in the 1911 reorganisation of municipal boundaries. In 1918 the number of seats in the city was increased to 12, but in reality, this merely drew clearer boundaries between the borough and county seats. The boundaries of Birmingham had actually grown between 1885 and 1918 to include portions of a further three seats, Staffordshire Handsworth, Tamworth, and Worcestershire East. The first had been represented by Liberal Unionists continuously since 1886 while the last had been Austen Chamberlain's seat for 22 years until 1914, which demonstrated their close affinity with Birmingham's pre-war politics. Nevertheless, the verdict of most Birmingham politicians was that the city had been 'favourably dealt with' as the city now had, 'more members than any other city outside London', apart from Glasgow.[82] This provoked a backlash from the agricultural interest in the region which lobbied one of the assistant commissioners of the boundary review at Birmingham Town Hall in August 1917. Lawrence Tipper, chairman of the Worcestershire chamber of agriculture, claimed that under the proposed distribution of seats in and around Birmingham, 'agriculturists would be overpowered and outvoted by the urban population'.[83] Reviewing the Representation of the People Act later in 1918, Arthur Hobbs suggested that Birmingham's increased electoral representation was partly as a result of the business premises qualification, which was designed, in his opinion 'to preserve the separate identities of the commercial constituencies such as the City of London and certain divisions of Birmingham … and other large towns'.[84]

One of the chief purposes of redistribution was supposedly to equalise the size of constituencies to reflect the changes in population since 1885 and the impact of the expansion of the franchise. While this produced a large number of seats where the electorate was between 30,000 and 40,000 there were a number of exceptions. County towns which retained a seat, even if the constituency expanded to include some of the surrounding countryside, such as Shrewsbury and Worcester, had significantly smaller electorates, both having less than 26,000 electors. On the other hand, Coventry, which had grown considerably due to pre-war expansion and wartime industry, saw the enfranchisement of its largely working-class population in 1918, which resulted in an electorate of 62,066. The local press had been concerned at this inequality and had reported, with some justified doubts, the view of the Boundary Commission that some boroughs (including Coventry) would not be given two seats, despite their large populations, because the increase was purely the result of recruitment to munitions factories and would not be permanent.[85] The *Coventry Standard*

[80] *The Times*, 5 Nov. 1917.

[81] When the Unionists had retained all the Birmingham seats in 1906, despite the national Liberal landslide, Chamberlain's supporters printed a postcard with the caption 'Well done Birmingham!! We are Seven!!!'; Andrew Reekes, 'Birmingham Exceptionalism, Joseph Chamberlain and the 1906 General Election', University of Birmingham PhD, 2014, p. 35.

[82] *Birmingham Daily Gazette*, 6 Oct. 1917.

[83] *Birmingham Daily Post*, 9 Aug. 1917.

[84] A.O. Hobbs and F.J. Ogden, *A Guide to the Representation of the People Act, 1918* (1918), 29.

[85] *Midland Daily Telegraph*, 9, 12, 13 Oct. 1917.

argued that Coventry's growth would be permanent, due to the expansion of the suburbs of Coundon, Foleshill, Keresley, and Binley in recent years, and that there was a danger that disparity between parliamentary and municipal boundaries would cause 'an increase of trouble and a diminution of satisfaction'.[86] Similarly, in Stoke-on-Trent, the increase in representation from two to three MPs was felt to be inadequate, given the huge growth of the population since 1885.[87] The issue in Coventry was raised by the City Council and then D.M. Mason, the Liberal MP for Coventry, took up the issue in parliament and moved an amendment on the Representation of the People Bill. However, he received no support in the House (possibly due to having been deselected by the Coventry Liberal Association before the war began), and in reply, the home secretary, Sir George Cave, merely commented that he hoped Coventry 'would do better in the next bill'.[88] Cave's dismissive attitude provoked an angry response from the local press and the Coventry Board of Guardians, but in truth, it was too late and Mason was too marginalised a figure in the Commons to achieve anything.[89]

Other areas were angered by the increase in the size of the constituency which redistribution brought. The leader column of the *Leamington Spa Courier* described the proposed expansion of the Warwick and Leamington constituency as 'unwieldy' as it now contained Kenilworth, Stratford-upon-Avon, and Alcester, as well as the two towns. The population of this area was 83,000 people, and the paper noted that this was far in excess of the 70,000 figure fixed by the Speaker's conference as the ideal size of a constituency. It was also far higher than the county borough seat of Worcester, which fell at least 40,000 people short of the ideal figure, yet which was retained in the redistribution.[90] The *Courier* also noted that agricultural and urban issues would be confused and that 'the historic continuity of such a historic borough as Warwick' would be destroyed.[91] The removal of the name Stratford-upon-Avon was regarded as 'a snub or rather a humiliation'.[92] The renaming of the North Worcestershire constituency as 'Stourbridge' also drew the ire of Oldbury District Council which objected that its town had not been named in the constituency, despite being almost the same size as Stourbridge.[93] Its concerns were not resolved, but when Evelyn Cecil raised the issue in the House that the proposed naming of a new Birmingham constituency as 'Hockley' would mean the end of the 'West Birmingham' constituency, famously associated with Joseph Chamberlain, Cave swiftly backed down and allowed the old name of the seat to survive, prompting cheers from the government benches.[94]

When the boundary commissioners visited the west midlands in July 1917, they were largely faced with apathy from a population focused on the increasingly-bitter conflict

---

[86] *Coventry Standard*, 6 July 1917.

[87] *Staffordshire Advertiser*, 14 July 1917.

[88] Herbert Local History Centre, PA68/5: Coventry Liberal Association minutes, 6 Feb. 1912–22 Oct. 1922; *Evening Despatch*, 29 Oct. 1917; *Midland Daily Telegraph*, 6 Nov. 1917.

[89] *Midland Daily Telegraph*, 7 Nov. 1917.

[90] *Birmingham Daily Gazette*, 30 June 1917.

[91] *Leamington Spa Courier*, 29 June 1917.

[92] *Coventry Standard*, 6 July 1917.

[93] *Birmingham Daily Gazette*, 30 June 1917.

[94] *Birmingham Daily Post*, 30 Nov. 1917.

in Flanders and a political class that had been 'quiescent' since 1914.[95] Only the size of the representation of Coventry and the constituency boundaries of South Warwickshire were seriously challenged.[96] In Warwick and Leamington, the challenge was quite ill-tempered, with the chairman of Warwickshire County Council claiming that the proposed redistribution of seats 'bore the stamp of having been drawn by some clerk in London who did not know much of the interior working of the county'.[97] The anger of the Unionist Association was also noted, largely as two fairly safe seats, Stratford and Warwick, would be combined into one. Ludford Docker, brother of the influential Birmingham industrialist, Dudley Docker, had been nominated as the successor to the sitting Stratford MP, and the amalgamation of the two urban areas left him without prospects.[98] The level of protest was relatively muted, however, and the boundary commissioners' initial recommendations were ultimately forwarded to parliament and accepted without revision.

If the redistribution of seats in 1918 had had little impact in the region, the clauses in the Representation of the People Act which attempted to reduce electoral corruption did more to transform the culture of politics in the west midlands. Worcester had been notorious as a corrupt borough before 1914. There had been allegations of 'treating' by Conservative candidates in the municipal elections of November 1904.[99] The relatively small size of the parliamentary electorate and the threat of a Liberal victory had encouraged the Conservative candidate's supporters to engage in similar tactics in 1906. The Liberals, defeated by a mere 129 votes that year, had petitioned parliament and a royal commission had been held. Although it did not find evidence of widespread corruption, the commission did conclude that 'a class of voters, numbering about 500 ... are prepared to sell their vote for drink or money'.[100] It was behaviour such as this that the act's expenses clauses aimed to stamp out. The banning of auxiliary organisations from campaigning for candidates, to ensure equality between candidates of different parties (and to restrict the influence of trade unionists in favour of the Labour candidate), did much to reduce the bitter antagonism that such bodies had brought to Edwardian politics.[101] This had the effect of reducing the extent of disturbance and destruction traditionally associated with elections, though this was, arguably, more influenced by the presence of women as political actors, which would have considerably affected the public behaviour of men in the political arena. To give one example of the sudden change in political street culture after the war, a shop opposite Worcester Guildhall (the site of the declaration in the constituency) was barricaded in the

[95] *Walsall Observer and South Staffordshire Chronicle*, 14 July 1917.

[96] *Coventry Standard*, 13 July 1917.

[97] *Leamington Spa Courier*, 13 July 1917. The lack of consultation with the local leaders was also 'strongly resented' in Staffordshire: *Staffordshire Advertiser*, 14 July 1917; *Walsall Observer*, 21 July 1917.

[98] *Birmingham Daily Mail*, 14 July 1917.

[99] *Worcestershire Echo*, 2 Nov. 1904.

[100] Royal Commission on the Worcester Election, *Report of Royal Commission Appointed to Enquire into the Existence of Corrupt Practices at the Last Election for the City of Worcester [together with Minutes of Evidence]* (2 vols, 1906).

[101] E.H.H. Green, *The Crisis of Conservatism: The Politics, Economics and Ideology of the British Conservative Party, 1880–1914* (1995); Thackeray, *Conservatism for the Democratic Age*, 117–18. Thackeray does note that newspapers largely ignored the legislation until 1922, when it was amended to include any corporate bodies which intervened in an election.

expectation of crowd trouble on 28 December 1918, but only 200 people were present for what the local paper described as the 'tamest declaration day ever seen in the city'.[102]

Under the terms of the 1883 Corrupt Practices Act, returning officers routinely sent the candidates' expenses to the press, and those that were printed indicate that Smith Child, the successful candidate in Stone in December 1918, spent £878 14s. 10d. in winning the seat. The maximum sum permitted in election expenses was 7d. for every registered voter in a county constituency, 5d. in a borough constituency.[103] From a survey of the expenses of other Staffordshire candidates, Smith Child's appears a fairly average amount, although it is noticeable that most Labour candidates spent less than their coalition rivals, a shrewd political move, given the contemporary national hostility towards 'profiteering' and 'waste'.[104] The statement printed in the *Staffordshire Advertiser* clearly indicated that Smith Child was not returning any personal expenses as he excluded the £61 10s. as 'paid by himself'. It was, however, striking that Child paid a mere £43 8s. 3d. for the hire of rooms, compared with his Liberal opponent, George Townsend, who spent £71 16s. 7d. on room hire, out of expenses that only amounted to £595 12s. 10d.[105] Possibly Smith Child had gathered that money spent on public meetings was increasingly wasted, as a smaller proportion of the electorate now attended these and he was choosing, instead, to spend more on advertising (Smith Child spent £462 14s. 11d. on 'goods supplied and work and labour done'). Or perhaps, given his position as commander in the royal artillery of the 46th (North Midland) Division of the Territorials, he had been offered premises *gratis* by patriotic and wealthy supporters.[106] Smith Child's large expenses, allowed given the increase of the electorate, were overshadowed by those of the Welsh architect, William Rees, who reported £979 2s. 4d. for his unsuccessful bid to unseat James Parker, the Coalition Labour candidate in Cannock.[107] But not even Rees's profligacy could match that of the hapless Willie Dyson, the National Democratic and Labour candidate for Nuneaton, who had expenses totalling £1,131 4s. 4d., despite only gaining 1,101 votes, which meant that each vote had cost over £1, as the Unionist *Tamworth Herald* somewhat gleefully pointed out.[108] The possibility of the misuse of taxpayers' funds which this suggests is borne out by curious expenses returns such as those of Ernest Pollock, who had spent £599 1s. 1d. at Warwick and Leamington, including nearly £200 for the employment of an agent, clerks and messengers and £43 5s. 7d. for 'miscellaneous expenses' in an election where he faced no opponent.[109]

None the less, by 1922, a correspondent to *The Times* noted that the unforeseen result of the election expenses clauses of the 1918 Reform Act, had, in fact, been a *de facto* glass

---

[102] *Worcester Herald*, 4 Jan. 1919.

[103] Sylvain Mayer, *Representation of the People Act 1918 and the Redistribution of Seats (Ireland) Act, 1918* (1918), 119.

[104] As the 1918 Staffordshire results reveal, this did not necessarily translate into electoral weakness. Samuel Finney spent £517 8s. 5d. in contesting Burslem, compared with his Unionist rival, Sampson Walker, who spent £613, but Finney won the seat with a majority of over 1,000 votes: *Staffordshire Advertiser*, 8 Feb. 1919.

[105] *Staffordshire Advertiser*, 1 Feb. 1919. William Ormsby-Gore, who likewise defeated a Labour candidate at Stafford, only spent £43 19s. on room hire: *Staffordshire Advertiser*, 25 Jan. 1919.

[106] *Staffordshire Advertiser*, 1 Feb. 1919.

[107] *Staffordshire Advertiser*, 8 Feb. 1919.

[108] *Tamworth Herald*, 22 Feb. 1919.

[109] *Leamington Spa Courier*, 10 Jan. 1919. By contrast, John Ward, unopposed in Stoke, reported £43 19s. 6d.: *Staffordshire Advertiser*, 11 Jan. 1919.

ceiling on the social class of potential candidates. As the Walsall-born Unionist MP, John Lort-Williams, commented:

> choice is restricted, generally, to candidates with means, such as professional, business or professional men in middle-age or older, profiteers, pensioners, what is left of the landed gentry and scions of the nobility with sufficient means and those who have succeeded in marrying wives with money.[110]

In the 1922 election, it is notable that several west midlands candidates returned expenses of over £1,000, indicating that the costs of campaigning were notably higher once normal times had returned after 1918.[111]

With the reduction of candidates' permitted expenses and the increase in the size of the electorate, the nature of political communication underwent a final shift away from the public meeting which had been a vital feature of pre-war political culture.[112] Hiring halls and paying to staff the meetings was a risky venture with limited funds when there were frequently few locations in a constituency which could house a reasonable audience and no guarantee that those who attended were undecided voters who the candidate most needed to persuade. Instead, the Edwardian explosion in printed, highly-visual propaganda continued, together with an increased use of publicity materials and commercial advertising, especially in leaflets and local newspapers.[113] The decline in direct confrontation between political opponents that the public meeting had traditionally provided also contributed, according to Jon Lawrence, to a far less rowdy and disruptive political culture in the interwar years.[114]

The 1918 Reform Act permitted the sending 'free of any charge for postage … one postal communication containing matter relating to the election only, and not exceeding two ounces in weight'.[115] This led to the development of increasingly-sophisticated publicity materials, best exemplified by Edward Manville's election leaflet, distributed across Coventry in November 1918. Manville and his local party association managed to present their electoral message using both sides of the small leaflet, even designing it to be read when it was folded for postage through voters' letterboxes and filled with dates of meetings, advice for voters, and attractive non-partisan slogans.[116] Given the limited number of posters that could be produced in time for the hastily-called contest in December 1918, this was a highly-effective alternative means of delivering the Unionist message, and Manville won the seat against five rival candidates with a majority of over 7,000 votes.

---

[110] *The Times*, 4 Feb. 1924.

[111] Those candidates in 1922 for whom figures are available who spent over £1,000 included David Wallace in Rugby, James Parker and Harold Abrahamson in Cannock, and Courtenay Warner and W.J. French in Lichfield: *Leamington Spa Courier*, 30 Dec. 1922; *Lichfield Mercury*, 29 Dec. 1922; *Staffordshire Advertiser*, 23 Dec. 1922.

[112] David Butler, *British Political Facts, 1900–1985* (1986), 247.

[113] James Thompson, ' "Pictorial Lies"? Posters and Politics in Britain, c.1880–1914', *Past & Present*, No. 197 (2007), 177–210.

[114] Jon Lawrence, 'The Transformation of British Public Politics after the First World War', *Past & Present*, No. 190 (2006), 185–216.

[115] Mayer, *Representation of the People Act 1918*, 70.

[116] Herbert Local History Centre, Coventry, PA1177/41/2: Manville leaflet.

The post-war politics of the west midlands was marked henceforth by press battles rather than by physical aggression. Once the dust had settled from the 1918 election, the Unionists of Birmingham, worried by the rise of Labour in the city after November 1919, discussed the 'urgent need for a local Unionist publication of some kind to counter-act the Socialistic propaganda'.[117] This 'propaganda' had chiefly appeared in the form of the *Town Crier* which had been relaunched by the Birmingham Labour Party, the ILP and the Birmingham Trades Council in October 1919, as well as the daily *Birmingham Gazette* which had backed Labour since the split in the Liberal Party in 1916.[118] It was agreed by the Birmingham Unionist Association management committee that the journal should be named *Straight Forward* and the first issue, costing 1*d.*, was printed in September 1920 with a mission statement 'to expose false prophets who seek to delude ignorant people'.[119] The Unionist Association then established a propaganda committee to promote a nuanced message suited to the working men and women of the city.[120]

The most significant change in political culture instigated by the 1918 Reform Act in the west midlands appears to have been a decline in the effect of denominationalism on political allegiance.[121] Before 1914, the alliance between nonconformist churches and Liberalism was already breaking down, as D.W. Bebbington observed when he commented that 'sections of nonconformity ... were swayed by their economic interest to transfer their votes from the Liberals ... to the Unionists', and he noted that wesleyan methodists were particularly prone to do so.[122] Once the bulk of the population had been enfranchised in 1918, this process was rapidly accelerated, as the indifference of working-class communities to religious denominationalism had long been a concern of Victorian and Edwardian christians. The issues of temperance, disestablishment and religious control of education, so central to Liberal politics and a crucial feature of their revival between 1902 and 1906, failed to resonate with a new class of voter, more concerned to see his or her children at the best possible school, to be able to afford a decent standard of living and looking for comfort following the sacrifices of the Great War.[123] Once the First World War began, as Arthur Burns has established, the Church of England proved itself better placed than the nonconformists to exploit its status as the 'national' church.[124] The cathedrals of the west midlands, such as Worcester, St Philips in Birmingham, Lichfield, and the newly-raised St Michael's in Coventry, became the location of chapels of remembrance, with tattered flags, books of remembrance, memorials to 'the glorious dead' and annual services on 11 November,

---

[117]Library of Birmingham, Archives and Heritage Service, 329.94249Con: Birmingham Conservative and Unionist Association publication subcommittee minutes, 31 Mar. 1920.

[118]Library of Birmingham, Archives and Heritage Service, 329.94249LAB: Birmingham Central Labour Party minutes, 14 Aug. 1919; *Town Crier*, new ser., no. 1, 3 Oct. 1919; Drake, 'The *Town Crier*', 104–8.

[119]Library of Birmingham, Archives and Heritage Service, 329.94249Con: Birmingham Conservative and Unionist Association management committee minutes, 28 May 1920; *Straight Forward*, no. 1, Sept. 1920.

[120]Library of Birmingham, Archives and Heritage Service, 329.94249Con: Birmingham Conservative and Unionist Association executive committee minutes, 21 Nov. 1921.

[121]K.D. Wald, *Crosses on the Ballot: Patterns of British Voter Alignment since 1885* (Princeton, NJ, 1983), 213–14.

[122]David Bebbington, 'Nonconformity and Electoral Sociology, 1867–1918', *Historical Journal*, xxvii (1984), 646.

[123]The removal of denominationalism from state schools in the 1918 Education Act also hastened this development.

[124]Arthur Burns, 'The Authority of the Church', in *Liberty and Authority in Victorian Britain*, ed. Peter Mandler (Oxford, 2006), 197–200.

to which thousands of different faiths (and none) flocked. Stanley Baldwin spoke of 'the grand old national church of England' in a fashion which transcended denominational lines of belief and secured the Church of England a place of respect and admiration in post-war Britain that it had scarcely enjoyed in the Victorian era.[125]

Among the Labour activists, the moderate 'Labour Church' movement which had been particularly powerful in pre-war Birmingham, was revived by the Birmingham branch of the ILP, but there is no indication from the pages of the *Town Crier* that this movement reached an audience beyond existing ILP members.[126] Neil Johnson goes so far as to suggest that the 'Labour Churches' were merely ILP meetings held on a Sunday evening, so called in order 'to placate certain sensitivities about political events taking place on the Sabbath'. He also theorises that the term 'Labour Church' was actually reanimated in post-war Birmingham as a (largely unsuccessful) ploy to overcome the peculiarly 'consensual nature of industrial relations in Birmingham' after 1918.[127] In the elections of 1918, 1922, 1923, and 1924, the lack of a clear denominational divide between the parties was consistently noted, and the attempts of long-serving Liberals to appeal to nonconformist consciences had very limited effect as Robert Outhwaite, David Mason, John Wilson, and Richard Fairbairn, all soon discovered.[128] Stanley Baldwin and Neville Chamberlain both continued the tradition, begun by Joseph Chamberlain in the 1880s, of appealing to the nonconformist tradition as part of British civic identity rather than as a separate entity, and then delivering the votes of this community to the Unionist cause.[129] The only religious group clearly excluded from the national collective was 'the Jew' who was frequently associated with Bolshevism in both Germany and Russia in Unionist publications and was frequently the butt of jokes regarding his assumed untrustworthiness and 'cosmopolitan' identity.[130] As Stuart Ball has noted, 'there certainly was an under-current of anti-Semitism in Conservative [and Unionist] circles' especially in the febrile atmosphere of post-war Europe.[131]

Shortly after becoming prime minister in 1923, Baldwin appointed Neville Chamberlain as his chancellor of the exchequer, forming an alliance which would last for the next 14 years. Baldwin and Chamberlain used the west midlands as the electoral base from which to control the Conservative Party and the politics of the nation. Only once, in 1929, was their

---

[125] Philip Williamson, 'The Doctrinal Politics of Stanley Baldwin', in *Public and Private Doctrine: Essays in British History Presented to Maurice Cowling*, ed. Michael Bentley (Cambridge, 1993), 181–208.

[126] Library of Birmingham, Archives and Heritage Service, A329.94249IND: ILP, Birmingham city branch minutes, 3 Mar. 1917; Barnsby, *Socialism in Birmingham and the Black Country*, 353–6; John Boughton, 'Working Class Politics in Birmingham and Sheffield, 1918–1931', University of Warwick PhD, 1985, pp. 286–9.

[127] N.W. Johnson, ' "So Peculiarly its Own" The Theological Socialism of the Labour Church', University of Birmingham PhD, 2015, pp. 262–4.

[128] Outhwaite came a poor third in Hanley in 1918. Mason came last in the poll of six candidates in Coventry in Dec. 1918 and Wilson lost the seat which he had held for 27 years in 1922 – the first time he had faced a Unionist candidate. Fairbairn lost three of the four elections he contested in Worcester in the period, in 1918, 1922, and 1924.

[129] Stephen Koss, *Nonconformity in British Politics* (1975), 174–7.

[130] See *Straight Forward*, esp. no. 1, Sept. 1920, no. 12, Sept. 1921.

[131] S. Ball, *Portrait of a Party: The Conservative Party in Britain 1918–1945* (Oxford, 2013), 65; G.R. Searle, *Corruption in British Politics, 1895–1930* (Oxford, 1987), 328–37. It must be noted that there was evidence of racial prejudice within the Birmingham Labour Party as well, as a meeting of the party in 1920 unanimously approved a motion which protested against 'the invasion of Germany by black troops' and called on the government 'to secure the withdrawal of this menace from Europe': Library of Birmingham, Archives and Heritage Service, 329.94249LAB: Birmingham Borough Labour Party minute book, i, 1919–21, 15 Apr. 1920.

dominance in the region challenged and this was soon rectified in the landslide of 1931 when they even made inroads into the only Labour area in the region, the Black Country.[132] Their appeal was, appropriately enough in the former 'fiefdom' of Joseph Chamberlain, based on liberal values of religious and wider cultural tolerance, social reform (in particular, housing) and, of course, protectionism in 1923 and 1931 (and its more limited industrial form of 'safeguarding' in 1924 and 1929). This programme was designed to offer a more convincing alternative to Labour than that offered by the fractious and increasingly-penurious Liberal Party or by Lloyd George and the ardent coalitionists (the latter including Neville's half-brother, Austen, who had, in Peter Marsh's words, 'lost touch with the grass roots of his party').[133] The west midland Unionists made it clear that they regarded the 'Labour' Party as a deception practised on the working man, by men 'who work hand in hand behind the scenes with Russian Bolshevists and German Jews'.[134] Neville Chamberlain's sincere commitment to social issues and his family's philanthropic efforts to improve housing in Birmingham paid rich political dividends in a city where, as Briggs explains in the official history of the city, 'housing [was pushed] into the centre of the picture before the war ended in 1918'.[135]

Baldwin's strategy, to trump both traditional local-sectarian and newly-emerging class-based politics with a seemingly non-political appeal to a nation hungry for a purpose in the aftermath of a shattering war, has been described as 'new Conservatism'.[136] But, in many ways, this approach was a partnership between Baldwin's rural traditionalists and the urban liberalism of Neville Chamberlain and his supporters. Very rarely have commentators noticed that the two men, whose partnership was the key to the Unionist dominance of the period between 1922 and 1937, were MPs for west midland constituencies that were a mere 20 miles apart. The key responses of Baldwin and Chamberlain to the 1918 Reform Act were a shared willingness to consider social and imperial reform, resistance to the demands of right-wing ideologues in their party and in the press, and tolerance of the legitimacy of the Labour Party (albeit a tolerance marked with vigorous political opposition). In this respect, the two men built on the traditions of 'Tory democracy' and radical Unionism and thereby managed to outmanœuvre challengers to their dominance from both within the Conservative Party (such as Winston Churchill) and without. In the west midlands, Conservative extremists such as Sir Richard Cooper and alternative right-wing parties such as the National Democratic and Labour Party, the National Party, and the Women's Party, were soon sidelined once their electoral appeal proved short-lived. Chamberlain and Baldwin realized that the decline of the Liberals, the sudden removal of the issue of Irish home rule and the more extreme policies of Labour, afforded the Unionists a political opportunity that might not come again. Less cynically, both men had been genuinely impressed by the patriotic response that the war had evoked from all social groups and they wished to articulate policies that would continue to bring the national community

---

[132] In 1931, the Unionists won Wednesbury, West Bromwich, Smethwick, and Kingswinford, all of which had been held continuously by Labour since 1918.

[133] Marsh, *The Chamberlain Litany*, 155.

[134] Neville Chamberlain, 'Our Task', *Straight Forward*, no. 1, Sept. 1920.

[135] Asa Briggs, *History of Birmingham. Vol. II: Borough and City, 1865–1938* (Oxford, 1952), 228.

[136] A.J. Taylor, 'Stanley Baldwin, Heresthetics and the Realignment of British Politics', *British Journal of Political Science*, xxxv (2005), 429.

together.[137] Despite their antipathy towards Lloyd George, both men had supported the coalition government until 1922 in the belief that it would promote and maintain the cross-class unity of the Great War.[138]

Baldwin is celebrated as a great communicator, rather than a great legislator, and Robert Self has shown that Neville Chamberlain also proved to be a very effective speaker, despite his personal reserve.[139] Both men sought to exploit radio and cinema to transmit their message of practical, non-ideological, common-sense responses to domestic and international problems to as wide a range of the mass electorate as possible. Both men enjoyed a (largely) positive relationship with the local press and both were careful to cultivate the support of John Reith, the anti-Churchillian director general of the recently-founded BBC.[140] They both endorsed a style of political campaigning which saw the Unionists in the west midlands routinely running regular 'surgeries' and visiting the homes and recreational clubs and institutes of their constituents (even though Neville Chamberlain clearly did not enjoy this experience, referring to it in private as 'slumming').[141] They ensured that the apparatus of party organisation and the staffing of party bodies remained in their hands, refusing to allow any democratisation or too much centralisation of the political system in the west midlands. The Unionists of the region may have successfully presented themselves as patriotic, moderate social reformers, but they remained paternalistic elites who largely saw the newly-enlarged electorates as entities to be 'managed' rather than consulted.

[137]See Baldwin's anonymous letter to *The Times*, June 1919, in *Baldwin Papers: A Conservative Statesman, 1908–1947*, ed. Philip Williamson and Edward Baldwin (Cambridge, 2004), 43–4.

[138]Powell, *British Politics, 1910–1935*, 91.

[139]John Ramsden, *An Appetite for Power: A History of the Conservatives since 1830* (1998), 253; Self, *Neville Chamberlain*, 261.

[140]James Curran and Jean Seaton, *Power Without Responsibility: The Press and Broadcasting in Britain* (5th edn, 1997), 111–27.

[141]*The Neville Chamberlain Diary Letters, ii: The Reform Years, 1921–27*, ed. Robert Self (Aldershot, 2000), 90: Neville Chamberlain to Ida Chamberlain, 7 Jan. 1922; Boughton, 'Working Class Politics', 415–19.

The 1918 Reform Act, Redistribution and Scottish Politics

EWEN A. CAMERON

This essay examines the effect of the 1918 Representation of the People Act on Scottish politics. It notes the extensive addition to the electorate with the enfranchisement of adult males and most women over the age of 30 years. The main focus of the essay is on the effect of the provisions of the act in terms of the redistribution of seats in Scotland. Although the overall level of Scottish representation increased from 70 to 71 seats, there was a profound shift from the rural areas of the north and south to the industrial areas of west central Scotland and the city of Glasgow, which was awarded a further eight seats. In addition, the majority of the 'Districts of Burghs', a legacy of the Union of 1707, were abolished. It is argued that these changes created new political conditions in Scotland which favoured the Labour Party in the interwar period, and especially in the 1920s. The arguments – economic, historical, and political – deployed in defence of seats scheduled for abolition by the Boundary Commission are analysed.

Keywords: Borders; Districts of Burghs; electoral reform; Glasgow; Highlands; Labour Party; Liberal Party; redistribution; Representation of the People Act 1918; Scotland

Although the features of the Scottish political landscape of the interwar period are fairly clear in the conventional interpretation – Liberal demise, Labour breakthrough, Unionist consolidation – the nature of the process which lay behind the demolition of the former pattern of Liberal dominance was complex.[1] The expansion of the Scottish electorate from 760,000 in 1910 to 2.2 million in 1918 gave politics a greater claim to the description 'democratic' and laid the foundations of many aspects of our modern political system.[2] The increase was greatest in urban industrial areas, where the expansion was of the order of 250%. The achievement of full adult male enfranchisement in the Representation of the People Act 1918 may have had a disproportionate effect on Scotland, since the level of enfranchisement prior to 1918 had been lower.[3] The impact of full adult male enfranchisement was less evident in the 1918 election than in later contests due to the low turnout. The enfranchisement of most women (around 80%) over the age of 30 years added a new factor to elections. The retention of property qualifications for this class of voters, their definition in relation to their husbands and discrimination against unmarried women, were

[1] E.A. Cameron, *Impaled upon a Thistle: Scotland since 1880* (Edinburgh, 2010), 150–74; the period has been subject to interesting new work by Malcolm Petrie: see his 'Public Politics and Traditions of Popular Protest: Demonstrations of the Unemployed in Dundee and Edinburgh, c.1921–1939', *Contemporary British History*, xxvii (2013) 490–513, and ' "Contests of Vital Importance": By-Elections, the Labour Party, and the Reshaping of British Radicalism, 1924–1929', *Historical Journal*, lx (2017), 121–48.

[2] Robert Blackburn, 'Laying the Foundations of the Modern Voting System: The Representation of the People Act 1918', *Parliamentary History*, xxx (2011), 33–52.

[3] I.G.C. Hutchison, *A Political History of Scotland, 1832–1924: Parties, Elections and Issues* (Edinburgh, 1986), 285.

Table 1: *Regional Distribution of Scottish Constituencies, 1885 and 1918*

	Number of seats		Percentage of seats	
	1885	1918	1885	1918
North East	10	9	14.2	12.6
Highlands	9	6	12.9	8.4
Western	23	32	32.8	45.0
Eastern	19	20	27.1	28.2
Southern	9	4	12.9	5.6

Source: Data reworked from *British Parliamentary Election Results 1918–1949*, ed. F.W.S. Craig (2nd edn, 1977).

regressive features and probably favoured the established parties rather than Labour. These problems were dealt with in 1928 when full adult female enfranchisement was granted.[4]

As well as the extension of the franchise in 1918 and 1928, there was significant redistribution. This was a crucial element of the new system, as the determination of the number of voters in each constituency and achieving something closer to parity was vitally important in establishing the equal value of votes across the country. Some progress was made in this regard but there were still wide disparities, and it cannot be said that the 1918 Reform Act achieved 'one vote, one value'.[5] In geographical terms, the beneficiary was Glasgow – which acquired a further eight seats – and the central lowlands. These changes disadvantaged the Liberal Party, as almost all of the 13 seats which were abolished had a Liberal history, and favoured Labour.[6] This essay will develop this theme and look in detail at the way in which the redistribution elements of the 1918 Reform Act changed the political landscape of Scotland. In a number of places, there was a feeling that the government had introduced these changes without sufficient consultation and that the midst of the war was not the most appropriate time to bring in such a major reform of the electoral system.[7] Attention will be given to the arguments that were used in the debates around these changes and, in particular, there will be a focus on the reduction in the number of the Districts of Burghs constituencies, especially in the Highland and Borders regions of Scotland.

If we divide the country into five electoral regions and compare the pattern in 1918 with that in 1885, we can see the shift which took place. Table 1 shows a shift in representation from the rural to the urban, from the west to the east, and from both southern and northern Scotland to the central industrial belt. Gordon Brown has argued that this meant that the 'electoral geography of Scotland ... was for the first time dominated by working-class constituencies'.[8] This also brought representation into line with population to a greater

[4]Michael Dyer, *Capable Citizens and Improvident Democrats: The Scottish Electoral System, 1884–1929* (Aberdeen, 1996), 113–17.

[5]R. Blackburn, *The Electoral System in Britain* (Houndmills, 1995), 113.

[6]Hutchison, *Political History*, 30; Dyer, *Capable Citizens*, 104–12, 118–21.

[7]*Scotsman*, 3 Apr. 1917, p. 4.

[8]G. Brown, 'The Labour Party and Political Change in Scotland, 1918–1929: The Politics of Five Elections', University of Edinburgh PhD, 1982, p. 27.

extent than ever before. The redistribution of 1918 was conducted according to entirely different principles from that of 1885.[9] There was a much clearer assumption of popular representation now that there was full male enfranchisement and most women over the age of 30 years were able to vote.

The boundary commissioners, who had the task of drawing the new electoral map of the UK, were enjoined to create seats with at least 50,000 people but also to pay attention to recognized administrative boundaries.[10] The Districts of Burghs were profoundly reorganised and reduced in number from 13 to six, as will be discussed below.

The first instruction contained a threat to the representation of rural Scotland but the latter provided some comfort. There might well have been a temptation among Unionists, who dominated the coalition government, to apply the rules in a rigorous manner given the recent electoral history of areas such as the Highlands. Interestingly, Sir George Younger, the chairman of the Conservative Party and former Scottish whip, made a plea for a relaxed application of the population formula in the Highlands. He tried to give the impression that this was contrary to his own party interest, in that the Highlands had a radical history. Lying behind this apparent generosity of spirit, however, lay political calculations. Younger may have been worried that reducing Highland representation in favour of the industrial lowlands could benefit the Labour Party. Further, he used older ideas of representation to make his argument. He argued that 'we ought to deal with areas with their characteristics and we ought to deal with historical and separate interests and so on'.[11] This was a conservative argument against popular representation. There were also voices arguing against the application of the arithmetical principle of representation.[12] Arguments in favour of a new constituency for the Western Isles, for example, were expressed in terms of its remoteness from the political centre in London and the special economic and social problems of the islands.[13] Although the electorate in the new seat created there in 1918 was small – with only 18,000 voters (out of a total population of around 60,000 according to the 1911 census) – it had greater geographical coherence and improved the quality of representation of the islands, which had formerly been divided between Inverness-shire (Harris, North Uist, Benbecula, South Uist, Barra) and Ross and Cromarty (Lewis). The boundary commissioners justified this recommendation with reference to 'the character of the constituency and the pursuits of the islanders'.[14]

This redistribution was at least as important as the extension of the franchise. The pattern of representation in Scotland was altered profoundly. The pre-war system had left urban industrial Scotland, where most of the population resided, considerably under-represented, and the rural fringes of the country over-represented. This was a pattern which went back to 1832, and even to 1707, and the anomalies had not been fully dealt with in the 19th

[9]Dyer, *Capable Citizens*, 104–12.

[10]D.J. Rossiter, R.J. Johnston and C.J. Pattie, *The Boundary Commissions: Redrawing the United Kingdom's Map of Parliamentary Constituencies* (Manchester, 1999), 51–61.

[11]Hansard, *Commons Debates*, 5th ser., xciv, col. 645: 11 June 1917.

[12]*Stornoway Gazette*, 18 Feb. 1918, p. 4.

[13]*Stornoway Gazette*, 27 July 1917, p. 3.

[14]*Representation of the People Bill, 1917: Redistribution of Seats: Report of the Boundary Commission (Scotland)*, Cd. 8759 (1917), 6.

century, even by the major redistribution which took place in 1885.[15] The redistribution of 1918 went a considerable way to resolving these issues, because it changed the electoral map of Scotland in a way which clearly benefited the Labour Party by increasing the number of seats in the geographical area of their greatest strength and diminishing the number of seats in the rural fringes of Scotland where they had little support. The results of this change were more clearly seen at the 1922 election, when 19 of the 29 seats won by Labour were in western Scotland. Nearly half (48.1% according to the 1921 census) of the electorate were located there and Labour's share of the vote was 44.1% in this region. The new electoral geography seemed to favour the Labour Party, at least in the 1922 election.

In the 32 seats of the industrial west central region, the Labour Party developed, for the first time, an electoral heartland in Scotland. This was not immediately evident in 1918, as the party won only six seats (Aberdeen North, Edinburgh Central, Glasgow Govan, South Ayrshire, West Fife, and Hamilton). The factors that produced this result were all temporary. They included the defective register, the disenfranchisement of many serving soldiers, the resulting low turnout, and the jingoistic appeal of the coalition government.[16] In comparison with other industrial cities in Britain, it has been argued that 'Glasgow undoubtedly did swing further to Labour in these years than other British cities, and retained its high degree of Labour loyalty through the inter-war years'.[17] In 1922, in an election more representative of the general trends of the period, Labour won nearly 42% of the vote in Glasgow; only Sheffield with 42.5% topped that, and many English industrial cites returned a much lower Labour vote. In Manchester, for example, it was 35%, in Leeds 26.5%, and in Liverpool 25%.[18]

In 1918, the Unionists had won ten seats in Glasgow as part of the coalition. Left to their own devices in 1922 – and it is worth remembering that Scottish MPs were keen to sustain the coalition – they won only four.[19] They did a little better in 1924, adding Partick and Maryhill to the prosperous seats in the south and west of the city in which they tended to do well, but, prior to the onset of renewed coalition politics in 1931, they remained a minority among the Glasgow MPs. In the four elections of the 1920s, after the demise of the coalition and prior to the split of 1931 and the disaffiliation of the Independent Labour Party (ILP) in 1932, the Labour Party won 38 of the 60 contests in Glasgow, the Unionists won 21 and the Liberals only once took a seat – Partick in 1922. This last point is a telling one. There was a strong Liberal tradition in Glasgow; in 1885, the party had taken all seven of the city's seats, and it performed strongly in 1906 and in both of the 1910 elections, although Liberal Unionism had become a significant force in the west of Scotland.[20] However, by the election of 1922, the Liberals were pushed to the geographical peripheries of Scotland in the Highlands and other rural areas.[21]

[15] Dyer, _Capable Citizens_, 11–32, 104–23.

[16] I. McLean, _The Legend of Red Clydeside_ (Edinburgh, 1983), 157.

[17] McLean, _Red Clydeside_, 158.

[18] McLean, _Red Clydeside_, 158–9.

[19] J.J. Smyth, _Labour in Glasgow, 1896–1936: Socialism, Suffrage, Sectarianism_ (East Linton, 2000), 93–4.

[20] J.F. McCaffrey, 'Politics Issues and Developments', in _Glasgow. Vol. 2: 1830–1912_, ed. W.H. Fraser and I. Maver (Manchester, 1996), 186–226.

[21] Brown, 'Labour Party', 499–500.

In the industrial west outside Glasgow, where there were 17 seats after 1918, the picture was more mixed. There were some seats, such as Hamilton, South Ayrshire, Bothwell, Coatbridge, and the surviving Dumbarton District of Burghs, where Labour dominated; another group of seats (North Lanarkshire, Rutherglen, and West Renfrewshire) where they did very well, and overall Labour won 39 out of the 68 contests in the 1920s. There were other seats where the picture was more varied: North Ayrshire and the Ayr District of Burghs were solid Unionist seats; Greenock and Paisley retained Liberal members in the 1920s, and Motherwell, returning tory and communist as well as Labour MPs in the interwar period, was in a category of its own.[22]

Another key element of the context in which the 1918 election was fought was the fact that the franchise had been radically altered compared with December 1910. In the prewar period, only around 60% of adult males – and substantially fewer in the poorer urban areas – were able to vote.[23] After the extension of the franchise in 1918, all adult males were able to vote, as were most women over the age of 30 years. Although the overall level of enfranchisement of women was roughly the same in Scotland (79.2%) as in England (79.5%), women were enfranchised on a slightly different basis. In Scotland it was a householder franchise or a tenancy of non-domestic property of at least £5 annual rental value. The system worked against domestic servants who lived with their employers. There were interesting variations in the extent to which the electorate in particular seats was female and the proportion of females who were enfranchised across the Scottish constituencies. Some seats, such as towns dominated by the textile industries, had higher levels of females in the population but relatively low levels of female enfranchisement because the system disenfranchised single, unmarried working women (who were less frequently occupiers of a dwelling house) constituted a relatively large proportion of the electorate in such towns. There was a direct contrast with towns based on engineering, metalworking or coalmining, where there were relatively few economic opportunities for women. The consequence in these cases was that single females over the age of 30 years and in employment were fewer than in textile towns and a higher proportion of the women over the age of 30 years were married and more likely to qualify as voters.[24]

A further key issue in considering the 1918 Reform Act in the Scottish context is the extent to which grievances about the extent, as well as the geography, of Scottish representation emerged in the debate. This stemmed from the way in which the boundary commissioners charged with the duty of redrawing the boundaries were operating. The number of Irish seats was to remain unaltered and the overall number of seats in Britain was originally intended to remain largely the same. Beyond this, however, there was no reference to Scotland. The commissioners were working on the assumption that 50,000 was the minimum population level for a parliamentary seat. Strict application of this rule would have created some seats of very large area in rural parts of Scotland, not only in the Highlands but also in the Borders.[25] An English MP, James Mason (who sat for Windsor),

[22] R. Duncan, 'Motherwell for Moscow: Walton Newbold, Revolutionary Politics and the Labour Movement in a Lanarkshire Constituency, 1918–22', *Scottish Labour History Journal*, xxviii (1993), 47–70.

[23] Smyth, *Labour in Glasgow*, 208–10.

[24] Dyer, *Capable Citizens*, 113–15; for a good discussion of the economic and employment patterns see R. Rodger, 'Employment, Wages and Poverty in the Scottish Cities, 1841–1914', in *Perspectives of the Scottish City*, ed. G. Gordon (Aberdeen, 1985), 25–63.

[25] Dyer, *Capable Citizens*, 107.

succeeded with an amendment to the instructions to the boundary commissioners to give them flexibility in order that redistribution did not create constituencies of 'inconvenient size and character'. After the redistribution was complete, Scotland had seven of its 71 constituencies below the 50,000 threshold, compared with ten out of 485 in England.[26] This gave the nature of Scottish politics in the post-1918 period a quite distinctive character, but the alternative would have been some huge seats that would have been virtually impossible to represent. The peripheries of Scotland, where most of these seats were located in the period after 1918, tended to have a different electoral history from the central belt. Over the course of the 20th century, most Liberal or Scottish National Party (SNP) representation was outside of the central belt. This could be seen as late as October 1974, when the two main parties received quite a low combined vote and the SNP gained 31.4% of the vote. Most of the eleven seats that they gained were outside the central belt, but they racked up large numbers of votes in central Scotland without gaining any seats. The history of Scottish Liberal representation has also been largely confined to these smaller seats. This, however, masks the fact that this 'periphery' was much smaller than it had been prior to 1918 and this, also, had a profound effect on Scottish electoral history, as will be discussed below.

One scholar has detected the articulation of 'nationalistic arguments' by Liberal and Labour MPs who argued for sustained or increased numbers of Scottish MPs when the case could not be made on 'democratic' grounds.[27] Reviewing the technical debates around the appointment of the boundary commissioners, a range of broad issues emerge. Principal among them was one of the longest running debates in modern Scottish politics, the extent of Scotland's representation in the house of commons and the role of the Scottish MPs. Eugene Wason, the MP for Clackmannan and Kinross, argued that there was a danger that, if Scottish seats were reduced, there could be a growing perception that the Union was not working to Scotland's best advantage:

> We are a separate nationality, we have our own system of laws, our own education system, and our own marriage laws. In Scotland the sexes are equal, and, as a matter of fact, we are constantly getting rebuked by our constituents that we do not act like the Irish party, and then they say we might be able to do something for Scotland. I am not one of those who want to see an independent Scottish party in this House in the same sense as there is an independent Irish party, nor do I begrudge Ireland its separate representation. But in Scotland we feel we are, and have been, somewhat severely neglected.[28]

Wason was a supporter of home rule for Scotland and some of the MPs who supported him in his amendment to ensure that there was no reduction in the number of Scottish MPs were members of the Young Scots Society. One of these, James Mylne Hogge, probably spoiled the case made by his colleague by arguing in an aggressive way that Scotland was always badly treated by the house of commons and that the issue of Scottish representation could not be dealt with until Scotland received its own parliament. He assumed that, if a Scottish

---

[26]Rossiter *et al.*, *Boundary Commissions*, 60.

[27]Dyer, *Capable Citizens*, 107–8.

[28]Hansard, *Commons Debates*, 5th ser., xciv, col. 863: 12 June 1917.

parliament was established, then that would end Scottish representation at Westminster. When Sir George Younger exclaimed 'Heaven forbid', Hogge replied:

> what we want is a Parliament in Scotland for our own affairs. If you give us that, we do not care a straw how many members come to Westminster. You can get rid of us altogether if you give us a Parliament of our own to deal with Scottish affairs.[29]

This is an issue that has echoed through every debate that has touched on the idea of Scottish home rule. It is mostly known today as the West Lothian question, after the constituency of the late Tam Dalyell, who articulated it incessantly in the debates over devolution in the 1974–9 period. Even in 1918, however, the question was not new, and it had figured in debates over Gladstonian home rule schemes in the 1880s and 1890s. As a devolutionist, Hogge was unusual in answering the question so unequivocally and in assuming that Scottish MPs would withdraw from Westminster in the eventuality of a parliament being established in Edinburgh. He deprecated the 'arithmetical' approach to the settlement of the representation question and argued that, if some Scottish seats were to be sacrificed in the redistribution, then the university seats were prime candidates for abolition. He called them 'undemocratic' and argued that the members who were elected for these seats were unrepresentative of Scotland.[30] Arguments were put forward to defend the relative overrepresentation of Scotland in the house of commons at this time: the distance from the centre of power in London, the sparsely-populated nature of some of the constituencies, and the dangers inherent in reducing the representation of the rural and agricultural areas in favour of the urban industrial areas. These points will be pursued in more depth later in this essay through consideration of the redistribution in the Highland and the Borders regions of Scotland.

It is interesting that the major reform that took place in 1918 has not attracted the same attention as the acts of 1832, 1868, and 1884–5.[31] In many ways, the electoral landscape was changed more profoundly in 1918 than on these earlier occasions. Scotland's system of representation went back to the Union of 1707 and, although the extent of Scottish representation in the house of commons was extended from 45 members then to the 70 seats that existed in December 1910 at the last election before the Great War, there were many continuities. Except for the addition of university seats in 1868, the essential structure of representation remained the same: the historic Scottish counties were represented, although some of them were divided in 1868 and 1885; the Scottish Burghs were represented, sometimes in groups or 'Districts'; although the larger ones – Glasgow and Edinburgh, for example – were divided into constituencies of roughly equal size.[32] There were strong links

---

[29] Hansard, *Commons Debates*, 5th ser., xciv, col. 871: 12 June 1917.

[30] Hansard, *Commons Debates*, 5th ser., xciv, cols 870–1: 12 June 1917; those arguing for the retention of seats in the Highlands were also critical of the retention of university representation, albeit at a reduced level: *Inverness Courier*, 20 July 1917, p. 2.

[31] W. Ferguson, 'The Reform Act (Scotland) of 1832: Intention and Effect', *Scottish Historical Review*, xlv (1966), 105–14; M. Dyer, 'Mere Detail and Machinery: The Great Reform Act and the Effects of Redistribution on Scottish Representation, 1832–68', *Scottish Historical Review*, lxii (1983), 17–34; I.M.M. MacPhail, 'The Highland Elections of 1884–1886', *Transactions of the Gaelic Society of Inverness*, l (1976–8), 369–92.

[32] M. Dyer, 'Burgh Districts and the Representation of Scotland, 1707–1983', *Parliamentary History*, xv (1996), 287–307.

here with the historic local administrative entities of Scotland. Some of these 'Districts' were quite coherent and composed of small Burghs that were reasonably close together. The Leith District included Leith, Portobello, and Musselburgh, all on the coast near Edinburgh. Others, however, were very different. The Ayr District, for example, included Ayr and Irvine, both in Ayrshire, and Campbeltown, Inveraray, and Oban, situated across the large Highland county of Argyll. Even taking into account the extent to which an MP was expected to be present in his constituency in this period, this seat would have presented a challenge. In 1918, the sitting MP was Sir George Younger and, during the debates on the bill, he described this seat as being 'divided by the Atlantic' and talked of the competing, even antagonistic, interests of the different Burghs, especially around the fishing industry.[33] The Wick District of Burghs, represented by the secretary for Scotland, Robert Munro, stretched from Cromarty on the 'Black Isle', just north of Inverness, through Dingwall and Tain in the eastern part of Ross-shire, to Wick in the northerly county of Caithness, and then to Kirkwall, the main town in Orkney. Other seats were composed of more closely-situated Burghs, but were simply awkward in other ways. This was true, for example, of the Stirling District, which was composed of the two major, but very different, towns of Stirling and Dunfermline, together with the smaller Burghs of Culross, Inverkeithing, and South Queensferry, which were spread across the north and south banks of the Forth. The politics of this seat, represented from 1868 to 1908 by Sir Henry Campbell-Bannerman, the Liberal Party leader from 1898 to 1908, presented difficulties in that the Liberals in Dunfermline, which had a radical tradition, behaved very differently from their counterparts in Stirling. This was resolved in 1918 when Stirling and Dunfermline were each made the centre of new Districts of Burghs.

The boundary commissioners' working assumptions posed a very severe threat to the Scottish Districts of Burghs and, although some press comment argued that their disappearance would 'occasion no regret', this was an issue of some significance.[34] The commissioners conceded that any Burgh with a population of more than 70,000 should survive and that a two-member Burgh (a single constituency electing two MPs, such as Dundee) should not be divided or lose members if it had a population of more than 120,000. They aimed to reorganise the Burgh Districts so that all the Burghs in a District were in the same county. Where Districts were abolished, the Burghs were included in their surrounding county; for example, Dingwall was absorbed into Ross-shire. The outcome was the reduction of the number of Districts constituencies from 13 to six, and the creation of more logical and geographically-coherent groupings (see Table 2).

There was a strong electoral implication in this change. In the 13 pre-1918 Districts, there had been a strong tradition of Liberal voting; in December 1910, only the Ayr District was held by the Conservatives and the St Andrews District by the Liberal Unionists (and the latter had been Liberal as recently as January 1910). The absorption by East Fife of the St Andrews District was a significant factor in Asquith's defeat in 1918, although the county seat was won by Liberals or National Liberals at each interwar election with the exception of a Unionist victory in 1924.[35] All of the others were represented by Liberals, although Leith Burghs was gained by a Conservative in a by-election in 1914. However, of the six

[33] Hansard, *Commons Debates*, 5th ser., xciv, col. 646: 11 June 1917.

[34] *Scotsman*, 1 Feb. 1917, p. 6.

[35] S.R. Ball, 'Asquith's Decline and the General Election of 1918', *Scottish Historical Review*, lxi (1982), 44–61.

Table 2: *Districts and Constituent Burghs*

District	Constituent Burghs
Ayr	Ayr, Ardrossan, Irvine. Prestwick, Saltcoats, Troon
Dumbarton	Dumbarton, Clydebank
Dunfermline	Dunfermline, Cowdenbeath, Inverkeithing, Lochgelly
Kirkcaldy	Kirkcaldy, Buckhaven, Methil, Burntisland, Dysart, Kinghorn
Montrose	Montrose, Arbroath, Brechin, Forfar, Inverbervie
Stirling	Stirling, Falkirk, Grangemouth

surviving Districts, in 1918, Ayr was held by the Conservatives, another four seats were held by Lloyd George Liberals and only one seat, Stirling, was won by an Independent Liberal. Looking at the interwar period as a whole, only in the Montrose District was there any tradition of Liberal representation in the interwar period, with victories for that party in 1923, 1924, and 1929. Overall, the six post-1918 Burgh Districts were another repository of support for the Labour Party over the interwar period. Aside from the Ayr and Montrose Districts, which never returned a Labour MP between the wars, Labour found these new seats relatively happy hunting grounds. Dumbarton (David Kirkwood) and Dunfermline were held by Labour MPs at each election from 1922 to 1935. In the cases of Kirkcaldy, and Stirling and Falkirk, there were four elections at which Labour MPs were returned, one of the exceptions being the special case of 1931.[36] In some ways, the abolition of the pre-1918 Districts was the most controversial result of the redistribution in the 1918 Reform Act, and it deserves to be discussed in more depth.

The general tone of historical discussion about the 1918 Reform Act has been dominated by its apparent democratisation of the UK's electoral system and, where caveats have been noted, they are largely centred on the failure to abolish plural voting, introduce proportional representation or a fully gender-equal franchise.[37] These points are valid, if the act is to be tested against the measure of a fully-democratic system, and they were voiced at the time. One northern newspaper with a radical Liberal tradition noted, at an early point in the process, that, although the scheme was a 'step forward', the reforms meant that 'we are still a long way from giving every adult British citizen a vote without reference to residence or property qualification'.[38] There were other worries hidden in the debate over the bill in its Scottish context and many of them can be explored through discussion of the abolition of the Districts of Burghs. The defenders of these seats were, of course, trying to protect their own interests, but the arguments that they used tell us much about Scottish political culture in the early 20th century and at a time of great change. The first argument that was used was that these were very old seats and represented a continuity to pre-Union Scotland and, therefore, to something genuinely 'Scottish'. This was not a period in which there was a particular romanticisation of Scotland's political system before 1707; indeed,

[36] Dyer, 'Burgh Districts', 304.
[37] David Powell, *British Politics, 1910–1935: The Crisis of the Party System* (Abingdon, 2004), 87.
[38] *Highland News*, 3 Feb. 1917, p. 4.

academic historiography tended to be rather dismissive of the Scottish parliament and other institutions, regarding them as corrupt, unsophisticated and dominated by the aristocracy.[39] Outside this body of literature there may have been a greater affection for an older Scotland. The town clerk of Kirkcaldy in Fife, resisting the addition of Methil and Buckhaven (which contained large numbers of working-class voters, especially coalminers), argued that the extant Kirkcaldy District had survived unchanged since 1707.[40] A similar point was made in the south of Scotland, where the Dumfries and Border Burghs were facing oblivion, and one local newspaper noted that the representation of the smaller towns of Scotland had been a central feature of the pre-Union system in that one of the 'estates' of the unicameral Scottish parliament were the Burgh and Shire Commissioners.[41]

If one argument used against the break-up of Burgh Districts was based on history, another was predicated on economics. The boundary commissioners were enjoined to keep industrial and agricultural areas separate in their work on county constituencies, but the diversity of economic interests in the Burghs made this more difficult to use as a basis for reorganisation. Nevertheless, it was resorted to by those who defended threatened Districts. In Fife, for example, in the Kirkcaldy Burghs there was an argument about the extent to which the mining areas of Buckhaven and Methil, which had 'special and peculiar problems', according to Kirkcaldy town council, would change the nature of the seat. In a similar argument, the town clerk of Dunfermline objected to his Burgh being grouped with Cowdenbeath and Lochgelly, both dominated by coalmining, and thought that the textile and service town of Dunfermline would be better grouped with the neighbouring and growing town of Rosyth.[42] In the event the new seat was constituted as Dunfermline, Cowdenbeath, and Lochgelly. There was an interesting three-sided contest there in 1918, which was won by a coalition Liberal candidate, but in 1922, a two-sided contest saw a victory for the Labour candidate and he held the seat until 1945.[43] In the north-east of Scotland, an argument was made by the 'leading citizens of Fraserburgh' that there should be a new District created composed of fishing ports from Peterhead to Buckie around the Aberdeenshire and Banffshire coast. No such seat was created.[44] Thus the antiquity and local identity of these seats was deployed in an attempt to retain their presence in the new Scottish electoral system after 1832.

If history was one argument that was used to defend the District of Burghs seats, another was related to the perceived modernity of the immediate post-war moment. Several MPs argued that this was a time of unprecedented change and that to introduce a new system

---

[39]See the essays published in the *Glasgow Herald* to mark the 200th anniversary of the Union of 1707 and gathered into a volume entitled *The Union of 1707: A Survey of Events by Various Writers with an Introduction by Peter Hume Brown and the Text of the Articles of Union* (Glasgow, 1907).

[40]*Fifeshire Advertiser*, 4 Aug. 1917, p. 2.

[41]*Dumfries and Galloway Standard*, 21 July 1917, p. 2; historical arguments were also adduced in early marshalling of the arguments to be used in defending the existence of the Inverness District, *Highland News*, 28 Apr. 1917, p. 5, and a petition prepared by the town clerk of Inverness and sent to parliament in the summer of 1917 noted that the District had sent a member to the UK parliament since 1707, *Inverness Courier*, 10 July 1917, p. 7.

[42]*Fifeshire Advertiser*, 21 July 1917, p. 4; 4 Aug. 1917, p. 2

[43]*Dunfermline Press*, 4 Jan. 1919, p. 4; Hutchison, *Political History*, 282–3.

[44]*Aberdeen Evening Express*, 19 July 1917, p. 2; the Unionist agent in Wick made similar arguments about the neglect of the fishing industry in his defence of the Wick Burghs and the separate county of Caithness, see *Northern Ensign*, 31 July 1917, p. 4.

before the demographic and social effects of the war were clear would be a mistake. As was noted above, local politicians in Dunfermline argued that a combination of that town and Rosyth, its massively-expanded neighbouring naval base and dockyard, would make more sense than hitching Dunfermline to two mining towns. A similar argument was made with reference to Gretna in the south-west of Scotland, during the discussion on the Dumfries Burghs.[45] In both these cases there had been massive expansion in the war years. Gretna was the site of a huge explosives factory which employed thousands of women during the war years. Rosyth was a rapidly-developing new town on the garden city principle, as the local authority and the admiralty sought to house the population associated with the naval base and dockyard. George Younger worried that it would be a mistake to 'wipe out' the Dumfries Burghs when a perfectly good constituency could be created in Gretna and Annan, especially after the government had spent massively to build up the factory.[46] The MP for Dunfermline, the pacifist, Arthur Ponsonby (who lost the new seat in the 1918 general election), supported Younger in arguing that Rosyth was a special case and that the 1914 level of population was quite the wrong baseline to use, as the town had expanded so much since then and was likely to continue to grow.[47]

In the north of Scotland, the reaction against the changes embodied in the 1917 bill, and largely enacted in 1918, was very marked indeed. The electoral history of the Highlands was quite striking. The expansion of the electorate there had been very considerable in 1885, and the political results were almost unique in a British context, in that the new electors used their new rights to reject the traditional parties and elect a series of 'Crofter' MPs at the elections of 1885 and 1886.[48] Although these were either neutered and drawn back into the Liberal fold or defeated in the elections of the 1890s, the tradition of apparent radicalism was quite strong and was reasserted from 1906. In the 1910 and 1918 elections, there were candidates in Argyll, Inverness, Ross and Cromarty, and the Western Isles, under the banner of the 'Highland Land League', a reference to the politics of the 1880s. None of them made much impact but their presence is worth noting. Although the new seat of the Western Isles was created out of insular parts of Ross-shire and Inverness-shire, the Highlands lost three other seats, due to the absorption of the Inverness and Wick Districts of Burghs into their surrounding county seats, and the amalgamation of Caithness and Sutherland into a single seat: the latter was a long-standing proposal which had been headed off in 1868.[49]

Radical opinion in the Highlands was confident that the new seats would still return Liberal MPs, and this did turn out to be the case in the interwar period, although the Western Isles elected a Labour MP in 1935.[50] It was noted that seats like Inverness-shire

[45] *Dumfries and Galloway Standard*, 21 July 1917, p. 2; J. Minett, 'Government Sponsorship of New Towns: Gretna, 1915–1917 and its Implications', in *Scottish Housing in the Twentieth Century*, ed. R. Rodger (Leicester, 1989), 104–24.

[46] Hansard, *Commons Debates*, 5th ser., xciv, col. 877: 12 June 1917.

[47] Hansard, *Commons Debates*, 5th ser., xciv, cols 884–5: 12 June 1917; the Rosyth case was an interesting one in that Dunfermline had extended its Burgh boundaries to include the new town, making it one of the biggest towns in Scotland by area.

[48] J.P.D. Dunbabin, 'Electoral Reforms and their Outcome in the United Kingdom', in *Later Victorian Britain, 1867–1900*, ed. T.R. Gourvish and A. O'Day (1988), 314–15; MacPhail, 'Highland Elections', 369–92.

[49] M. Dyer, *Men of Property and Intelligence: The Scottish Electoral System prior to 1884* (Aberdeen, 1986), 106.

[50] E.A. Cameron, ' "Rival Foundlings": The Ross and Cromarty By-Election, 1 February 1936', *Historical Research*, lxxxi (2008), 507–30.

were vast in area and the difficulties which candidates faced due to the 'absence of the means of easy communication, and to the mountainous ranges and stormy seas that divide one District from another, and make travel slow and tedious'. This was especially relevant when the proposal that the election be held within eight days of the nomination of the candidates is taken into consideration.[51] The lack of community of interest between Caithness and Sutherland was noted, they were deemed to be as different as a Welsh and an English county in 'race, language, traditions, customs, sentiments'.[52] A variety of themes in Highland history were mobilised in opposition to these proposals on the assumption that in this, as in so many other areas of politics and policy, there was a case for special treatment for the region.[53] Far from being seen as a democratising influence, the redistribution was seen as an attack on the Highlands for which the government had no mandate; this was seen as especially grievous when so many men from the Highlands were fighting 'to preserve our freedom'. Opponents of the scheme thought that the government was unduly distracted from the more important task of winning the war and that the redistribution was inappropriate and manipulative.[54] Newspapers across the political spectrum noted that the context of Highland depopulation ought to be considered, if that was the basis on which its representation was to be reduced. Highland towns were small because of 'misgovernment since the days of the "Forty-Five"' and:

> Depopulation started with the butchery of the Highlanders at Culloden by hired Germans. Then a foreign land system was thrust upon us … In a couple of generations it culminated in the Clearances, and if it has eased off since it is only because there are fewer victims left. It is not the existing population that ought to be the basis of representation in the Highlands but the latent or potential population. Because of what the Highlands has suffered, and is suffering, we ought not to have our voice stifled; we ought to have a larger say.[55]

Another newspaper argued that the Highlands were not being treated in a manner consistent with Ireland. Irish over-representation was seen as the result of an unwillingness to punish the Irish people for the mistakes of historical British policy in Ireland, and that there were grounds for dealing with the Highlands in a similar manner.[56] In a variant of the argument used in the discussions over Rosyth and Gretna, the Highland Land Settlement Association wrote to the Speaker of the house of commons arguing that the current population levels in the Highlands would likely be altered very significantly by the process of

---

[51]There were genuine difficulties here, not least in the case of a winter election, such as the Inverness-shire by-election of 1954.

[52]*Highland News*, 3 Feb. 1917, p. 4; 28 July, 1917, p. 4; see also *Inverness Courier*, 2 Feb. 1917, p. 3, and *Northern Ensign*, 31 July 1917, p. 4, for similar arguments.

[53]E.A. Cameron, 'The Scottish Highlands as a Special Policy Area, 1886 to 1965', *Rural History*, viii (1997), 195–215.

[54]*Northern Ensign*, 24 July 1917, p. 4.

[55]*Highland News*, 28 July 1917, p. 4; the same edition, however, carried (at p. 5) a letter from 'Unafraid', who argued that the 'deer forest wastes, ornamental parks and grounds "preserved" from national use' ought not to be represented in parliament to the same extent as 'Busy hives of humanity'; the editor published this below a headline of 'Disenfranchising the deer'.

[56]*Northern Times*, 1 Mar. 1918, p. 2.

land settlement and the demands of food production, both of which would repopulate the north of Scotland.[57] The strong levels of recruiting allegedly evident in the Highlands was also used to argue against the proposed redistribution. As campaigners against the amalgamation of Caithness and Sutherland argued: 'The government took the men away to fight for the Empire and now they want to blot us out as a separate constituency.'[58] This was also a point made by Alpheus C. Morton, the MP for Sutherland; in a letter to the boundary commissioners in August 1917, he contrasted the 'loyal and remarkable' wartime service of the people of Sutherland with their 'harsh' treatment by the boundary commissioners.[59] It is, perhaps, not surprising that we should find opposition to redistribution in an area, such as the Highlands, which stood to lose seats from the process. The depth of the opposition and the range of arguments that were deployed in the interests defending the seats slated for abolition is quite striking and provides evidence that this apparently democratising moment was not always seen as such.

The other areas of Scotland that stood to lose from the redistribution, to an even greater extent than the Highlands in fact, were the Borders and the south-west. In this case, the Border Burghs and the Dumfries Burghs were under threat, while the number of county seats was to be reduced to three – Galloway, Dumfries, and a single constituency of Roxburgh and Selkirk. Berwickshire was to be part of a new seat with Haddington, and Peebles was to be merged with South Midlothian, another mining constituency. This was very unpopular across southern Scotland.[60] The principal issue that was debated in this case was the awkward marriages of counties and Burghs with different industrial structures and socio-economic backgrounds. As in the Highlands, there was a feeling that the redistribution would give too much power to the industrial areas of Scotland and to Glasgow, and the inclusion of the Burghs in the county seats would mean that the constituencies in the south of Scotland would no longer be ones in which 'agriculture is the paramount interest'. It was also pointed out that the new Galloway constituency would be large, stretching 80 miles east to west from the River Nith to the Irish Sea and about 65 miles, from south to north, from the Solway Firth to the borders of Ayrshire. Even compared with the Highlands, which were relatively well penetrated by railways, this was an area with poor communications facilities and would be very difficult for an MP to represent.[61] In response to these difficulties, local political representatives tried to create a scheme for combining the two Burgh seats to produce a constituency of more than 70,000 population. This was controversial in Selkirk town council as some bailies argued that there was little community of interest between the agricultural service centres in the Dumfries District and the textile industries in the Hawick District and that this proposal would not result in a rational constituency.[62] The

[57] *Northern Times*, 17 May 1918, p. 3; this repopulation did not occur, although there was an extensive land settlement following an act of 1919.

[58] *Northern Times*, 26 July 1917, p. 5; 2 Aug. 1917, p. 5; see also *Northern Ensign*, 7 Aug. 1917, p. 4.

[59] *Northern Times*, 23 Aug. 1917, p. 5; see also letter from 'Landholder' from Halladale, Caithness, *Northern Ensign*, 14 Aug. 1917, p. 4, and from H. Henderson who simply condemned the redistribution as 'unpatriotic', *Northern Ensign*, 21 Aug. 1917, p. 4.

[60] *Southern Reporter*, 8 Feb. 1917, p. 6; *Dumfries and Galloway Standard*, 24 Feb. 1917, p. 6; Dyer, *Capable Citizens*, 109–10.

[61] *Dumfries and Galloway Standard*, 21 July 1917, p. 2.

[62] *Southern Reporter*, 12 July 1917, p. 6; some evidence of the strength of feeling aroused can be gauged by bailie Crichton's doubts that 'the majority of the inhabitants of Dumfries were really Scots'.

town councils of Hawick, Selkirk, and Galashiels were hostile to this scheme and it went no further.[63] There were wider questions raised about the possibility of an MP representing a constituency which combined agriculture and industry. One newspaper questioned the desirability:

> of placing upon one man the duty of attempting to represent adequately and efficiently such widely differing interests. The factory and the farm hold equally important positions in the internal economy of the district and both are entitled to send to parliament men whom they believe will best represent them respectively.[64]

Indeed, in the case of divided counties, the boundary commissioners had been enjoined to separate industrial and farming areas.[65] As in the Highlands, there were criticisms of the government for introducing such a wide-ranging scheme of redistribution without an electoral mandate and at a time 'when the public mind is on the great issues of the war'.[66]

A group of MPs from the south of Scotland combined to write to the boundary commissioners to argue against the scheme of redistribution. They referred to the long distances involved in representing constituencies of sparse population and argued that the new constituencies would make these problems much worse. They explicitly compared their area of Scotland with the Highlands, which, they argued, had been treated much more leniently. In their view, this was contrary to the instructions given to the boundary commissioners to avoid the creation of constituencies 'inconvenient in size or character'.[67] The boundary commissioners prepared two memoranda in response to this letter. They noted that the MPs defined the Highlands as stretching from Shetland and Orkney in the north to Argyll in the South and encompassed six seats. These seats had an average population of 50,842, compared with the seats in the south of Scotland, stretching from Berwickshire in the east to the new seat of Galloway in the south-west, with an average population of 68,666. On this basis, John Barran and his colleagues appeared to have a point, although there were only four persons per 100 acres in the Highlands, compared with ten persons in the south. The commissioners then took a slightly disingenuous line of argument. They added Perthshire and Kinross-shire, Moray and Nairn, Banff, Aberdeenshire and Kincardineshire and, particularly unconvincingly, the city of Aberdeen. This allowed them to build a comparison between the south of Scotland and the 'Highland and Northern Counties as a whole'. This brought the average populations per seat closer together: 68,666 in the south and 59,648 in the north. This was deemed to be a 'not undue disparity ... when all the relevant circumstances are taken into account' and they went on to argue that 'absolute

[63] *Southern Reporter*, 26 July 1917, p. 6.
[64] *Southern Reporter*, 26 July 1917, p. 4.
[65] Dyer, *Capable Citizens*, 10.
[66] *Southern Reporter*, 26 July 1917, p. 4; 30 Aug. 1917, p. 4.
[67] Edinburgh, National Records of Scotland [hereafter cited as NRS], HH41/1317: circular letter, 16 Aug. 1917. This letter was signed by John Barran, Hew Dalrymple, John W. Gulland, John D. Hope, John Jardine, Donald MacLean, Gilbert McMicking, P.A. Molteno, and H.J. Tennant. This group did not put forward an alternative scheme, but John Gulland later wrote to the Speaker with two five-seat schemes for the south of Scotland: see NRS, HH41/1317: Gulland to the Speaker, 8 Sept. 1917; he began his letter by recognizing the difficulties of redistributing in Scotland, especially the south, but argued that Scotland was being relatively badly treated compared with England and Wales and that the Scottish university seat could be traded for further territorial seats in order to settle this grievance.

equality of population – even if desirable – is unattainable under any scheme of parliamentary representation which has regard to existing administrative areas'. It was further noted that the constituencies in the Highlands were much further from Westminster and the internal communications were 'incomparably more difficult' in the north. These were, of course, arguments used by Highland MPs to argue against the redistribution.[68] The difference in tone between the arguments used by representatives of the south of Scotland compared with the Highlands is quite striking. The emotional and historical arguments used by the Highlanders was of a piece with the tone of debate about the region since the 1880s. Nevertheless, when comparing the two cases, the evidence of the boundary commissioners' response to the former suggests that it was broadly geographical and demographic arguments and recognition of the difficulty of travelling and communicating in the large Highland seats that were crucial in securing the relatively greater representation of the Highlands compared with the south of Scotland.

This essay has attempted to show that the redistribution inherent in the Representation of the People Act of 1918 had an important effect on the Scottish political landscape. The effect of these changes on the electoral map of Scotland requires some comment in conclusion. Many of the features of that landscape, which had helped to sustain Liberal domination of Scottish politics since 1832, were swept away. Alongside important social and economic changes and the extension of the electorate, a new landscape was formed that provided territory across which the Labour and Scottish Unionist Parties could stride. The Liberal Party declined as an electoral force but its legacy survived in a number of aspects of post-war Scotland. The progressive Unionism which was such a feature of the Scottish scene in the 1920s and 1930s owed more than a little to elements of Liberalism from the late 19th and early 20th centuries. The Labour Party, which broke through into the mainstream of Scottish politics in 1922, can be seen as an outgrowth of radical Liberalism, rather than an alternative to it. Towards the end of the decade, Scottish nationalism began to emerge in partisan form. Although it was not until the Second World War that it had any electoral effect, its central demand for Scottish home rule was one which would have been recognizable to Liberals who had been involved in the Young Scots Society (and who were involved in the debates reviewed in this essay), or to a slightly older generation who had founded the Scottish Home Rule Association in the 1880s. Nevertheless, the novel elements of the political system of the 1920s should not be denied. New forms of politics were required in order to appeal to a truly mass electorate, organised into constituencies of a type quite different from those which date from the redistribution of the 1880s. The electoral geography of Scotland caught up, at last it might be said, with the demographic geography of the nation. The urban-industrial western region punched its weight and this made an important contribution to the changed nature of politics in the post-war period.

[68] NRS, HH41/1317: memoranda by the boundary commissioners, 31 Aug., 10 Oct. 1917.

The Impact of the 1918 Reform Act in Ireland

JOHN COAKLEY

Ironically, the Representatiion of the People Act of 1918, the penultimate measure in democratising the electoral franchise in the United Kingdom, had the effect not of modernising and consolidating political structures there but rather of paving the way for the kingdom's break-up.
The near-threefold increase in the size of the Irish electorate opened the door to radical political forces, permitting the newly-minted republican-nationalist Sinn Féin party to win an
overwhelming majority of Irish seats. Since the Sinn Féin members refused to attend parliament
in Westminster and instead sought to establish an Irish republic, this effectively ended southern
Irish representation in the house of commons. The act also facilitated a tightening of the Unionist grip in the northern part of the island, leading to the partition of Ireland in 1921: Northern
Ireland continued as a near-independent component of the United Kingdom, while the rest
of Ireland left the United Kingdom in 1922. The essay explores the dynamics of this process,
considering five matters in turn: the Irish political context within which the 1918 Reform Act
was located; the nature of the act's provisions as they applied to Ireland; the outcome in Ireland
of the first general election under the act; the extent to which this outcome was conditioned by
the terms of the Reform Act; and the longer-term consequences of the act. It concludes that
the significance of the act for Ireland lay more in the domain of ideology than of constitutional
law, given its symbolic importance for later generations of Irish nationalist activists.

Keywords: constitution; electoral reform; general elections; Ireland; Irish nationalism; Northern
Ireland; parliament; representation; Representation of the People Act 1918; suffrage

1

A distinguished American professor of political science observed of the Representation
of the People Act of 1918 that it was 'a measure which history may pronounce more
momentous than any other passed by the British Parliament since the beginning of the
present war'.[1] The 1918 Reform Act joined the ranks of its celebrated predecessors of 1832,
1867, and 1884, as a landmark event in British constitutional and parliamentary history.
Perhaps surprisingly, though, its significance seems to have been assessed in a much more
low-key way by observers in the neighbouring island: studies of the seismic results of the
December 1918 election in Ireland largely ignore the significance of the Reform Act.[2] Yet,

---

[1] Frederic A. Ogg, 'The British Representation of the People Act', *American Political Science Review*, xii (1918),
498.

[2] A comprehensive historiographical review of the impact of the Reform Act on the election results in Ireland
would be impossible in an essay of this kind, but the range of typical approaches may easily be illustrated; e.g.,
Diarmuid Ferriter, *The Transformation of Ireland* (2004), 183–4, briefly notes the effects of a trebling of the Irish
electorate; Michael Laffan, *The Resurrection of Ireland: The Sinn Féin Party, 1916–1923* (Cambridge, 1999), 151–68,
notes the impact of the Redistribution Act on the outcome in Ulster; and F.S.L. Lyons, *John Dillon: A Biography*

for Irish republican activists, it was not just the election that mattered, but the fact that the voters were representative of the Irish people. This became important as a perceived legitimation of republican goals and methods. Thus, as pragmatic and traditionalist members of the Provisional Irish Republican Army (IRA) and Sinn Féin lined up for a battle over the future of their movement in 1986, an elderly veteran of the war of independence of 1919–21, Tom Maguire, intervened on the traditionalist side with an appeal for fidelity to the vote of the Irish people almost 70 years earlier:

> The Irish Republic, proclaimed in arms in Easter Week 1916 and established by the democratic majority vote of the people in the general election of 1918, has been defended by Irish republicans for several generations. Many have laid down their lives in that defence. Many others have suffered imprisonment and torture. I am confident the cause so nobly served will yet triumph.[3]

The significance of this interpretation will be addressed later, but first the contribution of the 1918 Reform Act needs to be considered. The present essay aims to revisit this issue by exploring the impact of the 1918 Reform Act on Irish political development. It begins by outlining the distinctive nature of the Irish constitutional and political experience, one aspect of which was that franchise law, like much other legislation, had followed a path that was a variant on, and not an extension of, that in Great Britain. It continues by looking at the implications of the act for voters and elections in Ireland. A critical test of the act, the outcome in the 1918 general election, is then examined. Following an assessment of the extent to which the Irish election outcome can be traced back to the 1918 Reform Act, the longer-term political consequences of the act are discussed.

2

The distinctiveness of the Irish position in respect of the electoral provisions which had evolved by 1918 may be seen in three domains. First, Ireland had remained a constitutionally distinct part of the United Kingdom, even after the union of 1800, in this respect mirroring the separate status of Scotland following the Union of 1707; this had implications for a wide range of areas, not least electoral law. Second, Irish social structure was marked by a sharper division between the ruling landed class and the subordinate peasant and labouring classes than was the case in England; and, crucially, this overlapped substantially with religious denominational differences. Third, the question of Ireland's membership of the Union was of growing importance and unpredictability, with the status quo challenged both in parliament by the Irish Nationalist Party (whose central demand was for home rule, or devolution) and outside parliament by the subterranean militant republican movement represented by the Irish Republican Brotherhood (IRB), which aimed for a complete break with Great Britain. The dominance of the Nationalist Party was illustrated by its electoral track record: it was comfortably able to see off such occasional challenges as were offered

---

2 *(continued)* (1968), 444–55, and Joseph Lee, *Ireland 1910–1985: Politics and Society* (Cambridge, 1989), 40, make no reference to the effects of the Reform Act.

[3] Robert W. White, *Provisional Irish Republicans: An Oral and Interpretive History* (Westport, CT, 1993), 148.

to it by Sinn Féin, a militant nationalist party formed in 1908, but rather less radical than the IRB.[4]

Ireland's constitutional distinctiveness under the Union was reflected most obviously in the continuing existence of an Irish government, headed ceremonially by the lord lieutenant, but with the chief secretary gradually emerging as the principal political officer in the course of the 19th century.[5] Irish electoral law also followed a separate trajectory: alongside the 'great' English Reform Acts of 1832 and 1867 were separate, but much less far-reaching, Irish Reform Acts in 1832 and 1868, as well as an additional act in 1850 that was a response to the collapse in the Irish electorate following the famine.[6] But significant differences between English, Scottish and Irish electoral law continued in respect of franchise provisions, valuation systems, and registration arrangements. These came to an end only in the 1880s: a substantial standardisation of electoral provisions was brought about by the Reform Act of 1884, together with the Parliamentary Registration (Ireland) Act 1885; and the Redistribution of Seats Act 1885, ensured a more even distribution of MPs within (but not between) the three jurisdictions.[7]

When the enfranchised section of the population is drawn only from one section of the community, as is the case when the threshold of eligibility rests on property, wealth or other such criteria, its relationship to the wider society acquires great importance, especially where there are elements of a cultural or ethnic division of labour – where the dominant social groups come from a fundamentally different background from the subordinate ones. Given the history of the relationship between protestants and catholics in Ireland, with the former maintaining a privileged position long after the Catholic Emancipation Act of 1829, it is not surprising that structural inequalities of this kind survived through the 19th century. The census of 1861, the first to provide reliable data on religious affiliation, showed that, while the male labour force was 78% catholic, the proportion of catholics dropped as occupational status rose: catholics accounted for only 42% of the learned professions, 41% of landed proprietors, 30% of 'gentlemen' and 13% of the titled nobility.[8] Since the right to vote depended on social status, it is likely that the relatively small electorate was disproportionately protestant. While there are no statistics that allow us to examine this systematically, windows have occasionally opened up, allowing a partial view of the position. Thus, we know that in Dundalk Borough the proportion of protestants in 1861 was 17.5%, but the proportion of protestant voters there in 1859 was 35.5%; and in Sligo Borough at the same time, while the population was only 21.7% protestant, the electorate was 52.6% protestant.[9]

---

[4]The original object of Sinn Féin was to establish a dual monarchy that would link Ireland to Britain on the model of the Austro-Hungarian *Ausgleich* of 1867, but the party's early electoral successes were confined to local elections, as in Dublin; see Richard P. Davis, *Arthur Griffith and Non-Violent Sinn Fein* (Dublin, 1974).

[5]See K. Theodore Hoppen, *Governing Hibernia: British Politicians and Ireland 1800–1921* (Oxford, 2016); *The Irish Lord Lieutenancy c. 1541–1922*, ed. Peter Gray and Olwen Purdue (Dublin, 2012).

[6]On the effects of the 1832 Irish act, see Norman Gash, *Politics in the Age of Peel: A Study in the Technique of Parliamentary Representation 1830–1850* (1953), 90; on 1850, see G. Locker Lampson, *A Consideration of the State of Ireland in the Nineteenth Century* (1907), 300; and on 1868, see Brian Mercer Walker, 'The Irish Electorate, 1868–1915', *Irish Historical Studies*, xviii (1973), 359–61.

[7]Walker, 'Irish Electorate', 361–6.

[8]John Coakley, 'Religion, National Identity and Political Change in Modern Ireland', *Irish Political Studies*, xvii (2002), 11.

[9]Derived from K. Theodore Hoppen, *Elections, Politics, and Society in Ireland 1832–1885* (Oxford, 1984), 37.

At the political level, there was a sharp difference between Ireland and the other parts of the United Kingdom. In the early 19th century, Irish MPs were generally loosely identified with one of the two great British parties, and were not separated by meaningful policy differences. But between 1830 and 1880 the tories (and later the Conservatives) became increasingly concentrated in the protestant counties of Ulster, with the whigs (and later the Liberals) substantially confined to the rest of the country.[10] Notable policy divergences, rather different from those characteristic of the British parties, began to divide the two sides: Conservatives increasingly stood for the protestant establishment, for the interests of landlords and for the British connection, Liberals for catholic rights, the welfare of tenants and specifically Irish interests. The Liberals were increasingly challenged by more radical Irish groups, culminating in the rise of the Home Rule Party in the 1870s and 1880s, a development which entirely marginalised the Liberals. Commonly known as the Irish Nationalist Party, it acquired a lasting position of electoral hegemony outside the northern counties in 1885, following the Reform Act of the previous year.[11] Furthermore, the party ultimately achieved its central political objective, with the passage of the Home Rule Act of 1914, even though implementation of the act was suspended on the outbreak of war and pending a resolution of the Ulster question.[12]

3

In assessing the significance of the 1918 Reform Act for Ireland, there is no need to outline its general provisions or the political background to its enactment, as these are covered in the introduction to this volume. But the areas that merit further examination may easily be highlighted. These derive from the distinctiveness of the Irish case, as outlined in the last section, and raise two important questions. The first concerns the political implications of extension of the suffrage to three-quarters of the adult population. The second has to do with the implications of the redistribution of seats for the character of party competition.[13]

The extension of the right to vote to virtually all adult males, to women aged at least 30 years (subject, in effect, to a valuation qualification), and to members of the armed forces, had a huge impact on the size of the electorate. The electoral register of 1915 showed a total of 8.4 million – all males, of course – entitled to vote.[14] Under the new register of 1918, this increased to 12.9 million men and 8.5 million women, to give a total electorate of 21.4 million (including almost four million soldiers, 68,000 university voters and less than

---

[10]John Coakley, 'Centres, Peripheries, and Party Systems: Nested Secession Processes in Great Britain and Ireland', *Political Geography*, xxvii (2008), 740–60.

[11]John Coakley, 'Critical Elections and the Prehistory of the Irish Party System', in *Dissecting Irish Politics: Essays in Honour of Brian Farrell*, ed. Tom Garvin, Maurice Manning and Richard Sinnott (Dublin, 2004), 134–59.

[12]Alvin Jackson, *Home Rule: An Irish History, 1800–2000* (2003), 165–202.

[13]For a useful overview of the act and its context, see Robert Blackburn, 'Laying the Foundations of the Modern Voting System: The Representation of the People Act 1918', *Parliamentary History*, xxx (2011), 33–52; and, for a detailed, annotated presentation of the act, see Sir Hugh Fraser, *The Representation of the People Act, 1918, with Explanatory Notes* (1918). The act is set in its broader historical context in Neil Johnston, *The History of the Parliamentary Franchise* (House of Commons Library Research Paper 13/14, 2013).

[14]*Return Showing, with Regard to Each Parliamentary Constituency in the United Kingdom, the Total Number … of Electors on the Register Now in Force* (House of Commons Paper 120, 1915), 20.

200,000 business voters).[15] Women now accounted for 40% of the electorate, and members of the armed forces for 18%.[16]

The Irish experience was broadly similar to the general pattern, but there were some important differences. The proportionate increase in the electorate was rather more than in Great Britain, from 700,000 to 1.9 million, with a slightly smaller proportion of women voters (36%) and, importantly, a much smaller proportion of voters from the armed forces (less than 6% of the total, one-third of the level in Great Britain).[17] This was, in part, attributable to the fact that conscription was never extended to Ireland, but also to politically-driven reluctance to enlist on the part of many Irish nationalists. In 1915, for example, a disproportionate number of Irish recruits (39%) were protestant, even though protestants made up only 26% of the Irish population at the time.[18]

The battle for women's suffrage had been fought vigorously, but with little success, in Ireland. A number of suffragist groups had sought to win the Nationalist Party around to supporting the extension of the right to vote to women.[19] However, the Irish suffragist movement was divided between 'constitutionalists', who deferred to the Nationalist Party and acknowledged the primacy of the campaign for home rule, and 'militants', for whom suffrage extension was the priority.[20] Ultimately, it was the campaign in Britain whose influence shaped the outcome; but the suffrage was deliberately restricted to prevent the unthinkable. This was the risk that women (who numbered 14 million) would outnumber men in the electorate; equality of women with men was 'never seriously considered'.[21] The consequence of the 1918 Reform Act in Ireland was that 97.5% of all adult males were enfranchised (up from 55.2%), but the combined effect of age and valuation restrictions was that only 53.3% of all adult women became entitled to the vote. Overall, the Irish electorate (including armed forces voters) amounted to 72.6% of those aged 21 years or over.[22]

Ireland was also a special case in the matter of soldiers' votes. Irish soldiers had made a remarkable contribution to the British army in the 19th century, their enlistment level being much higher than would be suggested by the Irish share of the population. In 1830,

---

[15]There were 159,000 business voters in England and Wales, and 15,000 in Ireland; however, the number in Scotland was not reported in the official return, and hence this estimated total.

[16]Calculated from *Return Showing, for Each Parliamentary Constituency in the United Kingdom, the Numbers of Parliamentary and Local Government Electors on the First Register Compiled under the Representation of the People Act, 1918* (House of Commons Paper 138, 1918). The armed services electorate included a small number of women (3,372).

[17]Calculated from *Return of Electors* (1915) and *Return of Electors* (1918).

[18]Calculated from *Chief Secretary's Office, Dublin Castle Intelligence Notes, 1913–16, Preserved in the State Paper Office*, ed. Breandán Mac Giolla Choille (Dublin, 1966), 180–2.

[19]Margaret Ward, ' "Rolling up the Map of Suffrage": Irish Suffrage and the First World War', in *Irish Women and the Vote: Becoming Citizens*, ed. Louise Ryan and Margaret Ward (Dublin, 2007), 136–53.

[20]Louise Ryan, 'Traditions and Double Moral Standards: The Irish Suffragists' Critique of Nationalism', *Women's History Review*, iv (1995), 492.

[21]Johnston, *History of the Parliamentary Franchise*, 45.

[22]Calculated from *Return of Electors* (1918) and *Census of Ireland, 1911: General Report*, Cd 6663 (1913), 74, 98. Note that the figure for males includes armed forces voters, many of whom were aged under 21 years. Since population was declining, it is likely that the proportion of the adult Irish population entitled to vote in 1918 was slightly higher. If the population base is adjusted to the mean of the 1911 and 1926 figures (assuming linear population decline), the proportion of the adult population entitled to vote increases to 74.0% (99.3% of men and 54.3% of women).

for example, there were actually more Irishmen than Englishmen in the army.[23] Although Irish recruitment levels had fallen in line with population decline, it remained substantial until 1914. But by then the issue of joining the British army had been politicised; the Irish Volunteers, a movement established to support home rule, split on the issue, with a majority responding to the Nationalist Party's call to enlist in the army following the outbreak of war.[24] The rest remained aloof, ultimately finding themselves at the centre of the 1916 rebellion and evolving into the IRA. In consequence, Ireland's contribution to the war effort was significantly less than Great Britain's; it has been estimated that a total of about 200,000 Irish soldiers served.[25]

The Reform Act was of particular interest to the Nationalist Party. From one perspective, the extension of the suffrage could be seen as helpful to it. In general, the outcome of elections was determined by the religious composition of a constituency: Unionists won all of the predominantly protestant ones, while the Nationalists won almost all of the predominantly catholic constituencies (though some of these were held by independent nationalists). But these outcomes were not quite symmetrical: there were three constituencies with catholic majorities that were not in Nationalist hands. Fermanagh North (51% catholic) had been a Unionist seat since 1892; Tyrone East (55% catholic), once a Unionist constituency, had been held by the Liberals since 1895; and Londonderry City (56% catholic) had been Unionist until lost to the Liberals in a by-election in 1913.[26] These outcomes were, in part, attributable to bias in the composition of the electorate, which was almost certainly still disproportionately protestant due to the higher social standing of the protestant population, as described above. But the introduction of near-universal suffrage was likely to bring all three of these seats within the grasp of the Nationalist Party, since the newly-enfranchised voters would probably be disproportionately catholic.

The Nationalists, however, had to contend with competition from another direction. A newly-envigorated, and now more radical, Sinn Féin party had been biting at its heels since shortly after the Easter Rising of 1916 and the spiral of political tension that followed. Sinn Féin had been reborn as a more militant party at its annual conference in October 1917, when the senior surviving figure from the Easter Rising, Eamon de Valera, took over as leader and the establishment of an independent Ireland rather than a dual monarchy became its objective. Sinn Féin had challenged the Nationalist Party at four by-elections during 1917, and had won on each occasion.[27] While suffrage extension was likely, then, to help the nationalist side in general, there was a good chance that Sinn Féin rather than the Nationalist Party would be the main beneficiary.

---

[23] E.M. Spiers, 'Army Organisation and Society in the Nineteenth Century', in *A Military History of Ireland*, ed. Thomas Bartlett and Keith Jeffrey (Cambridge, 1996), 336.

[24] See D.G. Boyce, ' "That Party Politics Should Divide Our Tents": Nationalism, Unionism and the First World War', in *Ireland and the Great War: 'A War to Unite Us All'*, ed. Adrian Gregory and Senia Pašeta (Manchester, 2002), 190–216.

[25] Philip Orr, '200,000 Volunteer Soldiers', in *Our War: Ireland and the Great War*, ed. John Horne (Dublin, 2008), 65.

[26] Derived from *Parliamentary Election Results in Ireland, 1801–1922*, ed. Brian M. Walker (Dublin, 1978), 325–82, and *Census of Ireland, 1911*, 218–21.

[27] *Parliamentary Election Results*, ed. Walker, 174–5. The Nationalist Party's thinking on the Reform Bill was shaped by these results; it performed better at by-elections in 1918, defeating Sinn Féin in three, losing one, and allowing one unopposed Sinn Féin return.

In addition, the Nationalist Party had to confront a second challenge, one that arose at the Speaker's conference of 1916–17 which agreed on the main provisions of the Reform Bill.[28] The conference's 32 members included four Nationalist MPs (P.J. Brady, Maurice Healy, T.P. O'Connor, and Thomas Sanlan).[29] The Nationalist group argued strongly for the exclusion of Ireland from the bill's redistribution provisions.[30] Redistribution could be seen as prejudging the new arrangements for reduced Irish representation in the house of commons under the provisions of the Home Rule Act of 1914, and the negotiations which were proceeding at that time between all of the Irish parties in the Irish Convention (July 1917–March 1918). But it was no doubt also influenced by the likelihood that a redistribution would weaken the position of the party itself. The difficulty was not Ireland's existing over-representation in Westminster, since there were no plans to reduce this, but the fact that many of the least-populous constituencies were catholic, and vulnerable to being merged, or otherwise altered to form larger units. The outcome of the dispute was a decision to deal separately with the question of redistribution in Ireland, and to refer it to another Speaker's conference. Though divided on the practical plan for redistributing territorial seats, the conference recommended that Ireland be given two additional seats, one for each of the two new universities that had been established there; the National University of Ireland and Queen's University, Belfast.[31] The new scheme was given legal force by the Redistribution of Seats (Ireland) Act 1918, which was distinct from, but associated with, the 1918 Reform Act itself.

In fact, Ireland, which had been seriously under-represented in the house of commons on a population basis in the early 19th century, was significantly over-represented by the early 20th century. Its share of the population, according to the 1911 census, suggested that it would be entitled to just 69 seats, not 103; and it emerged from the redistribution process with two extra seats, a total of 105 (Scotland, with a larger population, ended up with only 74 seats). But the redistribution *within* Ireland had considerable political signifi- cance. Alongside two university seats (both for Trinity College, Dublin), Ireland had exactly 100 territorial constituencies (99 single-member ones, with one two-member constituency, Cork City). Of the territorial constituencies, which had not been revised since 1885, 85 had a catholic majority and 15 a protestant majority – a distinct advantage to the Nationalist side, since the overall proportion of catholics in the population, according to the 1911 cen- sus, was 74%, and 74 Nationalist seats would have been more equitable. Taking account of changed demography, the Redistribution Act increased the number of MPs in urban areas: in Belfast from four to nine, in Dublin City from two to four, and in Dublin County from four to seven. To compensate for these additional ten seats, three small boroughs (Galway, Kilkenny, and Newry) were abolished, though the Newry seat was used to create an extra constituency in County Down; seven southern counties returning two members were re-

[28]The Speaker's conference of 1917 was an innovation in British parliamentary procedure, with the Speaker chairing a cross-party working group whose aim was to achieve a degree of consensus on the divisive question of electoral reform; see Isobel White and Andrew Parker, *Speaker's Conferences* (House of Commons Library Standard Note SN/PC/04426, 2009), 3–4.

[29]See *Conference on Electoral Reform: Letter from Mr Speaker to the Prime Minister*, Cd 8463 (1917), 3.

[30]Homer Lawrence Morris, *Parliamentary Franchise Reform in England from 1885 to 1918* (New York, 1921), 185–7.

[31]See *Report of the Boundary Commission (Ireland)*, Cd 8830 (1917), and *Redistribution of Seats in Ireland: Letter from Mr Speaker to the Prime Minister*, Cd 8919 (1918).

duced to one member; and one county (Tyrone) was reduced from four to three seats. Some less-significant consequential adjustments and boundary changes were also made. The net effect of the changes was to reduce the 'catholic' total by six (to 79 constituencies) and to increase the number of 'protestant' seats by the same amount (to 21 constituencies).[32]

4

The ultimate test of the effects of the 1918 Reform Act was the general election that took place under its provisions on 14 December 1918. As is well known, the election had a transformative effect on politics in Great Britain, but the party system remained recognizable. The electoral upset in Ireland, however, was on an entirely different scale. Before looking at the effects of the Franchise Act in the next section, the broad results of the election and the political factors associated with this outcome need to be considered.[33]

Notwithstanding its reservations about the probable effects of the Reform Act, at least superficially, the Irish Nationalist Party was not without resources as it entered the election. Since its victory in the pivotal election of 1885, it had normally held between 80 and 85 of Ireland's 103 seats in the house of commons.[34] Its electoral machine, the United Irish League, had a network of about a thousand branches spread across the country, and, while their level of activity might have diminished, they were a vital accessory in fighting the election.[35] Despite its by-election losses to Sinn Féin in 1917, it managed to hold that party at bay during 1918, defeating Sinn Féin in three out of four head-on battles between the two parties, although it handed a fifth seat to Sinn Féin without a contest. On the eve of the election there were 75 Nationalists in the house of commons, dwarfing the handful of abstentionist Sinn Féin MPs.[36]

The election outcome, however, confirmed the worst fears of Nationalist pessimists: Sinn Féin MPs were returned in 73 seats, while the Nationalists' share dropped to six; and 26 Unionists were elected. The election also generated some dramatic headlines. The Sinn Féin leader, de Valera, defeated the Nationalist leader, John Dillon, by a two to one majority in Mayo East, the constituency which he had held for 33 years. Indeed, only two of the six surviving Nationalist MPs had fought off the Sinn Féin challenge. The other four, all in Ulster constituencies, had benefited from an election pact between Sinn Féin and the Nationalist Party. Negotiated by the catholic primate, Cardinal Logue, the pact was designed

[32] Since no religious breakdown of the new constituencies was published, these calculations are based on a mixture of census and electoral data. The Unionist gains were in Belfast (five extra seats) and Dublin (Rathmines, one seat); the latter was the only Unionist seat in the south after 1918, apart from the Trinity College seats.

[33] For an overview of the election in Ireland, see John Coakley, 'The Election that Made the First Dáil', in *The Creation of the Dáil*, ed. Brian Farrell (Dublin, 1994), 31–46, on which this section draws heavily.

[34] This includes a small number of MPs belonging to breakaway nationalist factions. Unionists, including Liberal Unionists and a tiny number of independent unionists, won between 18 and 23 seats over the same period. The Liberals never won more than one seat at a general election after 1885.

[35] Police reports show decline in Nationalist organisation beginning already before the war and accelerating after 1916, especially outside what would become Northern Ireland; see TNA, CO 904/20: 'Returns Relating to United Irish League Meetings, etc., 1898–1921', 1921.

[36] Due to shifting party affiliations, classification cannot be definitive, but of the 75 Nationalists in the outgoing parliament, nine were independent nationalists, and there were 19 Unionists, seven Sinn Féin members and two Liberals, as described earlier; *Daily Express*, 13 Dec. 1918.

Table 1: *Estimates of the Relative Strength of Party Support in Ireland in the 1918 General Election*

Party	A %	B %	C %	D %	E %
Sinn Féin	24.6	32.7	47.0	51.5	64.0
Nationalists	14.9	19.8	21.7	22.9	19.3
Unionists	11.4	15.1	28.4	23.3	14.8
Others	1.5	1.9	2.8	2.3	1.9
Non-voters	47.6	30.5	–	–	–

Note: Estimates are based on expressing party support as a percentage of (A) the electorate in all constituencies, (B) the electorate in contested constituencies, (C) those voting in contested constituencies, (D) those voting in contested constituencies, but incorporating estimates of party strength in uncontested constituencies (overall strength of the parties in southern Ireland applied to each un-contested constituency, assuming a uniform turnout of 68%, the actual rate in southern Ireland), and (E) those voting in contested constituencies plus the entire electorate in uncontested constituencies, but attributing all votes in uncontested constituencies to Sinn Féin.
Source: See Appendix.

to prevent competition between the Nationalists and Sinn Féin in marginal constituencies from handing these seats to the Unionists. It had divided eight Ulster constituencies between Sinn Féin and the Nationalists, allocating four to each. The strategy was relatively successful, but it broke down in one constituency, where an unplanned Nationalist candidate split the vote, allowing the Unionist to win.[37] On the other hand, the Nationalist Party did not even put forward a candidate in 25 constituencies which it had traditionally dominated, leaving the seat to Sinn Féin.

As a consequence of these pacts and of the large number of constituencies where Sinn Féin returned a candidate unopposed, there are difficulties in assessing the true level of sup-port for Sinn Féin in the 1918 election – a vital question, given disagreement to the present over the actual result and its significance. Unfortunately, official results of this election for the Irish constituencies were never published, and the manuscript returns kept in the par-liamentary archives do not report the numbers of votes cast.[38] Other sources disagree on the details. For this reason, an effort is made in the Appendix to this essay to reconstruct the results (see below). But simply reporting the raw figures is not enough; there is a dispute also about their interpretation, given disagreement about the manner in which uncontested returns should be dealt with.

As Table 1 shows, the election results may be used to present the Sinn Féin victory in different ways. The most negative interpretation expresses the Sinn Féin vote as a percentage

[37]The deadline for nominations had closed before the pact was agreed, but in the four constituencies allocated to the Nationalists, Sinn Féin won between 33 and 79 votes; in two of the four allocated to Sinn Féin, the Nationalist candidate vote was only 120 and 132; in a third there was no Nationalist candidate; and in a fourth, Down East, the pact effectively broke down, as the Nationalist won 4,312 votes to Sinn Féin's 3,876, handing the seat to the Unionist (with 6,007 votes). In a ninth constituency, Fermanagh North, a plebiscite of nationalist voters had decided by a 65% to 35% majority to put forward only a Sinn Féin candidate; *Northern Whig*, 3 Dec. 1918. In the event, this candidate was narrowly defeated by a Unionist.

[38]Letter to the author from Dr Chris Pond, Public Information Office, House of Commons, 17 May 1994.

of the total electorate (24.6%; estimate A in the table), thus assuming that all who abstained were opponents of Sinn Féin, or it expresses the Sinn Féin vote as a percentage of the total electorate in contested constituencies (32.7%; estimate B); these were the preferred interpretations of the more hostile of Sinn Féin's opponents.[39] The most positive estimate treats all electors in uncontested constituencies won by Sinn Féin as party voters (64.0%; estimate E), an assessment given by the leader of Sinn Féin himself.[40] The true strength of Sinn Féin falls between these extremes, but the raw results, showing Sinn Féin with 47.0% of the vote (estimate C) understate the party's 'real' strength.[41] A fairer estimate would add its probable minimum support in uncontested constituencies, taking account of average levels of turnout and party support; this would put Sinn Féin on 51.5% of the total vote (estimate D).[42] However, even that is likely to be an underestimate.

The election results also showed a big north-south division in the island. In the 26 counties that now constitute the Republic of Ireland, Sinn Féin won 69 out of a total of 72 territorial seats, and its share of the vote in contested constituencies amounted to 65.3% (again, undoubtedly its real strength was greater than this, since this figure ignores party support in the 25 uncontested constituencies, which accounted for more than a third of all Sinn Féin seats in the south). In the territory that was to become Northern Ireland, however, Sinn Féin won only three seats, with 19.0% of the vote (the Nationalist Party won four seats with 11.1%, and the Unionists won the remaining 22 territorial seats, with 63.7%). This represented a significant consolidation of the Unionist Party in Northern Ireland, where it had now won 23 of the 30 seats (including the university constituency).[43]

A final question about the accuracy of the data has to do with the extent to which the election was fought in a free and fair manner. Were the results an accurate reflection of public opinion, or were they distorted by corrupt or other inappropriate methods? Undoubtedly, undue pressure was exerted on all sides. Sinn Féin's opponents accused it of intimidating candidates of other parties and their workers, of putting unfair pressure on voters, and of irregular behaviour at the polls, including impersonation.[44] A Sinn Féin activist in Meath, for instance, claimed to have voted at least 30 times, suggesting complicity by staff at polling stations: 'from midday onwards I used to be greeted with a friendly smile by the presiding officer at a particular booth, and his poll clerk would laughingly ask: "whose name is it this time?"'[45] It was, however, British government agencies which were responsible for the management of the election and most senior officials involved were Nationalist or Unionist Party supporters (though many of the polling clerks were not). In May 1918,

[39] See, e.g., Sir James O'Connor, *History of Ireland 1798–1924* (2 vols, 1926), ii, 293.

[40] Eamon de Valera, *The Foundation of the Republic of Ireland in the Votes of the People: Results of the General Election of December 1918 – A National Plebiscite Held under British Law and British Supervision* (New York, [1918]).

[41] Laffan, *Resurrection of Ireland*, 168; Tom Garvin, *The Evolution of Irish Nationalist Politics* (Dublin, 1981), 119.

[42] This calculation is based on the assumption that, in the 25 uncontested constituencies (all of which were in southern Ireland), the turnout was the same as that in the contested constituencies in the same area (68.0%), and that party support was at the same level (for instance, Sinn Féin won 65.3% of the vote in southern Ireland). It is reasonable to estimate that at least 44.4% (65.3% of 68.0%) of the 474,778 electors in the uncontested constituencies would have supported Sinn Féin had they had the opportunity of doing so.

[43] See Marie Coleman, *The Irish Revolution, 1916–1923* (2014), 42.

[44] See, e.g., W. Allison Phillips, *The Revolution in Ireland 1906–1923* (1923), 152–3.

[45] Cited in R.F. Foster, *Modern Ireland 1600–1972* (1989), 638.

the government had arrested many of Sinn Féin's leaders, alleging their involvement in a 'German plot'; by the time of the election, more than 100 Sinn Féin leaders were in prison, Sinn Féin was banned, a great part of the country was under military rule, censorship was in operation, and 47 out of 73 Sinn Féin candidates were in jail.[46]

These harsh measures were not entirely unwelcome to the party: ill-treatment by the British was by no means electorally damaging, and being imprisoned was a positive electoral asset to a candidate. It would be reasonable to conclude that, notwithstanding departures from conventional standards of good electoral practice, the result of the 1918 general election in Ireland was a reasonably fair expression of the electorate's preferences. Later observers of the election took this position, acknowledging it as a spectacular victory for Sinn Féin.[47] But the contemporary reaction of the press also confirms this. The main newspapers overwhelmingly supported the Unionist or Nationalist Parties.[48] Only the *Irish Independent* and the *Evening Herald* broke ranks by adopting a less-committed position, the latter urging its readers to assess candidates on their merits, rather ambiguously advising them to 'vote for Ireland'.[49] After the election, though, the press acknowledged the scale of the Sinn Féin victory, with even unionist newspapers acknowledging the emergence of a powerful new political force.[50]

It seems that a range of political factors led to the Sinn Féin victory. The first and most obvious was the radicalisation of public opinion that had been taking place since the 1916 rising. Initial public anger directed at the rebels had been transformed first into sympathy and then into support for Sinn Féin, as the harshness of the British response made martyrs of the executed leaders and heroes of their imprisoned followers, offering a new grievance that Sinn Féin was able to exploit. Second, British government plans in April 1918 to extend conscription to Ireland evoked vehement opposition from nationalists of all hues – from the catholic hierarchy to the trade union leadership – and precipitated the withdrawal of the Nationalist Party from the house of commons, as well as offering Sinn Féin an opportunity to present itself as the foremost opponent of this 'unwarrantable aggression'.[51] Third, Sinn Féin's militancy on the unresolved 'land question' stole the clothes of the Nationalist Party in this area too, notwithstanding the long tradition of agrarian agitation with which the party and its local organisation, the United Irish League, were associated. In the increasingly polarised climate, other parties that might have emerged stood aside. In October 1918, the All-for-Ireland League (a splinter group from the Nationalist Party that had dominated

---

[46]Dorothy Macardle, *The Irish Republic* (1968), 264–2, 274–7.

[47]Researchers who analysed the election in general saw it as a Sinn Féin triumph; see, e.g., Edgar Holt, *Protest in Arms: The Irish Troubles 1916–1923* (1960), 166–8; Garvin, *Evolution of Irish Nationalist Politics*, 118–9; F.S.L. Lyons, 'The New Nationalism, 1916–18', in *A New History of Ireland. VI: Ireland under the Union, II: 1870–1921*, ed. W.E. Vaughan (Oxford, 1996), 238–9.

[48]See the *Irish Times*, the (Dublin) *Daily Express*, the *Dublin Evening Mail*, the *Belfast News-Letter* and the *Northern Whig*, which supported the Unionist Party, and dismissed the Sinn Féin programme as fantasy; and the *Evening Telegraph*, the *Irish News*, the Cork *Examiner* and the *Freeman's Journal*, which also derided the Sinn Féin programme, all on 13 or 14 Dec. 1918.

[49]*Evening Herald*, 13 Dec. 1918.

[50]See, e.g., on the unionist side, the *Dublin Evening Mail*, and on the nationalist side, the *Evening Telegraph*; the *Irish Independent* and the *Evening Herald* blamed the ineffectiveness and corruption of the Nationalist Party; all on 30 Dec. 1918.

[51]Macardle, *Irish Republic*, 233.

Cork parliamentary representation since 1910) announced that it would not contest the election; and on 1 November, after some vacillation, Labour followed suit.[52]

5

Alongside the political determinants of voting in the 1918 election, it appears that a number of aspects of the Reform Act had an impact. First, though it was associated legislation rather than part of the act, the Redistribution of Seats (Ireland) Act 1918 resulted in a net transfer of six seats from predominantly catholic to predominantly protestant hands, as noted above. This was accurately translated into electoral reality: the number of Unionist MPs increased from 17 to 23, disregarding the university seats.

Second, the extension of the franchise is likely to have had a major effect: as mentioned already, the act had trebled the Irish electorate, making a huge section of the population available for mobilisation by political parties. In fact, the number of first-time voters in Ireland in 1918 was much greater than these figures suggest. Such was the dominance of the Nationalist Party that, at most general elections, most seats were uncontested; indeed, in 1886, 1900, and 1906, more than two-thirds of Irish MPs were returned without a contest.[53] In any case, it was eight years since the previous election in December 1910, but in many constituencies voters had not gone to the polls for a much longer period. In a quarter of the constituencies, the 1918 election was the first to be contested in the 20th century. In 17 of these, the most recent election had taken place in 1892, the year of an exceptionally bitter contest that followed the split over Parnell's leadership. The most extreme case was Donegal West, where voters had not gone to the polls in a general election since 1880.

Taking these factors into account, and allowing for natural wastage through death, we can estimate that, of the electorate of almost two million, only about 357,000 had previously voted in a parliamentary election.[54] These figures do not take account of voting in local elections, but they suggest that the electorate of 1918 was, for the most part, free from any prior habit of party voting; those who had voted previously accounted for a mere 18% of the new electorate, rather than the 36% suggested by comparing the new register with that of 1915. It was, therefore, in a position to be won over by Sinn Féin. In addition to the recruitment of new voters, Sinn Féin was able to convert existing ones; there is evidence of a considerable volume of defection from the Nationalist Party in 1917–18.[55]

It is not clear that the two other aspects of the suffrage extension of 1918 had much effect in Ireland. Although 700,000 women were given the right to vote (36% of the Irish electorate), little is known about how they used their votes. Sinn Féin nominated two women candidates, but one of these was in a strongly-protestant Belfast constituency where

---

[52] A Labour group, the Labour Representation Committee, did contest four seats in Belfast, but fell victim to the Ulster Unionist Labour Association, founded in Apr. 1914 by the Unionist Party leadership specifically to head off the threat of a defection to Labour by the protestant working class; its three MPs sat as Unionists; see J. Dunsmore Clarkson, *Labour and Nationalism in Ireland* (New York, 1925), 373–5.

[53] Of 101 Irish constituencies, the numbers for which MPs were returned unopposed at general elections were as follows: 1885, 21; 1886, 68; 1892, 20; 1895, 60; 1900, 70; 1906, 80; Jan. 1910, 64; Dec. 1910, 63.

[54] Calculated from *Parliamentary Election Results*, ed. Walker, 325–98, by computing the number of persons who voted at the previous contested parliamentary election in each constituency and estimating the number of survivors on the basis of a very crude measure, an annual mortality rate of 2%.

[55] David FitzPatrick, 'The Geography of Irish Nationalism 1910–1921', *Past & Present*, No. 78 (1978), 125–6.

there was no hope of success; the other, Constance Markiewicz, a colourful 1916 veteran of Anglo-Irish background, was elected comfortably in Dublin City, becoming the United Kingdom's first-ever woman MP.[56] However, it is hard to trace any link between this and the enfranchisement of women.

Similarly, there is little evidence that the introduction of votes for members of the armed forces had much impact. To start with, soldiers accounted for a much smaller proportion of the electorate than in Great Britain (6% as compared with 19%). In addition, turnout was very low: in Cork City, for example, only 27% of absent soldiers and sailors voted, while in Roscommon South the figure was 32%.[57] Nevertheless, since the military vote in Cork was quite sizeable (12.6% of the electorate), it appears that soldiers accounted for about 5% of those voting – not enough to make a difference in the context of a Sinn Féin landslide. A corresponding calculation for Roscommon South, a more typical constituency, suggests that soldiers made up only 0.8% of those voting. The military vote might have had an impact in other constituencies that were marginal, but there is no way of testing this.

A further technical feature of the 1918 Reform Act had to do with the role of proportional representation. Although the act finally only provided for this in multi-member university constituencies, the Nationalist Party was a late convert to this new electoral system, as it faced being overwhelmed by Sinn Féin.[58] It had pushed unsuccessfully for this in the course of the Speaker's conference on the Reform Act.[59] Proportional representation would undoubtedly have reduced the impact of the Sinn Féin victory, as may be seen if we consider its probable result in a notional constituency. A five-member constituency of North Leinster could have been created (merging the counties of Louth, Meath, Westmeath, and Longford); under proportional representation, Sinn Féin, with 65% of the vote, would have won three seats, to the Nationalists' two (with 35%). But, under the existing plurality system, this area consisted of five single-member constituencies, all of which were won by Sinn Féin. It is likely that a sizeable Nationalist Party would have survived under proportional representation. As it was, under the existing system, Sinn Féin was able to win 94% of the contested seats in the 26 counties with only 65% of the vote.

6

The 1918 Reform Act has a well-established place in British electoral evolution. Historically, it formed part of a series of measures that progressively democratised parliament between 1832 and 1928, with stepwise expansion rather than incremental increase in the size of the electorate. This narrative of steady progress sits alongside the much more turbulent set of changes with which the act was associated in Ireland. These may be reviewed in three broad areas: political, constitutional-legal, and, most remarkably, ideological.

The electoral enfranchisement that facilitated the rise of Sinn Féin in Ireland in 1918 had its counterparts elsewhere in Europe at that time, with the dislocation of war, the collapse of the old social order and the new climate of political change boosting support for radical

---

[56] See F.W.S. Craig, *British Parliamentary Election Statistics 1918–1968* (Glasgow, 1968), 62.

[57] *Cork Examiner*, 30 Dec. 1918; *Roscommon Messenger*, 4 Jan. 1919.

[58] Martin Pugh, *Electoral Reform in War and Peace 1906–18* (1978), 162–3.

[59] See Morris, *Parliamentary Franchise Reform*, 186.

parties and policies. Although Ireland's wartime experience had been significantly different, the outcome was similar: a popular appetite for revolutionary change. As the conservative press warned, the 'virus' of Bolshevism was at large, and not even Ireland was immune. The programme of the Irish radicals was, however, a political – rather than a social – one. Sinn Féin's election manifesto had outlined its four-point strategy: its members would refuse to attend the house of commons; it would use 'any and every means available to render impotent the power of England to hold Ireland in subjection by military force or otherwise'; its members would meet as a constituent assembly 'as the supreme national authority'; and it would appeal to the international peace conference for 'the establishment of Ireland as an independent nation'.[60] Even the party's critics in the press accepted that Sinn Féin now had a mandate. As the main nationalist newspaper put it: 'whatever democratic nationalists may think of the wisdom of the people's decision, whatever their doubts about the practicability of the republican policy, … as democrats, nationalists are bound now to give the republicans a fair field'.[61]

The first and most obvious consequence of the 1918 general election in Ireland and, by extension, of the Reform Act that facilitated the Sinn Féin victory, was, then, its role in paving the way for Irish independence. For the Sinn Féin candidates, the chamber to which they were seeking election was not the British house of commons, but their own proposed constituent assembly. As is well known, the Sinn Féin MPs met in January 1919 as the first Dáil, proclaimed an Irish republic, and in due course accepted responsibility for the activities of the IRA. The Government of Ireland Act 1920, which partitioned Ireland, created new institutions for Northern Ireland that duly appeared in 1921 and lasted until 1972. Sinn Féin chose to interpret the election to the proposed house of commons of Southern Ireland as an election to the second Dáil, and it won 124 of the 128 seats to this body without a contest. The 1921 Anglo-Irish Treaty brought effective independence, with the creation of the Irish Free State as a British dominion outside the United Kingdom. This extraordinary development was, perhaps, the most dramatic long-term consequence of the election of 1918 and the Reform Act.

Second, at the constitutional or legal level, Ireland moved quickly away from some of the central provisions of the 1918 Reform Act. The Government of Ireland Act of 1920 provided for proportional representation and this was duly adopted in both jurisdictions. In 1922, it was written into the constitution of the Irish Free State, and that document also provided for universal suffrage. Electoral law within both the Free State and Northern Ireland quickly diverged from that provided for in the 1918 Reform Act. In addition, the Free State was no longer represented in the house of commons and Northern Ireland's representation there was reduced to 13, well below the number to which its share of the population should have entitled it – a trade-off for its new autonomous status. By 1921–2, the 1918 Reform Act had, for the most part, been superseded in the two Irish states.

Third, as mentioned in the introduction to this essay, the general election of 1918 ac-quired iconic status in Irish republican ideology. Even conservative Irish constitutional lawyers accept a widely-used numbering system for the Dáil. The present Dáil, the 30th since Irish independence in 1922, is officially labelled the 32nd Dáil, since it traces its ori-gins not to its roots under the Irish constitution of 1922 but to the revolutionary assembly

---

[60] The text of the manifesto is reproduced in Macardle, *Irish Republic*, 842–4.
[61] *Freeman's Journal*, 30 Dec. 1918.

of 1919. More importantly, though, for militant republicans the 1918 general election had privileged status: it was seen as the only occasion on which Irish people had made a collective decision on the future of the island (subsequent elections were to parliaments which, in militant republican eyes, were illegitimate, British-imposed institutions). In this interpretation, the results of the 1918 election, their legitimacy underlined by the generous franchise arrangements, were an enduring expression of the voice of the Irish people. It was for this reason that, when the Good Friday agreement of 1998 was reached, one of its core principles was an all-Ireland plebiscite to approve its terms – a deliberate attempt finally to trump the verdict of 1918 and provide popular endorsement for the constitutional status quo.[62]

7

Within a narrow constitutional legal sense, then, the 1918 Reform Act had an impact in Ireland not dissimilar to that in Great Britain: it represented a further step along the road towards universal suffrage (which was introduced in the Irish Free State in 1922–3). When seen in its political clothing, however, the act had more far-reaching implications. It did not merely disrupt or reshape the existing party system, as was the case in Great Britain; it transformed it entirely, with the replacement of the relatively moderate Nationalist Party by the more militant Sinn Féin party. As well as doing nothing to resolve the looming question of the partition of Ireland, or perhaps even making that outcome more likely, it brought southern Irish representation in the house of commons to an effective end.

The act had a powerful impact in another area, one little known to those unfamiliar with the Irish republican tradition. In the view of uncompromising Irish republicans, the act, for the first time, gave a voice to the Irish nation (or at least to its adult male section, which in many eyes at the time was all that mattered); the nation spoke, demanding the creation of an independent, united Irish republic; and no subsequent election had the authority to annul this demand. This was because, in this view, none (at least until 1998) possessed sufficient island-wide legitimacy based on universal suffrage to supersede the Irish people's decision in 1918. Perhaps not surprisingly, then, the centenary of this event is likely to attract much more public attention in Dublin than in any party of the kingdom that was responsible for drawing up the 1918 Reform Act.

APPENDIX: A Note on the Results of the General Election of 1918

Because no definitive statement of the results of the general election in Ireland has been published, this Appendix seeks to reproduce the results as accurately as possible.[63] It does so separately for Southern Ireland and Northern Ireland, which came into being only in 1921.

[62]The Good Friday agreement specified that the agreement itself would be put to referendum of the Irish people on 22 May 1998, an unspoken commitment to revising the people's purported verdict of 1918 (which would undermine the ideological position of republicans). The form of the referendum was, however, different in the two jurisdictions. In Northern Ireland it was a consultative referendum explicitly on the terms of the agreement; in the Republic it was a referendum on amending certain articles of the constitution.

[63]An earlier version of this Appendix appeared in Coakley, 'Election that Made the First Dáil', Appendix, 160–4.

Electorate. Data on electorate, area, and population are from *Return of Electors, 1918*. Data on women, military, and business voters are included in the 'total' figure for the electorate.

Votes. F.W.S. Craig, compiler of the definitive collection of British election statistics covering this period, *British Parliamentary Election Statistics 1918–1968* (Glasgow, 1968), used the 1922 edition of *Debrett's Illustrated House of Commons and Judicial Bench* as the source for this election, citing (p. xi) the editors' claim to have checked their tabulations with the returning officers in each constituency, and this has in general been followed in *Parliamentary Election Results in Ireland*, ed. Walker. A check against other similar sources, including *Dod's Parliamentary Companion, 1920*; *Whitaker's Almanac, 1919* and *Thom's Directory, 1919*, and with the yearbooks of the major political parties, including *The Constitutional Year Book, 1919*; *The Labour Year Book 1919*; and *The Liberal Year Book for 1926*, confirms almost all of these, if certain obvious misprints are disregarded. In four cases (the Sinn Féin vote in Mid Armagh, Belfast Victoria, and Donegal East, and the Nationalist vote in Down East) all of these sources except the *Liberal Year Book* agree on a different figure from that in *Debrett's*, while in a fifth, the Nationalist vote in Roscommon South, all of these sources except *Thom's Directory* agree on a different figure. Contemporary newspaper reports (the *Freeman's Journal*, the *Irish Times*, the (Dublin) *Daily Express*, the *Cork Examiner*, the *Irish News*, the *Belfast Telegraph*, the *Belfast News-Letter*, and the *Northern Whig*, 30 Dec. 1918) in general confirm the accuracy of this consensus in the first four of these figures, but disagree on the fifth. The *Roscommon Herald*, 4 Jan. 1919, provides a detailed and internally-consistent account of the returning officer's announcement, which confirms the accuracy of the newspapers (except the *Freeman's Journal*) rather than the yearbooks. In Cork City each elector had two votes; following the procedure in Craig, *British Parliamentary Election Statistics*, xi, each vote in this constituency has been counted as half a vote, resulting in a minor rounding error in the Southern Ireland votes (the actual votes were Sinn Féin 41,307, Nationalists 14,642, and Unionists 4,773).

Candidates. Where sources disagree on party affiliations, the source closest politically to the attributed party label has been used (for example, five candidates in Belfast described variously as 'Labour Representation Committee' and 'Independent Labour' have been classified here as 'Labour', following the *Labour Year Book*). Unionists include three candidates of the Ulster Unionist Labour Association in Belfast (all elected; 30,304 votes). In the territorial constituencies, 'Others' include Labour (five candidates, all in Belfast; 12,823 votes) and eight independent candidates, of whom four were of a nationalist orientation (6,217 votes), three of a unionist orientation (8,738 votes) and one indeterminate (436 votes). There were eight candidates for the university seats (two Unionists, two Nationalists, one Sinn Féin and one independent unionist in the south, one Unionist and one Sinn Féin in the north). Four university members were elected (one Unionist, one independent unionist and one Sinn Féin in the south, one Unionist in the north). The total number of candidates was slightly less than the numbers reported here due to double (or even multiple) candidacies.

Seats. Sinn Féin candidates were returned unopposed in 25 constituencies.

Universities. Trinity College, Dublin returned two members using the single transferable vote.

	Southern Ireland		Northern Ireland		All Ireland	
	Number	%	Number	%	Number	%
Electorate						
Total	1,371,911	100.0	554,363	100.0	1,926,274	100.0
women	*485,426*	*35.4*	*210,609*	*38.0*	*696,035*	*36.1*
military personnel	*64,395*	*4.7*	*45,016*	*8.1*	*109,411*	*5.7*
business votes	*8,396*	*0.6*	*7,115*	*1.3*	*15,511*	*0.8*
Votes						
Total	610,056	100.0	398,608	100.0	1,008,664	100.0
Sinn Féin	398,619	65.3	75,922	19.0	474,541	47.0
Unionists	32,928	5.4	253,899	63.7	286,827	28.4
Nationalists	174,742	28.6	44,341	11.1	219,083	21.7
Others	3,768	0.6	24,446	6.1	28,214	2.8
Candidates						
Total	130	100.0	74	100.0	204	100.0
Sinn Féin	72	55.4	28	37.8	100	49.0
Unionists	9	6.9	27	36.5	36	17.6
Nationalists	46	35.4	9	12.2	55	27.0
Others	3	2.3	10	13.5	13	6.4
Seats						
Total	72	100.0	29	100.0	101	100.0
Sinn Féin	69	95.8	3	10.3	72	71.3
Unionists	1	1.4	22	75.9	23	22.8
Nationalists	2	2.8	4	13.8	6	5.9
Others	0	0.0	0	0.0	0	0.0
Universities						
Electorate	8,360	100.0	2,039	100.0	10,399	100.0
women	*504*	*6.0*	*141*	*6.9*	*645*	*6.2*
Votes	5,411	100.0	1,605	100.0	7,016	100.0
Sinn Féin	1,644	30.4	118	7.4	1,762	25.1
Unionists	1,904	35.2	1,487	92.6	3,391	48.3
Nationalists	1,070	19.8	0	0.0	1,070	15.3
Others	793	14.7	0	0.0	793	11.3

The Impact of the 1918 Reform Act on the House of Commons

MARTIN FARR

The victorious conclusion of the war, coupled with a great democratising reform for the peace, created a sense of expectation that the parliament elected in December 1918 could not more starkly have disappointed. There was widespread shock at the overnight transformation of party politics, and general disorientation and speculation. To the central criticism that the 1918 Reform Act had produced a deeply unrepresentative, and therefore undemocratic, house of commons, came complaints that the legislature had become merely an appendage of the executive, and parliamentary government had been supplanted by party government. Many opined that the authority of the house of commons had been undermined. This essay considers how the implications of the act were envisaged, and how they were experienced and reported. It will look at the legislature that resulted, its members, and how they adapted to, and changed, its procedures and conventions. Finally, it will reflect on the politics of the impact of the Reform Act, on the parties, on their policies, and on a new political environment that had been created. Through their writings at the time and their reflections subsequently, those who were members, and those who were observers, of parliament testified as to how they felt the house of commons had changed as a result of the impact of the 1918 Reform Act.

Keywords: Conservative Party; democracy; general elections; house of commons; Labour Party; Liberal Party; MP; parliament; Representation of the People Act 1918; Speaker of the house of commons

'The magnitude of the measure is so obvious as to be almost platitudinous; its significance, though not less certain, is perhaps more subtle.'[1]

1

'We have to face this morning the spectacle of the old British political system in ruins', one newspaper announced when finally the results, if not the consequences, of the general election were known.[2] A great 'reform parliament' – not to mention a 'victory parliament' – could expect to be exalted by high purposes; none served with such disrepute as that which followed the 1918 Reform Act. 'After the victory and the brief jubilations', a member remembered, 'there followed a period of confusion and squalor which one might

---

[1] J.A.R. Marriott in *Fortnightly Review*, Mar. 1918, p. 331. The author is grateful to Mari Takayanagi, and to Stuart Ball, Paul Seaward, and Richard Toye, for their comments on earlier drafts of this essay.

[2] *Westminster Gazette*, 30 Dec. 1918, p. 1.

© *The Parliamentary History Yearbook Trust 2018*

have expected only in defeat.'[3] 'It is mediocrity personified', opined another editorial, a year later.[4] It 'was quite the wickedest I have known', recalled one member of parliament who sat in ten; 'Some called them the hard-faced men, I should have said empty-headed.'[5] 'It had not been difficult to get into', another admitted, 'provided one stood either as a Conservative or a National Liberal and there were many men there uninterested in politics but merely attracted by the kudos of being an M.P.'[6] The preponderance of Conservatives and National Liberals meant that the Commons 'suffered principally from the lack of Parliamentary ability and authority in the ranks of the Opposition'; for the Free Liberals and for Labour, Asquith and Adamson were likened to Prospero and Caliban.[7] Outside, pessimistic screeds proliferated: '[g]rave dissatisfaction with Parliamentary government is widely felt and expressed', reflecting the 'undoubted decline in the prestige of Parliament'.[8] There was 'popular inattention', 'disconsideration', even a 'growing contempt of institutions'.[9] The Burke scholar, Frank Raffety, detected a 'great decline in the influence of the House of Commons'.[10] Hard it was perhaps that morning to recall during the 'war parliament' the recent triumph of peaceful progress, that 'remarkable legislative achievement', 'the most comprehensive measure of electoral reform enacted'; one which 'made the whole system of what we regarded as democratic representation seem rudimentary'.[11] The house of commons elected in 1918 was certainly not what was anticipated from 'the greatest revolution this country has seen'.[12] Unless by great revolutions was also meant great confusion.

It is actually a perfectly explicable irony that the impact of the Representation of the People Act 1918 on the place whence it came and where its consequences were first felt has yet to be studied. That one of Britain's most significant democratising reforms transformed the principal legislative chamber of the country is obvious; demonstrating in quite what forms that took is somewhat harder. Its impact being tied neither to a date nor to an issue, the evidence is almost all circumstantial; it is hard to disaggregate which aspects of what came after were direct consequences of the act, rather than the consequences of the consequences of the act. Although it created the world that found expression in the Commons, the act itself is metaphorically almost what it was literally: a backdrop, as if democracy were a *mise-en-scène* courtesy of the Office of Works and Public Buildings. Once the act

[3] Churchill Archives Centre, Churchill College, Cambridge [hereafter cited as CAC], Churchill Papers, CHAR/8/642/56: Winston Churchill, 'The House of Commons', [Dec. 1938].

[4] *New Statesman*, 29 Nov. 1919, p. 237.

[5] Josiah C. Wedgwood, *Memoirs of a Fighting Life* (1941), 146; J[.]R[.] M[acDonald], *Socialist Review*, Jan.–Mar. 1919, p. 15.

[6] Brunel Cohen, *Count Your Blessings* (1956), 59; Gershom Stewart, *Letters of a Back Bencher to His Son* (1926), 101.

[7] J.B. Firth, in *Fortnightly Review*, Apr. 1920, pp. 537, 545.

[8] D. Henry Rees in *Fortnightly Review*, Jan. 1920, p. 77; *Saturday Review*, 8 Feb. 1919, p. 1.

[9] *Time and Tide*, 5 Apr. 1919, p. 416; Herbert Sidebotham, 'The Inefficiency of Parliament', *Political Quarterly*, i (1930), 351.

[10] F.W. Raffety, *The Future of Party Politics* [1918], 67.

[11] A.O. Hobbs and F.J. Ogden, *A Guide to the Representation of the People Act, 1918* (1918), 1; *Daily Mail*, 24 Aug. 1918, p. 2.

[12] J. Renwick Seager, *The Reform Act of 1918* (1918), 25.

had passed its third reading on 7 December 1917, there was scarcely a mention of it – as distinct from its effect on the general election known to be impending – in newspapers, in campaign material or in the private papers and memoirs of members, candidates and parliamentary officials; all were similarly silent. Significantly, the act never acquired a moniker. Whereas that of 1832 was soon thereafter invariably known as the Great Reform Act, the 1867 act generally called the Second Reform Act and that of 1884 usually dubbed the Third Reform Act, the 1918 act was rarely called the Fourth Reform Act, and almost never by its full name. Variously it was the Franchise Act, Reform Act, or Electoral Reform Act. Other measures – pre-eminently the Parliament Act 1911 – lived longer in renown. After an initial fanfare of superlatives, more usually it was not mentioned at all.

Other than for those inside it, at the time the doings of the Commons were a preoccupation only of journalists and political scientists, for whom the act prompted a series of stocktakings and summary reports of varying degrees of portentousness. For subsequent scholarship, it was a subject overlooked rather than neglected. The act is significant because it sits at the fulcrum of broader historiographical debates about parties (demographic change, the consequences of the war), the results of the 1918 election, and the precise, perhaps exaggerated, role of the act in creating a new electoral environment.[13] Few historians have been concerned with its immediate impact; in the procedural over the political, and challenges to politicians and to party were more vital subjects than whatever changes there may have been in, or to, the Commons itself. Once the parliament was elected, the parties sought to adapt to the new system. The Commons itself was almost taken for granted. Retrospective studies have tended to be *longue durée*, or to deem other issues to be more prominent, or to identify changes the impacts of which were more discernible.[14] The 1918 parliament as such proved to be not especially privileged; centennial interest began to rectify that.[15] Aspects that might still profitably be considered include the act and its implications, as envisaged and experienced; the assembly it produced, its conventions, and the character and status of its members; the politics of impact, in terms of parties and their policies, and the meaning of the house of commons after the 1918 Reform Act.

---

[13] H.C.G. Matthew, R.I. McKibbin and J.A. Kay, 'The Franchise Factor in the Rise of the Labour Party', *English Historical Review*, xci (1976), 723–52; P.F. Clarke, 'Liberals, Labour and the Franchise', *English Historical Review*, xcii (1977), 582–90; M. Hart, 'The Liberals, the War, and the Franchise', *English Historical Review*, xcvii (1982), 820–32; D. Tanner, 'The Parliamentary Electoral System, the "Fourth" Reform Act and the Rise of Labour in England and Wales', *Bulletin of the Institute of Historical Research*, lvi (1983), 205–19; Michael Dawson, 'Money and the Real Impact of the Fourth Reform Act', *Historical Journal*, xxxv (1992), 369–81; Martin Farr, 'Waging Democracy: The British General Election of 1918 Reconsidered', *Cercles*, xxi (2011), 65–94; David Thackeray, *Conservatism for the Democratic Age: Conservative Cultures and the Challenge of Mass Politics in Early Twentieth Century England* (Manchester, 2013), 117–30.

[14] *The House of Commons in the Twentieth Century*, ed. S.A. Walkland (Oxford, 1979); S. Ball, 'Parliament and Politics in Britain 1900–1951', *Parliamentary History*, x (1991), 243–76; Michael Rush, *The Role of the Member of Parliament since 1868* (Oxford, 2001); Paul Seaward and Paul Silk, 'The House of Commons', in *The British Constitution in the Twentieth Century*, ed. Vernon Bogdanor (Oxford, 2003), 139–88; Philip Norton, 'The House of Commons 1911–49', in *A Short History of Parliament*, ed. Clyve Jones (2009), 271–82.

[15] Richard Toye, 'The Rhetorical Culture of the House of Commons after 1918', *History*, xcix (2014), 270–98; Richard Toye, ' "Perfectly Parliamentary"? The Labour Party and the House of Commons in the Inter-War Years', *Twentieth Century British History*, xxv (2014), 1–29; Richard Toye, 'The House of Commons in the Aftermath of Suffrage', in *The Aftermath of Suffrage: Women, Gender, and Politics in Britain, 1918–1945*, ed. Richard Toye and Julie Gottlieb (Basingstoke, 2013), 70–86.

2

Even had it wanted to, the house of commons was not to resume from where it had left off in August 1914. Preliminary to a new, and likely post-war, parliament, Speaker Lowther had chaired an inquiry – the first Speaker's conference – into electoral reform, the report of which he advised the prime minister to make public.[16] From its recommendations, members went on to show, Sir William Bull told them, 'characteristic British phlegm when, in the midst of a great war, we deliberately decided to have a Reform Bill'.[17] Two major anomalies had survived the previous one: the continuation of plural voting, and the denial of votes for women. The conference reached broad agreement on universal male suffrage, voter registration, plural voting, university representation, redistribution of seats, adoption of alternative votes for single member constituencies, and even the enfranchisement of women who had attained a specific age.[18] The subsequent bill embodied those recommendations, leaving proportional representation and votes for women to a free vote: to expedite its progress, electoral reform was decoupled from that of franchise; proportional representation was lost, for Labour 'the one serious blot in what is otherwise a most comprehensive Franchise Reform'.[19] While political scientists recognized the form as being of much broader modern constitutionalism, what was bullishly exceptionalist was that, though the act bore great fidelity to the report, it represented no consistent body of principles; it was a progressive, more than a radical, measure, as was noted at the time.[20]

There was general agreement that the act would mean profound change, though little consensus as to what that change would be.[21] The act was recognized as being more than merely a piece of franchise legislation; upon the basis of a doubled electorate 'it erects an electoral system which is almost entirely new'.[22] A 'greater Reform Act than any that have gone before it' had been passed 'without more than a ripple of excitement, dealing with questions which in pre-war days would have aroused bitterest feelings'.[23] The act repealed in whole or in part over 100 statutes, changed the conduct of elections, and transformed the character and size of the electorate, tidying up the 'chaotic concretion' of other acts and measures to extend the franchise.[24] The most significant outcome of the act was the redistributing, rationalising, and equalising of constituencies ('a sort of jigsaw puzzle', thought

---

[16] Parliamentary Archives [hereafter cited as PA], Lloyd George MSS, LG/F46/12/5: Lowther to Lloyd George, 27 Jan. 2017.

[17] Hansard, *Commons Debates*, 5th ser., clxx, col. 897: 29 Feb. 1924.

[18] Representation of the People Act 1918, 7 & 8 Geo. V, c. 64, [6 Feb. 1918].

[19] C. Willoughby Williams, *Rogers on Elections* (3 vols, 1918), ii, p. vii; People's History Museum, Manchester [hereafter cited as PHM], Labour Party Archive: *Report of the Annual Conference, 1918*, 21.

[20] Malbone W. Graham jr, 'Some Foundations of Popular Government in Contemporary Europe', *Southwestern Political and Social Science Quarterly*, iv (1924), 333.

[21] *Sunday Pictorial*, 17 Feb. 1918, p. 4; *Athenaeum*, Mar. 1918, p. 130.

[22] Frederic A. Ogg, 'The British Representation of the People Act', *American Political Science Review*, xii (1918), 499.

[23] W.H. Dickinson, 'The Greatest Reform Act', *Contemporary Review*, cxiii (1918), 249; Philip G, Cambray, *Politics Retold* (1925), 161.

[24] William R. Anson, *The Law and Custom of the Constitution* (1922), 107–8; *Dod's Parliamentary Companion for 1919* (1919), 225; J.M. Robertson, foreword to Seager, *Reform Act*, 1; D. Lindsay Keir, *The Constitutional History of Modern Britain 1485–1937* (3rd edn, 1946), 471–2; G.P. Warner Terry, *The Representation of the People Acts, 1918 to 1928* (1928), xxvi.

the Speaker, 'though rather more interesting').[25] The electorate was now so large that the state made it its business to ensure that qualified people were registered. The prospect of an election determined by 'slavish adherence' to the report struck 'terror in the soul of the party agent' standing 'on the brink of the unknown'.[26] In addition to commentarial surveys, guides to the perfecting of the new electoral machinery rapidly materialised.[27] With election expenditure now having to go through the agent, electioneering interest groups were cauterised; through the requirement of a £150 deposit, the act introduced a restriction – a capital requirement – on standing for election rare in democracies.[28] The new legal maxima on expenses benefited the coming party, Labour, although the result of the election ensured that the benefit was initially well disguised.[29] With the Conservatives, the socialists went on to defend the system by which they would be over-represented; the attractions of electoral reform waned for Labour as they waxed for the Liberals, who in 1922 belatedly included it in their manifesto. The Conservatives had been fearful more of the electoral consequences – the effect of the uncouth and the un-male – than of the institutional ones. As it was, not all the new male voters were working class, and only older women were enfranchised. Redistribution proved a boon as the areas of growth were where the tories were stronger, and the act still retained the plural franchise in the form of university members and business votes. With the self-denying absence of the 73 Irish Sinn Fein MPs, to Conservatives the new democracy could appear more propitious than the old.

When it came, as one candidate recalled, the 'outstanding feature of the 1918 election was apathy'.[30] With voting on a single day, the election created a national campaign, albeit one where activity was compromised by shortages of paper and petrol, and the outcome by questions of legitimacy. Only half of voters voted, and 'a *bare quarter of the electorate*', to the disgust of one newspaper, voted for the government. Turnout was 58.9%, by far the lowest of any 20th-century election. 'Not only is Parliament unrepresentative, but the people who have got themselves returned to power expressly "wangled" the electorate so that Parliament *should* be unrepresentative.'[31] There was much in the contest 'which redoubled little to the credit of "democracy"', a coalition Conservative admitted. 'Our victory proved to be too complete.'[32] The snap election had been 'a plan for the extinction of all independent opinion', for another editorial: 'there is serious danger that we shall discover too late that the credit of Parliament has suffered a disastrous blow'.[33] To one Labour man who lost his seat, and who risked sounding peevish, it was 'probably the most grotesque reflection of the votes cast which any Parliamentary vote has ever shown'. Ramsay MacDonald went on:

[25] James William Lowther, *A Speaker's Commentaries* (2 vols, 1925), ii. 206.

[26] *Conservative Agents' Journal*, Sept. 1919, p. 1; *Daily Mail*, 22 Aug. 1918, p. 2; 10 Oct. 1918, p. 2.

[27] *Daily Herald*, 31 Aug. 1918, p. 3; J. Renwick Seager, *Parliamentary Elections under the Reform Act, 1918* (1918); Hobbs and Ogden, *1918*; Philip Snowden, *The New Franchise Act Clearly Explained* [c.1919].

[28] Philip Cambray, *The Game of Politics* (1932), 123; Ivor R.M. Davies, *Trial by Ballot* (1950), 24.

[29] F.J.C. Hearnshaw in *Fortnightly Review*, Mar. 1919, p. 341.

[30] Frank Gray, *The Confessions of a Candidate* (1925), 71; Leo Amery, *My Political Life* (3 vols, 1953–5), ii, 174.

[31] *Daily Herald*, 4 Jan. 1919, p. 7; *Nation*, 4 Jan. 1919, pp. 403–4; Ramsay Muir, *How Britain is Governed* (1930), 163; Ivor Jennings, *The British Constitution* (1941), 21.

[32] John Marriott, *Memories of Four Score Years* (1946), 162, 163.

[33] *Westminster Gazette*, 13 Nov. 1918, p. 1.

'there has been no Parliament elected in the lifetime of any of us the existence and work of which ought to be more firmly challenged', by the extra-parliamentary, if necessary.[34]

3

From the public gallery it was evident that there was more than just a matter of seating protocol to be contended: there was a new geography of politics. From the press gallery it was evident that the 'Opposition front bench has almost completely disappeared'; 'Two constitutional parties are virtually wiped out', the *New Statesman* observed. 'These results destroy the party system, turning the House of Commons into an annexe of Government.'[35] The latter consequently found itself embarking 'on the experiment of governing a country without an Opposition'.[36] Even the most supportive press admitted that 'the size of the majority and the absence of any man of parliamentary standing to lead His Majesty's Opposition are grave evils'.[37] Remarkably, with estimates varying between 250 to over 400, 'no official or even semi-official pronouncement has been made as to what the majority really is'.[38]

'This congested House' first met on 4 February.[39] Because of a London underground strike, many members were late arriving, and there were rumours of a power cut by strikers to prevent them meeting at all.[40] The chamber 'was a seething mass of humanity', *Punch's* William Locker observed, 'enough to swamp the floor and surge over into the galleries' and so many coalitionists that they had to 'overflow' to the opposition benches.[41] Seating remained scarce, and its scarcity contentious. Those who were able to subside had then to survive a ventilation system 'most members feel the effect of ... some to the extent that it shortens their parliamentary existence, voluntarily or not',[42] In the dark adjacent lobbies, one new Member discerned 'a steady stream of beggars, sightseers, would-be statesmen, people with grievances, inventors and others seeking relief and advice demand their member's services'.[43] Many attested that as 'a workshop it is badly equipped; it is overcrowded, and it is unhealthy'.[44]

It was a neophyte, yet aged, assemblage.[45] Seasoned by life though they may have been, in parliament 'the majority of the members [were] new and inexperienced, [and] such a

---

[34]J.R. MacDonald in *Socialist Review,* Jan.–Mar. 1919, p. 12.

[35]*New Statesman,* 4 Jan. 1919, p. 271; *Nation,* 4 Jan. 1919, p. 1.

[36]*Westminster Gazette,* 30 Dec. 1918, p. 1.

[37]*Saturday Review,* 4 Jan. 1919, p. 4.

[38]*Forward,* 4 Jan. 1919, p. 1.

[39]CAC, Mancroft MSS, MNCR 1/6: Midleton to Arthur Samuel, 30 Dec. 1918.

[40]Earl of Winterton, *Orders of the Day* (1953), 90; *Morning Post,* 4 Feb. 1919, p. 4.

[41]*Punch,* 12 Feb. 1919, p. 125; *Daily Mirror,* 5 Feb. 1919, p. 2.

[42]William Bull, *The Parliamentary Pocket Book* (1920), 68–9; Kenneth Murchison, *Family Notes and Reminiscences* [c.1940], 125.

[43]Gerald Hurst, *Closed Chapters* (1942), 109.

[44]Lord Snell, *Men, Movements, and Myself* (1936), 208–9; Spencer Leigh Hughes, *Press, Platform and Parliament* (1918), 147; TNA, WORK 11/258: Ramsay MacDonald to George Lansbury, 21 Nov. 1929.

[45]J.F.S. Ross, *Parliamentary Representation* (2nd edn, 1948), 106–7; Philip Buck, *Amateurs and Professionals in British Politics* (Chicago, IL, 1963), 7; Harry Brittain, *Happy Pilgrimage* (1949), 45.

one-sided House was not a good training for them. There was a tendency to disregard traditions and precedents'.[46] 'It was not, as a rule, a well-attended House', as was apparent from the press gallery. 'An unusually small proportion of the new men, unskilled and unpractised, were desirous of Parliamentary distinction or interested in everyday work.'[47] Once questions were over, a 'House of fifty or sixty is not noticeably thin'.[48] Some blamed the members' dramatically improved social and leisure facilities of bars, restaurants and games rooms.[49] Despite being salaried since 1911, members without private means or an auxiliary profession found that salary hard to live on, and so, after Labour Party representations, expenses were paid to cover transport between the Commons and their constituency. That provision corresponded with the stated intention of Labour members that they should be constituency representatives, with the Commons both their 'dwelling place' and 'platform'.[50] Their request that salaries were paid from the date of the declaration of the poll rather than that of the oath being taken was, however, refused by a Speaker worried at a public 'already rather restive at the payment of salaries'; only after the oath could the £150 deposit be reclaimed, and 'in their zeal to be in a position to reimburse themselves Members crowded in such numbers to the tables that there was some danger that they would be overturned'.[51]

Those on whom the act had the greatest impact played no part. The ingress of the 40% of men who had been unenfranchised was much more apparent than that of the 100% of women who had been (those under the age of 30 years remained voteless). Of 1,623 candidates in the election, 17 were women; only one was elected, and she declined to take her seat. In the event that one might, there was the urgent provision of 'lavatory accommodation' – albeit for numbers unknown – and 'Quarters for the Feminine Contingent', with a refreshment room 'decorated with portraits of famous men'.[52] The act notwithstanding, women still, as one authority ambiguously put it, 'were incapable of being elected'.[53] The corrective Parliament (Qualification of Women) Bill, which would not long before have 'been laughed out of the House', in 1918 'was carried, after a couple of hours, by an overwhelming majority'.[54] Nevertheless, '[i]t took women quite a long time to get accustomed to politics and the atmosphere of Westminster', and not a few men, some of whom were at

[46] Lord Hemingford, *Back-Bencher and Chairman: Some Parliamentary Reminiscences* (1946), 17; Lord Conway, *Episodes in a Varied Life* (1932), 145.

[47] Alexander Mackintosh, *From Gladstone to Lloyd George* [1921], 306.

[48] Herbert Sidebotham, *Pillars of the State* (1921), 17.

[49] James Agg-Gardner, *Some Parliamentary Recollections* (1927), 85; TNA, WORK 11/292, Works of Art: photograph of Mr. Bonar Law and Sir W. Rutherford playing chess; WORK 11/301, House of Commons chessroom: showcase for chess trophy; Edward Fellowes, 'Changes in Parliamentary Life 1918–1961', *Political Quarterly*, xxxvi (1965), 256–65; Cohen, *Blessings*, 60.

[50] J.R. MacDonald in *Socialist Review*, Apr.–June 1920, p. 104.

[51] Hansard, *Commons Debates*, 5th ser., cxiii, col. 517: 5 Mar. 1919; PA, Bonar Law MSS, BL/97/1/14: Lowther to Bonar Law, 27 Mar. 1919; *Punch*, 12 Feb. 1919, p. 126.

[52] TNA, WORK 11/237: 'Admission of Women to the Legislature', memorandum, 1 Nov. 1918; *Illustrated London News*, 19 Jan. 1924, p. 111; 6 Dec. 1919, p. 917.

[53] Seager, *Parliamentary Elections*, 2. The present author takes this to mean in a legal, rather than a capacitive, sense.

[54] *Punch*, 30 Oct. 1918, p. 286.

least partly reconciled to the opposite sex by the sudden ease of locating a hat when raising a point of order.[55]

When, in 1931, a cabinet minister at the dispatch box was asked a question about the removal of two trees in Green Park in consequence of a proposed widening of Piccadilly, followed by a question about the granting of a new constitution for Burma, it was clear to him at least that the Commons was swamped in more than one sense. Central to one post-war critique from the Webbs was 'the submergence of the House of Commons in the flood of government activity'.[56] The cabinet minister in question concluded that the 'consequence is that hardly any of the work is done properly'.[57] Government programmes in the 1918 parliament were 'uncomfortably full'.[58] That that parliament, in addition to non-legislative business, placed an average of 79 acts annually on the statute book – a considerable increase compared with the 1910 parliament – was, at least in part, a reflection of the significant procedural changes effected within days of the session beginning. Though not dependent on the act, they and their timing were products of the opportunity it provided. The government continued the trend to take time for its business from that of private members. The system of standing committees was extended, relieving parliamentary business by sitting simultaneously with the House to consider bills as a matter of course. Changes to standing orders provided a technical, strictly regulated, enhancement of the old system. By giving the Speaker power to select amendments for debate, the House accepted arrangements that would limit individual members' ability to delay or disrupt the passage of a bill by flooding the order paper with amendments.[59] Not long into the parliament, the Speaker was presented with a 'very real and present danger' requiring him 'to guard the rights and privileges of the Commons against the encroachment by the Executive Government'.[60] Lowther had been prevailed upon to preside over the first two years of the new parliament, and the prime minister wanted the chairman of ways and means, J.H. Whitley, to succeed him.[61] This apparent abuse of authority produced a row with accusations of gross violations of the ancient privileges of the Commons of which private members were the trustees.[62] Such desecration notwithstanding, the prime minister's nominee prevailed. A member of the cabinet inadvertently revealed Whitley's allure: 'A minister in charge of a difficult bill and fighting an uphill battle against the clock could wish for no better ally.'[63]

---

[55] Arthur Baker, *The House is Sitting* (1958), 206; Gideon Murray, *A Man's Life* (1934), 245; Earl of Portsmouth, *A Knot of Roots* (1965), 107; Henry W.J. Stone, 'The Changing Scene', *Empire Review and Magazine*, cdxviii (1935), 286.

[56] Sidney Webb and Beatrice Webb, *A Constitution for the Socialist Commonwealth of Great Britain* (1920), 71. The author is indebted to Paul Seaward for his corrections to this paragraph.

[57] Sir Herbert Samuel, 'Defects and Reforms of Parliament', *Political Quarterly*, ii (1931), 305–18; Reginald Bassett, *The Essentials of Parliamentary Democracy* (1935), 256.

[58] *Time and Tide*, 22 Oct. 1910, p. 480.

[59] Sir Frederick Sykes, *From Many Angles: An Autobiography* (1942), 310; Lonsdale Webster, preface to Thomas Erskine May, *A Treatise on the Law, Privileges, Proceedings and Usage of Parliament* (1924), vii.

[60] Dennis Herbert in *The Times*, 13 Apr. 1921, p. 6.

[61] Huddersfield University Archives [hereafter cited as HUA], Whitley MSS, JHW/4/1/25: Lloyd George to Whitley, 22 Mar. 1921; JHW/4/1/2: Hoare to Whitley, [27 Mar.] 1921.

[62] *The Times*, 12 Apr. 1921, p. 12; Hansard, *Commons Debates*, 5th ser., cxl, cols 307–8: 27 Apr. 1921.

[63] HUA, Whitley MSS, JHW/4/1/32: Fisher to Whitley, 4 Apr. 1921.

The abiding antagonism between 'certainty of business' and 'liberty of discussion' for some had been settled. 'Parliament had little more to do than to ratify the decisions of the executive Government', one private member felt, 'and Parliament could do little more than approve, or disapprove.'[64] A cabinet minister confided: 'legislation is being passed by a mere handful of Members'.[65] There were signs for many that the act had produced effectively a dictatorship – the Labour leader called it 'Kaiserism'[66] – and that the Commons had become 'the charwoman of Whitehall'.[67] The position of leader of the House became more important – to the scepticism of some – but with the immediate benefit of ministers more reliably circulating important papers to private members.[68] The machinery of government committee recommended as a 'correlative an increase in the power of the Legislature as the check upon the acts and proposals of the Executive', while at the same time not 'disturbing the balance of authority'.[69] The sapping of initiative from the Commons – apart from debates over amendments to the address – was one reason why the executive conceded greater interrogative opportunities. The questioning of ministers constituted a 'Grand Inquest of the Nation' in which Labour members' 'influence of questions on policy and administration', a clerk averred, was 'considerable. They are very often the only means available of expressing the views of groups of members on the government.'[70] So determined was the Speaker to include as many as possible that, to some, the questioning of ministers had been reduced to 'a trivial catechism'.[71] Over 200 questions being asked in a day was not uncommon, a 'growing plague' which led to the eventual remedy of no more than four oral questions being allowed to be put down daily, freeing a minister from devoting 'so much of his valuable time to satisfying Parliamentary curiosity'.[72] Yet the ventilative functions of parliament were the primary instruments of private members.[73] Private members' bills offered the lowest prospect of return of all parliamentary investments, but Labour members were adept in exploiting the ballot as such bills were the principal way in which they could use their platform for the education of public opinion. Those who obtained the highest place had to introduce a bill to represent fundamental party policy even if there was no chance of it progressing. Friday, the only day when ministers were not expected to attend, effectively became the day for debates on Labour Party projects or, 'mere variations on hackneyed party themes'.[74]

[64] Hurst, *Closed Chapters*, 119.

[65] CAC, Bull MSS, BUL/4/19: Long to Bull, 20 May 1919; George R. Lloyd, 'The House of Commons System', *The Statist*, Oct. 1938, p. 432.

[66] Hansard, *Commons Debates*, 5th ser., cxii, col. 110: 12 Feb. 1919 (William Adamson).

[67] J.B. Firth, in *Fortnightly Review*, Feb. 1919, pp. 190–201; Ivor Jennings, 'The Technique of Opposition', *Political Quarterly*, vi (1935), 208–21; Sidebotham, 'Inefficiency of Parliament', 353.

[68] *Saturday Review*, 8 Feb. 1919, p. 122; PA, Bonar Law MSS, BL/93/2/6: Bonar Law to Curzon and others, 9 July 1919.

[69] *Report of the Machinery of Government Committee*, Cd. 9230 (1918), 15, 14.

[70] Robert W. McCulloch, 'Question Time in the British House of Commons', *American Political Science Review*, xxvii (1933), 975: Horace Dawkins; J.R.J. Macnamara, *The Whistle Blows* (1938), 144; Gervais Rentoul, *This Is My Case* (1944), 120.

[71] Sidebotham, 'Inefficiency of Parliament', 356.

[72] Hansard, *Commons Debates*, 5th ser., cxii, cols 1382–3: 24 Feb. 1919; *Punch*, 5 Mar. 1919, p. 185; 12 Mar. 1919, p. 205.

[73] H.B. Lees-Smith, 'The Time-Table of the House of Commons', *Economica*, xi (1924), 140–62.

[74] P.A. Bromhead, *Private Members' Bills in the British Parliament* (1956), 50; Sidebotham, 'Inefficiency of Parliament', 356.

Procedure struck some 'as being unduly cumbersome', not to say obsolete: 'hours march-
ing through the lobbies like sheep through a pen'.[75] Stricter whipping had 'tended to turn
the average back-bench member in to a voting machine'; when there was a division – the
result of which was nearly always known beforehand – 'the absent members pour in from
the smoke-rooms and elsewhere, and march through the division lobbies', three-quarters
of whom having 'not heard a word of the debate', or, if they were called, 'find themselves
on their feet without any remembrance of what their motions are'.[76] One new member
reflected how 'pride is chastened by disillusionment';[77] another of how a member was
swiftly disabused 'of the fancy that he influenced events'.[78] 'Ridiculed and reviled', private
members 'are deprived of the authority that they are elected to exercise.'[79] One said: 'I
used to wonder how I ever got here, but now I cannot help wondering how on earth any
of the others ever managed it.'[80] Outside diversions were essential: 'Complete devotion to
the pursuit of political life may lead to swifter advancement, but seems inevitably to bring
with it a loss of sense of proportion.'[81] Inside, more than one felt that initiative and independence of thought were discouraged.[82] Outside, local associations distributed candidate
'questionnaires' requesting return with detailed replies.[83] One member knew colleagues
'who bitterly regretted' giving 'some written pledge or promise which they found it difficult or objectionable to have to comply with'; another always refused. 'I cannot help
feeling that every Member of the House would be happier in his mind if he could go back
to Westminster on that explicit understanding.'[84] It was the antithesis of direct action.

4

One of the many epithets that the act generated was 'an experiment in politics without
party'.[85] In its absence could be heard what the leader of the House called the 'clatter
outside, which is reflected so much in some of the new speeches to which we have listened':
the press.[86] It was a clamour to which some suspected the prime minister listened more
attentively than he did to that of members. It evinced a sense that journalists effectively had
supplanted members; indeed, Austen Chamberlain's 'corporate feeling of the House' was

[75] Sir Ellis Hume-Williams, *The World, the House, and the Bar* (1930), 240; Sykes, *From Many Angles*, 310; W. Ivor Jennings, *Parliamentary Reform* (1934), 29.

[76] Muir, *How Britain is Governed*, 198–9, 193; Sidebotham, *Pillars of the State*, 17; Hansard, *Commons Debates*, 5th ser., cxxii, cols 233–4: 2 Dec. 1919; Lees-Smith, 'Time-Table', 158.

[77] Hurst, *Closed Chapters*, 101.

[78] Lord Brabazon of Tara, *The Brabazon Story* (1956), 115; Sir Philip Richardson, *It Happened to Me: Reminiscences* (1952), 182, 183.

[79] Viscount Esher, *After the War* (1918), 52–3.

[80] Unnamed back bencher, in Gervais Rentoul, *Sometimes I Think* (1940), 232.

[81] H.H. Balfour, *An Airman Marches* (1933), 253–4.

[82] Sykes, *From Many Angles*, 311; Sir Gilbert Campion, *An Introduction to the Procedure of the House of Commons* (2nd edn, 1950), 40.

[83] Hemingford, *Back-Bencher and Chairman*, 11–12.

[84] Brittain, *Happy Pilgrimage*, 131.

[85] *Pall Mall Gazette*, 1 Jan. 1919, p. 4.

[86] Hansard, *Commons Debates*, 5th ser., cxx, col. 566: 28 Oct. 1919 (Bonar Law).

felt most when the press sought to bully.[87] Some saw virtue in the lack of parliamentary opposition, others that, after years of coalition, government by party was overdue, not least as the present government majority was overlarge.[88] There were so many coalitionists it was even unclear where they would sit. Since separation on party lines may 'create an atmosphere of opposition', the Unionist chief whip told the Speaker; 'it would be wiser for all sections of Coalitionists to be mixed up'.[89] With such a large majority, discipline was lax, government back benchers rebelling sometimes with immunity and for their own amusement.[90] It was a problem for the Speaker. Not only were there parties both inside and outside of the government, there were 'a number of groups, Unionists, Liberals, Labour, Nationalists, Sinn Feiners, Cooperators etc who may or may not act together, or who may act together on some subjects and not on others', the Speaker told one member. 'Events alone and not I can determine which of these groups or what combination of groups will eventually become the regular opposition or whether there will be a regular opposition.'[91] From the aspect of the first commissioner of works, who had physically to accommodate them, 'it seems in the future we shall have more of the group system, rather than the two Party system of the past'.[92]

Arithmetic alone meant that 'the Coalition can safely ignore what such a tatterdemalion Opposition chooses to say or do'.[93] With the non-return of Asquith and Arthur Henderson, there was no obvious leader of it, and the two largest opposition parties in the Commons were divided as to which should be the official opposition. Aware that by-election results might lead to a weekly census, Lowther felt his responsibility extended to whom to call first. As it was, business was slowed – and Locker inspired – by the Liberal and Labour leaders as 'each of them thinks it necessary to speak whenever the other does, like the hungry lions on Afric's burning shore'.[94] The Speaker alternated the roars; attempts similarly to divide the opposition whip rooms were abandoned ('The narrow passage leading down to them make it impossible to divide them between 2 without great inconvenience and probably friction.')[95] The leaders of the groups could sit on the opposition front bench as well as members of the previous administration. The Speaker said: 'there would be no official opposition and no person who could claim (or whose claim would be admitted) to be leader of His Majesty's Opposition'.[96]

Donald Maclean led the opposition Liberal Party contingent, although few thought 'that they were the real "Simon Pure", with great historical traditions which should not be lightly

[87] Cadbury Research Library, University of Birmingham, Austen Chamberlain MSS, AC/5/1/142: Austen Chamberlain to Hilda Chamberlain, [c. 30 Oct. 1919].

[88] Cadbury Research Library, University of Birmingham, Neville Chamberlain MSS, NC/1/16/2: Neville Chamberlain to Ida Chamberlain, 29 Dec. 1919; Austen Chamberlain MSS, AC/5/1/105: Austen Chamberlain to Ida Chamberlain, 1 Jan. 1919.

[89] PA, House of Commons records, HC/S0/22/10: Lord Edmund Talbot to Lowther, 1 Jan. 1919.

[90] Hemingford, *Back-Bencher and Chairman*, 16; Colin Coote, *A Companion of Honour: The Story of Walter Elliot* (1965), 45; Conway, *Episodes*, 148; Marriott, *Memories*, 188.

[91] PA, House of Commons records, HC/SO/1/22/5: Lowther to Sir Thomas Whittaker, 10 Jan. 1919.

[92] PA, House of Commons records, HC/SO/1/22/3: Mond to Lowther, 16 Jan. 1919.

[93] J.B. Firth, in *Fortnightly Review*, Feb. 1919, p. 191.

[94] *Punch*, 19 Feb. 1919, p. 145.

[95] PA, House of Commons records, HC/SO/22/11: Talbot to Lowther, 17 Jan. 1919.

[96] PA, House of Commons records, HC/SO/1/22/[9]: Lowther to George Terrell [copy], 29 Jan. 1919.

set aside by reason of a passing failure at the polls'.[97] Maclean's colleague, Sir Thomas Whittaker, maintained that the Speaker should regard all Liberals as of one party, and thus 'the only possible alternatives to this government would be a Unionist or a Liberal Government'. Indeed, the chairman of the committee on parliamentary procedure went on, 'it would appear to be unnecessary and undesirable to depose a great historic party from that position simply because … [it] is not quite homogenous in regard to its leadership'.[98] Outnumbered they may have been by the coalition, but Labour still outnumbered the 'Wee Free' Liberals. The alternative leader of the opposition was thus William Adamson, to some ears the personification of the Parliamentary Labour Party. 'Speech seems hard for him and thought harder still', the leader of the House told the king; of Adamson's colleagues 'the average mentality is slow and lacks understanding of even comparatively simple propositions and except for the annoyance which obstinacy always causes my personal feeling is that they will not be a very formidable opposition'.[99] Speaker Lowther found the Labour men 'slack in attendance and ineffective in discussing details'.[100] Inside the party, concerns were raised about 'the poor attendance of Members on the Benches and the necessity for better organisation' as well as for individual initiative.[101] From outside the Commons, through a passing failure at the polls of his own, MacDonald complained that too many Labour men 'are not really interested in Parliamentary work, and are not being taught to be interested'.[102] A good parliamentary team increasingly being seen as essential, the organisation committee stepped in to support Adamson's scratch efforts. 'Two clerks, three typists – we cannot do with less', were requested, plus one of the Liberals' three messengers 'to fetch members to important divisions'.[103] And the National Executive Committee instructed the parliamentary party to 'make the necessary arrangements to become the Official Opposition'.[104] Thus did Adamson assert himself, asking the Speaker before parliament met to 'make whatever arrangements are necessary for the Party to assume the responsibilities of the Official Opposition'. 'There is no immediate hurry, of course', Adamson assured him, 'but tomorrow would suit us.'[105]

'Tranquillity' was the Conservative slogan in the subsequent general election, in November 1922. Tranquillity triumphed. Yet it was 'always inevitable that, if an adequate constitutional outlet were denied, the demand for drastic changes in the economic system would take shape in the industrial field'.[106] In 1922, the coming party arrived. More numerous and

[97]Lowther, *Commentaries*, ii, 251.

[98]PA, House of Commons records, HC/SO/1/22/8, TPW [Sir Thomas Palmer Whittaker] memorandum, c. Jan.–Feb. 1919.

[99]PA, Bonar Law MSS, BL/91/7: Bonar Law to George V [copy], 11 Feb. 1919; BL/91/7: [J.C.C. Davidson] to Stamfordham [copy], 14 Feb. 1919.

[100]Lowther, *Commentaries*, ii, 254.

[101]PHM, Labour Party Archive: Parliamentary Labour Party minutes, 11 Nov. [1919], p. 103; *Report of the Annual Conference, 1919*, 127–30.

[102]J.R. MacDonald, in *Socialist Review*, July–Sept. 1920, p. 196.

[103]London School of Economics Library, Passfield MSS, Passfield/1/3664: Beatrice Webb diary, 14 Jan. 1919; PHM, Labour Party Archive, LP/PA/19/1–2: H.S. Lindsay, report from organisation committee, Dec. 1919.

[104]PHM, Labour Party Archive: Parliamentary Labour Party minutes, 7 Jan. 1919, p. 1.

[105]PA, House of Commons records, HC/SO/1/22/1: Adamson to Lowther, 7 Jan. 1919; Hansard, *Commons Debates*, 5th ser., cxxii, cols 62–3: 11 Feb. 1919 (Adamson); PHM, Labour Party Archive: Parliamentary Labour Party minutes, 11 Mar. [1919], p. 26; 18 Mar. [1919], p. 31.

[106]*Nation*, 8 Feb. 1919, p. 1.

numinous, the Labour benches 'have been filled, whilst other benches have been scantily occupied, the work of the Whips has been reorganised, and in division after division we have been able to account for every man … The Labour Party has revived the life of Parliament.'[107] But then '[f]lushed with triumph … they were speedily disillusioned'.[108] Impatience defined the attitude of many Labour members to parliamentary procedure. Edward Fellowes, assistant clerk, felt 'they regarded the rules of debate in the Commons as having been framed solely to prevent their freedom of expression'.[109] Speaker Whitley decided to drive those elected in 1922 'with a loose rein' and for that purpose felt it politic to break on occasion with custom.[110] Whitley's secretary felt that 'he was out to help them to take their position as His Majesty's Opposition', the Rules of Order and recognized Procedures permitting.[111] It appeared to others that, for the Red Clydesiders, 'Mr Speaker was only a Lord Mayor'.[112] The reception that the new Labour members, few of whom had much formal education or training, received was, for one of them, 'contemptuous indifference strongly tempered with fear'.[113] The roots showed. Fellowes recognized that their 'experience was largely confined to the platform, where interruptions could be dealt with in language which was disorderly in the Commons'.[114] For the Speakers, tranquillity came to be a reminiscence. When their time came, both were happy to retire.[115]

5

That the 1918 house of commons was heralded was partly why it disappointed. One newspaper recalled 'the common cant of the election period. There was to be a "new world", and the House of Commons, elected on an extended franchise, was to be representative of aspirations and ideals of which the country had become actively conscious during its passage.'[116] That the act produced a 'complete travesty in the House of Commons of the verdict of the country' proved to Asquith, among others, that 'a not very legitimate use was made of it'.[117] An act which settled electoral arrangements for the rest of the century had been followed by an election on a system that all had condemned. Its very unrepresentativeness meant that the government's victory lacked moral authority; worse, was 'destructive

[107] J.R. MacDonald, in *Socialist Review*, Jan. 1923, p. 26.

[108] Murray, *A Man's Life*, 240; Rentoul, *Sometimes I Think*, 232.

[109] Edward Fellowes, 'Practice and Procedure in the House of Commons 1919–61', *Journals of the Parliaments of the Commonwealth*, xliii (1962), 105.

[110] Hemingford, *Back-Bencher and Chairman*, 31; Baker, *The House is Sitting*, 191.

[111] HUA, Whitley MSS, JHW/4/3/15/2: Sir Ralph Verney to Dennis [Herbert, Lord Hemingford] [copy], 5 Jan. 1945.

[112] 'An Old Member', *John Blunt*, 16 June 1928, p. 11.

[113] Sir Patrick Hastings, *The Autobiography of Sir Patrick Hastings* (1948), 229.

[114] Fellowes, 'Changes in Parliamentary Life', 261.

[115] PA, Bonar Law MSS, BL/107/1/17: Lowther to Bonar Law, 19 Apr. 1921; HUA, Whitley MSS, JHW/4/1/86: Whitley to Oliver Whitley, 21 June 1928.

[116] *New Statesman*, 29 Nov. 1919, p. 237.

[117] H.H. Asquith, *Liberalism and the Coalition* (1919), 16. Keir, *Constitutional History*, 473.

of the representative character of Parliament'.[118] Electoral reformers were emboldened.[119] Some commentators felt that the act meant that the Commons 'no longer performs some of the functions attributed to it by Bagehot and is not indispensable to the performance of any of them'.[120] It was incompetent in controlling the executive, had no point of view to oppose that of the government, and was ignorant of the principles of parliamentary government. Inasmuch as members reflected anything, they reflected 'interests'. 'Women produce life, and men produce property', Walter Elliot mused, 'and this is the reason of their respective bias, each stressing the value of the effort which they can realise'; by enfranchising women the act 'very greatly emphasised the position of the Commons as a Consumers' Council'.[121] More than after other such acts, members 'had to find means of satisfying the whole adult population, many of whom had neither the capacity nor the interest to assess serious arguments'.[122] What took place inside the chamber should not be separated from how it was considered outside: the specific – its conventions – and the general, 'its special business as a representative Assembly is to explore the causes of discontent, to hear and redress grievances, to anticipate and prevent disturbances of the peace'.[123] It was clear to some that the 'fair hopes of the fathers of modern democracy have not been fully realized. Universal suffrage has not proved to be a universal panacea.'[124] Coming at the conclusion of the war to end all wars, that may have been fitting.

Governing had to be adapted to the new conditions. 'The old oligarchic methods will not do', as a viscount told a cabinet secretary.[125] The majority undeservedly conferred on the government threatened the role of the Commons. 'What the House thinks or feels is no longer a question of importance with the government or anyone else', said the *New Statesman*. 'The supremacy of the Executive was complete.'[126] However propitious some tories may have found democracy to be, others felt that representative government, independent and critical thinking, and quality of debate, had become neglected, and that parliament must revive to defeat non-democratic ideas, such as direct action.[127] For Ivor Davies, the Liberal, too many members 'since 1918 have been shamefully reluctant to act according to their consciences' for fear of 'a candidate who could be relied upon by their Party to toe the line'.[128] With payment, perquisites, and presumption on the part of the public, came a class of professional politicians. It was this conception, not government, which subdued parliament – the prime minister's threat of dissolution, which was simultaneously an appeal to the people and a threat to legislators – 'but the Chief Whip, with his ultimate verdict as

[118]Parliamentary Committee for Proportional Representation, *The Proportional Representation Bill* [1921].

[119]J. Fischer Williams, in *Representation*, Mar. 1919, p. 5; PA, Stansgate MSS, ST/41/2: John Humphreys to Benn, 9 Feb. 1920; ST/41/2: Proportional Representation Society to Benn, 8 Mar. 1922.

[120]Robert Livingston Schuyler, 'The Decline of the House of Commons', *Columbia University Quarterly*, xxi (1919), 310–18; cf. Frank Fox, *Parliamentary Government: A Failure?* [1930].

[121]Walter Elliot, *Toryism and the Twentieth Century* (1927), 80.

[122]Davies, *Trial by Ballot*, 7.

[123]*Westminster Gazette*, 12 Feb. 1919, p. 1.

[124]R.L. Schuyler, 'Parliament and Revolution', *Political Science Quarterly*, xxxv (1920), 669–71.

[125]CAC, Esher Papers, ESHR/4/11: Viscount Esher to Sir Maurice Hankey, 15 Feb. 1919.

[126]*New Statesman*, 29 Nov. 1919, p. 238.

[127]Esher, *After the War*, 49.

[128]Davies, *Trial by Ballot*, 9–10.

to the re-election of all'.[129] One effect was to strengthen the party machine, not only over constituents, but also over members, who owed their election to it; a new oligarchic method.

More than being a place merely to raise issues, the House was vaunted as a place to do things, but the very purpose of the coming party was in danger of suffocation from the parliamentary embrace. For some Labour members their elevation was consummation. 'This was the House of Commons!' one remembered exclaiming: 'I was convinced that the workers were right in shaping their course to capture this citadel.'[130] Citadel, dwelling place, or platform, 'Socialists', MacDonald pronounced, 'should consider how to perfect the system.'[131] Their enemy agreed.[132] The complaint, as expressed by Austen Chamberlain, was that 'a great loquaciousness has seized upon the House', thereby providing a measure against which to disparage the unpractised Labour men.[133] The act had the effect of emphasizing that the person chosen by Labour MPs to be parliamentary leader was effectively the party leader; in 1921, Adamson was replaced.[134] In 1922, the Clydesiders 'came to Westminster with a reputation as revolutionaries', as Ellen Wilkinson recalled, 'and the House of Commons, which was only used to the solid trade union official type of Labour member, was thrilled to find that they really looked the part'.[135] With MacDonald as leader, they finally sounded it. Yet he appealed to his colleagues 'for a greater measure of self-restraint and for a realisation of the fact that when a Labour government arrives it will be greatly hampered if, in the meantime, Parliamentary Government has been destroyed'.[136] It was the case that '[i]f the Party fails in Parliament, it fails in the country, and the dream of a Labour government will vanish for a generation'.[137] So it was that 'as the years went by they steadily became more and more rigid upholders of the traditions of the house', as keen to stress that in 'defending Parliamentary method and Parliament, one must be careful not to be committed to defend Parliament in its existing form', but nor should anything be done to weaken the power of Labour for when it did win a majority.[138] The house of lords excepted, on parliamentary reform the party's 1918 constitution was silent given that its 'repeated demands largely [had been] conceded' by the act.[139] In consequence of the concerns that the Commons was becoming overwhelmed with reconstructing a nation and running an Empire, some advocated geographical, if not functional, devolution, and members agreed to 'the creation of subordinate Legislatures within the United Kingdom'.[140] Speaker Lowther chaired another inquiry, into devolution. His earlier jigsaw puzzle had

[129] Walter Elliot, 'The Inefficiency of Parliament', *Political Quarterly*, 1 (1930), 366.

[130] Jack Lawson, *A Man's Life* (1932), 259, 263; S.V. Bracher, *The Herald Book of Labour Members* (1923), v: Hamilton Fyfe.

[131] James Ramsay MacDonald, *Parliament and Revolution* (1919), 61, 64.

[132] *Spectator*, 25 Nov. 1922, p. 6.

[133] Austen Chamberlain, 'The House of Commons', *Empire Review*, xxxix (1924), 368.

[134] *Morning Post*, 4 Feb. 1919, p. 4; *New Leader*, 24 Nov. 1922, p. 1; TNA, MacDonald Papers, PRO/30/69/1165: J.R. Clynes to MacDonald, 14 Feb. 1921.

[135] Ellen Wilkinson, *Peeps at Politicians* (1930), 1.

[136] PHM, Labour Party Archive: Parliamentary Labour Party minutes, 3 July 1923.

[137] J.R. MacDonald, in *Socialist Review*, Jan. 1923, p. 27.

[138] J.R. MacDonald, *Parliament and Democracy* (1920), viii.

[139] Labour Party, *Labour and the New Social Order* (1918), 10.

[140] *Liberal Magazine*, Mar. 1919, pp. 95–6; Hansard, *Commons Debates*, 5th ser., cxvii, cols 2063–129: 4 June 1919.

rationalised the conception of the electorate: all were free and equal, 'but interchangeable. No account is taken of the difference in function of the voters, which the early constituencies at least tried to respect.' In the interests of rationalising and equalising, a fishing or agricultural constituency brought up to the average of constituents 'is nowadays loaded with any block of population, mining, urban-dormitory, what you will'. For Walter Elliot, 'This is a very new development.'[141] Rational it may not have been, but at least with the old boroughs there was a rationale.

'It is the fashion to decry the Parliament of 1918.'[142] Illegitimate issue of a cynical and peremptory consummation that was the 'Coupon Election'; for Asquith, it was 'from first to last an artificial business'.[143] Such an election, at least, would not happen again: in 1945 the dislocation may have been greater but the polity more settled. Moreover, in the testimony of one who witnessed both, the quality of the later intake was much more practised.[144] By then, the act had contributed to the greater nationalisation of voting in terms of class, politics, and religion; by compounding fishwives and farmers. Changes to constituency boundaries in 1918 were considerable, but a similar number of members was returned so the matter was of party, more than parliamentary, significance. The story of franchise extension meant that, just as the determinant of the government passed from the Commons to the country, legislative dominance passed from Commons to cabinet, and, once electoral reform had been dropped, party triumphed. As one of those moved to take stock then acknowledged, 'to oppose the Party System in this Year of Grace, 1919, is a work of supererogation'.[145]

Party government undermined parliamentary government; alongside the anomalous election outcome, the authority of the Commons was undermined, as if political principle had been by partisan chicanery. The 1918 election had inevitably disordered the two-party system. Only in 1924 was that system restored, albeit with a different two parties. Three general elections in three years between 1922 and 1924 gave scope to consider electoral reform, but there was little appetite outside Westminster and the commentariat. The system remained stable, and direct action and syndicalism were marginalised. The new prominence of party leaders served to reinforce the notion that, as the chamber was directed by the executive, members followed their leader more than they did their judgment. The Commons appeared merely as a legislature, rather than as the authority which could determine the existence of the executive. So far as women and redistribution were concerned, the war impeded but also impelled, rather as the great decline in the influence of the Commons detected by the Burke scholar, Frank Raffety, was 'by no means due to the War'; it 'has almost meant an eclipse'.[146] The war suspended its power to determine, and the decline in its prestige followed.[147]

The aftermath of Armageddon was as conducive to great hyperbole as it was to sheer confusion. Much was said to be 'on trial' – parliamentary institutions in general, and the

[141] Elliot, *Toryism*, 80–1.

[142] Sidebotham, *Pillars of the State*, 24.

[143] H.H. Asquith, *The Duty of the Liberal Party* (1919), 5.

[144] Winterton, *Orders of the Day*, 83.

[145] Edward Melland, *A Plea for Parliamentary Government* [1919], 8.

[146] Raffety, *Future of Party Politics*, 67.

[147] J.A. Spender, *The Public Life* (2 vols, 1925), i, 125.

house of commons in particular: '[i]t is not too much to say that the constitutional method is upon its last trial – and the sands are running out'.[148] Single member plurality voting had survived and was unthreatened thereafter; female suffrage, proportional representation, and Lords' reform remained unresolved. Questions as to whether individual opinion had been transmitted into public action, or whether a system that was too centralised had been rectified, continued unanswered. The appeal of decentralisation, devolution and direct action was evident to some; to others, parliament should be such voice as the nation possessed. That was why, as important as it was that the franchise had been extended and that redistribution had taken place, the election which followed undermined much of the sense that good had been done. Such counsels were of perfection. It neither violated tradition nor broke from precedent that the house of commons should not be representative of the people, but it had been subject to an act of reform.

---

[148] *Daily Herald*, 8 Feb. 1919, p. 7.

The British Press and the 1918 Reform Act

ADRIAN BINGHAM

This essay provides the first comprehensive study of the British press's reporting of, and discussions about, the electoral reform proposals that became the Representation of the People Act 1918. It shows that, in responding enthusiastically to calls for substantial constitutional change, newspapers from across the ideological spectrum revealed a deep disillusionment with partisan politics and party machines, and imagined a re-energised democracy that would rise to the complex tasks of post-war reconstruction. Female voters were to have a significant role in this more inclusive political system, and even long-standing opponents of women's suffrage chose this moment publicly to alter their position – although by repeatedly framing enfranchisement as an outcome of service to the nation, the language of democratic rights was sometimes blurred. Many newspapers also argued for proportional representation (PR) to create a fairer, less cynical and less strictly-managed type of politics. These debates marked an important moment in the redefinition of British democracy, and they would have a lasting influence on post-war political culture. After 1918, the press generally defended this new democracy, even if some commentators expressed anxieties that certain voters lacked the capacity or inclination properly to exercise their political responsibilities. Set against the political turbulence across Europe, and the inevitable disquiet generated by economic dislocation and mass unemployment, it is the resilience of democracy in Britain, rather than its weakness, that is notable. In these difficult times, the press played a crucial role in legitimising and stabilising the parliamentary system and celebrating a more inclusive politics.

Keywords: democracy; female voters; feminism; franchise; Lloyd George; newspapers; press; proportional representation (PR); Representation of the People Act 1918; suffrage

1

Welcoming, in March 1917, the introduction into the house of commons of the comprehensive programme of electoral reform that would become the Representation of the People Act 1918, a *Daily Telegraph* editorial predicted that any opposition to the measures would be restricted to a small number of MPs who had not grasped the new world brought about by the Great War. 'All men who are facing the future and not the past, whatever their political predilections', the paper contended, 'know that one consequence of this war, to which the whole nation has devoted itself, is to render the demand for a fully democratised franchise irresistible, both morally and practically'.[1] The *Telegraph* succinctly articulated a set of ideas that was expressed repeatedly across the pages of the national press – namely that war had transformed the basis of British politics; that service to the nation had rendered almost irresistible the claims to representation of the disenfranchised; and that the partisan

[1] *Daily Telegraph*, 29 Mar. 1917, p. 4.

struggles of the past should be forsaken for a constructive, forward-looking spirit. As the reforms worked their way through the parliamentary system to become law in February 1918, the chorus of newspaper support and approval did not falter.

The exceptional circumstances of the Representation of the People Act, and its relatively consensual passage, has meant that it has received less attention from historians than did earlier measures of enfranchisement or redistribution.[2] Lacking the drama of the party political battles, constitutional crises and high-profile extra-parliamentary campaigns that marked previous moments of reform, the 1918 Reform Act has been widely regarded as the inevitable, and long-awaited (near) endpoint of a characteristically British process of incremental democratisation.[3] The intellectual case for extending the suffrage had effectively been won; the war merely provided the conditions in which a political *impasse* could be unblocked, individuals could justify withdrawing from deeply-entrenched positions by applauding service to the nation, and partisan electoral calculations no longer seemed quite so urgent.[4] It is perhaps not surprising, therefore, that historians of the press have been drawn far more frequently to the bitter political conflict of the pre-1914 period, the role of the 'press barons' in unseating Asquith as prime minister in 1916, or newspaper attempts to appeal to the expanded electorate after 1918, than to the apparently routine debates about the Reform Act.[5] Indeed, Ian Machin has suggested that the press assumed that the public were more interested in developments on the battlefield, and therefore 'gave only brief references' to the reform of the electoral system.[6]

If one is looking for the vigorous cut-and-thrust of partisan journalistic confrontation, or the elaboration of innovative justifications for franchise extension, the newspaper coverage of the reform debates between 1916 and 1918 might well disappoint. But this is to miss the real significance of the press's contribution in this period. Given the space constraints imposed by newsprint rationing, most newspapers did provide serious and detailed reporting of the passage of this legislation, and staked out clear positions on contested issues such as women's suffrage and proportional representation (PR). In so doing, they played an important role in helping to reformulate ideas about the nature of British democracy, the definitions of citizenship, and the process of representation. Indeed, the fact that there was widespread agreement among mainstream papers made these ideas even more influential, and therefore all the worthier of attention. This essay seeks to explore the debates about reform to tease out and analyse the attitudes and arguments underpinning the acceptance of reform. How did the *Telegraph*, and other papers, conceive the future that it encouraged

[2] For a recent overview of the scholarship, see R. Blackburn, 'Laying the Foundations of the Modern Voting System: The Representation of the People Act 1918', *Parliamentary History*, xxx (2011), 33–52.

[3] Ian Machin, *The Rise of Democracy in Britain, 1830–1918* (Basingstoke, 2000); John Garrard, *Democratisation in Britain: Elites, Civil Society and Reform since 1800* (Basingstoke, 2001).

[4] Martin Pugh, *The March of the Women: A Revisionist Analysis of the Campaign for Women's Suffrage, 1866–1914* (Oxford, 2000).

[5] Stephen Koss, *The Rise and Fall of the Political Press in Britain. Vol. 2: The Twentieth Century* (1984); J.M. McEwen, 'The Press and the Fall of Asquith', *Historical Journal*, xxi (1978), 863–83; Adrian Bingham, 'Enfranchisement, Feminism and the Modern Woman: Debates in the British Popular Press, 1918–1939', in *The Aftermath of Suffrage*, ed. Julie Gottlieb and Richard Toye (Basingstoke, 2013), 87–104; Adrian Bingham, ' "An Organ of Uplift?" The Popular Press and Political Culture in Interwar Britain', *Journalism Studies*, xiv (2013), 651–62; Laura Beers, *Your Britain: Media and the Making of the Labour Party* (Cambridge, MA, 2010).

[6] Machin, *Rise of Democracy*, 142.

its readers to face? How had the fact that the 'whole nation' had 'devoted itself' to war altered the nature of citizenship, and made a 'fully democratised franchise irresistible'? What did democracy mean in this new world? This essay will contend that the emergence of a broad consensus about many of these questions was of major significance when Europe was about to enter a period in which democratic systems would be critiqued, rejected and overthrown. If the consensus frayed in Britain after 1918, it remained strong enough to sustain mainstream confidence in the legitimacy and effectiveness of parliamentary democracy and to limit the strength of the challenge from fascist and communist movements.

The essay will proceed in four sections. The first will consider the press's general appetite for parliamentary reform, which became increasingly evident once prime minister, Herbert Asquith, raised the question of updating the voting register in August 1916. In responding to calls for a substantial change to the existing system, newspapers revealed a deep disillusionment with partisan politics and party machines, and looked ahead to a re-energised democracy that would be able to rise to the complex tasks of post-war reconstruction. There was some irony in this, given that the press was deeply complicit in the polarisation of political life before 1914, but the wholehearted embrace of democracy, and the suggestion that it was a key part of what the allies were fighting for, helped to smooth the transition to the new arrangements after 1918.

The second section examines the debates about citizenship and the reconstitution of the political nation. Newspapers from across the political spectrum accepted the claim of servicemen to the franchise, and even long-standing opponents of women's suffrage chose this moment publicly to alter their position. By repeatedly framing enfranchisement in terms of service to the nation, however, the language of democratic rights was sometimes blurred, which had a lasting impact on how women voters, in particular, were viewed; it also paved the way for the temporary exclusion of conscientious objectors from the electorate.

The third section discusses the proposals for reforming the operation of the electoral system by introducing a measure of PR. It is striking how enthusiastic many leading newspapers were for dismantling the first-past-the-post system in the name of developing a fairer, more responsive type of politics. This became a central theme of idealistic commentaries about creating a purer, less cynical, and less strictly managed form of democracy, and lends weight to the argument that this was the greatest missed opportunity for PR in the modern period.[7]

The final part briefly outlines how the press represented the functioning of the new system in the 1918 election and thereafter. Although the basic principles of the new democracy were never seriously threatened in the pages of the mainstream press – with the partial exception of the *Daily Mail* and the *Daily Mirror* under Lord Rothermere – some journalists and commentators expressed anxieties that certain voters lacked the capacity or inclination properly to exercise their political responsibilities. There was also some nostalgia for a time when smaller electorates made political campaigning more straightforward and ensured that each individual vote had greater weight. Set against the political turbulence across Europe, and the inevitable disquiet generated by economic dislocation and mass unemployment, it is the resilience of democracy in Britain, rather than its weakness, that is notable. In these difficult times, the press played a crucial role in legitimising and stabilising the system.

[7]Blackburn, 'Laying the Foundations of the Modern Voting System', 145–7.

This essay is based on a detailed study of the output of the leading national daily and Sunday newspapers – notably the *Daily Chronicle, Daily Express, Daily Mail, Daily Mirror, Daily News, Daily Telegraph, Manchester Guardian,*[8] *Morning Post, Observer, The Times,* and *Sunday Times* – as well as the leading political weeklies, the *New Statesman,* and the *Spectator.*[9] The analysis focuses more intently on the responses of the right-wing publications. Liberal and Labour newspapers had few difficulties in embracing democratic reform and supporting the enfranchisement of women; in most cases, they had campaigned for these very changes for years. Of far greater significance for the emergence of a consensus around the reformed political system was the way in which cautious, sceptical, and often anxious, conservative voices came to terms with the new democracy. The essay is also concerned primarily with the press's contribution to public debates about parliamentary reform – examining how it reflected and shaped wider opinion – rather than tracing its private influence in the corridors of power. It therefore concentrates on the published content of the newspapers, particularly leading articles, comment pieces, and reports of parliamentary proceedings, rather than the personal correspondence and internal policy decisions of editors, proprietors and journalists.[10] While the war restricted how much the papers could print, it increased the public appetite for news of all sorts. The all-consuming nature of this 'total war' inevitably directed attention away from local concerns to Britain's various campaigns on the global stage, and helped to reinforce a growing nationalisation of politics and culture that would be further consolidated by the democratic reforms of 1918.[11] The influence of the London-based press was steadily increasing: once newsprint rationing ended, the circulations of national newspapers rose significantly, with a near doubling of circulations in the interwar period, and the combined sales of the national papers passing those of the provincial papers in 1923. If the powers of the 'press barons' were not as far-reaching as some feared - 'What England thinks is largely controlled by a very few men', lamented the journalist, author and peace campaigner, Norman Angell, in 1922[12] – newspapers were central to British political and popular culture in this period, and, especially before the rise of radio broadcasting, they had a very significant role in setting the political agenda and framing public discussion.[13]

2

For opponents of reform, the midst of war – and no less than the bloodiest conflict the nation had ever experienced – was not a moment for raising controversial questions of constitutional reorganisation. The proposals 'ought to be laid aside as a waste of our more precious

---

[8] The *Manchester Guardian* was, of course, strictly speaking a provincial paper, but its reputation ensured that its voice was heard nationally and internationally.

[9] The Labour-supporting *Daily Herald* was unable to sustain daily publication throughout the war, and published a short, and rather idiosyncratic, weekly edition, which is only considered very briefly here: for more on the *Herald,* see Huw Richards, *The Bloody Circus: The Daily Herald and the Left* (1997), ch. 1.

[10] For editorial policies and the preoccupations of proprietors, see Koss, *Rise and Fall of the Political Press;* Kevin Williams, *Read All About It! A History of the British Newspaper* (2010); Adrian Bingham, *Gender, Modernity, and the Popular Press in Inter-War Britain* (Oxford, 2004).

[11] Paul Ward, *Britishness since 1870* (2004); Thomas Hajkowski, *The BBC and National Identity in Britain, 1922–53* (Manchester, 2013).

[12] Cited in Williams, *Read All About It!,* 164.

[13] Bingham, ' "An Organ of Uplift?" '.

time', grumbled the *Morning Post*, the only leading paper consistently against changes to the system of representation.[14] Most press commentators argued, by contrast, that the war, and the meanings ascribed to it, made reform necessary, morally, intellectually, and practically. 'Whatever the war may have been in its earlier stages, it has now assumed definitely the complexion of a war for democracy', argued the *Manchester Guardian* in May 1917. Britain's international reputation as a defender of democracy, the paper continued, made it essential that it get its own house in order:

> If this country is to maintain the place which is its due in the vanguard of the Allies it must show that it is in the vanguard of democracy. With our present wretched electoral system any such claim on our part is open to dispute, and indeed is being contested. We need a franchise reform to maintain our moral hegemony during the war, so that our full influence may tell in determining the course of the war and the character of the peace.[15]

The 'march of democracy is the cardinal fact of the war', agreed the *Daily News*.[16] If stirring celebrations of democracy might have been expected in Liberal newspapers, though, similar sentiments were also voiced by more Conservative publications. The *Observer*, edited by the widely-respected, and fiercely-independent, J.L. Garvin, published a substantial editorial in June 1917 entitled 'The New Democracy' which argued that the war represented 'the struggle of a great principle', namely that of democracy against absolutism:

> in truth and in fact our war with Germany is in its essence a war between these two ideas: a war between the idea that the State should be as much like an Army as possible and the idea that it should be the living expression of the minds of the men and women who compose it … The stake, indeed, is nothing less than this: Whether military absolutism or democratic freedom shall emerge from this war with the prestige of success and all the immense consequences that victory and defeat for one or other of those ideas must bring upon Europe and the world.[17]

The *Observer*, like the *Manchester Guardian*, was very conscious of what it saw as Britain's world historical role, especially given the United States' recent entry into the war and the February revolution in Russia. The proposals to widen the franchise, in conjunction with Lloyd George's recently-made promise that Ireland be allowed to become 'a free member of the Empire', were momentous steps that would buttress Britain's position as a moral exemplar: 'Both decisions bring to our nation an immediate strength, for they rally to us all the hopes and dreams of a world that bases on democracy, as never since the day of the fall of the Bastille, its passionate longing for peace and progress and freedom'.[18] The *Daily Express* was more pithy, but had a similar opinion: 'since we have acclaimed the fact that we are fighting to preserve democracy, it is ridiculous to decline to make Great Britain a

[14] *Morning Post*, 28 Mar. 1917, p. 6.
[15] *Manchester Guardian*, 16 May 1917, p. 4.
[16] *Daily News*, 17 May 1917, p. 1.
[17] *Observer*, 24 June 1917, p. 6.
[18] *Observer*, 24 June 1917, p. 6.

truly democratic nation'.[19] For papers of both left and right, British national identity at this moment of crisis was deeply wedded to the notion of being a champion of democracy.

These defences of democratic principle revealed both a disdain for the habits and practices of pre-war politics, and a yearning for a parliamentary system that worked in different ways. There was, in particular, a widely-professed contempt for the cynicism of party machines and the narrow-mindedness of the partisan battles. Such commentaries required some strategic forgetfulness, if not outright hypocrisy, on the part of the press, given that editors, proprietors and journalists had not only been fully committed to the bitter arguments about house of lords reform, Irish home rule and female suffrage before 1914, but had often been guilty of polarising debates and sensationalising conflict.[20] Neal Blewett has, for example, demonstrated that leading national papers dedicated huge amounts of space and resources to the coverage of the general elections in 1910.[21] Nevertheless, the frequent articulation of a desire for a different form of politics, at a time of (relative) party truce and administration by coalition government, should not be dismissed as simply press opportunism or insincerity. This was, after all, a highly-unusual moment of fluidity in British politics, with the Liberals riven by splits, the teenage Labour Party poised to grow into adulthood, and the imminent prospect of millions of unaligned voters being added to the register. There were real possibilities for reshaping the British political scene, not least given Lloyd George's popularity as a war leader standing above party conflict, and there were also genuine anxieties about the dangers that lay ahead if the political system was insufficiently responsive.

The *Daily Telegraph* was, perhaps, the most vociferous in its criticism of pre-war politics. 'The country will never go back to the conditions of July, 1914', declared an editorial in March 1917, in which the repetition of the cursed word 'party' emphasized the paper's contempt:

> After a considerable experience, the British nation had begun very seriously to doubt if its affairs were best transacted by an apparatus of party caucuses, party funds, party programmes, party speechmaking. The party system was visibly decaying … The idea of reverting after this war to the old machinery, the old spirit, the old dead level of scheming professionalism, is one which the nation as a whole entirely refuses to entertain, and which no one takes seriously except those who found their livelihood in party management, and those who are afflicted permanently with the looking-backward temperament.[22]

The *Telegraph* was under no illusion that parties would disappear, but it hoped that they would rally around a 'living principle of one sort or another, and not round a machine'.[23] Without a shift to a more idealistic form of politics, warned another editorial, not only would parties risk losing support, the whole political system would be imperilled:

---

[19] *Daily Express*, 24 May 1917, p. 2.

[20] Koss, *Rise and Fall of the Political Press*; Susanne Stoddart, 'The New Liberalism, the New Journalism and Emotion in Edwardian Liberal Newspapers', Royal Holloway, University of London PhD, 2014.

[21] Neal Blewett, *The Peers, the Parties and the People: The British General Elections of 1910* (1972), ch. 15.

[22] *Daily Telegraph*, 30 Mar. 1917, p. 4.

[23] *Daily Telegraph*, 30 Mar. 1917, p. 4.

If anything could totally wreck Parliamentary government in this country it would be the spectacle of a Legislature, formed by the old methods, flourishing the old weapons, and egged on by the old wirepullers, devoting itself to a protracted wrangle of that sort with all the life of a nation awaiting reconstruction.[24]

The liberal *Daily Chronicle* likewise argued that only by seizing the present opportunity for reform would the legitimacy of the political system be secured:

our pre-war failure to set our electoral house in order had exposed us to a great danger and a great handicap … the nation has been extraordinarily lucky in having a way of escape from this danger and handicap … posterity would never forgive us if we threw such a great piece of good fortune away.[25]

Central to the arguments for reform was the belief that the enormous challenges of post-war reconstruction would require parliament to be more efficient and agile than ever before: there simply would not be time for what *The Times* called 'the old fruitless controversies of long years before the war'. Those who contemplated addressing these tasks with an unreformed parliament, the paper argued, 'must either be the blindest of partisans or they can have no conception whatever of the volume of work which will inevitably descend upon parliament the very moment the war is over'; doing so would inevitably mean leaving 'our Parliamentary institutions to fall still further into disrepute'.[26] The *Observer* made similar predictions, and was equally concerned about the risks of preserving the status quo:

Social, industrial and Imperial needs will demand our whole time for constructive legislation. Otherwise, there would be inefficiency, distraction, confusion – a disastrous barrenness and bitterness of party strife in the old manner. This for some years to come, as we value our lives, we must banish like the plague.[27]

The *Sunday Times* called upon politicians to maximise and build upon the 'new spirit of reasonableness and compromise that is in the air', while the *Express* echoed the prime minister's call not to 'leave ourselves the helpless slaves of party machines'.[28] 'We need a new machine for new work', stated the *Daily News* bluntly.[29] Perhaps most striking of all, even the *Morning Post*, the paper most resistant to constitutional reform, recognized the need 'to get a new spirit into our system of government', because before 1914 it 'had fallen into a state of rottenness which boded ill for the future of this country'.[30] Indeed, central to the *Post*'s case against change was the fact that the wartime house of commons was not representative of the nation, and had been elected 'solely upon party issues and by means of the powerful and secret operation of the great party machine and the subsidised caucus

[24] *Daily Telegraph*, 29 Mar. 1917, p. 4.
[25] *Daily Chronicle*, 28 May 1917, p. 2.
[26] *The Times*, 19 June 1917, p. 7.
[27] *Observer*, 1 Apr. 1917, p. 6.
[28] *Sunday Times*, 1 Apr. 1917, p. 6; *Daily Express*, 29 Mar. 1917, p. 1.
[29] *Daily News*, 27 Mar. 1917, p. 2.
[30] *Morning Post*, 28 Mar. 1917, p. 6.

on both sides'; since then, however, 'the whole sentiment and opinion of the country' had changed and 'the very name of party politics ha[d] become odious'.[31] Opponents of reform had no desire to stake their position on a defence of a form of partisan politics that was widely perceived as unpopular and ineffective.

This wholesale rejection of party had an important impact. In the short term, it helped to legitimise the maintenance of Lloyd George's coalition government not only until the end of the war, but into the 1918 general election and several years beyond. More deeply, though, it influenced the nature of interwar political culture. In particular, it fed some of the tendencies identified by Jon Lawrence and Helen McCarthy – notably the 'low-key and homely' tone of much political discourse, the focusing of party propaganda on 'the vast numbers of less partisan, largely inactive citizens whose votes were said to decide elections', and the flowering of voluntary associations which defined themselves against the partisanship of the Westminster parties.[32] If partisan politics resumed in the 1920s – with the press more than playing its part during election campaigns – the wartime reaction against party machines, nevertheless, left a significant legacy.

3

The new politics that wartime commentators envisioned was to be based, it was almost universally agreed, on a broader, and more inclusive, franchise. The unprecedented demands and sacrifices of the Great War transformed the dynamics of the debates about who should be enfranchised. Citizenship could not be denied to those who had given so much. 'Every soldier or sailor, by the mere fact that he has fought for the country, should be entitled to a vote and should be permitted to exercise it', declared the *Daily Mail*; 'A vote is a small thing to offer a man who has been ready to give his blood' agreed the *Manchester Guardian*.[33] No mainstream politician or journalist was inclined to dissent. The *Mail* was also one of the leading proponents of following this argument to its logical conclusion, by disbarring those 'who have ignobly shirked fighting': the conscientious objector, the paper argued, 'is one of the most contemptible products of our time and richly deserves the disgust with which the public regard him'.[34] The *Express* used similar language to voice its disdain: 'It is intolerable that the contemptible creatures who have discovered a "*conscience*" to save their precious skins should ever be allowed to enter a polling booth and take any part in the grand inquest of the nation.'[35] The pressure from popular newspapers, and magazines such as *John Bull*, helped to create a climate of opinion in which parliament agreed temporarily to enfranchise 19-year-old servicemen, while disqualifying conscientious objectors from voting for five years.

[31] *Morning Post*, 30 Mar. 1917, p. 4.

[32] Jon Lawrence, *Electing Our Masters: The Hustings in British Politics from Hogarth to Blair* (Oxford, 2009), 96, 111, 113; Helen McCarthy, 'Parties, Voluntary Associations, and Democratic Politics in Interwar Britain', *Historical Journal*, 1 (2007), 891–912; Helen McCarthy, 'Whose Democracy? Histories of British Political Culture between the Wars', *Historical Journal*, lv (2012), 221–38.

[33] *Daily Mail*, 16 May 1916, p. 4; *Manchester Guardian*, 23 May 1917, p. 4.

[34] *Manchester Guardian*, 23 May 1917, p. 4.

[35] *Daily Express*, 29 Mar. 1917, p. 2.

Inevitably, though, it was the proposal to grant suffrage to women that dominated the headlines and generated the most commentary. Before 1914, the press had been deeply divided on the issue. While the *Manchester Guardian*, the *Daily News*, and the *Daily Herald* were avowed supporters of female enfranchisement, *The Times*, the *Daily Mail*, and the *Morning Post* were consistently hostile; other papers condemned suffragette violence, while wavering about the broader principle.[36] By 1917, however, there was an enthusiastic press consensus around giving women the vote at age 30 years, and, indeed, allowing them to stand as parliamentary candidates. Opposition was now presented as unreasonable and outdated, the preserve of an obstinate and out-of-touch minority. 'There can be no case against women suffrage now' insisted the *Express*; 'no other course is possible' agreed the *Telegraph*.[37] Even the *Spectator*, a bastion of resistance, accepted that 'we are faced now by a strong popular desire to give women the vote which cannot possibly be mistaken'.[38] Of the leading papers, only the diehard *Morning Post* maintained its resistance, arguing that this reform was 'designed to swamp the voter who has political experience and sagacity', and concluding defiantly that 'a nation of men which hands its responsibility in government over to women is not adding to its reputation in the world of men'.[39]

Few historians now make a straightforward connection between the war and the success of the suffrage cause. 'The intellectual case for enfranchising women had long been won', suggests Geoffrey Searle, building on the research of Martin Pugh: 'The war simply created circumstances in which Votes for Women could be granted with minimum political disturbance', and provided opponents such as Asquith with 'an escape from the impossible position' in which they found themselves.[40] This is a persuasive argument. Several Conservative newspapers made clear that they would have been reluctant to agree to any reform that could have been perceived as a concession to violent campaigning. 'We think a great deal more of "Votes for Women" to-day than we did three years ago, when the cry was accompanied by church burnings and window smashing', observed an *Express* editorial in August 1916.[41] *The Times* highlighted that enfranchisement was not a 'triumph of agitation, for agitation has long been stilled', while the *Telegraph* was keen to reach agreement so that parliament did not 'relight the flames of the miserable sex controversy over the suffrage which poisoned public life in England before the war'.[42] Nor did Liberal and left-of-centre titles, apart from the *Herald*, dissent from this position. The *Daily Chronicle* suggested that 'some measure' of enfranchisement 'would almost certainly have become law ere now but for the antagonism aroused at Westminster and in the country by the methods of the Pankhurst agitation'. Only once 'the painful impression created by those follies and crimes' had subsided could the question be considered on its own merits. For the *New Statesman*, indeed, 'Perhaps the war's best help to the cause was the excuse with which it provided the militants for stopping militancy', given that in the immediate pre-war

[36] Pugh, *March of the Women*, 229–31; Bingham, *Gender, Modernity, and the Popular Press*, 111–13.
[37] *Daily Express*, 24 May 1917, p. 2; *Daily Telegraph*, 8 Jan. 1918, p. 6.
[38] *The Spectator*, 22 June 1917, p. 2.
[39] *Morning Post*, 8 Jan. 1918, p. 6.
[40] G.R. Searle, *A New England? Peace and War 1886–1918* (Oxford, 2004), 791.
[41] *Daily Express*, 15 Aug. 1916, p. 4.
[42] *The Times*, 29 Mar. 1917, p. 7; *Daily Telegraph*, 8 Jan. 1918, p. 6.

years their activism 'ceased to have any but an obstructive effect'.[43] If press opposition to the Pankhursts had softened, due to Emmeline and Christabel's conspicuous patriotism and support of the war effort, there was little inclination to show any generosity to the Women's Social and Political Union (WSPU); more credit tended to go to the peaceful campaigns of Millicent Fawcett's National Union of Women's Suffrage Societies (NUWSS), whose 'patient exercise of persuasion', in the *Chronicle*'s admiring words, 'brought opinion round to their side'.[44]

Instead, and with a remarkable consistency of tone and language, newspapers pointed to women's wartime service as demonstrating their suitability as full citizens. The outpouring of editorials and articles developing this argument should not be read, in the main at least, as a reflection of journalistic insincerity or pragmatism. Martin Pugh has suggested, for example, that 'the positive welcome given to women's wartime work proved to have been very superficial and short-lived'.[45] Yet even if historians can see the limits to the wartime renegotiation of gender, and rightly dismiss simplistic claims that the conflict brought a 'liberation' for women, we should also not dismiss the very real impact on contemporaries of women moving into unfamiliar roles and bearing the burdens of the home front; the perception that women had 'proved' themselves during the war remained a cliché well into the 1920s.[46] The argument that the vote was conceived as a 'reward' for wartime service is undermined, as both contemporaries and historians have recognized, by the continuing exclusion from the franchise, on age grounds, of many young female munition workers. But this is too narrow an understanding of the debates. As Nicoletta Gullace has argued, the war involved a redefinition of citizenship around notions of patriotism, duty and sacrifice, and women's new and high-profile public roles, as well as their private suffering as wives and mothers, included them within these freshly-drawn boundaries.[47] An editorial in *The Times* in March 1917, indeed, made this very distinction. The idea that the 'vote is a mere reward for good behaviour' was one that 'every patriotic women resents', the paper argued: 'It is based wholly on the palpable injustice of withholding such protection as the vote offers from a sex which has for the first time taken its full share in the national effort and will have sufficient difficulty in any case to maintain the position which it has won.'[48] It was not necessarily assumed that women would be able to 'maintain the position' they had won, but by taking a 'full share' in the 'national effort' they deserved their place in the political system and a voice in the reconstruction work to come. Such arguments, of course, patronised women both by rendering invisible the full range of their pre-war work, paid and unpaid, and by silencing women's own campaigns for equality. In the circumstances

---

[43] *New Statesman*, 3 June 1917, p. 268.

[44] Martin Pugh, *The Pankhursts* (2002); *Daily Chronicle*, 21 June 1917, p. 2.

[45] Martin Pugh, 'Suffrage and Citizenship', in *20th Century Britain: Economic, Cultural and Social Change*, ed. Francesca Carnevali and Julie-Marie Strange (2nd edn, Harlow, 2007), 101.

[46] *Behind the Lines: Gender and the Two World Wars*, ed. M.R. Higonnet, J. Jenson, S. Michel, M. C. Weitz (New Haven, CT, 1987); Gail Braybon and Penny Summerfield, *Out of the Cage: Women's Experiences in Two World Wars* (1987); Adrian Bingham, ' "An Era of Domesticity"? Histories of Women and Gender in Inter-War Britain', *Cultural and Social History*, i (2004), 225–33; Bingham, *Gender, Modernity, and the Popular Press*, ch. 2.

[47] Nicoletta F. Gullace, *'The Blood of Our Sons': Men, Women, and the Renegotiation of British Citizenship during the Great War* (New York, 2002).

[48] *The Times*, 29 Mar. 1917, p. 7.

of the war, however, they provided very little discursive space in which opponents could counter or resist the logic of enfranchisement.

Considering the 'greatest change in our electoral law projected in modern times', for example, a *Daily Telegraph* editorial in June 1917 rehearsed arguments that were becoming very familiar in the pages of the press. A 'great and decisive difference' had been made by the 'experience of war-time', it noted: 'those who needed that experience to persuade them of women's strength of patriotism, their capacity for public service, their steadiness in even the least familiar aspects of duty, must have had their fill of conviction after the first two years of war'.[49] Over the following months, as the decisive votes in parliament loomed, it returned to these themes time and again. In January 1918, on the eve of a debate in the house of lords, the paper was adamant that there was only one legitimate option available, namely:

> to extend the franchise to women in view of the part which they have played in the war and the multitudinous public, industrial, and social services which they are now rendering, and but for which the war work of the nation – in the widest sense of the term – would come to a standstill. The war could not be carried on as it is without the willing co-operation of the women, and still greater and greater calls will be made upon them in the near future. Whether, therefore, one has regard chiefly to their present war work or to the colossal task of Reconstruction which will confront the State after the war is over, the result is the same. It is now plain that the active co-operation of women is essential to the well-being of the State.[50]

The debate, concluded the *Telegraph*, 'has been irrevocably settled by the war.'[51]

Other papers made very similar arguments, declaring women's wartime contribution as unimpeachable evidence of their readiness for citizenship, and framing any contrary opinions as almost incomprehensible in the changed circumstances.[52] Opposition to reform, declared the *Express* in March 1917, 'that might have been reasonable before the war becomes mere stubborn reaction after the creation of a citizen army and its heroic achievements'. Women had 'shown their eager desire to fulfil the duties of citizenship even before they possess its privileges'.[53] Another editorial the following January likewise insisted that 'Women demonstrated their right to the privileges of citizenship by the enthusiasm for service that they have shown since the beginning of the war.'[54] 'If there is one thing that the war has brought about', contended the *Mail*, 'it is a change in the national feeling towards this question, a change that amounts to an almost universal conviction that the State will be all the better for the active participation of women in its public life'.[55] By the end of the

---

[49] *Daily Telegraph*, 19 June 1917, p. 4.

[50] *Daily Telegraph*, 8 Jan. 1918, p. 6.

[51] *Daily Telegraph*, 8 Jan. 1918, p. 6.

[52] Sarah Pedersen has recently found similar language in the Scottish Press: 'Suffragettes and the Scottish Press during the First World War', *Women's History Review*, published online 22 Feb. 2017, DOI: 10.1080/09612025.2017.1292620.

[53] *Daily Express*, 29 Mar. 1917, p. 2.

[54] *Daily Express*, 11. Jan. 1918, p. 2.

[55] *Daily Mail*, 11 Jan. 1918, p. 2.

war, indeed, the *Mail*, a long-time opponent of reform, could hardly conceive of women being excluded from citizenship:

> Now that we have admitted and realized the rights of women it seems almost incredible that we should ever have attempted to touch even the fringes of such problems [of social reform] while more than half of the population were excluded from any share in the management of the nation's affairs.[56]

The power of these arguments was such that even papers that had consistently supported the principle of female enfranchisement still drew upon them. The *Manchester Guardian*, a long-standing and consistent proponent of the women's cause, nevertheless informed its readers that 'The war has taught us many things, and among others the immense power, both moral and economic, which women command within the State'; women had proved themselves 'capable and worthy' as 'workers in every unaccustomed field, as nurses and doctors actually on the scene of conflict'.[57] Even when the paper described reform as a matter of 'elementary justice', as it did in an editorial of January 1917, it could not resist reinforcing its case in a similar way – it was 'a justice which the lessons of the war have brought home as never before to all thoughtful and patriotic people'.[58] Similarly, while the *Daily News* made clear its view that women's citizenship belonged 'to her as one who has an equal share in the burdens, responsibilities, and restraints of an organised society', it nevertheless added that the claim had been 'strengthened in these days beyond challenge even from those who have opposed that claim in the past on the infantile ground that women can have no part in the defence of the country'.[59] A headline after a key vote in the house of commons read 'Suffrage Earned by Magnificent Work During the War', and when female enfranchisement was finally accepted by the house of lords in January 1918, the paper argued that it had been conferred by 'the popular feeling aroused by the importance of women's contribution to the war'.[60] This was precisely where the longer-term dangers for feminism lay. The invocation of women's wartime contribution was, by and large, genuine, and had a discursive power that opponents could not counter. It muted, however, the language of democratic rights and equality, and the 1918 Reform Act could not be straightforwardly claimed as a feminist victory. By so effusively encouraging readers to admire women's wartime contributions and service, newspapers may, indeed, have challenged some perceptions about female 'capabilities', but they may also have obscured the challenge that suffrage campaigners wanted to pose to conventional understandings of representation and citizenship.

4

If votes for women generated the most headlines, the most controversial and fiercely-contested proposals proved to be those related to the introduction of a measure of PR.

[56] *Daily Mail*, 26 Nov. 1918, p. 2.

[57] *Manchester Guardian*, 15 May 1916, p. 4.

[58] *Manchester Guardian*, 19 Jan. 1917, p. 4.

[59] *Daily News*, 27 Mar. 1917, p. 2.

[60] *Daily News*, 29 Mar. 1917, p. 1; 11 Jan. 1918, p. 2.

The Commons and the Lords ultimately failed to reach an acceptable compromise, other than the appointment of a royal commission, and the status quo prevailed.[61] Historians have not sufficiently appreciated how enthusiastic the press was for reform of the first-past-the-post system in 1917–18. The disillusionment with pre-war partisan politics, discussed earlier, ensured that there was widespread support for a new system that would better reflect the variety of public opinion, and would be less susceptible to management by party machines. Papers as different as the *Daily Telegraph* and the *Manchester Guardian* devoted considerable amounts of space to defending the merits of PR, and many press commentators agreed that some form of experiment was worth taking given the inequities and rigidities of the existing system. Such a groundswell of support would not be seen again for the rest of the century: here was the great missed opportunity for the implementation of PR.

For its advocates, PR brought a measure of rationality and transparency to an electoral system that was unrepresentative, opaque and unnecessarily complex. It would, papers of both left and right argued, strengthen the position of moderate and independent voices in the house of commons, which at present was too beholden to party whips and managers. 'Proportional representation, by abolishing the "swing of the pendulum" and giving to each political party a representation in the House of Commons substantially equal in proportion to the votes it can command in the country, would have an extraordinarily steadying effect on the composition of the House', argued the *Manchester Guardian* in January 1917. It would also 'attract men of character, ability and influence' and would thereby 'raise the character of the House of Commons, and restore to it its due independence of the Executive'.[62] For the *Observer*, PR was the ideal way of ensuring that the wartime idealism surrounding politics and democracy was consolidated, and a return of the despised old ways avoided:

> The rigid and narrow traditions of party conflict, in our hope, belong to the past. Proportional Representation would be welcome as tending to strengthen the independent forces in political life, and the present moment, when men are speaking and thinking along new lines, breaking free from many an iron law of the past, would be very suitable for its introduction.[63]

It was, the paper affirmed in another editorial, 'a sane and excellent policy' hobbled by a 'ponderously impossible term': 'Why do not its supporters recognise this at once, and advocate PR henceforth as "Fair Voting"?'[64] The *Daily Telegraph* used similar language. The main argument in favour of PR was 'that it is fair; that in the absence of it there can be no fairness, and representation is an empty word; that it gives to majorities and minorities alike the weight that they ought to have if "representation of the people" is to be a real thing'. PR would inevitably triumph, it predicted, 'by virtue of its own intrinsic reasonableness and justice'.[65] The *Daily Chronicle* printed a column written by John Humphries, the secretary of the Proportional Representation Society; under the headline 'How "P. R." Gives Every Vote A Value', he explained that 'It stands for the embodiment in our electoral laws of two

[61] Blackburn, 'Laying the Foundations of the Modern Voting System'.
[62] *Manchester Guardian*, 19 Jan. 1917, p. 4.
[63] *Observer*, 24 June 1917, p. 6.
[64] *Observer*, 13 Jan. 1918, p. 3.
[65] *Daily Telegraph*, 11 Jan. 1918, p. 4.

democratic principles – Justice and Freedom.[66] The paper ultimately argued in favour of the alternative vote system, which it described as 'a very reasonable and unrevolutionary proposal', which would avoid 'all the evils of three-cornered contests'.[67] 'P.R. is essential to a really representative system', concluded the *Daily News*.[68] There was no need for the government to be 'shy' of the 'novelty' of PR agreed *The Times*, a paper hardly known for its embrace of change: 'we should be sorry to see the total disappearance from the scheme of an interesting and very limited experiment in minority representation'. Intellectual ballast for the reform was provided in a detailed letter from the author, H.G. Wells, who labelled PR as 'A Necessary Remedy'.[69] This was an impressive consensus for a relatively-novel proposal, and the language of justice and fairness had an extra power in the context of a society bearing all the sacrifices of total war.

There was a subsidiary case, put most strongly by the *Daily Telegraph*, for PR as a defensive measure that would limit the political turbulence that could result from the greatly-expanded electorate. It was, argued an editorial in March 1917, 'a very necessary safeguard against the complete swamping, in many constituencies, of independent and moderate opinion under the proposed extension of the franchise'. Three months later, the paper spelled out the dangers with greater urgency, having received no satisfactory assurances about the risks of the expanded electorate (an expansion which it fully supported):

> No one, so far as we know, has attempted to meet the argument upon which we have laid most emphasis; that a measure which doubles the numbers of the electorate to-day makes certain an enormous and sweeping addition to the Socialist and extreme Radical elements in the representation of the country, if that representation is obtained by the fallacious and often glaringly unjust method pursued until now. Any man who looks even a little way beyond the conditions of the moment, or the temporary situation in his own Parliamentary constituency, might well tremble for the future if it is to be wholly without guarantees for the fair representation of minority opinion.[70]

The *Telegraph* reported in great detail, and with some concern, the twists and turns of the stand-off between the Commons and the Lords over PR, before reaching the 'melancholy' recognition that it was not going to be accepted. As Blackburn has argued, a more determined government probably could have 'swayed opinion in the Commons'; Lloyd George's ambivalence on the measure ensured that MPs' perceptions of their own self-interest, and anxieties about losing their seats, fortified them to resist the considerable pressure placed upon them by newspapers and campaigners.[71] As anxieties about the expanded electorate faded, and the new system bedded in, the momentum for reform was lost. Yet if the PR cause did not triumph, the significant press support made clear, once again, the considerable dissatisfaction with the existing system, and a yearning for a new politics, based on a fairer representation of a wider range of voices.

[66] *Daily Chronicle*, 10 Jan. 1918, p. 3.

[67] *Daily Chronicle*, 6 Feb. 1918, p. 2.

[68] *Daily News*, 20 June 1917, p. 2.

[69] *The Times*, 7 Feb. 1918, p. 7; 30 Mar. 1917, p. 7.

[70] *Daily Telegraph*, 20 June 1917, p. 6.

[71] Blackburn, 'Laying the Foundations of the Modern Voting System', 47, 51.

5

If a more-principled, less-managed, politics did not emerge after the Armistice in the form imagined by idealists, nor was there a return to the *status quo ante bellum*. The widely-expressed dissatisfaction with party machines and partisan conflict helped to sustain Lloyd George's government until 1922, and continued to resonate in a number of voluntary and campaigning organisations. The decline of the Liberals, and the rise of the Labour Party, ensured that politics looked and sounded different after 1918, and the house of commons became (marginally) more representative of the broader public. The emergence of Labour as the second party, as well as the growth in power of trade unionism, helped to consolidate a gradual shift in Westminster debates away from constitutional and religious issues to those connected to economics, social policy and welfare.[72] Partly in response to the new female electorate that made up much of the 'silent majority' that fascinated party strategists, there was a more domesticated tone in political discourse, typified by the reassuring radio broadcasts of Stanley Baldwin.[73] There was no escaping the transformation that the 1918 Reform Act had wrought in British political life, and the press debates discussed here played a vital role in explaining and justifying these changes to the electorate.

The press was generally staunch in the defence of the new democracy that it had helped to usher in. In the first general election involving the expanded electorate, in December 1918, newspapers repeatedly highlighted the diligence and maturity of the new female voters. If the overall turnout, at 58.9%, was disappointing, women were conspicuously excluded from any blame. For the *Daily Telegraph*:

> The General Election has provided the justification – if, indeed, justification were needed – of the policy of admitting women to the franchise. Their eagerness to fulfil the new duty of taking a full share of responsibility in a decision so vital to the country was the outstanding feature of polling day.[74]

'Not even the most ardent women suffragists … anticipated such a remarkable demonstration of women's interest in their new prerogative', declared the *Express*: 'While the men were apathetic, the women turned out everywhere.'[75] The *Mirror* agreed: 'This election has been marked by a great number of abstentions: not amongst the women. The women voted.'[76] 'Two facts stand out from the polling' noted the *Mail*. 'First the public apathy; second the great strength of the women's vote … nearly as many women voted as men.'[77] Similar observations were made in subsequent elections. Women 'have taken their elective function seriously and responsibly', wrote the *Telegraph* the day after the general election in November 1922, and had 'gone to the poll in great numbers': 'The result is a full justification of that sweeping act of reform which the late Government placed upon the Statute

[72]Ross McKibbin, *Parties and People: England 1914–1951* (Oxford, 2010).

[73]Lawrence, *Electing our Masters*; McCarthy, 'Parties, Voluntary Associations, and Democratic Politics'; David Jarvis, 'Mrs Maggs and Betty: The Conservative Appeal to Women Voters in the 1920s', *Twentieth Century British History*, v (1994), 129–52.

[74]*Daily Telegraph*, 16 Dec. 1918, p. 7.

[75]*Daily Express*, 16 Dec. 1918, p. 7.

[76]*Daily Mirror*, 31 Dec. 1918, p. 5.

[77]*Daily Mail*, 16 Dec. 1918, p. 5.

Book.[78] At the general election two years later, the paper was similarly optimistic, suggesting that women 'have voted in greater numbers than ever before'.[79] Female voters, in short, were demonstrating their worth as citizens.

While the new female voters received the greatest attention from columnists and commentators, it was also widely agreed that the inclusion of more working-class male voters had altered electoral dynamics. When Labour won an eye-catching victory in the Spen Valley by-election in January 1920, for example, *The Times* speculated that the 'decisive votes were recorded in the main by men and women who were enfranchised for the first time by the Representation of the People Act passed two years ago'.[80] The act was, the paper contended, 'a constitutional revolution, and it is only now that its effects are being felt':

> There are over 20 million electors now, with a vast expanse of virgin soil for a fresh political force. The 12 million new voters are of two classes, married women and young men … They are the classes who were most profoundly influenced by the war, and who retain after it the fewest of the old national prejudices and illusions. They offer a unique opportunity for the teaching of a new political creed, and there can be hardly any doubt that it is the swing of the women and ex-Service voters to Labour which is the chief lesson to be learnt from Spen Valley and other recent by-elections.[81]

In such circumstances, it was clear to moderate right-wing opinion that the Conservatives would have to work hard to attract some of these new working-class voters – which was a central part of Stanley Baldwin's appeal as party leader. An editorial in *The Times* in September 1924 warned that the 1918 Reform Act had 'revolutionized' the political situation, and there would be 'nothing but a slow death before the party which does not strive to be truly national by enlisting the cordial cooperation of every man and woman who shares its ideals, irrespective of the class to which they belong':

> The importance of associating the wage-earning class more closely with the Conservative Party becomes increasingly urgent with every day that lengthens the period separating the country from the two-party system and the relatively small electorate … The Conservative Party should not be behind the Labour Party in encouraging the youth of the nation to enlist under its banner with the possibility of satisfying its proper ambitions of public service. The time has gone by for putting up a few working-men candidates for hopeless seats at a General Election and forgetting their very existence when a safe seat falls vacant at a by-election.[82]

Such were the necessary challenges of the new democratic politics, and they were, in most cases, accepted with equanimity as an inevitable consequence of a more inclusive franchise.

[78] *Daily Telegraph*, 17 Nov. 1922, p. 10.
[79] *Daily Telegraph*, 30 Oct. 1924, p. 8.
[80] *The Times*, 7 Jan. 1920, p. 13.
[81] *The Times*, 7 Jan. 1920, p. 13.
[82] *The Times*, 17 Sept. 1924, p. 11.

This is not to suggest, of course, that there were no questions about the suitability of the new electors, or that nostalgia for the pre-1918 system was entirely absent. At the gentlest end of the spectrum, some voices expressed frustration that not all citizens fulfilled their duties at election times. The number of 'unpolled votes' in the 1923 general election was, the *Daily Telegraph* asserted, 'a mocking commentary upon democracy's assumed eagerness for the franchise'.[83] Others argued that the expansion of the electorate had gone so far that any single voter could easily feel insignificant. 'No one can doubt that the individual elector is today of less importance than he was sixty years ago', lamented the *Evening Standard* in 1928 when contemplating the granting of the vote to women at 21 years of age.[84] 'If women under thirty really want votes of ever decreasing value, they might as well have them', grumbled another editorial in the same paper.[85] It was happy to accept, however, that the enlarged democracy was 'not an experiment concerning which there can be any thought of revocation'.[86]

More scathing in tone were those who argued that the franchise reform had allowed the electorate to become dangerously unbalanced. Harold Cox, an occasional columnist in the *Sunday Times* during the 1920s, insisted that ratepayers and companies did not have sufficient weight in the new system, and denounced the 'Scandal of the Pauper Vote'.[87] By the late 1920s, the *Daily Mail*, under the idiosyncratic proprietorship of Lord Rothermere, was complaining that many electors lacked the political knowledge and civic responsibility to be worthy of the franchise:

> The fact is that quite a large number of people now possess the vote who ought never to have been given it. It is obviously unjust to the community, for example, that persons in receipt of public relief, who are living on the taxes paid by workers out of their earnings, should have the power to dictate policy and decide elections. It is curious that the more widely the vote is given, the less it appears to be desired. It ceases to be a sign of capacity and is even sometimes regarded almost with contempt.[88]

This concern famously developed into a crusade against equalising the franchise, under the slogan 'Stop the Flapper Vote Folly'. 'Nothing could be madder than at this present moment yet further to extend the franchise', argued a typical editorial: 'But by adopting this ridiculous proposal of "votes for flappers" Ministers are preparing to add millions of irresponsible voters to the total of electors.'[89] Ultimately, though, this campaign was motivated by the vehement anti-socialism of a 'press baron' who was increasingly out of touch with mainstream opinion in Britain, and it failed to resonate widely. Rothermere's main anxiety was that young women would disproportionately vote Labour, and therefore enable a left-wing domination of British politics. Other Conservative papers felt such anxieties less keenly, and accepted that equalisation was both an inevitability and not to be feared; the

[83] *Daily Telegraph*, 28 Oct. 1924, p. 8.

[84] *Evening Standard*, 4 Feb. 1928.

[85] *Evening Standard*, 30 Mar. 1928.

[86] *Evening Standard*, 4 Feb. 1928.

[87] E.g., *Sunday Times*, 4 Sept. 1921, p. 7; 7 Feb. 1926, p. 8; 8 July 1926, p. 8.

[88] *Daily Mail*, 7 Apr. 1927.

[89] *Daily Mail*, 30 Mar. 1927, p. 10.

Mail's alarmist editorials also jarred badly with its encouragement over the previous decade of women's participation in the political arena.[90] As with Rothermere's campaign in support of the British Union of Fascists in 1934, this step outside the mainstream failed to move public or parliamentary opinion, and was fairly quickly disavowed; before long it was viewed as an embarrassment.

These fulminations against unqualified voters should not be ignored, but, viewed in the context of the serious, and often successful, attacks on democracy throughout Europe in the interwar period, nor should they be blown out of proportion. The national newspaper market in Britain was certainly dominated by a handful of rich men and their heavily-capitalised companies; right-wing voices tended to drown out radical and socialist alternatives, and readers were offered a diet of celebrity, crime and consumerism that made many critics despair.[91] At the same time, mainstream newspapers helped to sustain the legitimacy of Britain's parliamentary system and did much to integrate new voters into the post-war democracy. The press's enthusiasm for wide-ranging measures of reform eased the passage of the Representation of the People Act through parliament by framing opposition as unreasonable and outdated, and editors and journalists also offered an important platform for frustrations about the bitter partisanship that had become entrenched before 1914; on the question of PR, indeed, the press's appetite for change was far greater than that within parliament. Newspapers across the political spectrum urged their readers to be politically informed and to exercise their vote, and right-wing commentators encouraged the Conservative Party to adapt to the new electorate and find new ways of appealing to working-class and female electors. The language of rights certainly remained rather muted, especially in relation to women, and the press, like politicians, tried to direct and control the ways in which readers and voters were mobilised, by pushing their own agendas and crusades. But as the western world was about to be plunged into depression and democracy would undergo its fiercest challenges, the British press remained relatively secure in its faith in the political wisdom of its people. Twelve years after welcoming the 'fully democratised franchise', the *Daily Telegraph* could celebrate the 'calm' that characterised the general election of May 1929, even though its favoured party would be defeated: 'the people of Great Britain, at all times the least revolutionary-minded of peoples, are at the moment less disposed to militant and extremist courses than ever'.[92] The paper could still 'face the future' with confidence.

[90] Adrian Bingham, ' "Stop the Flapper Vote Folly": Lord Rothermere, the *Daily Mail*, and the Equalization of the Franchise 1927–28', *Twentieth Century British History*, xiii (2002), 17–37.

[91] James Curran and Jean Seaton, *Power Without Responsibility: The Press, Broadcasting, and New Media in Britain* (7th edn, 2009).

[92] *Daily Telegraph*, 31 May 1929, p. 12.

Women and the Vote: The Parliamentary Path to Equal Franchise, 1918–28

MARI TAKAYANAGI

Following the Speaker's conference on electoral reform of 1916–17, the Representation of the People Act 1918 gave women over the age of 30 years who met minimum property qualifications the parliamentary vote for the first time. After a decade of continued suffrage campaigning and pressure in parliament, the Representation of the People (Equal Franchise) Act 1928 gave women the vote on the same terms as men, at age 21 years, with no age or any other restrictions. Although important in itself, votes for women also carried along a wider agenda of legislation relating to gender equality and issues affecting women and children during the interwar period. This essay gives an overview of how the Speaker's conference and the 1918 act affected women, considers the immediately-related legislation in 1918–19 which allowed women to become MPs and removed other sex disqualifications, and traces progress in parliament towards equal franchise over the next decade, including a pledge by Stanley Baldwin in 1924 and an undertaking by William Joynson-Hicks in 1925. It explains the changes in personnel and attitudes over time which finally enabled a Conservative government to grant equal franchise in 1928.

Keywords: Equal Franchise Act 1928; house of commons; Representation of the People Act 1918; Speaker Lowther; Speaker's conference; Stanley Baldwin; suffrage; William Joynson-Hicks; women

1

I remember my feeling of indignation that one could be considered fit for such a post and not be considered fit to vote.[1]

In 1918, Vera Laughton was serving in the Women's Royal Navy Service (WRNS) as a unit officer when the Representation of the People Act was passed. Twenty-five years later, she recalled her indignation at the news of her exclusion from the franchise. She was 29 years old in February 1918, just a little too young to qualify. A former suffragette, as Vera Laughton Mathews she was later director of the WRNS during the Second World War.

The 1918 act gave a woman the parliamentary vote subject to gender specific provisos: she had to be at least 30 years old, and she (or her husband) had to meet the minimum property qualification for the local government franchise, meaning occupying either a dwelling-house of any value, or land or premises of a yearly value of not less than £5. She was also given the university franchise, providing she was 30 years old and would be entitled to be

---

[1] London Metropolitan Archives [hereafter cited as LMA], Willoughby Hyett Dickinson MSS, F/DCK/052/29: article in *The Catholic Citizen: Organ of the St Joan Alliance*, 15 Feb. 1943.

so registered if she were a man.[2] The provisos excluded approximately one-third of the adult female population, and approximately one-third of those excluded were aged over 30 years.[3] All this followed more than 50 years of campaigning by women's suffrage supporters, including peaceful 'suffragists' led by Millicent Fawcett, and militant 'suffragettes' led by Emmeline Pankhurst and others.[4]

The terms of the 1918 act were grounded in the recommendations of the Speaker's conference on electoral reform of 1916–17. Approximately 40% of men were not entitled to vote before 1914 because of residential and property qualifications.[5] By 1916 it was clear that the next general election could not take place using the pre-war electoral register, as men on military service would not have been entitled to vote, which was not politically acceptable. Conservative MPs argued for a 'soldier's vote'; Liberal and Labour politicians argued that this had to be extended to other workers on militarily-useful service, and it became necessary to at least consider women in this context.[6]

A cross-party conference of 32 MPs and peers was set up to consider the franchise and other electoral issues, chaired by the Speaker of the house of commons, James W. Lowther. There had never been a Speaker's conference before; this unusual mechanism was suggested by Walter Long.[7] The Speaker's conference first met in October 1916 and reported in January 1917 after 26 sittings, twice a week throughout parliament's recess. Its terms of reference were to examine, and, if possible, submit agreed resolutions, on four matters: franchise reform, redistribution of seats, electoral registration reform, and the method and cost of elections.[8] Although an 'anti-suffragist', Speaker Lowther was judged by Millicent Fawcett as justly famed for his 'courtesy, humour, and power of balancing contending factions'.[9] A list of proposed conference members was prepared by whips, from which the Speaker chose the members, attempting to represent the interests concerned fairly.[10] Its eventual mem-

---

[2]Representation of the People Act 1918, c. 64. More on the detail and implications of all this for women is below.

[3]David H. Close, 'The Collapse of Resistance to Democracy: Conservatives, Adult Suffrage, and Second Chamber Reform, 1911–1928', *Historical Journal*, xx (1977), 913.

[4]It is beyond the scope of this essay to detail the enormous suffrage historiography. Works which cover the period up to 1928 include: Cheryl Law, *Suffrage and Power: The Women's Movement, 1918–1928* (1997); Johanna Alberti, 'A Symbol and a Key: The Suffrage Movement in Britain, 1918–1929', in *Votes for Women*, ed. June Purvis and Sandra Stanley Holton (2000); Elizabeth Crawford, *The Women's Suffrage Movement: A Reference Guide, 1866–1928* (1999).

[5]Neal Blewett, 'The Franchise in the United Kingdom, 1885–1918', *Past & Present*, No. 32 (1965), 27–56; D. Tanner, *Political Change and the Labour Party 1900–1918* (Cambridge, 1990).

[6]Nicoletta F. Gullace, *'The Blood of our Sons': Men, Women and the Renegotiation of British Citizenship during the Great War* (New York, 2002), 170–7.

[7]David Rolf, 'Origins of Mr. Speaker's Conference during the First World War', *History*, lxiv (1979), 33–46. For an overview of Speaker's conferences, see House of Commons Library, 'Speaker's Conferences', Standard Note SN/PC/04426 (2009).

[8]*Conference on Electoral Reform: Letter from Mr Speaker to the Prime Minister*, Cd. 8463 (1917). Studies of the Speaker's conference include Homer Lawrence Morris, 'Parliamentary Franchise Reform in England From 1885 to 1918', *Studies in History, Economics and Public Law*, xcvi (New York, 1921), ch. ix; Martin Pugh, *Electoral Reform in War and Peace 1906–18* (1978); J.D. Fair, 'The Political Aspects of Women's Suffrage during the First World War', *Albion*, viii (1976), 274–95; Robert Blackburn, 'Laying the Foundations of the Modern Voting System: The Representation of the People Act 1918', *Parliamentary History*, xxx (2011), 33–52; Close, 'Collapse of Resistance to Democracy'.

[9]Millicent Garrett Fawcett, *What I Remember* (1924), 236.

[10]James William Lowther, *A Speaker's Commentaries* (2 vols, 1925), ii, 197.

bership included approximately 17 women's suffrage supporters and ten anti-suffragists, with others undecided or unclear, even to the Speaker, who reported: 'On the question of Woman Suffrage I endeavoured to obtain an equal division of opinion ... but many obvious difficulties presented themselves in discovering the views of gentlemen upon that important topic.'[11]

The Speaker deliberately left discussion of women's suffrage as long as possible, to obtain agreement on other matters first and, on the departure of three members in December 1916, he replaced anti-suffragists with pro-suffragists.[12] Possibly he found the eventual debate to be easier than he feared; of the eight conference members he particularly chose to thank in his memoirs, virtually all were women's suffrage supporters.[13] One of these was Willoughby Dickinson MP, a long-standing and committed supporter of women's suffrage. Dickinson recorded that the issue was discussed on 10–11 January 1917, when the Speaker, 'who presided over the conference with great skill and fairness', suggested informal divisions. The conference agreed by 18 votes to four to consider the question of women suffrage; then agreed by 15 votes to six that there should be some measure of women's suffrage; but a motion to give the vote on the same terms as men was lost, ten votes to 12. Various age limits were then considered, including 25, 30, and 35 years, but the number of women enfranchised by each of these seemed either too high or too low for consensus. At this point, as described by Dickinson: 'I made my proposition that the vote should go to occupiers or wives of occupiers, and this was carried 9 to 8. Thus by a majority of one, the suffrage clause went forward!'[14]

The conference therefore decided by a majority to recommend that the franchise be conferred on all women who were on the local government register, or whose husbands were, provided they had reached a specified age 'of which 30 and 35 received most favour'.[15] Women's suffrage campaigners from various bodies including the Women's Freedom League were lobbying sympathetic politicians extensively in this period.[16] Foremost among them was Millicent Fawcett, president of the National Union of Women's Suffrage Societies (NUWSS). The NUWSS had offered to give evidence to the conference, and,

---

[11] *Conference on Electoral Reform.* Historians who have attempted to categorise the conference members include Pugh, *Electoral Reform*, 206–7; Fair, 'Political Aspects of Women's Suffrage', 294–5.

[12] Lowther, *Commentaries*, ii, 198. Lord Salisbury and Frederick Banbury (certain antis) were replaced by Lord Stuart-Wortley and George Touche (known pro). James Craig (representing Ulster, a pro) was replaced by Edward Archdale (a likely pro). Two others also left the conference without being replaced: Earl Grey (pro) due to illness, and Robert Finlay (anti) on being made lord chancellor.

[13] Lowther, *Commentaries*, ii, 205. Lord Burnham, William Bull, Willoughby Dickinson, Maurice Healy, John Simon, and Aneurin Williams, were known suffragists, with Ryland Adkins as a possible late convert; only Harry Samuels was a certain anti-suffragist.

[14] LMA, Willoughby Hyett Dickinson MSS, F/DCK/052/023: rough notes by Dickinson, 10 Jan. 1917; F/DCK/052/028: letter from Dickinson to Miss Barry, 20 Jan. 1943; F/DCK/028/001: paper, 'The Speaker's Conference on Electoral Reform', 1918.

[15] *Conference on Electoral Reform.*

[16] Recent scholarship is clear that, although the Women's Social & Political Union suspended militancy on the outbreak of war, suffrage campaigning did not cease but, instead, took different forms, influenced by either support for the war or for pacifism. A recent case study is Alison Ronan, 'The Legacy of the Suffragettes: Women, Peace and the Vote in Manchester 1914–1918', in *Suffragette Legacy*, ed. Camilla Mørk Røstvik and Ella Louise Sutherland (Cambridge, 2015). 'The Suffragettes of the WSPU', a breakaway organisation founded by Rose Lamartine-Yates, who disagreed with the suspension of militancy, redoubled its lobbying efforts during the Speaker's conference and picketed its members outside the house of commons (my thanks to Alexandra Hughes-Johnson for this point).

when this was refused, they drew up a memorandum outlining what they wanted to say and sent it to every conference member individually.[17] Following the report of the conference, Fawcett presided over a deputation of women war workers to prime minister, Lloyd George, on 29 March 1917. Fawcett declared that all campaigners were resolved to support the conference, as 'we would greatly prefer an imperfect scheme that can pass to the most perfect scheme in the world that could not pass'. Other speakers at the deputation included Emmeline Pankhurst, who said in wartime she wanted to see this done 'with as little disputes and as little difference as possible'.[18]

The Representation of the People Bill introduced in May 1917 embodied the conference's resolutions on a wide variety of electoral reform issues. In relation to the male franchise, the act as passed enabled a man aged 21 years or older to vote if he occupied a residence for six months (regardless of the value of the premises or rates paid, as had previously been the case), with a possible second vote for business premises in a different constituency, or the university franchise. Men on military or naval service in connection with the current war were allowed to vote from the age of 19 years (although women on military or naval service, like Vera Laughton, still had to be aged 30 years), while conscientious objectors (who had not performed other war services or alternative work of national importance) were disqualified from voting for five years.[19]

The women's suffrage clause in the bill was to be decided by a free vote of the house of commons, and hedged with provisos. A 30-year age limit was imposed, in order that women should not comprise the majority of the electorate.[20] William Bull later credited the fact that the age was 30, rather than 35 years, to the actions of Walter Long during drafting,[21] although the Speaker explained, 'It was thought desirable that women and men should be somewhere about on a parity and we took the age of thirty which was the nearest we could get to make the number of women voters equal to the number of men.'[22] It was estimated at the time that this would give the vote to six million women (an underestimate, as it turned out, the actual figure was 8.4 million).[23] There was also the requirement for women to meet the local government franchise eligibility. As advocated by Willoughby Dickinson:

> I believe you will get a very fair system of representation of women. It practically comes to this, that under this scheme you do not give the vote to servant maids, daughters and other people in that position in a family, but you give the vote to the head of the household. You practically give to women what the men were first of all given in former

[17] Millicent Garret Fawcett, *The Women's Victory – and After* (1920), 138.

[18] LMA, Willoughby Hyett Dickinson MSS, F/DCK/052/024: pamphlet, 'Women's Suffrage Deputation to the Prime Minister', 29 Mar. 1917. Sylvia Pankhurst was virtually alone among suffrage leaders in continuing to advocate equal franchise at this point.

[19] There were 8,357,648 male voters on the 1915 electoral register and 12,913,166 in 1918, an increase of approximately 35%. *Parliamentary and Local Government Electors (United Kingdom)*, HC 138 (1918).

[20] Hansard, *Commons Debates*, 5th ser., xciv, col. 1818: 20 June 1917 (Dickinson).

[21] 'I attended the meeting of the Drafting Committee. Lord Long took the Chair, and there were also present the Home Secretary and the draftsman. When we came to the question of the age, Lord Long said, "This is rubbish," and he struck out 35, and put in 30.': Hansard, *Commons Debates*, 5th ser., clxx, col. 898: 29 Feb. 1924 (Bull).

[22] Hansard, *Commons Debates*, 5th ser., cxiv, col. 1612: 4 Apr. 1919 (Mr Speaker).

[23] Women electors in the 1918 general election totalled 8,479,156. A slightly larger number of women, 8,515,438, received the local government franchise: *Parliamentary and Local Government Electors*.

years; you give them a household franchise. The head of the house, the mother of the family in every family, rich and poor, would have the vote.[24]

As passed, the act stipulated that, to qualify to vote, a woman or her husband had to occupy a dwelling-house (of any value), or occupy land or premises of a yearly value of not less than £5. Occupying a 'dwelling-house' meant living in a house or a separate part of a house, as an owner (i.e., a freehold owner) or a tenant (i.e., paying rent). Occupying 'land or premises' meant living as a lodger in rooms within a house, let in an unfurnished state, to the annual value of £5 (the gross estimated rental or gross value as assessed for rates, as determined by the registration officer). Therefore, living as a lodger in furnished rooms at any value, or in unfurnished rooms to a value of less than £5, did not qualify.

This meant in practice that women over the age of 30 years who lived at home with parents or other family members, were resident servants, or lived in furnished rooms or hostels, could not vote. The number of women excluded from the vote in 1918 was approximately one-third of the adult female population; and about one-third of those women were aged over 30 years.[25] Many of these women would have been domestic servants: although numbers employed in domestic service declined immediately after the war, there were considerable regional variations and numbers recovered during the 1920s. The nature of domestic service changed; more typical than the large 19th-century household of staff in great houses was the one- or two-servant households of working and middle classes – suburban homes employing 'chars', washerwomen, or sewing women as casual help.[26] Despite this, the 1931 census shows that 60% of 1.3 million female servants still 'lived in'[27] – these women would have been unable to vote before 1928, even if over 30 years old, while many women working instead in factories, shops and offices would have been living at home with parents or in furnished rooms, and so similarly voteless at any age.

Women had a potential second vote in the university franchise, even if their university did not admit women to degrees,[28] but unlike men were not eligible for the business premises franchise. No woman aged under 30 years could vote, even if a university graduate or on military or naval service. Thus, gender equality and rewarding war service were not as important principles of reform as retaining traditional considerations of electoral eligibility, such as age, respectability, class, property, and education. As Nicoletta Gullace has described, it was 'incongruous but not unacceptable' to give votes to women ostensibly for their patriotic war service, while excluding actual young female munitions workers.[29] Although a compromise, pro-suffrage MPs were clear that this was the best possible result. Lloyd

---

[24] Hansard, *Commons Debates*, 5th ser., xciv, col. 1820: 20 June 1917 (Dickinson).

[25] Close, 'Collapse of Resistance to Democracy', 913. In 1928, 5.2 million women were enfranchised, of whom 34% were over the age of 30 years: Hansard, *Commons Debates*, 5th ser., ccxv, col. 1369: 29 Mar. 1928.

[26] Lucy Delap, *Knowing Their Place: Domestic Service in Twentieth Century Britain* (Oxford, 2011), 9. Domestic service was, however, in long-term decline, and only 5% of women worked in domestic service by 1951: Selina Todd, *Young Women, Work and Family 1918–1959* (Oxford, 2005), 22.

[27] S. Ball, *Portrait of a Party: The Conservative Party in Britain 1918–1945* (Oxford, 2013), 119; Delap, *Knowing Their Place*, 13.

[28] Provided they had passed the final examinations and kept the conditions required by the university for residence, as were necessary for a man to obtain a degree. Only Oxford and Cambridge Universities did not admit women to degrees in this period (Oxford did from 1920, Cambridge from 1947).

[29] Gullace, *Blood of our Sons*, 185.

George told the deputation of women that the age limit was illogical and unjustifiable, unpalatable and undesirable, but necessary for consensus.[30] Dickinson recognized that young war workers would not get the vote, but at least 'their mothers, their sisters and the women who know what they have been doing and who are quite as well capable of exercising it in their behalf as themselves' would.[31]

There was significant opposition to any measure of women's suffrage from some long-standing opponents in parliament, such as Arnold Ward and Sir Frederick Banbury, who tried to introduce wrecking amendments to the bitter end. However, the crucial division was passed decisively, with 385 votes to 55 at committee stage in the Commons.[32] Including tellers, Liberals voted for the bill 184 to 12 and Conservatives 140 to 45, while all Irish Nationalists and Labour MPs backed it. Comparisons to pre-war divisions are complex, as the bills then were different in nature, but it is clear that there was a large reversal among both Liberals and Conservatives, with high-profile conversions such as Asquith and Long; the Conservatives also had much less reason to fear limited women's suffrage once universal male suffrage was granted.[33] Millicent Fawcett wrote to thank supportive MPs and added that she hoped the big majority would 'provide deep waters enough to float over the rocks of the House of Lords'.[34] It passed by 134 votes to 71 in the Lords, with Lord Curzon, president of the National League for Opposing Woman Suffrage, abstaining on the grounds that he did not want to bring the Lords into conflict with the Commons on an issue affecting their own constitution.[35] The act received royal assent on 6 February 1918, the first step on the path to equal franchise.

2

A woman shall not be disqualified by sex or marriage from being elected to or sitting or voting as a Member of the Commons House of Parliament.[36]

Women did not stand for parliament before 1918 as a matter of common law, not statute law. Some 3,000 women stood successfully for local government positions between 1870 and 1918. However, the majority of these were on poor law and education boards; women were only eligible to stand for county and borough councils from 1907, and found it much

[30] LMA, Willoughby Hyett Dickinson MSS, F/DCK/052/024: pamphlet, 'Women's Suffrage Deputation to the Prime Minister', 29 Mar. 1917.

[31] Hansard, *Commons Debates*, 5th ser., xciv, col. 1820: 20 June 1917 (Dickinson).

[32] Hansard, *Commons Debates*, 5th ser., xciv, col. 1751: 19 June 1917.

[33] Labour had always supported women's suffrage, while the Irish Nationalists were supportive but had not been inclined to support suffrage bills before the war when home rule was their priority; full analysis in Pugh, *Electoral Reform*, 148–50.

[34] LMA, Willoughby Hyett Dickinson MSS, F/DCK/052/022: correspondence between the Provisional Committee for Adult Suffrage and the prime minister, Aug. 1918.

[35] Hansard, *Lords Debates*, 5th ser., xxvii, cols 524–5: 10 Jan. 1918 (Earl Curzon of Kedleston).

[36] Parliament (Qualification of Women) Act 1918, c. 47. For more detail on this section, see Mari Takayanagi, 'Parliament and Women c.1900–1945', King's College London PhD, 2012, ch. 1; Mari Takayanagi, ' "One of the most revolutionary proposals that has ever been put before the House": The Passage of the Parliament (Qualification of Women) Act 1918', in *Labour, British Radicalism and the First World War*, ed. Lucy Bland and Richard Carr (Manchester, forthcoming).

more difficult to stand for, or make an impact on, these.[37] Helen Taylor was the first woman to be selected as a prospective parliamentary candidate and to run an election campaign in 1885, but the returning officer refused to accept her nomination as a woman.[38] Feminist organisations in the late 19th and early 20th centuries had focused efforts on the right to vote, not the right to stand. In early 1918, however, with the principle now established that at least some women could vote, the question immediately arose as to whether they could also become MPs.

The pioneer this time was Nina Boyle, a Women's Freedom League activist, who put herself forward for a by-election in Keighley in April 1918. Boyle was one of the founders of the Women Police Volunteers during the war, and keen to stand as a test case. Her nomination was refused only on a technicality with her papers; the returning officer stated he would have accepted her nomination otherwise.[39] However, the legal advice given to the government was that women were not eligible. Bonar Law explained to the house of commons in August: 'In the unanimous opinion of the Law Officers of England, Scotland, and Ireland a woman is not entitled to be a candidate for Parliament.'[40] By October, with a number of women candidates selected, a general election approaching, and the possibility of chaos across the country if the situation was not determined one way or the other, the cabinet decided that the decision should be left to a free vote in the Commons.[41]

On 23 October 1918, Liberal MP, Herbert Samuel, introduced a resolution, 'That in the opinion of this House, it is desirable that a Bill be passed forthwith making women eligible as Members of Parliament.' He argued that it was a logical consequence of the vote, necessary to avoid different decisions being made by individual returning officers, that women had proved themselves in local government, and women MPs would make a valuable contribution to the work of the house of commons. Opponents argued that it was far too radical a move, so soon after the franchise extension, that women had failed to make a mark in parliaments elsewhere, and that the culture of the Commons was not suited to women.[42] The resolution passed overwhelmingly on division, 274 to 25.[43] The Parliament (Qualification of Women) Bill was introduced shortly afterwards, and piloted through by Lord Robert Cecil, an MP with a long-standing record of support for women's equality causes.[44]

---

[37] Patricia Hollis, *Ladies Elect: Women in English Local Government, 1865–1914* (Oxford, 1987). There is no comparable study of the interwar period. Anne Baldwin has identified some trends, finding that, by 1928, women in London were being elected in greater numbers, but elsewhere many counties and boroughs continued to have a low representation of women: Anne Baldwin, 'The Relationship between Changing Party Politics and the Elected Representation of Women in Local Government, 1919–1939', University of Huddersfield MA, 2007.

[38] Helen Taylor was selected by the Camberwell Radical Club as Independent Radical Democrat candidate for Camberwell North. I am grateful to Janet Smith from the Women's Legal Landmarks project for this point.

[39] *The Times*, 20 Apr. 1918.

[40] Hansard, *Commons Debates*, 5th ser., cix, col. 1534: 8 Aug. 1918 (Bonar Law).

[41] TNA, CAB 23/8, f. 30.

[42] More in Takayanagi, 'Parliament and Women'.

[43] Hansard, *Commons Debates*, 5th ser., cx, col. 856: 23 Oct. 1918.

[44] As well as women's suffrage, Cecil represented Gwyneth Bebb in the Court of Appeal in *Bebb v. the Law Society* [1913 B. 305], the unsuccessful test case for women to enter the legal profession: Rosemary Auchmuty, 'Whatever Happened to Miss Bebb? Bebb v The Law Society and Women's Legal History', *Legal Studies: The Journal of the Society of Legal Scholars*, xxxi (2011), 175–343.

The Parliament (Qualification of Women) Act was more radical than the Representation of the People Act, as it allowed women to stand without any restrictions as to age or property. Women could therefore stand as MPs from the age of 21 years, the same as men, while unable to vote for themselves. Samuel and Cecil argued that it was not necessary for a parliamentary candidate to be able to vote,[45] and there was insufficient appetite by opposing MPs to fight this so late in the parliamentary session. An attempt to introduce an age restriction was lost without a division, and the act was passed on the last day of the session, 21 November 1918 – just a few weeks before the general election on 14 December 1918.

Seventeen women stood in the general election, but the only one to be elected was Constance Markievicz for Dublin St Patricks, who did not take her seat at Westminster as a member of Sinn Fein. It is, in fact, doubtful that Markievicz was eligible to be a parliamentary candidate, although not because of her age or gender. In common with a number of other Sinn Fein MPs elected in 1918, she had been found guilty of treason in 1916 and not been pardoned or endured her punishment, and as a woman she had an additional disqualification: she had lost British nationality on her marriage to a Pole.[46] However, her position was never challenged and she went on to sit as a member of the first Dáil Éireann in Ireland. Nancy Astor became the first woman to take her seat in parliament in 1919, followed by a very slow trickle of other women over the next ten years. Numbers of women candidates were also small, with none of the major political parties selecting women in more than a very few winnable seats.[47]

Despite the small number of women directly affected, the equalitarian nature of the Parliament (Qualification of Women) Act was crucial in opening up candidacies to all women, including those who could not vote. Over the next ten years, a number of women under the age of 30 years stood for all parties. Examples include: Ursula Williams, who stood in the 1923 general election as Liberal candidate for Consett, Durham, aged 27 years;[48] Irene Ward, who stood in the 1924 general election as Conservative candidate for Morpeth, aged 29 years;[49] and Jennie Lee, who was elected Labour MP in a by-election for North Lanark in March 1929, aged 24 years, still too young to vote before the Equal Franchise Act 1928 came into force at the 1929 general election.[50] Ellen Wilkinson also became an MP while unable to vote; when elected for Middlesbrough East in 1923, she was over the age of 30 years but did not meet the property qualification. She explained: 'When I was first elected to this House, I happened to live in furnished rooms, and having neither a husband nor

---

[45] The whig statesman, Charles James Fox, became an MP at the age of just 19 years in 1768. Samuel claimed during debates that he himself had stood for parliament before becoming an elector, presumably disqualified due to registration requirements.

[46] Mari Takayanagi, 'The Eligibility of Constance Markievicz', *History of Parliament blog*, 14 Dec. 2015, available at *https://thehistoryofparliament.wordpress.com/2015/12/14/the-eligibility-of-constance-markievicz/* (accessed 29 July 2016).

[47] Pamela Brookes, *Women at Westminster: An Account of Women in the British Parliament, 1918–1966* (1967); Elizabeth Vallance, *Women in the House* (1979); Brian Harrison, 'Women in a Men's House: The Women MPs 1919–1945', *Historical Journal*, xxix (1986), 623–54.

[48] *Sunderland Daily Echo and Shipping Gazette*, 14 Nov. 1923. She was the daughter of Speaker's conference member, Aneurin Williams MP, who lost the seat in 1922.

[49] Ward later became one of the longest-serving female MPs: Helen Langley, 'Ward, Irene Mary Bewick, Baroness Ward of North Tyneside (1895–1980)', *ODNB*.

[50] Jennie Lee, *My Life with Nye* (1980), 66.

furniture, although I was eligible to sit in this House, I was not eligible for a vote.'[51] Only equal franchise could remove such anomalies.

3

A person shall not be disqualified by sex or marriage from the exercise of any public function, or from being appointed to or holding any civil or judicial post, or from entering or assuming or carrying on any civil profession or vocation.[52]

Following the 1918 act, the first parliamentary opportunity to introduce equal franchise came as early as 1919 with the passage of the Sex Disqualification (Removal) Act 1919. However, despite great efforts by the Labour Party and indeed the house of commons as a whole, the coalition government refused to support it and this act did not, in the end, affect the franchise.

The act originated in a Labour private members' bill, the Women's Emancipation Bill, introduced by Benjamin Spoor in March 1919: 'To remove certain restraints and disabilities imposed on women.' The bill proposed to remove the disqualification of women from holding civil and judicial appointments, introduce equal franchise, and allow women to sit and vote in the house of lords.[53] The Women's Emancipation Bill enjoyed a very high degree of success in the house of commons. It passed a division at second reading in April 1919, 119 votes to 32 – a major triumph for a private members' bill. It then went through committee stage without amendment, when the government tried to remove the equal franchise clause but failed without even managing to force a division. Finally, it passed third reading in July 1919 in a division, 100 votes to 85, against whipped government opposition, before falling in the Lords. So, although equal franchise was not achieved until 1928, the house of commons actually passed a bill in favour of equal franchise as early as 1919.[54]

Only the substance of the first of the Women's Emancipation Bill clauses, on civil and judicial appointments, was adopted by the government to include in the Sex Disqualification (Removal) Bill. Equal franchise was still too controversial at this date. Some MPs who were otherwise supportive felt it was too soon after the Representation of the People Act, such as Speaker's conference member, Ryland Adkins:

It was only in the last Session of Parliament that a great franchise Act, which, with all its faults, did go much further than any preceding Act to the institutions of our country, was passed with something approaching common consent … I, for one, feel absolutely pledged to maintain the so-called compromise of Mr. Speaker's Conference, on the faith

[51] Hansard, *Commons Debates*, 5th ser., ccxv, col. 1405: 29 Mar. 1928 (Wilkinson).

[52] Sex Disqualification (Removal) Act 1919, c. 71.

[53] Women's Emancipation Bill, HC Bill 38 (1919). For women in the Lords, see Duncan Sutherland, 'Peeresses, Parliament, and Prejudice: The Admission of Women to the House of Lords, 1918–1963', *Parliaments, Estates and Representation*, xx (2000); Mari Takayanagi, 'A Changing House: The Life Peerages Act 1958', *Parliamentary History*, xxvii (2008), 380–92.

[54] For more detail on the passage of the Sex Disqualification (Removal) Act, see Takayanagi, 'Parliament and Women', ch. 2; Mari Takayanagi, 'Establishing the Known: The Parliamentary Passage of the Sex Disqualification (Removal) Act 1919', in *First Women Lawyers in Great Britain and the Empire Record, Vol. i*, ed. Judith Bourne (2016), 19–24.

of which it was put into the Report of that Conference and in the ensuing Bill, which I ardently desired.[55]

The lord chancellor similarly explained the absence of equal franchise in the Sex Disqualification (Removal) Bill:

> The franchises for men and women were settled last year by the Representation of the People Act as the result of the Speaker's Conference, which was representative of all political parties … it is contrary to the constitutional practice to extend the franchise in the first session of a new Parliament … a General Election, unless untoward and unanticipated events arise, should not take place until the country has had some further time to settle down after the war.[56]

Subsequent debate in both Houses focused on women being able to exercise public functions, holding civil or judicial posts, and entering professions. Women's organisations and MPs supportive of equal franchise were disappointed, but found it necessary to concentrate on amending these aspects to make them as palatable as possible, or risk losing the bill altogether. As a government replacement for a more radical private members' bill, the Sex Disqualification (Removal) Act was a compromise, and disappointing to some feminist campaigners at the time and historians subsequently, in particular regarding equal franchise. Areas of lobbying and extensive discussion included attempting to remove the practice of women being required to leave paid employment on getting married (the 'marriage bar'), and to amend provisos which enabled women to be excluded from the foreign and diplomatic services and for judges to be able to call all-male juries. However, full consideration of the parliamentary passage shows that it was the most that could be achieved at the time.[57]

4

> I have been a consistent supporter of women's suffrage and even at the time that the Franchise Bill of 1918 was passed I felt that the discrimination in age between men and women could not be permanent. I think so still.[58]

In 1922, the Conservative leader, Andrew Bonar Law, declared that unequal franchise could not be permanent. An election message was published in the form of a letter from him to Caroline Bridgeman, chair of the Women's Unionist Organisation; Malcolm Fraser, the

---

[55] Hansard, *Commons Debates*, 5th ser., cxiv, col. 1575: 4 Apr. 1919 (Adkins); in the end, he did vote for the Women's Emancipation Bill.

[56] Hansard, *Lords Debates*, xxxv, 5th ser., col. 894: 22 July 1919 (lord chancellor). Lord Birkenhead (previously F.E. Smith MP), had opposed women's suffrage before the war, although as attorney general he had to pilot the Representation of the People Bill 1918 through the Commons. As lord chancellor, he was responsible for ending Viscountess Rhondda's attempt to take her seat in the house of lords in 1922: Angela John, *Turning the Tide: The Life of Lady Rhondda* (2013).

[57] Takayanagi, 'Parliament and Women', ch. 2.

[58] Bodl., Conservative Party Archive, PUB 212/1: letter from Bonar Law to the National Union of Societies for Equal Citizenship during the 1922 general election, in *Home and Politics*, Dec. 1922.

principal agent at the Conservative and Unionist Central Office, sent this to her on 8
November 1922, explaining:

> I thought it was essential to get some letter specially for women from Mr Bonar Law. I
> consulted your advisers here and they were all in agreement. With their help we drafted
> the points necessary to be brought out in such a letter, and Mr Bonar Law has kindly
> written it to you. I hope you will forgive me taking your name in vain like this, but I
> am having this letter used as a leaflet and also sent out to the press.[59]

However, Bonar Law's statements were viewed as personal opinion rather than party manifesto, and did not lead to any Conservative government bill. Between 1920 and 1923, no
fewer than six equal franchise bills were introduced into the house of commons, but these
were all private members' bills, from MPs of all parties.[60]

It was not until a Labour minority government came to power in 1924 that the UK had
a government with a manifesto commitment to equal political rights for women. Many
Conservatives had also individually pledged themselves in support of equal franchise, with
the former cabinet minister, Sir Robert Sanders, recording in his diary: 'The matter is
difficult because so many of our people have pledged themselves to the principle.'[61] A
private members' bill was introduced by a Labour MP, William Murdoch Adamson, on 29
February 1924, which was not only concerned with equal franchise but also reforming
the business vote, local government franchise, and residence qualifications. Although it ran
out of time, before the fall of the government in October, this bill allowed for debate of
the principles and consideration of details, and came closest to achieving equal franchise
before 1928. There were now women MPs to contribute, including, for the first time, three
Labour women. Dorothy Jewson used her maiden speech to second the bill:

> We believe that the 1918 Act was a compromise. It was only accepted, very reluctantly,
> by women's organisations in the country because it was agreed that to add 7,000,000
> or 8,000,000 of new electors to the register was a very big experiment. I think no hon.
> Member will deny that that experiment of 1918 has been amply justified.[62]

However, the focus of opposition to Adamson's bill also came from a woman MP. The
duchess of Atholl moved a delaying amendment asking for a conference to be held on the
issue. Her fellow Conservative, Nancy Astor, said of Atholl, 'she is like Canute, trying to
keep the waves back'.[63] Atholl's amendment was defeated on a division, 288 votes to 72,
on the first occasion that women MPs (Jewson and Atholl) acted as tellers.

Adamson's bill was considered in standing committee between May and June 1924. Arguments mostly circled around the age restriction, with serious consideration given to a

[59] Shropshire Archives, Shrewsbury, Bridgeman MSS, 4929/1/1922/359: Fraser to Caroline Bridgeman, 8 Nov.
1922. She was also the wife of William Bridgeman MP, who had been appointed home secretary by Bonar Law
in Oct. 1922.

[60] A full list and discussion is in Takayanagi, 'Parliament and Women', ch. 4; see also David Butler, *The Electoral
System in Britain since 1918* (Oxford, 1963), 15–38.

[61] *Real Old Tory Politics: The Political Diaries of Sir Robert Sanders, Lord Bayford, 1910–35*, ed. John Ramsden
(1984), 215: 24 June 1924.

[62] Hansard, *Commons Debates*, 5th ser., clxx, col. 863: 29 Feb. 1924 (Jewson).

[63] Hansard, *Commons Debates*, 5th ser., clxx, col. 938: 29 Feb. 1924 (Astor).

voting age of 25 years for both sexes.[64] There were also points made about the property qualification: Ben Turner MP told the committee that he had daughters over the age of 30 years who could not vote because they were unmarried and not property owners.[65] In one last splendidly-ridiculous attempt at a wrecking amendment, Samuel Roberts proposed a new clause that votes cast by voters over the age of 35 years should count as two votes, and their ballot papers would be a different colour so that they could be distinguished. Susan Lawrence declared that some members were previously inclined to laugh about this clause, but now 'I feel the awful pathos of it ...' and, if taken to its logical conclusion, 'agents of all the parties would be found crowding around the precious centenarian to bring him tottering out with his perhaps 20 or 30 votes on his shoulders'.[66] The amendment was wisely withdrawn.

The prime minister, Ramsay MacDonald, finally announced on 16 July 1924 that the government would support the bill, and the cabinet duly noted it as one of the more 'important and urgent' bills to which they were committed.[67] However, parliament was then in recess between 7 August and 30 September, and the government fell almost directly after parliament returned, on 8 October, before the bill reached report stage. Even if it had finished its passage through the Commons, the minority Labour government would have had an impossible task in getting it through the house of lords; the Conservatives were prepared to use the Lords to block the bill if necessary.[68]

5

The Unionist Party are in favour of equal political rights for men and women and desire that the question of the extension of the franchise should if possible be settled by agreement. With this in view they would if returned to power propose that the matter be referred to a Conference of all political Parties on the lines of the Ullswater Committee.[69]

At the general election of 29 October 1924, the Conservative Party won by a large majority and Stanley Baldwin became prime minister. Although the Conservatives had not included equal franchise in their manifesto, Baldwin made a pledge, 'An Appeal to Women', on behalf of his party during the campaign in favour of 'equal political rights for men and women' and for a conference. This was in the form of a letter to Caroline Bridgeman, published in the press.[70] But the pledge was not simply Baldwin's personal opinion; as with Bonar Law's

---

[64] Hansard, *Standing Committee A Debates*, col. 592: 3 June 1924.

[65] Hansard, *Standing Committee A Debates*, cols 539, 549: 22 May 1924 (Turner).

[66] Hansard, *Standing Committee A Debates*, cols 666–7: 19 June 1924 (Roberts); col. 669: 19 June 1924 (Lawrence).

[67] Hansard, *Commons Debates*, 5th ser., clxxvi, col. 368: 16 July 1924 (prime minister (Ramsay MacDonald) in answer to a question from Mrs Wintringham); TNA, CAB 23/48: meeting 30 July 1924.

[68] 'I am now assured that even if it passes the Commons the Lords will not let it go through', *Real Old Tory Politics*, ed. Ramsden, 215: 24 June 1924.

[69] Stanley Baldwin's pledge, quoted as a 'statement' in *The Times*, 18 Oct. 1924. The Ullswater Committee was the 1916–17 Speaker's conference.

[70] *Morning Post*, 27 Oct. 1924. The letter was mainly about the cost of living for housewives, coming to equal franchise only at the end.

statement in 1922, it was drafted in Conservative central office. Pembroke Wicks, from the policy department, wrote to Caroline Bridgeman on 20 October 1924:

> I enclose a draft of the letter which it is proposed that Baldwin should write to you as his message to the Women of Great Britain for the Election. It has been approved by the Principal Agent. If you have no corrections to make, it would save valuable time if you would wire to me accordingly in order that I may put it before Mr Baldwin at once.[71]

The pledge was duly published, widely publicised, and Baldwin never repudiated it. His biographers find that his personal commitment to equal franchise was unquestionable.[72]

His government had other priorities, however, and when there was no mention of equal franchise in the king's speech, a Labour MP, William Whiteley, presented a private members' bill. At the second reading of Whiteley's bill on 20 February 1925, the home secretary, Sir William Joynson-Hicks ('Jix'), put down an amendment to postpone the bill until later in the parliament. This was designed to kill the bill, and an interesting action from the point of view of parliamentary procedure. Arthur Henderson said it was the first time in 22 years that he had known a government put down an amendment to a private members' bill. Baldwin responded: 'when private Members try to introduce Government Bills, it becomes the Government's business'.[73] A crucial exchange took place during the debate between Joynson-Hicks and Nancy Astor. Jix quoted Baldwin's pledge, declaring 'I am not afraid of young women voters', and (correctly) predicted that the government would last until 1929, so a conference could take place in a couple of years' time. Jix then said there would be 'Equal votes for men and women', and Astor jumped in: 'Does the right hon. Gentleman mean equal votes at 21?':

> Sir W Joynson-Hicks: 'It means exactly what it says.' [Hon Members: 'Answer!'] ' … I will say quite definitely that means that no difference will take place in the ages at which men and women will go to the poll at the next election.'[74]

Baldwin was present, and did not contradict his home secretary. Equal franchise therefore came to be regarded as government policy, and the fact that Joynson-Hicks's undertaking was made in the house of commons gave it credibility.[75] However, the fact that it had been expressed in an exchange during a debate on a private members' bill, rather than through any more deliberate statement, opened it up to subsequent doubt and some derision. The Conservative back bencher, Sir Cuthbert Headlam, complained in his diary: 'Jix apparently made it one Friday afternoon and the PM unfortunately was sitting beside him and never

[71] Shropshire Archives, Shrewsbury, Bridgeman MSS, 4629/1/4/9: Wicks to Caroline Bridgeman, 20 Oct. 1924.

[72] Stuart Ball, 'Baldwin, Stanley, first Earl Baldwin of Bewdley (1867–1947)', *ODNB*; Keith Middlemas and John Barnes, *Baldwin: A Biography* (1969), 468.

[73] Hansard, *Commons Debates*, 5th ser., clxxx, col. 1495: 20 Feb. 1925 (Henderson); col. 1560 (prime minister, Baldwin).

[74] Hansard, *Commons Debates*, 5th ser., clxxx, cols 1500–3: 20 Feb. 1925 (Astor and Joynson-Hicks).

[75] A suggestion was made at one point in 1927 that the 'House of Commons be invited to relieve the government from the 1925 undertaking', but this would be seen as 'the breach of a Parliamentary bargain': TNA, CAB 27/336: Equal Franchise Cabinet Committee, 21 Feb. 1927.

said a word – really our leaders are somewhat casual in their methods.'[76] Lord Salisbury, the Conservative leader in the house of lords, wrote: 'exuberant Jix, he positively likes pledging himself and the Government', while Lord Birkenhead, the India secretary, referred to 'our light-hearted colleague, the Home Secretary' giving 'a pledge which was delivered without even the pretence of consulting the Cabinet'.[77] Other ministers, including William Bridgeman and Winston Churchill, were sure that Jix had gone well beyond what the cabinet had agreed, which was simply for a Speaker's conference.[78]

Historians have subsequently argued that this image of an accident-prone Jix caught off guard is false, and that certain quarters of the Conservative Party constructed this idea to explain the anomaly of Joynson-Hicks, usually an unremitting 'Diehard', becoming an unlikely champion of equal franchise.[79] However, Jix's own defence, in an unpublished autobiographical fragment, has the ring of hindsight to it and he does not quite dare claim that the cabinet supported him:

> Every action I took was taken with the assent of the PM and our colleagues, none of whom carried their objections to the point of resigning or threatening resignation, and who therefore, according to all rules of Cabinet solidarity, were for ever debarred from criticizing the decision which was taken and acted upon.[80]

That both the prime minister and home secretary apparently had to use roundabout tactics to manœuvre their party into supporting their view shows the extent of cabinet disagreement. The government had their way on Whiteley's bill; the division was lost 153 to 220, with ten Conservatives, including Astor, going into the lobby against it.

6

Birthday present from Baldwin. Legislation next session. Votes at 21. Conference not mentioned. Greetings and happy returns.[81]

[76] *Parliament and Politics in the Age of Baldwin and MacDonald: The Headlam Diaries 1923–1935*, ed. Stuart Ball (1992), 118: 1 May 1927.

[77] *Conservative Politics in National and Imperial Crisis: Letters from Britain to the Viceroy of India 1926–31*, ed. Stuart Ball (Farnham, 2014), 132: Birkenhead to Irwin, 13 Apr. 1927; 135: Salisbury to Irwin, 24 Apr. 1927.

[78] The cabinet agreed 'to state that the Government intended to give effect to [Baldwin's pledge] later in the life of the present Parliament by proposing a Conference of all political parties': TNA CAB 23/49: cabinet meeting, 18 Feb. 1925, item 11; *The Modernisation of Conservative Politics: The Diaries and Letters of William Bridgeman 1904–1935*, ed. Philip Williamson (1988), 233: Nov. 1929; *Winston S Churchill, v, Companion Part 1: Documents – the Exchequer Years 1922–1929*, ed. Martin Gilbert (1979), 963: memorandum by Churchill, 8 Mar. 1927. Tantalisingly, David Butler says: 'one member of the 1925 Cabinet recalls that the Home Secretary went to the 1925 debate without Cabinet instructions on equal franchise because, owing to lunch, that part of the Cabinet was never reached', but does not give a source: Butler, *Electoral System*, 30.

[79] Jonathon Hopkins, 'Paradoxes Personified: Sir William Joynson-Hicks, Viscount Brentford and the Conflict between Change and Stability in British Society in the 1920s', University of Westminster MPhil, 1996; Huw Clayton, 'The Life and Career of Sir William Joynson-Hicks, 1865–1932: A Reassessment', *Journal of Historical Biography*, viii (2010), 1–38. Clayton finds some evidence as to Jix's possible sympathy with women's rights, even suggesting that his addition of 'Hicks', his wife's name, to his own on marriage in 1895 might be an early expression of this.

[80] East Sussex RO, Joynson-Hicks MSS, Acc. 9851, 1/2: 'Votes for women', autobiographical note, 9 Aug. 1931.

[81] Diana Hopkinson, *Family Inheritance: A Life of Eva Hubback* (1954), 93: Eleanor Rathbone to Eva Hubback, telegram, 13 Apr. 1927; Rathbone and Hubback were leaders of the National Union of Societies for Equal Citizenship, and 13 April was Hubback's birthday.

Encouraged by Baldwin's pledge and Jix's undertaking, over the next two years a coalition of women's organisations, the Equal Rights Political Campaign Committee, threw themselves into organising demonstrations, mass meetings, deputations and publications.[82] In parliament, MPs bombarded the government with questions, and private members' bills continued to be doggedly introduced. All of this was against the background of a prominent campaign in the *Daily Mail* against the 'flapper' vote; its proprietor, Lord Rothermere, feared the political consequences for the Conservative Party.[83] In late 1926, the Equal Franchise Cabinet Committee was formed to investigate the issues, and it considered the effect of equal franchise on the Conservatives very carefully, with much consideration on whether it would be preferable at age 25 years (thus excluding the 'flappers') or at 21 years.[84] The decision was taken at a special meeting of the full cabinet on 12 April 1927, as described by Leo Amery:

> At the Cabinet Stanley [Baldwin] opened with a short resume of the position with regard to our pledges on the women's vote concluding that the only thing we could do was to give it all round at 21. Winston [Churchill] led the opposition with great vehemence and our opinions were then taken all the way round … In the end 21 without a conference prevailed by a considerable majority.[85]

Lord Birkenhead said afterwards: 'The Cabinet went mad yesterday and decided to give votes to women at the age of 21', while Bridgeman's assessment was more measured: 'It was the only honourable course after so many foolish pledges had been given.'[86] Churchill had hoped for MPs to be given a free vote, and felt sufficiently strongly to insist that a separate secret cabinet minute was recorded, presumably for posterity's sake. This note, handwritten by Maurice Hankey, states that the decision to go for the equal franchise at age 21 years was taken by a majority, and the chancellor of the exchequer asked that his dissent be placed on record.[87] The cabinet decision was announced in a statement in the Commons the following day.[88]

Women's organisations continued to keep up the pressure over the following year. The government formally committed to equal franchise in the king's speech on 7 February 1928,[89] and the second reading of the Equal Franchise Bill took place on 29 March 1928. The atmosphere can be conveyed by the *Evening Standard* headlines:

---

[82]Law, *Suffrage and Power.*

[83]Adrian Bingham, ' "Stop the Flapper Vote Folly": Lord Rothermere, the *Daily Mail*, and the Equalization of the Franchise 1927–28', *Twentieth Century British History*, xiii (2002), 17–37; Close, 'Collapse of Resistance to Democracy'.

[84]TNA, CAB 27/336: Equal Franchise Cabinet Committee, 15 Dec. 1926, 14, 21 Feb. 1927; more in Takayanagi,' Parliament and Women', ch. 4.

[85]*The Leo Amery Diaries. i: 1896–1929*, ed. John Barnes and David Nicholson (1980), 504: 12 Apr. 1927; TNA, CAB 23/54: cabinet meeting, 12 Apr. 1927.

[86]*Conservative Politics*, ed. Ball, 132: Birkenhead to Irwin, 13 Apr. 1927; 138: Bridgeman to Irwin, 4 May 1927.

[87]TNA, CAB 23/90B: note by Hankey, 12 Apr. 1927.

[88]Hansard, *Commons Debates*, 5th ser., ccv, cols 358–60: 13 Apr. 1927.

[89]Hansard, *Commons Debates*, 5th ser., ccxiii, col. 8: 7 Feb. 1928.

"Jix" Leads Forth: Home Secretary Unabashed by the Fear of Feminine Rule, MRS PANKHURST IN GALLERY. Protests from Women MPs.[90]

The debate went on for more than seven hours. Joynson-Hicks painted the bill in terms of the 'logical conclusion of a series of Reform bills beginning with that of 1832'; Philip Snowden, from the opposition, took satisfaction in painting a picture of the Labour Party convincing the two older parties over time, and gave credit to '60 years of valiant work on the part of women suffrage organisations'.[91] The women MPs were prominent in the debate, including the countess of Iveagh, Ellen Wilkinson, and Nancy Astor. Although the discussion was mostly about the age limit, Margaret Bondfield drew attention to the property disqualification: 'Since I have been able to vote at all, I have never felt the same enthusiasm because the vote was the consequence of possessing property rather than the consequence of being a human being.'[92] There were still men prepared to argue against, such as Frederick Hall:

> I have always believed that, as was the case prior to 1918, the country should be repre-
> sented in this House by the male sex. Some hon. Members may think that is a rather
> surprising view to take, but that had been the practice and the recognised custom during
> hundreds of years of Parliamentary government, and the legislation of this country had
> been conducted in a very satisfactory manner. [Interruption].[93]

The bill passed overwhelmingly at second reading, with 387 ayes and just ten noes.[94] The lord chancellor later remarked on events in the house of lords: 'There were in the Division Lobbies I will not say ten just men but just ten men who were found to register their opposition to it.'[95] Rothermere's *Daily Mail* saw a Conservative Party split with many anti-suffragists, including Churchill, having absented themselves: 'Flapper Vote Sensation – 146 Missing Conservatives – Party Dissension Talk',[96] and some politicians also thought there was a large number of abstentions.[97] However, an analysis of voting numbers across the session shows that the number of MPs in attendance to vote was substantially *above* average.[98] Churchill was absent at second reading, but present at committee stage when there was a division on age 21 versus 25 years, and followed the government line in favour of age 21 years. The bill also passed readily through the house of lords, with Lord Birkenhead describing himself during the debate as its 'paradoxical champion'.[99]

---

[90] *Evening Standard*, 29 Mar. 1928.

[91] Hansard, *Commons Debates*, 5th ser., ccxv, col. 1359: 29 Mar. 1928 (Joynson-Hicks); cols 1371, 1375: 29 Mar. 1928 (Snowden).

[92] Hansard, *Commons Debates*, 5th ser., ccxv, col. 1415: 29 Mar. 1928 (Bondfield).

[93] Hansard, *Commons Debates*, 5th ser., ccxv, col. 1443: 29 Mar. 1928 (Hall).

[94] Hansard, *Commons Debates*, 5th ser., ccxv, cols 1359–482: 29 Mar. 1928.

[95] Hansard, *Lords Debates*, 5th ser., lxxi, col. 161: 21 May 1928 (lord chancellor (Lord Hailsham)).

[96] Bingham, ' "Stop the Flapper Vote Folly" ', 21.

[97] *Conservative Politics*, ed. Ball, 216: Crawford to Irwin, 3 Apr. 1928.

[98] Takayanagi, 'Parliament and Women', 137–8.

[99] Hansard, *Lords Debates*, 5th ser., lxxi, col. 253: 22 May 1928 (earl of Birkenhead). Lord Crawford wrote on the bill's passage through the Lords: 'Rothermere apparently expected that the queer old gentlemen would turn

An Act to assimilate the franchises for men and women in respect of parliamentary and local government elections; and for purposes consequential thereon.[100]

The Equal Franchise Act 1928 removed the limits placed on women voting, namely the age limit of 30 years and the possession or husband's possession of the local government franchise. Men and women now had the same qualifications, based on residence, business premises, or being the husband or wife of a person with a business premise qualification, and the university franchise. The result was the enfranchisement of 5,250,000 women, of whom 1,800,000 (34%) were over the age of 30 years.[101] The act also equalised the local government franchise, and made provision for consequential issues on election expenses and the electoral register.

Unlike in 1918, there was no scope for other electoral reform, such as proportional representation or redistribution of seats. The title of the bill had been chosen with care: it was 'to assimilate' the law, not 'to amend', and it was deliberately drafted to ensure that no wider constitutional changes could be made.[102] One result was that a husband gained a vote if his wife qualified for the business vote, meaning an estimated 16,000 *men* in England and Wales actually gained a second vote in respect of their wives' occupation of business premises.[103] It has been argued that this was 'a deeply conservative move, propping up the last remnant of the property qualification'.[104] However, abolition of the business vote through the Equal Franchise Act was never a realistic prospect. As Astor declared: 'The question before us is equality, and I feel that, as long as men have this absurd vote, women should have it too.'[105]

The achievement of 'votes for women' went well beyond the franchise itself. Suffrage campaigners had always sought the vote as a means to other ends, and equal franchise was only one of many women's causes campaigned for in the ten years after 1918. Thanks to efforts by feminist organisations, work by women MPs, and the influence of women voters, legislation passed between 1918 and 1939 equalised property inheritance rights; improved training for nurses and midwives; reformed the marriage and divorce laws; removed the automatic death penalty for infanticide and created the offence of child destruction; raised the age of consent and the age of marriage to 16 years; introduced equal guardianship, and widows and orphans pensions; regulated the sale of drink to children, and reformed

---

99 *(continued)* up from the provinces and swamp the lobby. On the contrary, some of the oddest old Peers put in an appearance and actually voted for the Bill': *Conservative Politics*, ed. Ball, 223: Crawford to Irwin, 1 June 1928.

[100]Representation of the People (Equal Franchise) Act 1928, c. 12.

[101]Hansard, *Commons Debates*, 5th ser., ccxv, col. 1369: 29 Mar. 1928 (Joynson-Hicks).

[102]TNA, HO 45/13153: correspondence between parliamentary counsel and the home office on the Representation of the People (Equal Franchise) Bill 1928.

[103]*Return showing in respect of each Parliamentary Constituency in England, Wales and Scotland, the estimated increase in the electorate under the provisions of the Representation of the People (Equal Franchise) Bill, 1928*, Cmd. 3119 (1928).

[104]Melinda Alison Haunton, 'Conservatism and Society: Aspects of Government Policy 1924–1929', Royal Holloway, University of London PhD, 2002, pp. 178–9.

[105]Hansard, *Commons Debates*, 5th ser., ccxvii, col. 68: 7 May 1928 (Astor).

legitimacy law and adoption law.[106] It is impossible to imagine that much, if any, of this would have happened if women had not achieved the vote; the partial franchise won in 1918 was a necessary step to enable feminist organisations to campaign on other issues.

In 2018, as we mark the centenary of 1918 and the 90th anniversary of equal franchise, we can reflect on the importance of the vote as a huge step forward in enabling women to play a full part in politics and society. This is not to say that equal franchise made women full and equal citizens with men; for example, British women continued to lose their nationality (and therefore also their right to vote and to stand as MPs) on marriage to non-British men, until 1948.[107] But the vote was a necessary first step in giving women rights and responsibilities; a stake in the country. Marking the silver jubilee of the Representation of the People Act in 1943, Vera Laughton-Mathews, now director of the WRNS and in the middle of another world war, reflected:

Twenty-five years ago the young women coming forward for the war were keen but diffident, and very inexperienced. Today I see them in their thousands … At the work bench, in the repair shops, in the busy and essential offices. … I see them, children of the first generation of politically free women, looking outward with fearless eyes, calm, confident, on a world which they share … One in which they have a stake, a responsibility, and please God, an opportunity of helping to build something new.[108]

[106] Martin Pugh, *Women and the Women's Movement in Britain, 1914–1999* (2nd edn, 2000); Pat Thane, 'What Difference did the Vote Make?', in *Women, Privilege and Power: British Politics 1750 to the Present*, ed. Amanda Vickery (Cambridge, 2001), 253–88.

[107] M. Page Baldwin, 'Subject to Empire: Married Women and the British Nationality and Status of Aliens Act', *Journal of British Studies*, xl (2001), 522–56.

[108] LMA, Willoughby Hyett Dickinson MSS, F/DCK/052/029: article in *The Catholic Citizen: Organ of the St Joan Alliance*, 15 Feb. 1943.

Chronology of the 1918 Reform Act

The figures for parliamentary votes are those given in the official record of debates, which in the case of the house of commons do not include the two tellers in each lobby.

12 July 1916	The prime minister of the coalition government, Herbert Asquith, tells the house of commons that the cabinet has been unable to find a practical solution to the issue of compiling a new electoral register and the possible extension of the franchise, and suggests that the House set up a select committee.
16 August	Walter Long, the president of the local government board, proposes a 'representative conference' be held under an impartial chairman.
1 October	The Speaker of the house of commons, James Lowther, accepts the invitation from Asquith to chair the conference.
12 October	First meeting of the Speaker's conference.
30 November	The government withdraws its proposed Special Register Bill.
6 December	David Lloyd George replaces Asquith as prime minister and forms a new coalition government.
26 January 1917	Final meeting of the Speaker's conference, after 26 meetings.
27 January	The report of Speaker's conference is sent to Lloyd George.
6 February	The cabinet considers the report, but is unable to decide on the best way to proceed.
26 March	The cabinet decides to bring forward a bill based upon the report's recommendations.
28 March	The house of commons debate on the report opens: Asquith's motion to thank the Speaker for his services and that 'legislation should promptly be introduced' is carried by 341 to 62. During the debate, Lloyd George indicates his lack of enthusiasm for proportional representation, but strong support for women's suffrage.
29 March	Lloyd George meets with a deputation of suffragists and says that women's suffrage is 'an open question'.
15 May	The first reading of the Representation of the People Bill is passed without a division.
22 May	The second reading debate in the house of commons begins, and is passed on 23 May, by 329 to 40.
6 June	The committee stage in the house of commons begins.
12 June	The single transferable vote scheme is defeated by 149 to 141 in a division to amend the instructions to the boundary commissioners.
18 June	After the continuation of the debate from 12 June, the amended instructions to the boundary commissioners are approved without a division; these give them flexibility to avoid creating constituencies 'inconvenient in size or character' and instruct them to proceed on the basis that proportional representation will not be implemented.

19 June	Sir Frederick Banbury's amendment to exclude women's suffrage by deleting section 4, subsections 1 and 2, of the bill is defeated by 364 to 23; after this the section is passed unamended by 385 to 55, with the age limit of 30 years and restriction to women who qualify for the local government franchise or whose husbands do so.
26 June	Ronald McNeill's amendment to disenfranchise conscientious objectors is refused by the home secretary, Sir George Cave, and defeated in a whipped vote by 141 to 71.
4 July	In a division on section 15, subsection 1, the single transferable vote is, again, rejected by 201 to 169.
9 August	The alternative vote is approved by 125 to 124.
20 November	The chairman of the Conservative Party, Sir George Younger, moves an amendment to disenfranchise conscientious objectors; on 21 November the home secretary concedes a free vote and the amendment is carried by 209 to 171.
22 November	The single transferable vote scheme is, again, rejected in the house of commons by 202 to 126; later the same day, the alternative vote is reaffirmed by 150 to 121.
5 December	The house of commons approves the use of the single transferable vote for constituencies in Ireland by 181 to 117.
7 December	The bill passes its third reading in the house of commons.
18 December	The bill passes its second reading in the house of lords without opposition.
8 January 1918	Debate during the committee stage in the house of lords on the inclusion of women's suffrage; following the speech accepting this by Lord Curzon, it is carried by 134 to 71.
22 January	During the committee stage in the house of lords, the single transferable vote scheme is inserted by 131 to 42, and the alternative vote removed by 57 to nine.
30 January	The bill returns to the house of commons, which rejects the amendments made by the house of lords by 223 to 113.
31 January	The house of commons reinstates the alternative vote by 178 to 170.
4 February	The house of lords reverses this and restores the single transferable vote scheme by 86 to 35.
5 February	The bill returns to the house of commons, which, again, removes the single transferable vote by 238 to 141, and restores the alternative vote – but only for borough constituencies – by 195 to 194.
6 February	In the house of lords, Lord Lansdowne moves an amendment that a royal commission be appointed to draw up a scheme for the application of proportional representation in 100 seats, and this is agreed without a division; the house of lords then, for the third time, removes the alternative vote by 74 to 33. The bill returns to the house of commons, which rejects the amendments by 184 to 166, but then due to concern that the whole bill may be lost, drops the alternative vote and accepts the compromise proposal of the royal commission. The bill then passes its final stage and receives the royal assent.
13 April	The royal commission publishes its proposed scheme for 24 large constituencies of three to seven MPs, returning a total of 99 MPs.
13 May	The house of commons rejects the proportional representation scheme recommended by the royal commission by 166 to 110, which has the effect that the single transferable vote is used only in the four university seats that elect two or three MPs, and all other constituencies are on the first-past-the-post system.

INDEX

Aberdeen 114
Aberdeen North 104
Aberdeenshire 122
Adamson, W. 79, 134, 144, 147
Adamson, W. Murdoch, 178
Adkins, R. 176–7
agriculture 16
All-for-Ireland League 126
alternative vote, *see* proportional representation
Amalgamated Society of Engineers 71, 73
Amery, L. 182
Anderson, M., *see* Macarthur, M.
Andrews, E. 78
Angell, N. 153
Anglo-Irish Treaty (1921) 6, 37, 53, 55,129
Anti-Proportional Representation Committee 8
anti-semitism 98
Argyll 4, 111, 114
Asquith, H. 21, 27, 28, 37, 49, 50, 51, 52, 55, 65, 108, 134, 143, 145, 148, 158
    Liberal decline 53, 56, 59–60, 61, 62–3
    women voters 52, 173, 179–82
Associated Society of Locomotive Engineers and Firemen 66
Astor, Lady 44, 175, 178, 180, 181, 183, 184
Atholl, duchess of 178
Austin, Sir H. 84
Ayr District of Burghs 105, 108, 109
Ayrshire North 105

Baldwin, S. 22, 43–4, 82, 98–100, 164, 165
Balfour, A. 12, 65
Banbury, Sir F. 173
Banff 114
Barker, E. 77
Barran, J. 114
Barrow 76
Bath 26
Battersea North 74
Belfast 122
Beresford, J. 77
Berwickshire 113, 114
Bethnal Green 4
Beveridge, W. 76
Bird's of Wolverhampton Ltd. 86
Birkenhead, earl of 181, 182, 183
Birmingham 14
    Conservative Party 83, 84–5, 87–8, 97, 99
    increase of electorate 81
    Labour Party 82, 85–6, 98
    Liberal Party 85
    local government elections 82, 85, 91
    redistribution 92

Birmingham Daily Post (from May 1918, *Birmingham Post*) 88, 91
Birmingham Duddeston 82
Birmingham Gazette 97
Birmingham King's Norton 84
Birmingham Ladywood 85, 86, 90, 91
Birmingham Small Arms Ltd. 86
Birmingham West 93
Blackburn 76
Black Country 82, 85, 99
Blackpool 58, 60
Bolshevism 33, 53, 78
Bonar Law, A. 25, 27, 28, 43, 49, 174
    women's suffrage 177–8
Bondfield, M. 183
Border District of Burghs 110, 113
Bothwell 105
Boundary Commissions 12, 38, 92, 103, 105, 108, 113, 114
Boyle, N. 174
Brady, P. 122
Bridgeman, C. 177, 179
Bridgeman, W. 86, 181, 182
British Broadcasting Corporation 100
British Union of Fascists 167
Bromley, J. 66
Bull, Sir W. 136, 171

Cadbury, G. 86
Caithness and Sutherland 111, 112
Campbell-Bannerman, Sir H. 108
Cannock 95
Carson, Sir E. 26
Catholic Emancipation Act (1829) 118
Cave, Sir G. 29, 93
Cecil, E. 93
Cecil, Lord R. 174–5
Chamberlain, Anne 89, 91
Chamberlain, Austen 82, 92, 99, 142–3, 147
Chamberlain, B. 89
Chamberlain, J. 82, 93, 98
Chamberlain, N. 83–4, 86, 89, 90, 91, 98–100
Chertsey 73
Chesterfield 59
Child, S. 95
Church of England 97–8
Churchill, W. 99, 181, 182, 183
Clackmannan and Kinross 106
Clydesiders 145, 147
Clynes, J. 66, 76, 78, 79
coal mining 14, 55
Coatbridge 105
Combined English Universities 6

conscientious objectors 4, 29, 53
Conservative Agents' Journal 89–90
Conservative Private Members' (1922) Committee 42
Conservative and Unionist Party
 agriculture 13, 29–30
 appeal 87, 99
 democracy 28, 46
 effects of 1918 Reform Act 30, 32, 34–7, 39, 45–6
  safe seats, increase 14–16, 37–8
 electoral fortunes 23–4, 46, 68, 99–100
  in cities 14–15, 104
  in university seats 7
  in west midlands 82, 98–9
  lost deposits 11, 35
 electoral reform, attitude to
  before First World War 24–5
  during First World War 25–7, 83, 169
  manhood suffrage 24, 32
 equalisation of franchise 43–5, 182
 house of lords reform 29, 42–3
 Ireland 24, 36, 55, 119, 125
 National Unionist Association
  annual conference 39, (1917) 25, 27, 28
  Central Council 28, 39, 42
  Executive Committee 26, 27, 28
  Sub-committees 28, 29, 32
 party organisation
  deputy party chairman 56
  Central Office 27, 38, 44, 83–4
  constituency associations 38, 41
  Junior Imperial League 41–2
  local agents 26, 41, 80, 89
  Midland Union 83, 84, 89, 90
  party chairman 4, 28, 29, 39, 44
  trade unionists 50–1, 54
  West Midland Women's Unionist Organisation 89
  women 39–40, 54, 87, 177
 passage of reform bill 28–32
 patriotism 28
 propaganda 39, 87
 provisions of 1918 Reform Act
  conscientious objectors 29
  deposits 35
  election expenses 35
  plural voting 30, 34
  proportional representation 8–9, 30–2
  redistribution of seats 26–7, 35–9, 69
  registration 68
  women's suffrage 24, 25, 27, 33–4, 39, 173
 religion 97
Conservative and Unionist Women's Franchise Association 24
Consett 175
Cooper, Sir R. 99
Co-operative Party 73, 76
Cork 122, 127, 128
Corn Production Act (1917) 70
corrupt practices 11
cost of living 70
Cottrell, M. 91

Coventry 82, 86, 91, 92–4, 96
Coventry Standard 92–3
Cox, H. 166
Crofter MPs 111
Curzon, marquess of 173

Dail Eirann 129–30, 175
Daily Chronicle 153, 156
 proportional representation 162–3
 women's suffrage 158, 159
Daily Express 153, 154, 156, 157
 women's suffrage 158, 160
Daily Herald 75, 158
Daily Mail 77, 90, 152, 153, 157
 'flapper vote' 44, 166–7, 182–3
 women's suffrage 158, 160–1, 164
Daily Mirror 152, 153, 164
Daily News 52, 153, 154, 156
 proportional representation 163
 women's suffrage 158, 161
Daily Telegraph 150, 153, 166, 167
 party politics 155–6
 proportional representation 162, 163
 women's suffrage 158, 160, 164
Dalyell, T. 107
Davidson, J. 41
Davies, I. 146
de Valera, E. 121, 123
Defence of the Realm Act (1914) 70
democracy 28, 46, 52, 68, 83, 109, 137, 146, 150, 151, 154, 164–7
Deptford 74
Derby 76
Derbyshire 84
Despard, C. 74
devolution 147–8
Dickinson, W. 170, 171–2, 173
Dillon, J. 123
Disraeli, B. 27
Docker, D. 94
Docker, L. 94
Donegal West 127
Dorset East 72
Down, County 122
Dublin City 122, 128
Dublin, County 122
Dublin St Patrick's 175
Dublin, University, *see* Trinity College, Dublin
Dumbarton District of Burghs 105, 109
Dumfries 113
Dumfries District of Burghs 110, 113
Dundalk 118
Dundee 45, 108
Dunfermline District of Burghs 4, 108, 109, 110
Dyson, W. 95

Easter Rising (1916) 121
Edinburgh Central 104
electorate
 increase 2
 nature 53, 91

Elliot, W. 146, 148
Elvin, H. 67
Equal Franchise Cabinet Committee 182
Equal Rights Political Campaign Committee 182
Esher, Lord 78
Essex 14
Evening Herald 126
Evening Standard 166, 182–3
Evesham 86

Fawcett, M. 159, 169, 170–1, 173
Fellowes, E. 145
Fenn, L. 75
Fermanagh North 121
Fife East 4, 37, 55, 108
Fife West 4, 104
First World War 23, 25, 28, 32, 70–1
Fisher, V. 83–4
'flapper vote', *see* franchise, equalisation
Forest of Dean 74
franchise 2–3
    absent voters 10–11
    armed services 4, 120–1, 128
    before 1918 Act 3, 12, 24, 117–18, 169
    business premises 5–6, 30, 34, 53, 120, 184
    conscientious objectors 4, 29, 53
    enfranchisement, proportion 3–4, 33, 101, 105,
        120
    equalisation 16, 43–4, 176–84
        Cabinet decision on 182
    extension (1969) 16
    local government 4–5, 69
    lodgers 3
    female 4–5, 33, 101–2, 105, 127–8, 168–72
        after 1928 Act 45
        business franchise 6
        exclusions 16, 33–4, 169, 172
    registration system 2–3, 10–11, 41, 56, 68
    university 6–7, 73, 169, 172
Francis, G. 75
Fraser, M. 177

Galloway 4, 113, 114
Galway 122
Garvin, J. 154
Gateshead 79
general elections
    (1918) 49, 52, 59, 60–1, 72–4, 82, 95, 96, 104, 133,
        137, 148
        in Ireland 123–32
        women 39, 139, 164–5
    (1922) 58, 78–9, 96, 104, 144–5, 164
    (1923) 55, 78–9, 86
    (1924) 79
    (1929) 45, 167
    (1974) 106
    campaigning 11–12, 41, 96
    expenses 11, 35, 94–6
Gibbs, W. 84
Gladstone, H. 50, 51

Gladstone, W. 36, 60
Glasgow 14, 75, 79, 102, 104, 113
Glasgow Govan 104
Glasgow Maryhill 104
Glasgow Partick 104
Gleanings and Memoranda 83
Gloucestershire 84
Goldstone, F. 65
Good Friday Agreement (1998) 130
Gould, J. 68
Government of Ireland Act (1920) 129
Greenock 4, 105
Gretna 111, 112
Guest, F. 53

Haddington 113
Hall, F. 183
Hallas, E. 82, 83
Hamilton 104, 105
Handsworth 92
Hankey, Sir M. 78, 182
Harborough 60
Hardie, A. 75
Harrow 35
Hawick District of Burghs 113–14
Headlam, C. 180
Healy, M. 122
Henderson, A. 72, 73, 74, 76–7, 143, 180
    electoral reform 65, 67, 68
    party reorganisation 65, 71, 74
Highland Land League 111
Highland Land Settlement Association 112
Hobbs, A. 92
Hogge, J. 106–7
house of commons
    attendance 139
    back-bench MPs, role 142, 143
    effects of 1918 Reform Act 41–2, 149
    executive, dominance 140–1, 146
    facilities 139
    Irish seats 35–6
    Leader of the House 141
    legislation, increase 42, 140
    opposition, lack 138, 143
    overcrowding 138, 143
    passage of 1918 reform bill 8–9, 13, 27, 28,
        30–1
    plural voting 25
    private members' bills 141
    procedure 140, 145
        divisions 142
        questions 141
    size 37, 73, 91
    standing committees 140
    ventilation 138
    women 139, 146
house of lords
    passage of reform bill 8–9, 30–1
    plural voting 25
    proportional representation 8–9

reform 24, 42–3, 66
  Labour Party 67
Hudson, Sir R. 54, 56
Humphries, J. 162–3

Increase of Rent and Mortgages Interest (War
  Restrictions) Act (1915) 70
Independent Labour Party 75, 79, 85, 87, 98, 104
Inverness-shire 103, 111
Ireland
  armed services 120–1, 128
  effects of 1918 Reform Act 127–30
  electorate, increase 2, 119–20, 127
  franchise before 1918 Act 117–18
  general election (1918) 123–8, 130–2
    significance 117, 129–30
  over-representation 24, 35–6, 122
  proportional representation 128–9
  redistribution 14, 55, 122, 127
  republicanism 117, 129–30
  social and religious composition 118
  women's suffrage 120
Irish Convention (1917–18) 122
Irish Free State 7, 55, 129, 130
Irish Home Rule 117, 119, 122, 154
Irish Independent 126
Irish Nationalist Party 36, 55, 117–18, 119, 121–2,
  123–8
  proportional representation 9, 128
  women's suffrage 173
Irish Republican Army 121, 129
Irish Republican Brotherhood 117, 118
Irish Volunteers 121
Iveagh, countess of 183

Jewson, D. 178
John Bull 157
Jones, J. 74
Joynson-Hicks, Sir W. 22, 43–4, 180–3
Junior Imperial League, *see* Conservative and Unionist
  Party, organisation

Keighley 174
Kilkenny 122
Kincardineshire 114
Kinross-shire 114
Kirkcaldy District of Burghs 109, 110
Knightley, Lady 24

Labour Church Movement 98
labour movement 28
Labour Party
  advance 28, 42, 45, 48–9, 59, 77–9
  appeal 86
  conference (1914) 67, (1918) 66, 67, (1923) 72
  conscientious objectors 67
  constituency organisation 86
  constitution 75, 147
  effects of 1918 Reform Act 32, 64, 65, 69–70, 72,
    79–80, 137

electoral fortunes 73–4
  coal mining 14
  in Scotland 104, 115
  in university seats 7
  in west midlands 82–3, 85
  lost deposits 11
finances 71, 72
First World War, effects 70–1, 76
general election (1918) 72–4, 77, 79
house of commons 141, 147
  in 1918–22 parliament 144
  in 1922–24 parliament 145
house of lords 67
leadership 147
National Executive Committee 65, 144
payment of MPs 139
plural voting 24, 34
poor relief disqualification 69
proportional representation 8–9, 32, 67–9, 80, 136
redistribution 55, 69
registration system 68
reorganisation 65, 74
Speaker's conference (1916–17) 65, 66
subcommittee on electoral reform 64–5
trade unions 71–3
women 66, 74–6
Labour Party (Irish) 127
Lanarkshire North 105, 175
Lansbury, G. 69
Laughton-Mathews, V. 168, 171, 185
Law, A. Bonar, *see* Bonar Law, A.
Lawrence, S. 179
Leamington Courier 93
Lee, J. 175
Leeds 104
Leith District of Burghs 108
Liberal Party
  agricultural seats 16, 37
  decline 47, 51
    1918 election 48, 49–50, 63, 73
    impact of First World War 48
    leadership 59–60, 61
  deposits 56, 62
  disunity 28, 49, 54, 56, 60, 61
    effects on grass-roots 50
  effects of 1918 Reform Act 48, 56, 59, 61–2
    election expenses 19, 56
    loss of Districts of Burghs 108–09
    redistribution of seats 35, 54–55
  electoral fortunes 68, 79
    in Ireland 119
    in Scotland 102, 104, 106, 115
    in west midlands 85
    lost deposits 11
  finances 56
  grass-roots 50, 54, 55, 58
  in 1918–22 parliament 143–4
  lack of policies 52, 53, 60, 62
  local agents 57
  new electorate 51–2, 54, 62
  New Liberalism 60

nonconformity 97–8
paralysis 54, 55, 56
party organisation 51, 54, 88
  Home Counties Liberal Federation 54
  Liberal Central Association 54
  Midland Liberal Federation 50, 53, 55, 58
  National Liberal Federation 51, 58
plural voting 24–5, 62
proportional representation 8–9, 32, 57–8, 137
revival (1927–29) 45
university seats 7, 53
Liberal Unionist Party 82, 104, 108
Lichfield 86
Liebknecht, K. 85
Liverpool 30, 32, 104
Liverpool Everton 4
Llanelli 73
Lloyd George, D. 8, 28, 30, 32–3, 45, 62, 90, 99, 100,
  154, 155
  Liberal decline 49, 54, 56
  proportional representation 8, 30–1, 163
  women's suffrage 171, 173
Lloyd George Coalition government (1916–22) 26,
  33, 157, 164
Locker, W. 138, 143
Logue, Cardinal 123
London 3, 8, 14, 69, 79
London, City of 34, 92
London County Council 78
Londonderry 121
Long, W. 25, 26, 169, 171, 173
Longford 128
Lort-Williams, J. 96
Louth 128
Lowestoft 72
Lowther, J. 9, 12, 26, 136, 140, 143, 144, 148, 169
Luton 50

Macarthur, M. 66, 74
MacDonald, J. Ramsay 67, 68, 72, 137–8, 144, 147, 179
Mackenzie, M. 74
Maclean, Sir D. 54, 56, 62, 143
Maclean, J. 85
Maguire, T. 117
Manchester 14, 37, 104
Manchester Guardian 52, 53, 153, 154, 157
  proportional representation 162
  women's suffrage 158, 161
Manchester Rusholme 74
Manville, E. 88, 96
Markiewicz, C. 128, 175
Mason, D. 93, 98
Mason, J. 105–6
Maurice debate (1918), 62
Maxwell-Fyfe Report (1949) 35
Mayo East 123
Meath 128
Members of Parliament, *see* parliament
Middlesbrough East 175
Middlesex 14, 35

Middleton, J. 66
Midland Union, *see* Conservative and Unionist Party,
  party organisation
Midlothian South 113
Military Service Act (1916) 4
Miners' Federation of Great Britain 71, 73, 79
Mitchell, C. 91
Mitchells & Butlers Ltd. 86
Montgomery Boroughs 4
Montrose District of Burghs 109
Moray and Nairn 114
Morning Post 153, 154, 156
  women's suffrage 158
Morpeth 175
Morris, T. 86
Morton, A. 113
Motherwell 105
Munitions of War Acts (1915–17) 70
Munro, R. 108
Murray of Elibank, Lord 61

National Democratic and Labour Party 83, 99
National Federation of Women Workers 74, 88, 89, 90
National League for Opposing Woman Suffrage 173
National Party 99
National Society of Conservative Agents 68
National Union of Clerks 67
National Union of General Workers 71
National Union of Railwaymen 71
National Union of Shop Assistants 75
National Union of Women's Suffrage Societies 159,
  170
National Unionist Association, *see* Conservative and
  Unionist Party, organisation
National University of Ireland 6, 122
New Statesman 138, 146, 153, 158
Newcastle 64, 79
Northcliffe, Lord 77
Northern Ireland 55, 129
Newry 122
Newton 73
Nuneaton 95

Observer 153, 154, 156
  proportional representation 162
O'Connor, T. 122
Oswestry 85, 86–7
Outhwaite, R. 98
Oxford 4

Paisley 52, 105
Pankhurst, C. 90, 159
Pankhurst, E. 158, 159, 169, 171
Parker, J. 95
parliament 133–4, 137–9, 145–6
  devolution 147–8
  members of parliament
    payment 139
    role 145–7
  role 140–1, 146, 148

see also house of commons
see also house of lords
Parliament Act (1911) 36, 42, 60
Parliament (Qualification of Women) Act (1918) 139, 174–5
Parliamentary Registration (Ireland) Act (1885) 118
Peebles 113
Perthshire 114
Pethick-Lawrence, E. 74
Phillips, M. 74, 75
plural voting 5–8, 24–5, 26, 30, 34
Pollock, Sir E. 95
Ponsonby, A. 111
Poplar 69
Postmen's Federation 71
Potteries, Staffordshire 82
press
    democracy 152, 154, 164–7
    franchise, extension 150–2, 157
    origins of Reform Act 153
    party politics 155–7
    proportional representation 152, 161–3
    role 142–3, 153, 167
    women's suffrage 158–61
press barons 153, 166
Primrose League 89
proportional representation
    in Ireland 128
    in university seats 7, 10
    opposition to 8–9, 13, 17, 30–2
    possible effects 32, 57–8
    Royal Commission (1918) 9–10
    support for 8–9, 67–9, 161–3
Proportional Representation Society 162
Provisional Irish Republican Army 117
Punch 138

Queen's University, Belfast 6, 122

Raffety, F. 134, 148
redistribution of seats, *see* Representation of the People Act (1918), redistribution of seats
Redistribution of Seats (Ireland) Act (1918), 122, 127
Rees, W. 95
Reform Act, Fourth (1918), *see* Representation of the People Act (1918)
Reform Act, Third (1884–5) 12, 30, 118
Reith, J. 100
Renfrewshire West 105
Representation of the People Act (1918)
    historiography 17–20, 109, 116, 135, 151
    'franchise factor' debate 17–19, 47–8, 69–70, 83
    impact 16, 19, 41–2, 53, 69, 79–80, 81, 83–4, 104, 105, 134, 136–7, 148–9, 164–7
    in Ireland 127–30
    name 1, 135
    origins 25–7, 64–5, 150, 157
    passage 8–9, 13, 28–32, 135, 171–3, 186–7
    principles 136

proportional representation 8–10, 13, 30–2, 57–8, 67–9, 136
    in Ireland 128
    in university seats 7
provisions
    conscientious objectors 4, 29, 53
    deposits 11, 35, 56, 62, 137, 139
    expenses 11–12, 19, 41, 56, 68, 72, 83, 94–6, 137
    electorate, increase 1–2, 5, 81, 101, 119–20, 127
    franchise, armed services 4, 29, 128
    franchise, business premises 5–6, 30, 34, 53, 120, 184
    franchise, female 4–5, 33–4, 101–2, 105, 120, 127–8, 168–72
    franchise, male 2–4, 18–19, 47–8, 69, 169, 171
    franchise, university 6–7, 73, 169, 172
    legal incapacity 2 (note 6)
    plural voting 5–8, 30, 53, 62
    polling day 12, 35, 59
    poor relief disqualification 3, 69
    postal delivery 12, 35, 74, 96
    registration system 2–3, 10–11, 41, 56, 68
    school premises 11–12, 35
    two-member boroughs 14
redistribution of seats 12–16, 26, 30, 35–7, 54–5, 62, 69, 81, 91–4
    after 1918 Act 16–17
    effects 37–9, 55, 91–4
    in Ireland 122, 127
    in Scotland 102–5, 107–11
    principles 103, 104, 148
    see also Boundary Commissions
Representation of the People Act (1948) 7, 34
Representation of the People (Equal Franchise) Act (1928) 6, 16, 43–5, 68, 182–4
Roberts, S. 179
Rochdale 64
Romford 35
Roscommon South 128
Ross and Cromarty 103, 111
Rosyth 110, 111, 112
Rothermere, Lord 152, 166–7, 182–3
Roxburgh and Selkirk 113
Rugby Advertiser 88
Runciman, W. 54
Russian Revolution (Feb. 1917) 28, 154
Russian Revolution (Nov. 1917) 53
Rutherglen 105

Salisbury, marquess of 44, 180–1
Samuel, H. 174–5
Sanders, R. 178
Sanlan, T. 122
Scarborough 4
Scotland
    effects of 1918 Reform Act 105
    increase in electorate 4, 101
    national feeling 106–7, 115
    nature of politics 106, 110
    political change 101

redistribution 14, 35, 102–7
  Districts of Burghs 14, 37, 103, 107–12
regions
  borders 102, 105, 113–15
  highland 102, 103, 105, 111–13, 115
  industrial west 104–5
  lowland 102
Scottish Home Rule 106–7, 115
Scottish National Party 106
second chamber reform, *see* house of lords, reform
Selborne, countess of 24
Selborne, earl of 25
Sex Disqualification (Removal) Act (1919) 176
Sheffield 79, 104
Shepherd, G. 76
Shrewsbury 38–9, 85, 91, 92
Silvertown 74
single transferable vote, *see* proportional representation
Sinn Fein 49, 117, 118, 137, 175
  electoral advance 121
  general election (1918) 123–8
  mandate 129, 130
  manifesto 129
Sligo 118
Smethwick 90
Smillie, R. 78
Smuts, J. 78
Snowden, P. 183
Speaker, The 139, 140, 143, 145
Speaker's conference (1916–17)
  meetings 26, 85, 128, 169
  membership 26, 65, 122, 169–70
  origins 25–6, 65, 169
  report 4, 8, 11, 13, 26, 57, 67, 93, 136
  women's suffrage 6, 26, 170
Spectator 153, 158
Spen Valley 52, 165
Spoor, B. 176
St Andrews District of Burghs 55, 108
Staffordshire Advertiser 95
Steel-Maitland, A. 26, 45
Steel Smelters' Association 71
Stirling District of Burghs 108, 109
Stoke-on-Trent 93
Stone 95
Stourbridge 84, 88, 93
Straight Forward 82, 86, 88, 97
Stratford-upon-Avon 93, 94
Sunday Times 153, 156, 166
syndicalism 28

Tamworth Herald 95
Taylor, H. 174
Textile Factory Workers' Association 71
Thomas, J. 78
Times, The 68, 92, 95, 153, 165
  party politics 156
  proportional representation 163
  women's suffrage 158, 159
Tipper, L. 92

Tory Democracy 99
Town Crier 86, 97, 98
Townley, A. 75
Townsend, G. 95
Townswomen's Guild 89
trade unions 70–1, 72–3, 77, 82
Trades Union Congress 65
Trinity College, Dublin 6, 7, 122
Turner, B. 179
Tyrone 123
Tyrone East 121

Ullswater Committee, *see* Speaker's conference
Ulster 124
Unionist Labour Movement, *see* Conservative and
  Unionist Party, organisation
Unionist Party, *see* Conservative and Unionist Party
United Irish League 123, 126
United States of America 28, 154
University of Wales 6
university seats 6–7, 10, 32, 34, 53, 74, 107, 122

Wake, E. 67
Wales 14
Walsh, S. 65
Walthamstow 35, 58
War Emergency Workers' National Committee 65,
  66, 75, 76, 85
Ward, A. 173
Ward, I. 175
Wardle, G. 65
Warwick & Leamington 93, 94, 95
Wason, E. 106
Waterson, A. 76
Watford 76
Webb, B. 76, 140
Webb, S. 73, 76, 77, 140
Wednesbury 82, 88
Wells, H. 163
West Ham Plaistow 74
West Lothian Question 107
West Midland Women's Unionist Organisation, *see*
  Conservative and Unionist Party, party organisation
west midlands
  Conservative Party
    organisation 83, 84, 89, 91, 100
    success 82, 98–100
    effects of 1918 Reform Act 94–6
    general election (1918) 82
    increase of electorate 81
  Labour Party
    advance 82–3, 85
    organisation 86, 90
  Liberal Party 88
  political culture 97–8
  redistribution 91–4
Western Isles 103, 111
Westmeath 128
Westminster Gazette 59, 60, 61
Weymouth 40

Whiteley, W. 180, 181
Whitley, J. 140, 145
Whittaker, Sir T. 144
Wick District of Burghs 108, 111
Wicks, P. 180
Wilkinson, E. 147, 175–6, 183
Williams, U. 175
Wilson, J. 98
Wimbledon 35, 72
Wolverhampton 82
women
    attitudes towards 88–9
    candidates 74, 173–6
    disqualifications, removal 176–7
    enfranchisement 4–5, 105, 120, 158–61, 170–2
        effects 94, 146, 165–7, 184–5
        press support 158–61
        restrictions 4–5, 34, 159, 168–9, 172
    equalisation of franchise 43–5, 166–7, 177–84
    general election (1918) 164–5
    marriage and occupations 16, 33, 105, 172–3, 177
    party appeals 33, 87–8
    trade unions 70–1, 77

    war work 70–1, 159–61
Women Police Volunteers 174
Women's Amalgamated Unionist and Tariff Reform
    Association 39, 89
Women's Emancipation Bill (1919) 176
Women's Freedom League 170, 174
Women's Institute 89
Women's Labour League 75
Women's Party 90, 99
Women's Royal Navy Reserve 169
Women's Social and Political Union 159
Women's Unionist Organisation, *see* Conservative and
    Unionist Party, organisation
Woolwich 75
Worcester 92, 93, 94
Worcestershire East 92
Wrekin, The 86

York 76
Young, R. 73
Young Scots Society 106, 115
Younger, Sir G. 4, 29, 39–40, 103, 107, 108,
    111